IMISCOE Research Series

Now accepted for Scopus! Content available on the Scopus site in spring 2021.

This series is the official book series of IMISCOE, the largest network of excellence on migration and diversity in the world. It comprises publications which present empirical and theoretical research on different aspects of international migration. The authors are all specialists, and the publications a rich source of information for researchers and others involved in international migration studies. The series is published under the editorial supervision of the IMISCOE Editorial Committee which includes leading scholars from all over Europe. The series, which contains more than eighty titles already, is internationally peer reviewed which ensures that the book published in this series continue to present excellent academic standards and scholarly quality. Most of the books are available open access.

More information about this series at http://www.springer.com/series/13502

Carmelo Danisi • Moira Dustin • Nuno Ferreira
Nina Held

Queering Asylum in Europe

Legal and Social Experiences of Seeking
International Protection on grounds of Sexual
Orientation and Gender Identity

Carmelo Danisi
School of Law, Politics and Sociology
University of Sussex
Brighton, UK

Department of Political and Social Sciences
University of Bologna
Bologna, Italy

Nuno Ferreira
School of Law, Politics and Sociology
University of Sussex
Brighton, UK

Moira Dustin
School of Law, Politics and Sociology
University of Sussex
Brighton, UK

Nina Held
School of Law, Politics and Sociology
University of Sussex
Brighton, UK

ISSN 2364-4087   ISSN 2364-4095   (electronic)
IMISCOE Research Series
ISBN 978-3-030-69443-2   ISBN 978-3-030-69441-8   (eBook)
https://doi.org/10.1007/978-3-030-69441-8

© The Editor(s) (if applicable) and The Author(s) 2021. This book is an open access publication.
Open Access This book is licensed under the terms of the Creative Commons Attribution 4.0 International License (http://creativecommons.org/licenses/by/4.0/), which permits use, sharing, adaptation, distribution and reproduction in any medium or format, as long as you give appropriate credit to the original author(s) and the source, provide a link to the Creative Commons license and indicate if changes were made.
The images or other third party material in this book are included in the book's Creative Commons license, unless indicated otherwise in a credit line to the material. If material is not included in the book's Creative Commons license and your intended use is not permitted by statutory regulation or exceeds the permitted use, you will need to obtain permission directly from the copyright holder.
The use of general descriptive names, registered names, trademarks, service marks, etc. in this publication does not imply, even in the absence of a specific statement, that such names are exempt from the relevant protective laws and regulations and therefore free for general use.
The publisher, the authors, and the editors are safe to assume that the advice and information in this book are believed to be true and accurate at the date of publication. Neither the publisher nor the authors or the editors give a warranty, expressed or implied, with respect to the material contained herein or for any errors or omissions that may have been made. The publisher remains neutral with regard to jurisdictional claims in published maps and institutional affiliations.

This Springer imprint is published by the registered company Springer Nature Switzerland AG
The registered company address is: Gewerbestrasse 11, 6330 Cham, Switzerland

Carmelo dedicates these volumes to Marta, Maria and Mario.
Moira dedicates these volumes to Ben.
Nuno dedicates these volumes to Giuseppe, Codie and Kayden.
Nina dedicates these volumes to all the wonderful human and non-human beings in her life.
We dedicate these volumes to all those who participated in our fieldwork, by offering their time and sharing their experiences with us, and all SOGI asylum claimants and refugees in the world – may your strength never falter.

Preface for Volume 1

These volumes are the main output of the project 'Sexual Orientation and Gender Identity Claims of Asylum: A European human rights challenge – SOGICA' (www.sogica.org). This project has been funded by the European Research Council (ERC) under the European Union's Horizon 2020 research and innovation programme (grant agreement No 677693).

Although these volumes are a collective work, each co-author has taken the lead in producing the first draft of a selection of chapters and sections, as follows: Carmelo Danisi led on Chaps. 3 (Sect. 3.2), 5 and 6; Moira Dustin led on Chaps. 3 (Sects. 3.1, 3.3 and 3.5), 9 and 10; Nuno Ferreira led on Chaps. 1, 4, 7 and 11; and Nina Held led on Chaps. 2, 3 (Sect. 3.4) and 8. All material originally in a language other than English – including primary and secondary sources – has been translated into English by the authors (sometimes with the assistance of online tools), unless otherwise indicated.

Further to these volumes, during the project's lifetime we have published a range of other outputs on the theme of sexual orientation and gender identity (SOGI) asylum. Here we provide a comparative analysis of SOGI asylum in the three countries selected (Germany, Italy, UK), while other project publications cover subjects that emerged as important in our fieldwork but that did not fit with the structure of these volumes or which we wanted to discuss in greater detail than would be possible in these volumes taking a broad, pan-European perspective.[1] These volumes should be seen as part of that broader body of work, as an overall contribution to the debate on SOGI asylum in Europe and beyond.

Throughout the life of the SOGICA project, we worked with NGOs, lawyers and policy-makers, amongst others, to facilitate improvements in SOGI asylum, in

---

[1] All other relevant publications can be found at http://www.sogica.org/en/publications/. Many of these have been presented at public events throughout the life of the SOGICA project: http://www.sogica.org/en/events/. One can also find in the project's website tables of case law regarding each one of the case studies adopted in this project, which besides the country case studies also include the European Union (EU) and Council of Europe (CoE) (http://www.sogica.org/en/case-studies/).

particular by developing a database of resources,[2] as well as creating a network of individuals working or with an interest in this field. We hope these resources will survive the formal life of our project. Many events took place after this project was conceived, such as the Brexit referendum and subsequent negotiations, and the further rise of right-wing populist movements in several European countries and beyond. Such developments have important implications for the quality and consistency of asylum standards across Europe, which we hope to continue to analyse in future publications.

Within the life of the SOGICA project, we have benefitted from the generous input of a range of people who deserve recognition and our utmost gratitude. We would like to thank in particular the members of our Advisory Board, namely Giorgio dell'Amico (Italy), Rute Caldeira (Germany), Prossy Kakooza (UK), Maggie Merhebi (Germany), Vitit Muntarbhorn (Thailand), Barry O'Leary (UK) and Anbid Zaman (Germany), for their valuable support.[3] We would also like to thank all those who became Project Friends throughout the life of the project, including individual asylum claimants and refugees, researchers involved in asylum, human rights, socio-legal studies and SOGI, as well as lawyers, NGO representatives and service providers.[4] Thanks are also due to the Department of Political and Social Sciences, University of Bologna, and Marco Balboni for co-hosting a SOGICA conference in Forlì (Italy), and to the Cornelia Goethe Centre at the Frankfurt Goethe University and Uta Ruppert for co-hosting a SOGICA conference in Frankfurt (Germany). Finally, our sincere thanks to all organisations and individuals that in one way or the other supported our fieldwork, especially by facilitating the use of certain spaces and helping us to recruit participants.

We are also very thankful for the time and dedication offered by all those who undertook placements with SOGICA, namely Ibrahim Abdella (co-founder of the online initiative 'Solidarity with Egypt LGBTQ+'), Valentina Canepa (University of Sussex), Silvia Ciacchi (University of Trento), Elif Dama (University of Istanbul), Federico Di Persio (University of Bologna), Rose Gordon-Orr (Goldsmiths, University of London), Melody Greaves (Wilfrid Laurier), Oscar Kennedy (Dorothy Stringer School), Marita Haakonsen (University of Sussex), Lisa Harrington (University of Sussex), Ssu-Chi Ho (Goldsmiths, University of London), Alessandro Pigoni (University of Sussex / University of Bologna), Marie Pritchard (University of Sussex), Isabel Soloaga (University of Sussex), and Alba Trabandt (University of Sussex / Freie Universität Berlin), as well as others who preferred to remain anonymous. Thanks are also due to: our supportive research assistants Rosa Jones, Vítor Lopes Andrade, Natalie Pearson and Anbid Zaman; Giuseppe Mascia, who created our project logo and did other design work; and Silan Anil, Ammar Cheema, Shahrzad Fouladvand, Roberto Gangemi, Ali Kassem and Khalid Khan for the

---

[2] The database contains a range of items that relate specifically to SOGI asylum (http://www.sogica.org/en/sogica-database/).
[3] http://www.sogica.org/en/the-project/the-advisory-board/.
[4] http://www.sogica.org/en/the-project/project-friends/.

support with translations into languages besides English, German and Italian. We would also like to thank all colleagues at the University of Sussex for their support for this project, in particular Eleanor Griggs, Rachael Phelps and Charlotte Shamoon, for their help in producing SOGICA resources as well as assistance in organising our final conference, Liz McDonnell, for her support on ethical guidance, and Jo Bridgeman, Bal Sokhi-Bulley and Samantha Velluti, for their feedback on earlier drafts of this work. Many thanks, equally, are owed to colleagues and reviewers at IMISCOE and Springer for their feedback and support throughout this journey. Finally, our deepest gratitude goes to all SOGICA participants – without you, this project would not have been possible. We hope that we have reflected your experiences and views adequately.

A couple of last notes: these volumes discuss issues and contain language that – by their very nature – some readers may find offensive or disturbing. While acknowledging this, we believe that a thorough and serious analysis of our subject-matter could not circumvent such issues or avoid the language in question.

All information is correct to the best of our knowledge as of January 2020.

Brighton, UK
January 2020

Carmelo Danisi
Moira Dustin
Nuno Ferreira
Nina Held

Preface for Volume 2

This is Vol. 2 of *Queering Asylum in Europe*, which constitutes the main output of the project 'Sexual Orientation and Gender Identity Claims of Asylum: A European Human Rights Challenge – SOGICA' (www.sogica.org). This project has been funded by the European Research Council (ERC) under the European Union's Horizon 2020 research and innovation programme (grant agreement No 677693). For an extensive preface to both volumes, please refer to Vol. 1.

These volumes are constituted by 11 chapters. Vol. 1 gathered Chaps. 1, 2, 3, 4, 5 and 6 and Vol. 2 gathers Chaps. 7, 8, 9, 10 and 11. Chapter 1 offered an introduction to both volumes; Chap. 2 discussed the methodology used in the research underlying these volumes; Chap. 3 set out the theoretical underpinnings of our research; Chap. 4 explored the legal and policy framework that applies to SOGI asylum in the case study jurisdictions; Chap. 5 considered the lives of individuals before fleeing persecution, the journey and arrival in Europe; and Chap. 6 analysed SOGI asylum in the context of decision-making procedures.

Volume 2 goes on considering the legal treatment of SOGI asylum claims in the country case studies and then dissects as well the broader social experiences of SOGI asylum claimants and refugees. Chapter 7 considers how the substance of SOGI asylum claims is dealt with, Chap. 8 explores the lived experiences of SOGI asylum claimants in relation to housing and accommodation, and Chap. 9 analyses SOGI claimants' and refugees' access to healthcare services, the labour market and educational provision.

This volume is concluded with Part III, which presents our vision for a better future for SOGI asylum in Europe. Chapter 10 discusses legal and social experiences of harassment, isolation and oppression of SOGI claimants and refugees, focusing on four key themes: identities, discrimination, space and agency. Finally, Chap. 11 offers a range of policy recommendations addressed to decision-makers, policy-makers, NGOs and service providers, for improving the socio-legal framework that applies to SOGI asylum.

As forewarned in Vol. 1, this work discusses issues and contains language that – by their very nature – some readers may find offensive or disturbing. While acknowledging this, we believe that a thorough and serious analysis of our subject-matter could not circumvent such issues or avoid the language in question.

All information is correct to the best of our knowledge as of January 2020.

Brighton, UK
January 2020

Carmelo Danisi
Moira Dustin
Nuno Ferreira
Nina Held

Foreword: On the Importance of Intersectionality Within Policy and Research

As the United Nations Independent Expert on sexual orientation and gender identity, I hold the protection of the rights of LGBT asylum seekers, migrants, and refugees at the core of my mandate's work. It's hard to imagine a population of persons who reunite in their body a greater simultaneous intersection of both marginalized identities and far-too-often challenged rights. The plight of LGBT asylum seekers is then further compounded by the fact that their successful (or unsuccessful) navigation of a complex, foreign, and often unfriendly bureaucratic asylum process will impact the trajectory of the rest of their life. We owe this community our deepest admiration, support, and most importantly, our strongest advocacy.

For LGBT asylum seekers, diversities of gender identity, race, ethnicity, socioeconomic status, religion, disability, health, language, documentation status, and age *all* intersect and interplay with a number of rights which, unfortunately, are far too often ill-considered or outright rejected by state authorities.

From the right to have one's gender identity properly noted on state documents to the right to safe and inclusive temporary housing; from a fair and respectful interview process to the basic principle of non-refoulement, asylum agencies owe LGBT asylum seekers no "special" or "new" rights, but rather to simply extend the same basic rights afforded to them under the letter of the law with due consideration to LGBT persons unique and individual context.

As the current COVID-19 pandemic has shown, when state authorities fail to consider the underlying structural issues and barriers affecting marginalized groups like the LGBT community – even when enacting seemingly "neutral" policies – there can be dire unintended consequences. That is why, within those contexts, it is more important than ever that academe and civil society work to exhaustingly highlight and investigate all possible intersections of rights with identities, as well as always use data that is grounded directly in input from stakeholders who will be impacted by any proposed policy.

This fact makes applying the principle of intersectionality to all stages of the policy formulation process, especially during the early research and data collection stage, all the more important. Intersectionality is absolutely essential to creating asylum and migration policies that are not just inclusive, but ultimately also effective in the long run for all stakeholders involved. The colorful yet complex intersection of identities with and within the LGBT community requires civil society, academia, and state authorities to not only identify how to protect the most basic of their rights under the law, but to also take into consideration the numerous other identities that members of the LGBT community may also simultaneously hold and navigate life through with which may require additional forward-thinking in order to safeguard everyone's interests.

The sad reality is that we still live in a world where 69 countries criminalize the expression of LGBT persons' lives, love, and identities. In countless more jurisdictions, prevailing socio-cultural attitudes towards LGBT persons make their lives (whether they live openly or not) a de-facto internal prison sentence. Until the scourge of both criminalization and pervasive discrimination is ended around the world, LGBT persons must always be guaranteed the right to a safe and fair asylum process.

The work that all at SOGICA have done to study these issues from an intersectional and wide a perspective as possible is not only commendable, but also crucial to fixing what many believe is a broken asylum system in Europe. The research done so far in support of vulnerable LGBT persons around the world is of fundamental importance, and I exhort all stakeholders to continue it while bringing in as many new voices and perspectives into this discussion as possible.

We are all stronger when we fight this fight together.

Victor Madrigal-Borloz
United Nations Independent Expert on the prevention of violence and discrimination on the basis of sexual orientation and gender identity

Contents

VOLUME 1

Part I Contextualising SOGI Asylum Research

1 **Why Sexual Orientation and Gender Identity Asylum?** 3
   1.1 Seeking Asylum: Why Focus on Sexual Orientation
        and Gender Identity 3
   1.2 The International and European Legal, Policy
        and Social Context 8
   1.3 Framing Our Research 12
   1.4 The Structure of These Volumes 15
   References 17

2 **Researching SOGI Asylum** 23
   2.1 Introduction 23
   2.2 Methods 25
        2.2.1 Semi-structured Interviews 28
        2.2.2 Focus Groups 33
        2.2.3 Observations in Courts 34
        2.2.4 Online Surveys 35
        2.2.5 Documentary Analysis 39
        2.2.6 Freedom of Information Requests 40
   2.3 Ethical Implications: Doing Research with SOGI Refugees .. 42
   References 47

3 **A Theoretical Framework: A Human Rights Reading
   of SOGI Asylum Based on Feminist and Queer Studies** 51
   3.1 Introduction 51
   3.2 A Human Rights Approach to SOGI Asylum: What Role
        for Rights? 52
        3.2.1 Human Rights and SOGI: Reconsidering Personhood
               Through a SOGI and Anti-stereotyping Lens 54

xv

		3.2.2	Human Rights and the Refugee Convention: Establishing the Right Relationship.	58
		3.2.3	Human Rights as an Independent Basis for Protection in SOGI Asylum: From Procedural Guarantees to Substantive Fairness	61
	3.3	A Feminist Approach to SOGI Asylum		64
		3.3.1	Feminism and Multiculturalism.	67
		3.3.2	Intersectional Feminist Writing	68
		3.3.3	Anti-essentialism	70
		3.3.4	Recognising Agency	73
	3.4	Queer Theoretical Approaches to SOGI Asylum.		75
		3.4.1	Queer Theoretical Understanding of Sex, Gender, Sexuality and Identity	76
		3.4.2	Intersectional Queer Approaches.	79
		3.4.3	Queer Geographies.	81
	3.5	Concluding Remarks		84
	References			85

Part II The Legal and Social Experiences of SOGI Asylum Claimants and Refugees

4	**The Policy and Guidance**			97
	4.1	Introduction		97
	4.2	Social and Legal Dimensions of SOGI		101
	4.3	The National Asylum Systems.		104
		4.3.1	The Key Legal Instruments and Actors	104
		4.3.2	Degree of Compliance with Supranational and International Obligations.	109
	4.4	SOGI Dimensions of Domestic Asylum Systems		111
		4.4.1	Milestones in Policy and Guidance	112
		4.4.2	Vulnerability and SOGI Asylum	115
	4.5	Refugee Status Determination (RSD) Outcomes and Life After the Decision on a SOGI Asylum Claim		119
	4.6	From Policy to Law, from Law to Practice		127
	References			129

5	**Life in the Countries of Origin, Departure and Travel Towards Europe**			139
	5.1	Introduction		139
	5.2	Life in the Countries of Origin.		141
		5.2.1	'Ordinary' Lives.	142
		5.2.2	Treatment of SOGI Minorities in Countries of Origin	145
	5.3	'It Suddenly Happened'		150
		5.3.1	Forced Departures	152
		5.3.2	Journey Experiences	155

	5.4	The Arrival in Europe	160
		5.4.1 Information on SOGI Asylum	162
		5.4.2 Initial Screenings	166
		5.4.3 Initial Reception and Detention	170
	5.5	Concluding Remarks	174
	References	176
6	**The Decision-Making Procedure**	179
	6.1	Introduction	179
	6.2	The Preparation of Asylum Claims and Legal Aid	185
		6.2.1 The Preparation for the Main Interview and Judicial Hearing(s)	186
		6.2.2 Access to, and Quality of, Legal Representation	192
		6.2.3 Training of Volunteers, Lawyers and Staff Working with SOGI Claimants	201
	6.3	The Main Interview: Actors and Procedures in SOGI Asylum	204
		6.3.1 The Interview Setting	205
		6.3.2 The Selection and the Training of Caseworkers	209
		6.3.3 The Conduct of Interviews	213
	6.4	The Judicial Procedure	222
		6.4.1 The Appeal Setting	222
		6.4.2 The Conduct of Hearings and the Adoption of Decisions	227
	6.5	Country of Origin Information	234
	6.6	Interpretation	240
	6.7	Other Procedures	247
	6.8	Concluding Remarks	252
	References	253

VOLUME 2

Part II (cont.)

7	**The Asylum Claim Determination**	259
	7.1	Introduction	259
	7.2	Using the Grounds for the Recognition of Refugee Status	260
		7.2.1 Choosing from the Five Refugee Convention Grounds	261
		7.2.2 SOGI and 'Particular Social Group'	263
	7.3	Reaching the Persecution Threshold	269
		7.3.1 The Criminalisation of Same-Sex Acts	273
		7.3.2 The 'Discretion Argument'	277
		7.3.3 The 'Internal Relocation Alternative'	283
	7.4	Proving Claims Based on SOGI	285
		7.4.1 Standard and Burden of Proof	285
		7.4.2 Types of Evidence	289

	7.5	The Assessment of Credibility	300
		7.5.1 Stereotyping 'Gayness'	303
		7.5.2 Be 'Out and Proud' – The Western Way	307
		7.5.3 A Persisting Culture of Disbelief	312
	7.6	Outcomes of the RSD Process and What Lays beyond SOGI – Through an Intersectional Lens	317
	7.7	Concluding Remarks: Assessing the Assessor	321
	References		324
8	**Housing and Accommodation**		**331**
	8.1	Introduction	331
	8.2	Asylum Accommodation Policies	333
	8.3	Standard of Asylum Accommodation	339
	8.4	Living in Shared Accommodation, Being 'in the Closet' and Experiencing Discrimination and Hate Crime	344
		8.4.1 Accommodation of Couples	351
		8.4.2 Intersectional Dimensions of Accommodation	352
		8.4.3 Accommodation of Non-binary, Trans and Intersex Claimants	356
	8.5	Rural/Urban	359
	8.6	Homelessness and Destitution	366
	8.7	Housing After the Asylum Claim Process	368
	8.8	SOGI Accommodation	372
	8.9	Detention	377
	8.10	Concluding Remarks	382
	References		384
9	**Health, Work and Education**		**389**
	9.1	Introduction	389
	9.2	Physical and Mental Health	391
		9.2.1 Access to Healthcare	391
		9.2.2 Access to Specialist Treatment	392
		9.2.3 Experiences of Sexual Violence and Torture	395
		9.2.4 Mental Health	398
	9.3	Work	403
		9.3.1 The Right to Work	403
		9.3.2 Voluntary Work and Community Involvement	405
		9.3.3 Sexual Exploitation and Sex Work	406
		9.3.4 Discrimination and Exploitation in Employment	408
	9.4	Education and Training	411
	9.5	Concluding Remarks	414
	References		414

Part III Forging a New Future for SOGI Asylum in Europe

10 SOGI Asylum in Europe: Emerging Patterns 421
    10.1   Introduction 421
    10.2   Identities.. 422
            10.2.1   Homogenisation 422
            10.2.2   Stereotypes 423
            10.2.3   Language and Culture 426
    10.3   Discrimination 429
            10.3.1   Racism... 429
            10.3.2   Homophobia, Transphobia and Cross-Cutting
                        Discrimination................................. 431
    10.4   Place... 433
            10.4.1   Receiving Country and Region 433
            10.4.2   Isolation....................................... 436
    10.5   Agency.. 438
            10.5.1   Losing Agency................................. 438
            10.5.2   Taking Control................................. 441
    10.6   Concluding Remarks 443
    References... 444

11 Believing in Something Better: Our Recommendations 445
    11.1   So What? 445
    11.2   The Journey to Europe and Reception..................... 447
    11.3   The Asylum Application Process......................... 449
            11.3.1   Institutional and Policy Framework 450
            11.3.2   Procedural Rules 454
            11.3.3   The Asylum Claim Determination 459
    11.4   Detention and Accommodation 464
    11.5   Life 'Beyond Papers' 466
    11.6   Building Capacity and Enhancing Competences............. 467
    11.7   Something to Look Forward To 472
    References... 474

Index 479

List of Acronyms and Abbreviations

AASC	Asylum Accommodation and Support Services Contracts
AIDA	Asylum Information Database
APPG	All Party Parliamentary Group
ARE	Appeal Rights Exhausted
ASGI	Associazione Studi Giuridici sull'Immigrazione
BAMF	Bundesamt für Migration und Flüchtlinge (Federal Office for Migration and Refugees)
BMI	Bundesministerium des Innern, für Bau und Heimat (Federal Ministry of the Interior, Building and Community)
CEAS	Common European Asylum System
CFR	Charter of Fundamental Rights
CJEU	Court of Justice of the European Union
CoE	Council of Europe
COI	Country of Origin Information
COMPASS	Commercial and Operational Managers Procuring Asylum Support Services
CPIN	Country Policy Information Notes
EASO	European Asylum Support Office
ECHR	European Convention on Human Rights
ECRE	European Council on Refugees and Exiles
ECtHR	European Court of Human Rights
EU	European Union
FGM	Female Genital Mutilation
FOI	Freedom of Information
FRA	European Union Agency for Fundamental Rights
GG	Grundgesetz (German Basic Law)
GIC	Gender Identity Clinic
GOT	Giudici onorari (Honorary Judges)
GP	General Practitioner
HRC	Human Rights Council
HRW	Human Rights Watch

ICIBI	Independent Chief Inspector of Borders and Immigration
ICCPR	International Covenant on Civil and Political Rights
ICESCR	International Covenant on Economic, Social and Cultural Rights
IHRL	International Human Rights Law
ILGA	International Lesbian, Gay, Bisexual, Trans and Intersex Association
IO	Immigrazioni e Omosessualità
IOM	International Organization for Migration
IRL	International Refugee Law
LeTRa	Lesbentelefon e.V.
LGBTIQ+	Lesbian, Gay, Bisexual, Trans, Intersex, Queer and Others
LISG	Lesbian Immigration Support Group
MIT	Movimento Identità Transessuale
MSM	Men Who Have Sex with Men
MSF	Médecins sans Frontières
NGO	Nongovernmental Organisation
ORAM	Organization for Refuge, Asylum and Migration
PSG	Particular Social Group
PTSD	Post-Traumatic Stress Disorder
RSD	Refugee Status Determination
SOGI	Sexual Orientation and/or Gender Identity
TGEU	Transgender Europe
UDHR	Universal Declaration of Human Rights
UK	United Kingdom
UKBA	United Kingdom Border Agency
UKLGIG	UK Lesbian and Gay Immigration Group
UKVI	United Kingdom Visas and Immigration
UN	United Nations
UNHCR	UN High Commissioner for Refugees
USA	United States of America
VCLT	Vienna Convention on the Law of the Treaties

Part I
Contextualising SOGI Asylum Research

Chapter 1
Why Sexual Orientation and Gender Identity Asylum?

> *I'm here, stuck. I'm invisible in this country, nobody sees me, nobody sees my accomplishments, I am invisible.*
>
> (Marhoon, Germany)
> (Throughout these volumes, asylum claimant and refugee participants will be referred to only by first name/pseudonym and host country to safeguard their anonymity; references to other categories of participants will specify the capacity in which they were interviewed. Survey participants will be referred to by codes: C corresponds to claimants and S to supporters. More details about our methodology can be found in Chap. 2.)
>
> *The situation [for SOGI claimants] is disastrous...*
>
> (Maria Grazia, decision-maker, Italy)
>
> *Where to start! The whole system is broken and not fit for purpose, so of course this affects LGBTQI+ people along with everyone else.*
>
> (S110, NGO volunteer, UK)

1.1 Seeking Asylum: Why Focus on Sexual Orientation and Gender Identity

Forced migration – no matter how we wish to define it – has been high in the political agendas and debates across the world for several decades. Forced migrants become claimants of international protection, or 'asylum claimants',[1] and then find themselves trapped in convoluted, constraining and highly politicised systems. Often accused of being 'bogus' asylum claimants, they are also regularly accused of abusing the hospitality of the host country, violating countries' borders and

---

[1] 'Asylum' will be used throughout these volumes as encompassing both those claims for refugee status on the basis of the 1951 Refugee Convention and those claims for subsidiary protection and humanitarian protection, where available.

© The Author(s) 2021
C. Danisi et al., *Queering Asylum in Europe*, IMISCOE Research Series,
https://doi.org/10.1007/978-3-030-69441-8_1

territorial sovereignty, and simply seeking economic benefits (Ford 2009; UNHCR 2007). Conversely, asylum legal instruments have been repeatedly criticised for inadequately addressing the rights and needs of asylum claimants, therefore preventing those with legitimate claims from being granted protection. These debates have more recently been rehashed in the context of the negotiations behind the Global Compact for Safe Orderly and Regular Migration, a non-legally binding agreement negotiated under the aegis of the United Nations (UN) and endorsed by the UN General Assembly.[2] In this atmosphere of permanent politicised and humanitarian 'crisis' (McAdam 2014), a group warranting specific attention is constituted by those asylum claimants presenting a claim based on their sexual orientation or gender identity (SOGI).[3]

The precariousness affecting asylum claimants' legal and social experiences, in general, affects SOGI asylum claimants in very particular ways. This should come as no surprise, as queer migration studies have long revealed sexuality and gender to interact with several other characteristics to be key elements in the power relationships that shape migration (Luibhéid 2004, 2008). A key aspect in this context can be found in rights discourses. Human rights have been increasingly recognised irrespective of one's SOGI both at an international (Human Rights Council 2011; Various 2017) and domestic level. Yet, the legal frameworks of European and other countries, the European Union (EU), and the Council of Europe (CoE) have been slow in tackling the violation of such rights. Members of SOGI minorities across the world often find themselves trapped within borders of territories where they cannot vindicate their rights or secure minimum levels of safety and well-being.[4] Such state borders are compounded by legal, social and economic borders that further isolate and marginalise SOGI minorities.

It is thus entirely predictable that these minorities often see no alternative to leaving their countries of origin and seeking protection in other countries, where they frequently continue to endure various degrees of harassment, discrimination and violence, perpetrated by both private and public actors (IOM and UNHCR 2016; Luibhéid 2008, p. 170; Muntarbhorn 2017; UNHCR 2015, p. 27). As Terry, a member of the European Parliament, puts it:

> I think there is more awareness today around the problems, that there is persecution because of sexual orientation and gender identity, and that this should actually lead to people having the possibility to find safe haven inside of the European Union. At the same time, we also see that there is a general trend in asylum policies, for the European Union and also the member states of the European Union, to become more restrictive, and so I see that it is

---

[2] Seventy-third Session, 60th and 61st Meetings, GA/12113, 19 December 2018.

[3] For a clarification on the meaning of the terminology used in these volumes, see glossary here: http://www.sogica.org/en/the-project/glossary/

[4] We use the term 'minorities' for ease of communication, but are conscious that such groups are in reality 'minoritised', in the sense that they are constituted by active processes of 'othering' that designate certain attributes of groups in particular contexts as being in a 'minority' (Gunaratnam 2003, p. 17).

harder for asylum seekers to get asylum granted in the end, that it is harder to make their case, and in some member states so hard as if they want to get juridical support, consultancy from NGOs for example, they are restricted to access and so on and so on.

In these volumes we explore the legal and social experiences of those people who flee persecution in their home countries and somehow manage to travel to Europe, where they eventually present asylum claims relating to their SOGI. These claims are commonly perceived by judges, practitioners and academics alike as being particularly problematic. This is due to a mixture of factors, including the increasing number and awareness of such claims, the perceived unfairness in the adjudication of these claims, and the heavily politicised decision-making environment, with some evidence pointing to a disproportionately high rate of refusals on these grounds (UKLGIG 2010). These claims also raise particular issues in relation to different aspects of asylum adjudication, especially the intense social prejudice against these claimants in their country of origin, the role of legislation – namely criminalisation – in the country of origin in endorsing that prejudice, the assessment of credibility, the lack of possibility of internal relocation, and the role of private actors in persecution. Finally, these claimants face particular psycho-social challenges in terms of personal identity and community integration in the host state (Jansen and Spijkerboer 2011; UKLGIG 2010, 2013).[5] SOGI asylum claims are thus of a striking complexity and significance for the purposes of assessing the efficiency and fairness of an asylum adjudication system (Saiz 2004; Tunstall 2006). Importantly, SOGI claimants experience much suffering, as our participants have told us. Ali (UK), for example, asked himself 'why am I humiliating myself, why am I doing this to myself', and Lutfor (UK) told us that 'when I was in the asylum system, I felt it was like I came from another hell to this hell'.

These volumes deliver a much needed European comparative study of SOGI-based asylum claims, thereby contributing to improvements in the standards of law, decision and policy-making. So far, comparative works have for the most part concentrated on discrete matters in two or three countries, or attempted to compare a larger number of countries but being unable to offer a theoretically and empirically-informed in-depth treatment of the subject-matter. We combine the best of both approaches, by drawing from insights from a range of countries, as well as offering a theoretically and empirically-informed in-depth analysis of the subject-matter in a selection of key countries in this field. Such comparative approach addresses the urgent need to tackle the lack of reliable data that is currently perpetuating misunderstandings about the plight of SOGI asylum claimants and, in turn, perpetuating discriminatory and exclusionary treatment. Simultaneously, we aim to test whether

---

[5] We will use the term (social or community) 'integration' throughout these volumes for ease of communication, while acknowledging that it is a problematic notion, critiqued by scholars from various angles (Ager and Strang 2008; Castles et al. 2001). As this is not a central notion to our analysis, we will not expand on our use of it or the relevant critique. For our purposes, we will use this term loosely, as encompassing a range of aspects of the lives of asylum claimants and refugees (such as education, health and employment), without suggesting any degree of assimilation or loss of cultural identity.

the racialised, gendered, classist, heteronormative and homonormative legal and social experiences that SOGI asylum claimants undergo in other jurisdictions also take place in Europe (Aberman 2014; see, on intersectionality, Chap. 3). In doing so, we hope to re-politicise, de-criminalise and re-historicise the actions of SOGI asylum claimants escaping persecution and seeking international protection (Judge 2010; Chaps. 5 and 7).

Nobody knows exactly how many SOGI claimants there are in Europe, as asylum statistics generally only refer to the overall number of claims/decisions, nationality of asylum claimants, and outcome of procedures (including type of status granted). To our knowledge, only Belgium and Norway (which are not amongst the most statistically significant EU asylum host countries: EUROSTAT 2019) collect statistics regarding the claimants' SOGI (European Migration Network 2016), and the UK has – and only since 2017 – released experimental statistics regarding asylum claims on the basis of sexual orientation (Home Office 2017, 2018a, 2019). The very limited (and often poor) collection of this data (ICIBI 2014, p. 42 ff), despite decades of advocacy, can be seen as strategic – and even a tool of control by public authorities – to limit the strength of advocacy efforts on behalf of these claimants and force advocates into the realm of speculation (Kadir, NGO worker, Germany). Although it is recognised that statistics should be as thorough as possible, there are practical issues and deficiencies that prevent statistical high standards across the EU, and, as a European Commission staff member has told us, including information regarding claimants' SOGI is also problematic owing to the sensitive nature of this data. The judiciary also seems to oppose collection of this data: Harry, a UK senior judge, suggested to us that 'it would be too controversial, wouldn't it, really?', and Adrian, another UK judge, also stated that 'we don't keep statistics of that sort, obviously, it would be quite wrong to do so'. Similarly, according to the German government, it is the claimant's decision to inform government institutions about their SOGI. This cannot be asked routinely, as SOGI can be of relevance during the asylum process but may not be. In contrast to the UK, the German government argues that the right to freedom of choice with regard to the use of personal information needs to be respected, and 'the offensive interrogation and storage of intimate and highly personal information on sexual identity or other vulnerabilities' would interfere with this right (BMI 2019, p. 5).

In the absence of reliable figures, in 2011 (pre-'refugee crisis'), Jansen and Spijkerboer have roughly estimated an annual overall number of 10,000 LGBTI (lesbian, gay, bisexual, trans and intersex) asylum claimants in the EU (Jansen and Spijkerboer 2011, pp. 15–16),[6] and according to the German LGBTIQ+ (lesbian, gay, bisexual, trans, intersex, queer and others) rights organisation Schwulenberatung, there are an estimated 3500 SOGI asylum claimants in Berlin alone (Thomson Reuters Foundation 2016). Nonetheless, no statistical correlations between countries, claimants' SOGI, claim basis, and outcomes of the claims can be established

---

[6] This figure thus relates to the identity of the asylum claimant, as opposed to the grounds for the asylum claim, even if in practice there may be no substantial difference in the estimate achieved.

1.1 Seeking Asylum: Why Focus on Sexual Orientation and Gender Identity   7

at present. Within this grouping of claims, it appears that the number of female claims is smaller than those of male claims, possibly owing to the lower number of female claims in general (due to limited financial resources and independence enabling women to escape persecution), less social visibility of lesbians in many countries compared to gay men, and less severe legal punishments (although only on the statute books and not in reality) for lesbian same-sex conduct (Dawson and Gerber 2017, pp. 305 and 318; Neilson 2005, p. 419; Ramón Mendos 2019; Terry, member of the European Parliament).[7] The numbers of trans, bisexual and intersex claims is perceptibly smaller still, but again unquantifiable.

We set out to include in our research both SOGI asylum *claimants*, on the one hand, and SOGI-based asylum *claims*, on the other, as overlapping but conceptually different categories. SOGI asylum claimants may lodge asylum claims on non-SOGI-related grounds, either feeling reluctant to 'out' themselves during the asylum procedure and fearing that friends and family will find out about their SOGI (Held et al. 2018; Kalkmann 2010); because another ground is more relevant to their experience of persecution (for example, political or religious persecution); or because they may not know that claiming asylum on grounds of SOGI is a possibility (Chap. 5). Moreover, SOGI-based asylum claims may be lodged by heterosexual and cis-gender individuals, for example, when a certain minority sexual orientation is merely imputed to the claimant by the persecutors. Yet, the focus of this work is more squarely on SOGI as grounds for an international protection claim, as in our fieldwork we only met SOGI asylum claimants who were primarily claiming on the basis of SOGI.

We endeavour to place the experiences of individuals claiming asylum at the centre of this work. We do so by combining a comparative study (Germany, Italy, and the UK), an interdisciplinary approach (socio-legal), and an empirical methodology (semi-structured interviews, focus groups, judicial observations and a survey). Our analysis is grounded in human rights, feminist, intersectional and queer theoretical and analytical frameworks. This combined empirical and theoretical treatment secures new insights, laying the ground for policy-relevant recommendations of benefit to the academic community and asylum practitioner community alike. We begin by contextualising our subject matter in the international and European legal and policy frameworks.

---

[7] In the UK, for example, in 2016, of 30,747 asylum applicants, 23,066 were men (Home Office 2018b).

1.2 The International and European Legal, Policy and Social Context

The 1951 Convention Relating to the Status of Refugees (Refugee Convention),[8] along with the 1967 Protocol Relating to the Status of Refugees,[9] were developed in the aftermath of World War 2 and built on the 1949 Geneva Convention relative to the Protection of Civilian Persons in Time of War,[10] to regulate the movements of refugees across Europe and beyond (Rabben 2016). Article 1(A)(2) of the Convention defines refugees as someone who:

> owing to well-founded fear of being persecuted for reasons of race, religion, nationality, membership of a particular social group or political opinion, is outside the country of [their] nationality and is unable or, owing to such fear, is unwilling to avail [themselves] of the protection of that country; or who, not having a nationality and being outside the country of [their] former habitual residence as a result of such events, is unable or, owing to such fear, is unwilling to return to it.

Although simply a part of a much more complex system of assistance to displaced persons and regulation of refugee movements (Ferreira et al. 2020), this definition and, more generally, these UN instruments stand as the cornerstone of this system. Complementing this system, each domestic jurisdiction has introduced constitutional norms and/or ordinary statutes that enshrine the right to international protection.

Later in time, the EU also developed its own system of norms and policies applicable to people seeking asylum: the work-in-progress Common European Asylum System (CEAS).[11] CEAS is a system designed to set minimum standards across the EU member states with regard to different aspects of asylum, especially the standards for the reception of claimants for international protection, the qualification of third-country nationals or stateless persons as beneficiaries of international protection, and the procedures for granting and withdrawing international protection (Gorlick 2003; Noll 2000). CEAS aims to fulfil two main aims: to be fair and to be effective (Ippolito and Velluti 2011). Yet, the success of the CEAS has been undermined by a lack of harmonisation and consistency in standards across EU member states, which has remained the case even after the introduction of the recast EU Directives 2011/95/EU on qualification for international protection (Qualification

---

[8] UN General Assembly, *Convention Relating to the Status of Refugees*, 28 July 1951, United Nations, Treaty Series, vol. 189, p. 137.

[9] UN General Assembly, *Protocol Relating to the Status of Refugees*, 31 January 1967, United Nations, Treaty Series, vol. 606, p. 267.

[10] Adopted on 12 August 1949 by the Diplomatic Conference for the Establishment of International Conventions for the Protection of Victims of War.

[11] For further discussion on some specific rules in this system, see Chaps. 4, 6 and 7.

Directive),[12] 2013/32/EU on asylum procedures (Procedures Directive),[13] and 2013/33/EU on reception conditions (Reception Directive) (De Baere 2013; Velluti 2014).[14] Furthermore, the EU has become an anxious and eager player in this field, especially in light of the increased number of people claiming asylum in Europe in 2014–2017, a number that has gone down to 634,700 applications in the EU, Norway and Switzerland in 2018, an approximate 10% decrease compared to 2017 (EASO 2019). The starkly different number of claimants received by each EU member state and the considerable variation of refugee recognition rates across the EU remain two of the major challenges to the CEAS, awaiting a political solution that struggles to materialise in the current politically-charged migration and refugee debates in Europe.

Within an increasingly complex and politicised asylum policy context, domestic jurisdictions started granting international protection – including refugee status – to SOGI asylum claimants in the early 1980s, under the 'particular social group' (PSG) ground, with the Netherlands leading on this development in 1981.[15] This development gradually, but very slowly took place across other jurisdictions in Europe and around the world,[16] as a combined reaction to socio-cultural factors (growing movements across Western countries on 'gay' rights and the fight against AIDS), institutional and personnel changes in the asylum system, the gradual tendency to build on incremental progress in asylum authorities' procedures and policies, theoretical breakthroughs (including pioneering feminist and queer theories), international and supranational legal and policy advancements (particularly at EU

---

[12] Directive 2011/95/EU of the European Parliament and of the Council of 13 December, 2011 on standards for the qualification of third-country nationals or stateless persons as beneficiaries of international protection, for a uniform status for refugees or for persons eligible for subsidiary protection, and for the content of the protection granted, OJ L 337, 20.12.2011, p. 9–26, which replaced Council Directive 2004/83/EC of 29 April 2004 on minimum standards for the qualification and status of third country nationals or stateless persons as refugees or as persons who otherwise need international protection and the content of the protection granted, OJ L 304, 30.9.2004, p. 12–23.

[13] Directive 2013/32/EU of the European Parliament and of the Council of 26 June 2013 on common procedures for granting and withdrawing international protection, OJ L 180, 29.6.2013, p. 60–95, which replaced Council Directive 2005/85/EC of 1 December 2005 on minimum standards on procedures in Member States for granting and withdrawing refugee status, OJ L 326, 13.12.2005, p. 13–34.

[14] Directive 2013/33/EU of the European Parliament and of the Council of 26 June 2013 laying down standards for the reception of applicants for international protection, OJ L 180, 29.6.2013, p. 96–116, which replaced Council Directive 2003/9/EC of 27 January 2003 laying down minimum standards for the reception of asylum seekers, OJ L 31, 6.2.2003, p. 18–25.

[15] Judgment of 13 August 1981, Afelding Rechtspraak (Judicial Commission of the Council of State) no. A-2, 1113 Rechtspraak Vluchtelingenrecht no. 51981.

[16] In the USA, decision of the Board of Immigration Appeals (BIA), *Matter of Acosta*, A-24159781, 1 March 1985; in Germany, judgment of the Federal Administrative Court, BVerwG 9 C 278.86, 15 March 1988, 79 BVerwGE 143; in Canada, judgment of the Supreme Court, *Canada (Attorney General) c. Ward*, n. 21,937, 30 June 1993 (4DLR 103; 1993 2 RCS 689). The German judgment did not refer to PSG but political persecution. See, also, Millbank 2009b, p. 13.

level), and the growing recognition of SOGI as the basis for rights claims (Ferreira 2015; Hamila 2019, pp. 160–161; Kobelinsky 2015; Various 2017). This, however, has been a contentious and arduous trajectory, reflecting tensions between an increasingly progressive LGBTIQ+ equality agenda, on the one hand, and a strategy aimed to prevent the arrival of migrants to Europe (including people in need of international protection), an ever more hostile environment for all migrants, and a large degree of deference by international bodies to member states regarding migration and asylum matters, on the other hand (Danisi 2018; Dembour 2015; Ferreira 2021). This siloed approach to the LGBTIQ+ equality agenda, on the one hand, and migration and asylum, on the other, is a common feature of current debates, reflected in institutional reports and policy papers (for example, FRA 2019).

Against this background, international bodies have increasingly dotted their recommendations and reports with positive references to SOGI asylum claimants, with the UN Independent Expert on protection against violence and discrimination based on sexual orientation and gender identity (Victor Madrigal-Borloz), in particular, highlighting the 'unique vulnerability and specific needs of lesbian, gay, bisexual, trans, intersex and gender diverse (LGBTI) asylum-seekers and refugees' (OHCHR 2019). Nonetheless, the protection of SOGI asylum claimants has failed to attract sufficient support from UN quasi-judicial bodies. In 2003, for example, the UN Committee Against Torture addressed the *K.S.Y.* case,[17] involving a gay Iranian man who sought asylum in the Netherlands and saw his claim denied. He then filed a complaint before the Committee Against Torture, on the grounds that his deportation to Iran would violate Article 3 of the Convention against Torture and Other Cruel, Inhuman or Degrading Treatment or Punishment (on prohibition of return in case of danger of subjection to torture, also known as the principle of non-refoulement). K.S.Y reported having been tortured and sentenced to death in Iran due to his homosexuality. Both the torture suffered and post-traumatic stress disorder (PTSD) were confirmed by medical reports. In a surprisingly short and superficial consideration of the complaint's merits, the Committee subscribed to the Dutch authorities' arguments: there was no active policy of prosecution of homosexuals in Iran, and the claimant's account lacked credibility. More recently, the UN Human Rights Committee dealt with the *M.Z.B.M v. Denmark* case,[18] relating to a transgender Malaysian woman who claimed that her deportation from Denmark would violate her rights under Article 7 of the International Covenant on Civil and Political Rights (ICCPR) (on prohibition of inhuman and degrading treatment), in conjunction with Articles 17(1) (on privacy and family life), 18(1) (on freedom of thought, conscience and religion) and 26 (on non-discrimination). Although admitting the claim regarding gender identity, the Committee accepted the domestic authorities' assessment of lack of credibility and found there would be no violation of ICCPR rights upon her removal to Malaysia.

---

[17] UN Committee Against Torture in *K. S. Y. v. The Netherlands*, Communication No. 190/2001, 15 May 2003, CAT/C/30/D/190/2001.

[18] *M.Z.B.M v. Denmark* (Communication no. 2593/2015), 119th Session (6 March 2017–29 March 2017).

Despite this somewhat bleak picture at UN level, the UN High Commissioner for Refugees (UNHCR) has been proactive in protecting the rights of SOGI asylum claimants and refugees for more than a decade. While it had already expressed an interest in SOGI-related persecution in the late 1990s (Bissland and Lawand 1997), it was in 2008 that the UNHCR issued a 'Guidance Note on Refugee Claims Relating to Sexual Orientation and Gender Identity' (UNHCR 2008), subsequently replaced by the 2012 SOGI Guidelines (UNHCR 2012). Building on the UNHCR 2002 'Guidelines on International Protection No. 1: Gender-Related Persecution' (UNHCR 2002), the SOGI Guidelines offer valuable assistance to decision-makers and support organisations in the field, encouraging them to become more sensitised to the needs and specificities of SOGI asylum claims. Although by 2008 many countries across the world already granted refugee status to SOGI asylum claimants within the scope of membership of a PSG ground (Chap. 7), the UNHCR Guidance gave these claims a new and welcome prominence, raising hopes of greater fairness and appropriateness in the adjudication of these claims. Subsequent work – including staff operational guidance, risk identification tools, and resettlement assessment tools – has reinforced the UNHCR's commitment to improving the conditions of SOGI asylum claimants (Türk 2013; UNHCR 2015).

While the UNHCR's efforts in this field are commendable, there are still strong signs that the SOGI dimensions of asylum claims are treated in a particularly insensitive way in many countries, often inappropriately at legal, cultural and social levels. This has been explored by some scholarship and other literature over the years and has focused, for example, on asylum claimants' proof of belonging to a PSG, their identity, past and future risk of persecution, and credibility (Balboni 2012; Dustin 2018; Güler et al. 2019; ICIBI 2014; Jansen 2019; Jansen and Spijkerboer 2011; Millbank 2009a, b). Evidence of stereotyped adjudication processes presents a challenge to the claimed impartiality and objectivity of the legal system. Our survey with people who work with or support SOGI claimants confirmed that there are still significant problems in the asylum legal process, namely in relation to credibility assessment (81%), stereotyping (60%), Country of Origin Information (COI) (48%), 'discretion' reasoning (40%), the claimants' unawareness that SOGI can be the basis for claiming asylum (39%), and the 'internal relocation alternative' argument (34%). The jurisprudence at European level – both from the Court of Justice of the EU (CJEU) and European Court of Human Rights (ECtHR) – has either not addressed these issues appropriately, or only addressed them in a partially satisfactory way (Ferreira 2018, 2021).

The reported unfairness of the legal system is compounded by these asylum claimants being 'doubly' isolated, that is, not only as asylum claimants, but also as members of SOGI minorities. Often they cannot rely for support on their families or expatriate communities of other individuals who share their ethnicity and/or nationality to live freely and safely (Çalik and Hayriye 2016). Furthermore, SOGI claimants are frequently affected by serious psychological trauma and mental health conditions – including recurrent depression, dissociative disorders, panic disorder, generalised anxiety disorder, social anxiety, traumatic brain injury, substance abuse and PTSD – on account of the persecution they suffered in their home countries and their journeys to host countries (Hopkinson et al. 2017; Kahn et al. 2017; Shidlo and Ahola 2013). Yet, the asylum adjudication process often makes unreasonable expectations of asylum claimants; expectations that they will feel able to be entirely open, and give full, consistent and lucid accounts of their SOGI and experiences of persecution.

SOGI claimants' experiences are also highly variable amongst themselves. While considering SOGI claimants' experiences collectively may have value for the purposes of activism and service provision (for example, when advocating for targeted accommodation or community groups), it is important to disaggregate the identities of SOGI claimants in many contexts in order to offer more adequate and tailored services (Chap. 11). This can be clearly seen, for example, in relation to individuals claiming asylum on grounds of their gender identity – or who may present their claims on other grounds but identify as trans. There are reports of inadequate staff training, erroneous recording of these claims as pertaining to sexual orientation, and inappropriate assessments of lack of credibility (TGEU 2016, p. 6). In terms of social integration, trans asylum claimants face difficulties in finding specific social support and community groups, which leads to particular forms of isolation (TGEU 2016, p. 7). Many further issues may go unreported, leaving us with only a partial picture of these individuals' experiences.

Despite substantial scholarly and activist efforts in some countries to address the SOGI dimensions of asylum matters, NGOs' efforts and scholarly criticism concerning SOGI claims are still scarce in many European jurisdictions. This prevents the improvement of procedural and substantive decision-making and social integration in cases involving SOGI asylum claims. There is still need for a more comprehensive, theoretically and empirically-grounded analysis of the legal and social experiences of SOGI asylum claimants across several European jurisdictions. This is what these volumes aim to do.

1.3 Framing Our Research

Although there are instances of SOGI asylum claimants being resettled to European countries (Taylor 2019), their limited number and the nature of our fieldwork have led us to focus almost exclusively on claimants who undergo the refugee status determination (RSD) process in European countries. In other words, our analysis is limited to instances of territorial asylum, where claimants have reached the territory of the country where international protection is sought, as opposed to other forms of asylum such as diplomatic asylum. Our analysis is also limited to the individual assessment of international protection needs, rather than group assessment, as may happen in relation to group arrivals or groups of claimants from certain countries of origin (for example, Syria).

Focus will remain on developments that have taken place since the creation of the EU CEAS, in other words, post-1999 (Ferreira 2018), which has framed most key features of the asylum systems in EU countries. We focus mostly on the

1.3 Framing Our Research

SOGI-specific dimensions of the asylum experiences of SOGI claimants, and how these intersect with other dimensions (such as 'race', class, religion, etc.), rather than analysing their entire experiences.

Three levels of analysis are employed throughout these volumes: i) macro-level, through the examination of the incorporation by current legal frameworks of the emergent SOGI dimensions of human rights, the different scopes and approaches of asylum policies in European countries with regard to SOGI, and the fairness of the asylum adjudication process in SOGI-related claims; ii) meso-level, through the examination of the way in which the asylum adjudication system interrelates with these claimants' self-perceptions and integration both in the host communities and in the established diaspora of fellow nationals; iii) micro-level, through the examination of how, in the course of the asylum adjudication process and beyond, asylum claimants' identities evolve and adapt.

These volumes rely on a combined comparative, socio-legal and empirical methodology, as further explored in Chap. 2. As case studies for our comparative approach, we have adopted Germany, Italy and the UK. The rationale behind this choice is explained in Chap. 2. While acknowledging a range of other interests and perspectives (including states' sovereignty over borders, security and societal fears), we unapologetically adopt a normative approach that draws above all from the theoretical and analytical underpinnings expounded in Chap. 3, thus favouring human rights, feminist, queer and intersectional perspectives.

Terminology in the field of asylum/refugee policy and gender/sexuality has become a veritable minefield, both in academia and activism. This makes it important to dedicate space to explaining our terminological choices and offer some caveats before proceeding. While writing these volumes, the first choice before us was to decide how to refer to asylum and refugee matters. The term 'asylum seeker' has become negatively loaded in political and public debates and is rightly seen as dehumanising by many people, so there have been calls to replace it with 'people seeking asylum' (African Rainbow Family 2017). Endorsing this position, we thus either refer to people seeking asylum or asylum claimants throughout these volumes. We also explicitly refute the expression 'failed asylum seeker', because:

> [t]he use of the term "failed" evokes fault of the individual that he or she has not succeeded in obtaining international protection just as students who fail their exams did not study sufficiently or were inadequate. The individual is responsible for his or her fate, the authorities warned him or her of the risk of a poor application but he or she persisted in pursuing, inadequately, the claim. (Guild 2012, p. 20)

We favour instead the expression 'unsuccessful claim' or 'rejected claim', thus putting the emphasis on the lack of success of the claim, not the person. More generally, we will refer to 'refugees' in a non-technical way, thus including all beneficiaries of international protection, unless we specify the legal status granted.

Other fundamental terminological choices refer to whether to adopt characteristics (sexual orientation, gender identity, etc.) or identities (gay, lesbian, trans, etc.) as the key focus of our analysis (to use the common, if potentially reductive choice of terminologies available in this field of research). As one can deduce from this introduction, we have opted for the former. We chose a characteristic, as opposed to an identity-focused analysis, because a focus on certain identities and the use of terms such as 'LGBT' creates a greater risk of replicating Westernised concepts of personhood for individuals claiming asylum (something further explored throughout these volumes). Focusing on certain characteristics and using terms such as 'SOGI' reflects, or aims to consolidate, a more universal and cross-cultural basis for discussion, more sensitive to an intersectional approach to SOGI asylum (Dayle et al. 2010; Dustin and Ferreira 2017). As one of our participants said, 'I chose to say that I am gay, it's easy to understand and accept here [Europe]. Even if I keep thinking that being LGBTQ as definition is reductive' (C61, Italy). Moreover, as we explore further in Chap. 3, while:

> queers may reject the [LGBT+] acronym altogether, often because of its identitarian, culturally specific, or geo-politically loaded reference points (…) SOGI is used by the UN and is often used outside the West because of its capacity to be distant from the Western cultural and identitarian forms usually associated with the categories in the LGBT+ acronym. (Langlois 2018, p. 155)

Where appropriate to refer to an identity-based acronym, we have either opted for the acronym used by the author being discussed, or for LGBTIQ+, conscious of the scope to expand this acronym with a practically infinite number of other specific identities (for example, asexual, pansexual, unsure, polyamorous, etc.). While conscious that the UN opts for the acronym LGBTI (United Nations Human Rights Office 2019), we have found it important to add Q for queer, as 'identity categories are burdened by legacies that must be interrogated, do not map neatly across time and space, and become transformed through circulation within specific, unequally situated local, regional, national and transnational circuits' (Luibhéid 2008, p. 170).

Four further clarifications are relevant in this context. First, sexual orientation and gender identity constitute separate characteristics, but persecution related to these two notions raises common issues in terms of individuals' non-compliance with held social and cultural conceptions of gender roles (Kendall 2003; Miller 2000; Stichelbaut 2009, p. 70; UNHCR 2002). In essence, both sexual orientation and gender identity asylum claims are a consequence of 'failing to conform to gender-prescribed social norms and mores or for claiming their rights' (CEDAW 2014, par. 15). So, both these characteristics need to be considered if we are to tackle the insufficiencies of the asylum system, even if recognising along the way their autonomy, hence predominantly adopting the acronym SOGI throughout these volumes. Further characteristics such as sexual characteristics (or intersex variations) and gender expression, while distinct from SOGI, are also deeply connected to oppression on account of gender roles and are thus relevant to our subject-matter. This would have made the acronym SOGIESC (sexual orientation, gender identity and expression, and sexual characteristics) appropriate as well. While not adopting SOGIESC as our core acronym, we consider sexual characteristics and gender expression where relevant. However, we remain focused on SOGI, as that is where our empirical data has, for the most part, led us.

Second, where it is more appropriate to refer to certain SOGI-related identities in the light of the issues or data in question, we favour, wherever possible and known, the identities ascribed by those concerned to themselves. When not specified by the individuals in question, we have avoided ascribing an identity. And when wishing to refer to non-heterosexual and non-cisgender people generally, we also use the terms 'sexual minorities' and 'gender minorities'.

Third, 'sexual identity' is a term that is sometimes used to encompass a range of SOGI-related characteristics, and employed to replace 'SOGI' or 'SOGIESC'. As 'sexual identity' is not yet a term that is widely used and acknowledged, or consensually understood, we have opted not to use this term as our main terminology, despite its potential and merits, unless when referring to other sources that use that expression. Similarly, we do not use the words 'homosexual' and 'homosexuality', owing to their negative connotations, being increasingly disfavoured and replaced with the words 'gay' and 'lesbian' in English-speaking contexts. Yet, they are still frequently used in judicial decisions, policy documents and in other languages, and so we use the terms in the context of such sources without endorsing them.

Finally, we acknowledge that not everyone we wish to refer to, in the context of our fieldwork and beyond, may identify as a member of a 'sexual minority' or a 'gender minority', or see the matters discussed as a matter of 'sexual orientation' or 'gender identity'. We try to respect our participants' preferences as far as possible, while retaining the consistency needed for the purposes of these volumes.

1.4 The Structure of These Volumes

These volumes are constituted by 11 chapters, with Vol. 1 gathering Chaps. 1–6 and Vol. 2 gathering Chaps. 7–11. Chapters are divided into three Parts, with Part I in Vol. 1, Part II straddling the two volumes, and Part III in Vol. 2. Part I is aimed at contextualising our research on SOGI asylum and is constituted by four chapters. Following this introductory chapter, Chap. 2 offers an overview of the methodology used in the research underlying these volumes, including a discussion of the range of empirical methods employed. The chapter will also explore insights gained through our research in relation to conducting empirical research with refugees. Chapter 3 sets out the theoretical underpinnings of our research, derived from human rights, feminist theory, queer studies and intersectionality. This chapter identifies and explores a number of debates within these three vast and diverse bodies of literature, debates chosen for the novel contribution they can make to our understanding of SOGI asylum. After a critical analysis of these contributions, we use them to identify key underpinning principles or themes that will guide and inform the subsequent data analysis in the chapters that follow to provide a coherence to our approach, while avoiding a restrictive or orthodox approach to SOGI asylum. Chapter 4 concludes Part I by exploring the legal and policy framework that applies to SOGI asylum in the case study jurisdictions, including an exploration of key actors and instruments, the degree of domestic asylum systems' compliance with supranational and international obligations, specific SOGI asylum policy and guidance, and the range of outcomes an asylum claimant may expect, amongst other issues.

Part II offers an analysis of the legal and social experiences of SOGI asylum claimants and refugees across the three case study jurisdictions and further across Europe. Chapter 5 considers the lives of individuals before fleeing persecution, the journey and arrival in Europe, including a range of social and legal aspects. These include the availability in the three countries under comparison of information on SOGI asylum upon arrival, as well as what assessment is carried out, especially in relation to SOGI claimants' initial accommodation. Chapter 6 – the last one in Vol. 1 – proceeds to exploring SOGI asylum in the context of decision-making procedures, including: the interview setting; the training and conduct of caseworkers, judges, interpreters and other people working with SOGI claimants; how COI is produced and used in relation to SOGI asylum claimants; the impact of individuals' personal background and prejudices; and access to and quality of legal representation at initial decision-making stage and appeal stage.

Volume 2 starts with Chap. 7, which considers how the substance of SOGI asylum claims is dealt with. In particular, its analysis focuses on how decision-makers assess whether a SOGI asylum claimant is a member of a PSG (including whether the claimant's SOGI self-identification is influential), how the notion of 'persecution' is assessed (including the role of criminalisation of same-sex acts in the claim assessment), and to what extent the notion of 'internal relocation' is a relevant consideration. This chapter will also explore the evidentiary standards and how they are applied to SOGI claimants, exploring how decision-makers assess the 'credibility' of SOGI asylum claimants and whether a 'culture of disbelief' still persists amongst asylum authorities.

Chapter 8 shifts the focus to the lived experiences of SOGI asylum claimants in relation to housing and accommodation. This includes an analysis of SOGI asylum claimants' perceptions of reception and accommodation centres, experiences of detention, longer-term accommodation, homelessness and destitution, and post-refugee status housing arrangements. To conclude Part II, Chap. 9 focuses on a range of other aspects in the lives of SOGI asylum claimants and refugees that have a significant impact on their feelings, well-being and quality of life, but are often inappropriately regulated, namely access to healthcare services, the labour market and educational provision. The chapter explores access to mental health services, experiences of torture and sexual violence, the impact of being denied the right to work, experiences of volunteering, and issues related to language tuition and access to higher education, as well as emotional health more generally.

Part III presents our vision for a better future for SOGI asylum in Europe, one where all actors place greater trust in the asylum system and are confident of its fairness, as defined by the analysis carried out in these volumes. Chapter 10 brings together experiences of harassment, isolation and oppression that participants shared with us. The analysis revolves around four key themes – identities, discrimination, space and agency – all of which affect both the legal and social experiences of SOGI claimants. Finally, Chap. 11 offers a range of policy recommendations addressed to decision-makers, policy-makers, NGOs and service providers, for improving the socio-legal framework that applies to SOGI asylum. These focus mainly on domestic level contexts, but also refer to the European level to offer a more encompassing analysis. This chapter also functions as the conclusion to these volumes, and offers some final observations on the theme of SOGI asylum in Europe.

References

Aberman, T. (2014). Gendered perspectives on refugee determination in Canada. *Refuge: Canada's Journal on Refugees, 30*(2), 57–66.

African Rainbow Family. (2017). We are human – Manchester declaration. *African Rainbow Family*. https://africanrainbowfamily.org/2018/04/23/we-are-human-manchester-declaration/

Ager, A., & Strang, A. (2008). Understanding integration: A conceptual framework. *Journal of Refugee Studies, 21*(2), 166–191. https://doi.org/10.1093/jrs/fen016.

Balboni, M. (2012). *La protezione internazionale in ragione del genere, dell'orientamento sessuale e dell'identità di genere*. Giappichelli.

Bissland, J., & Lawand, K. (1997). Report of the UNHCR symposium on gender-based persecution. *International Journal of Refugee Law, 9*(Special_Issue), 11–31. https://doi.org/10.1093/reflaw/9.

BMI – Bundesministerium des Innern, für Bau und Heimat. (2019). *Kleine Anfrage der Abgeordneten Ulla Jelpke u.a. Und der Fraktion DIE LINKE: Situation von LSBTI-Geflüchteten (BT-Drucksache19/10308)*. https://www.ulla-jelpke.de/wp-content/uploads/2019/06/19_10308-LSBTI-Gefl%C3%BCchtete.pdf

Çalik, D., & Hayriye, K. (2016). *Waiting to be "safe and sound": Turkey as LGBTI refugees' Way Station*. Kaos Gay and Lesbian Cultural Research and Solidarity Association. https://www.asylumineurope.org/sites/default/files/resources/lgbti_refugees-_english-_multeci_raporu2016.pdf

Castles, S., Korac, M., Vasta, E., & Vertovec, S. (2001). *Integration: Mapping the field*. Centre for Migration and Policy Research and Refugee Studies Centre. https://pure.royalholloway.ac.uk/portal/en/publications/integration-mapping-the-field(ccb640e6-1466-471d-9957-2bf270c69a49)/export.html

CEDAW – Committee on the Elimination of Discrimination against Women. (2014). *General recommendation No. 32 on the gender-related dimensions of refugee status, asylum, nationality and statelessness of women (CEDAW/C/GC/32)*. https://documents-dds-ny.un.org/doc/UNDOC/GEN/N14/627/90/PDF/N1462790.pdf?OpenElement

Danisi, C. (2018). What 'safe harbours' are there for people seeking international protection on sexual orientation and gender identity grounds? A human rights reading of international law of the sea and refugee law. *GenIUS – Rivista di studi giuridici sull'orientamento sessuale e l'identità di genere (Special Issue on SOGI Asylum), 5*(2), 9–24.

Dawson, J., & Gerber, P. (2017). Assessing the refugee claims of LGBTI people: Is the DSSH model useful for determining claims by women for asylum based on sexual orientation? *International Journal of Refugee Law, 29*(2), 292–322. https://doi.org/10.1093/ijrl/eex022.

Dayle, P. L., DeJarlais, N. A., Grungras, N., Hutton, M. A., Kim, H. J., Levitan, R. S., Lo, K. C., Plant, D. A., Şengün, O., & Travis, A. A. (2010). *Rights & protection of Lesbian, gay, bisexual, transgender & intersex refugees & asylum seekers under the Yogyakarta principles*. ORAM–Organization for Refuge, Asylum & Migration. https://www.rainbowwelcome.org/uploads/pdfs/Yogyakarta%20Principles%20Article%20by%20ORAM%20September%202010.pdf

De Baere, G. (2013). *The court of justice of the EU as a European and international asylum court*. Leuven Centre for Global Governance Studies Working Paper (118). https://ghum.kuleuven.be/ggs/publications/working_papers/new_series/wp111-120/wp118-de-baere.pdf

Dembour, M.-B. (2015). *When humans become migrants: Study of the European Court of Human Rights with an Inter-American counterpoint*. Oxford University Press.

Dustin, M. (2018). Many rivers to cross: The recognition of LGBTQI asylum in the UK. *International Journal of Refugee Law, 30*(1), 104–127. https://doi.org/10.1093/ijrl/eey018.

Dustin, M., & Ferreira, N. (2017). Canada's Guideline 9: Improving SOGIE claims assessment? *Forced Migration Review, 56*(October), 80–83.

EASO – European Asylum Support Office. (2019). *Latest asylum trends—2018 overview*. https://www.easo.europa.eu/asylum-trends-overview-2018

European Migration Network. (2016). *Ad Hoc query on NL AHQ on national asylum policies regarding LGBT-asylum seekers*. https://ec.europa.eu/home-affairs/sites/homeaffairs/files/what-we-do/networks/european_migration_network/reports/docs/ad-hoc-queries/ad-hoc-queries-2016.1061_-_nl_ahq_on_national_asylum_policies_regarding_lgbt-asylum_seekers.pdf

EUROSTAT. (2019). *Asylum statistics—Statistics explained*. https://ec.europa.eu/eurostat/statistics-explained/index.php/Asylum_statistics

Ferreira, N. (2015). Portuguese refugee law in the European context. *International Journal of Refugee Law, 27*(3), 411–432. https://doi.org/10.1093/ijrl/eev032.

Ferreira, N. (2018). Reforming the Common European Asylum System: Enough rainbow for queer asylum seekers? *GenIUS – Rivista di studi giuridici sull'orientamento sessuale e l'identità di genere (Special Issue on SOGI Asylum), 5*(2), 25–42.

Ferreira, N. (2021). An exercise in detachment: The Strasbourg Court and sexual minority refugees. In R. Mole (Ed.), *Queer Migration and Asylum in Europe* (pp. 78–108). UCL.

Ferreira, N., Jacobs, C., Kea, P., Hendow, M., Noack, M., Wagner, M., Adugna, F., Alodat, A. M., Ayalew, T., Etzold, B., Fogli, C., Goumenos, T., Hatziprokopiou, P., Javed, M. M., Kamanga, K. C., Kraler, A., Momani, F. A., & Roman, E. (2020). *Governing protracted displacement: An analysis across global, regional and domestic contexts* (TRAFIG working paper 3). BICC.

Ford, R. (2009, November 3). Minister admits: We got it wrong on immigration. *The Times*.

FRA – European Union Agency for Fundamental Rights. (2019). *Fundamental rights report 2019*. FRA – European Union Agency for Fundamental Rights. https://fra.europa.eu/sites/default/files/fra_uploads/fra-2019-fundamental-rights-report-2019_en.pdf

Gorlick, B. (2003). Common burdens and standards: Legal elements in assessing claims to refugee status. *International Journal of Refugee Law, 15*(3), 357–376.

Guild, E. (2012). From persecution to management of populations: Governmentality and the Common European Asylum System. *Nijmegen Migration Law Working Papers Series, 2012*(4). http://repository.ubn.ru.nl/bitstream/handle/2066/105845/105845.pdf?sequence=1.

Güler, A., Shevtsova, M., & Venturi, D. (Eds.). (2019). *LGBTI asylum seekers and refugees from a legal and political perspective: Persecution, asylum and integration*. Springer. https://www.springer.com/us/book/9783319919041.

Gunaratnam, Y. (2003). *Researching 'race' and ethnicity: Methods, knowledge and power*. Sage. https://uk.sagepub.com/en-gb/eur/researching-race-and-ethnicity/book217580

Hamila, A. (2019). Les persécutions liées à l'orientation sexuelle: Un «nouveau» motif pour octroyer le statut de réfugié en Belgique? *Politique et Sociétés, 38*(1), 157–177. https://doi.org/10.7202/1058294ar.

Held, N., Rainbow Refugees Cologne-Support Group e.V., Aidshilfe Düsseldorf e.V., You're Welcome – Mashallah Düsseldorf, Kölner Flüchtlingsrat, Projekt Geflüchtete Queere Jugendliche, & Fachstelle Queere Jugend NRW/Schwules Netzwerk NRW e.V. (2018). *Projektbericht: Erfahrungen mit der Anhörung von LSBTIQ* Geflüchteten*. https://schwules-netzwerk.de/wp-content/uploads/2018/10/Projektbericht-zur-Anh%C3%B6rung-von-LSBTIQ-Gefl%C3%BCchteten.pdf

Home Office. (2017). *Asylum claims on the basis of sexual orientation. Experimental statistics*. GOV.UK https://www.gov.uk/government/uploads/system/uploads/attachment_data/file/663468/asylum-claims-basis-sexual-orientation.pdf

References

Home Office. (2018a). National statistics – *Experimental statistics: Asylum claims on the basis of sexual orientation*. GOV.UK https://www.gov.uk/government/publications/immigration-statistics-year-ending-september-2018/experimental-statistics-asylum-claims-on-the-basis-of-sexual-orientation

Home Office. (2018b). *National statistics: List of tables* (Asylum Data Tables, Volume 2). GOV.UK. https://www.gov.uk/government/publications/immigration-statistics-year-ending-march-2018/list-of-tables

Home Office. (2019, August 22). *Experimental statistics: Asylum claims on the basis of sexual orientation*. GOV.UK. https://www.gov.uk/government/publications/immigration-statistics-year-ending-june-2019/experimental-statistics-asylum-claims-on-the-basis-of-sexual-orientation

Hopkinson, R. A., Keatley, E., Glaeser, E., Erickson-Schroth, L., Fattal, O., & Sullivan, M. N. (2017). Persecution experiences and mental health of LGBT asylum seekers. *Journal of Homosexuality, 64*(12), 1650–1666. https://doi.org/10.1080/00918369.2016.1253392.

Human Rights Council. (2011). *Resolution adopted by the human rights council on 14 July 2011: Human rights, sexual orientation and gender identity* (A/HRC/RES/17/19). United Nations.

ICIBI – Independent Chief Inspector of Borders and Immigration. (2014). *An investigation into the Home Office's handling of asylum claims made on the grounds of sexual orientation March–June 2014*. GOV.UK. https://assets.publishing.service.gov.uk/government/uploads/system/uploads/attachment_data/file/547330/Investigation-into-the-Handling-of-Asylum-Claims_Oct_2014.pdf

IOM – International Organization for Migration, & UNHCR – UN High Commissioner for Refugees. (2016). *Module 02: Facilitation guide—Working with Lesbian, Gay, Bisexual, transgender and Intersex (LGBTI) persons in forced displacement and the humanitarian context*. IOM/UNHCR. https://lgbti.iom.int/sites/default/files/Module%202%20Conducting%20interviews/Module%2002_Facilitation%20Guide_Nov2016.pdf

Ippolito, F., & Velluti, S. (2011). Recast process of the EU asylum system: A balancing act between efficiency and fairness. *Refugee Survey Quarterly, 30*(3), 24–62.

Jansen, S. (2019). *Pride or shame? Assessing LGBTI asylum applications in the Netherlands following the XYZ and ABC judgments*. COC Netherlands. https://www.coc.nl/wp-content/uploads/2019/01/Pride-or-Shame-LGBTI-asylum-in-the-Netherlands.pdf

Jansen, S., & Spijkerboer, T. (2011). *Fleeing homophobia: Asylum claims related to sexual orientation and gender identity in Europe*. Vrije Universiteit Amsterdam. https://www.refworld.org/docid/4ebba7852.html.

Judge, R. (2010). Refugee advocacy and the biopolitics of asylum in Britain: The precarious position of young male asylum seekers and refugees. *RSC Working Papers Series, 60*. https://www.rsc.ox.ac.uk/files/files-1/wp60-refugee-advocacy-biopolitics-asylum-britain-2010.pdf

Kahn, S., Alessi, E., Woolner, L., Kim, H., & Olivieri, C. (2017). Promoting the wellbeing of lesbian, gay, bisexual and transgender forced migrants in Canada: Providers' perspectives. *Culture, Health & Sexuality, 19*(10), 1165–1179. https://doi.org/10.1080/13691058.2017.1298843.

Kalkmann, M. (2010). German report. *Fleeing Homophobia, Seeking Safety in Europe, Best practices on the (legal) position of LGBT Asylum Seekers in the EU Members States*. https://www.yumpu.com/en/document/view/21133881/draft-questionnaire

Kendall, C. N. (2003). Lesbian and gay refugees in Australia: Now that 'acting discreetly' is no longer an option, will equality be forthcoming? *International Journal of Refugee Law, 15*(4), 715–749.

Kobelinsky, C. (2015). *Juger l'homosexualité*. La Vie Des Idées. https://laviedesidees.fr/Juger-l-homosexualite-attribuer-l-asile.html

Langlois, A. J. (2018). Review article: Curiosity, paradox and dissatisfaction: Queer analyses of human rights. *Millennium, 47*(1), 153–165. https://doi.org/10.1177/0305829818783262.

Luibhéid, E. (2004). Heteronormativity and immigration scholarship: A call for change. *GLQ: A Journal of Lesbian and Gay Studies, 10*(2), 227–235. https://doi.org/10.1215/10642684-10-2-227.

Luibhéid, E. (2008). Queer/migration: An unruly body of scholarship. *GLQ: A Journal of Lesbian and Gay Studies, 14*(2–3), 169–190. https://doi.org/10.1215/10642684-2007-029.

McAdam, J. (2014). Conceptualizing 'crisis migration': A theoretical perspective. In S. Martin, S. Weerasinghe, & A. Taylor (Eds.), *Humanitarian crises and migration: Causes, consequences and responses* (pp. 28–49). Routledge.

Millbank, J. (2009a). From discretion to disbelief: Recent trends in refugee determinations on the basis of sexual orientation in Australia and the United Kingdom. *The International Journal of Human Rights, 13*(2–3), 391–414. https://doi.org/10.1080/13642980902758218.

Millbank, J. (2009b). The ring of truth: A case study of credibility assessment in particular social group refugee determinations. *International Journal of Refugee Law, 21*(1), 1–33.

Miller, A. M. (2000). Sexual but not reproductive: Exploring the junction and disjunction of sexual and reproductive rights. *Health and Human Rights, 4*(2), 68–109.

Muntarbhorn, V. (2017). *Report of the independent expert on protection against violence and discrimination based on sexual orientation and gender identity, 35th Session of the Human Rights Council (A/HRC/35/36)*. https://documents-dds-ny.un.org/doc/UNDOC/GEN/G17/095/53/PDF/G1709553.pdf?OpenElement

Neilson, V. (2005). Homosexual or female—Applying gender-based asylum jurisprudence to Lesbian asylum claims. *Stanford Law & Policy Review, 16*(2), 417.

Noll, G. (2000). *Negotiating asylum: The EU acquis, extraterritorial protection and the common market of definition* (Vol. 6). Martinus Nijhoff Publishers.

OHCHR – Office of the High Commissioner for Human Rights. (2019). *UN rights experts urge more protection for LGBTI refugees*. OHCHR - Office of the High Commissioner for Human Rights. https://www.ohchr.org/EN/NewsEvents/Pages/DisplayNews.aspx?NewsID=24764&LangID=E&fbcl id=IwAR0OADx9qNc_Vs9tc9XR4ybl9L3_e1QS6VTdm8MzGKN_YbqCsJof3i5IpTA

Rabben, L. (2016). *Sanctuary and asylum: A social and political history*. University of Washington Press.

Ramón Mendos, L. (2019). *State-sponsored homophobia 2019: Global legislation overview update*. ILGA. https://ilga.org/downloads/ILGA_World_State_Sponsored_Homophobia_report_global_legislation_overview_update_December_2019.pdf

Saiz, I. (2004). Bracketing sexuality: Human rights and sexual orientation: A decade of development and denial at the UN. *Health and Human Rights, 7*(2), 48–80.

Shidlo, A., & Ahola, J. (2013). Mental health challenges of LGBT forced migrants. *Forced Migration Review, 42*, 9–11.

Stichelbaut, F. (2009). L'application de la Convention sur les réfugiés aux demandeuses d'asile lesbiennes: De quel genre parlons-nous? *Nouvelles Questions Féministes, 28*(2), 66–79.

Taylor, D. (2019). Four LGBT Syrian refugees arrive in UK in time for pride. *The Guardian*. https://www.theguardian.com/uk-news/2019/jul/05/four-lgbt-syrian-refugees-arrive-in-uk-in-time-for-pride

TGEU – Transgender Europe. (2016). *Welcome to Stay*. http://tgeu.org/wp-content/uploads/2016/10/TGEU_TransAsylumBrochure_WEB.pdf

Thomson Reuters Foundation. (2016). Gay rights group to open center for LGBT asylum seekers in Berlin. *Reuters*. https://uk.reuters.com/article/us-germany-refugees-lgbt-idUKKCN0V02D8

Tunstall, K. (Ed.). (2006). *Displacement, asylum, migration: The Oxford Amnesty Lectures 2004*. Oxford University Press.

Türk, V. (2013). Ensuring protection for LGBTI Persons of Concern. *Forced Migration Review, 42*, 5–8.

UKLGIG – UK Lesbian and Gay Immigration Group. (2010). *Failing the grade. Home Office initial decisions on lesbian and gay claims for asylum*. UKLGIG.

UKLGIG – UK Lesbian and Gay Immigration Group. (2013). *Missing the mark. Decision making on Lesbian, Gay (Bisexual, Trans and Intersex) Asylum Claims*. UKLGIG.

UNHCR – UN High Commissioner for Refugees. (2002). *Guidelines on international protection no. 1: Gender-related persecution within the context of Article 1A(2) of the 1951 convention and/or its 1967 protocol relating to the status of refugees* (HCR/GIP/02/01). UNHCR – UN High Commissioner for Refugees http://www.unhcr.org/publications/legal/3d58ddef4/guidelines-international-protection-1-gender-related-persecution-context.html

References

UNHCR – UN High Commissioner for Refugees. (2007). Refugee or migrant? Why it matters. *Refugees*, 148.

UNHCR – UN High Commissioner for Refugees. (2008). *UNHCR guidance note on refugee claims relating to sexual orientation and gender identity*. UNHCR – UN High Commissioner for Refugees. http://www.refworld.org/docid/48abd5660.html

UNHCR – UN High Commissioner for Refugees. (2012). *Guidelines on international protection no. 9: Claims to refugee status based on sexual orientation and/or gender identity within the context of Article 1A(2) of the 1951 convention and/or its 1967 protocol relating to the status of refugees* (HCR/GIP/12/09). UNHCR – UN High Commissioner for Refugees. http://www.unhcr.org/509136ca9.pdf

UNHCR – UN High Commissioner for Refugees. (2015). *Protecting persons with diverse sexual orientations and gender identities*. A global report on UNHCR's efforts to protect lesbian, gay, bisexual, transgender, and intersex asylum-seekers and refugees. UNHCR - UN High Commissioner for Refugees. http://www.refworld.org/pdfid/566140454.pdf

United Nations Human Rights Office. (2019). *UN free & equal*. UN Free & Equal. https://www.unfe.org/

Various. (2017). *The Yogyakarta Principles plus 10 (YP+10): The Application of international human rights law in relation to sexual orientation and gender identity*. ICJ – International Commission of Jurists. https://yogyakartaprinciples.org/

Velluti, S. (2014). *Reforming the common European asylum system—Legislative developments and judicial activism of the European courts*. Springer. https://www.springer.com/gp/book/9783642402661.

Open Access This chapter is licensed under the terms of the Creative Commons Attribution 4.0 International License (http://creativecommons.org/licenses/by/4.0/), which permits use, sharing, adaptation, distribution and reproduction in any medium or format, as long as you give appropriate credit to the original author(s) and the source, provide a link to the Creative Commons license and indicate if changes were made.

The images or other third party material in this chapter are included in the chapter's Creative Commons license, unless indicated otherwise in a credit line to the material. If material is not included in the chapter's Creative Commons license and your intended use is not permitted by statutory regulation or exceeds the permitted use, you will need to obtain permission directly from the copyright holder.

Chapter 2
Researching SOGI Asylum

I wish you all the best with this study, really. I'm so happy to do this interview with you.
　　　　　　　　(Fares, focus group no. 6, Lower Saxony, Germany)

It was a cathartic experience for participants.
　　　　　　(Giulio, referring to focus groups no. 1 and 2, northern Italy)

I want to live a free life, and encourage others that they shouldn't give up.
　　　　　　　　　　(Tiffany, focus group no. 2, Glasgow, UK)

2.1 Introduction

The SOGICA project ran from September 2016 until August 2020.[1] In these four years, the project consisted of different phases: (1) delineating the project's methodology and theoretical and analytical frameworks, in particular how human rights, feminist and queer studies and the concept of intersectionality can be used as particular lenses for the analysis of SOGI asylum claims; (2) preparing and conducting fieldwork in Germany, Italy, the UK and at EU and Council of Europe levels; (3) analysing the data, writing up the results and producing detailed policy recommendations.

As explained in Chap. 1, we adopted an interdisciplinary, comparative and intersectional approach to explore the social and legal experiences of SOGI claimants.

---

[1] Asylum law and policies are constantly changing and in all three countries changes (and reforms) were implemented during the 4 years of our project. Important to note, therefore, are the timeframes when we conducted our interviews. In Germany, interviews and focus groups were conducted between 2 November 2017 and 16 October 2018; in Italy between 22 September 2017 and 4 January 2019, in the UK between 6 November 2017 and 26 October 2019, and at EU and CoE levels between 9 March 2018 and 5 July 2018.

© The Author(s) 2021
C. Danisi et al., *Queering Asylum in Europe*, IMISCOE Research Series,
https://doi.org/10.1007/978-3-030-69441-8_2

The interdisciplinary approach encapsulates legal and sociological theoretical and analytical frameworks and methods and therefore contributes to the developing field of refugee studies that take a socio-legal approach (Anderson et al. 2014; Güler et al. 2019; Khan 2016; Lukac and Eriksson 2017; Venturi 2017). As McConville and Chui (2007, p. 5) explain: 'The non-doctrinal approaches represent a new approach of studying law in the broader social and political context with the use of a range of other methods taken from disciplines in the social sciences and humanities'. Employing a wide range of quantitative and qualitative methods,[2] socio-legal approaches look at the social factors involved and the social impact of law and practice (McConville and Chui 2007, p. 20). In the context of these volumes, these approaches are especially useful for exploring the relationship between sexuality, gender (identity) and the law, and their intersections with other social relations of power. As McConville and Chui (2007, p. 22) argue, 'the law cannot be objectively isolated'. For analysing the complexities of the social as well as the legal experiences of SOGI claimants, doctrinal positivistic approaches focusing on case law would not have been sufficient.

In order to address the issue of disparate (and occasionally low) standards across the EU's and CoE's member states in asylum legal adjudication, a comparative approach is necessary (El-Enany 2008; Ferreira and Kostakopoulou 2016; FRA 2010a, b; Lomba 2004; Whittaker 2006). As we will explore further in Chap. 4, disparities still exist, even if they have to some extent been addressed by the establishment of the EU CEAS. By focusing on Germany, Italy and the UK, we aim to explore better and worse practices, as well as some distinctive trends that may guide asylum decision and policy-making.

The selection of the three countries was done on the basis of three factors:

- Volume of asylum claims – these countries are among the top six EU host countries in terms of numbers of applications (EUROSTAT 2019).
- Different adjudication procedures. While Germany adopts an inquisitorial system (where the decision-maker should take the lead in gathering evidence), and the UK adopts an adversarial system (where the evidence gathering burden is theoretically shared between decision-maker and asylum claimant, but in practice most of the burden lies on the claimant), Italy adopts a mixed system. The inquisitorial or adversarial character of the asylum adjudication system has been identified as a crucial feature that may have a bearing on the outcome of asylum claims (Committee on Migration, Refugees and Population 2009; Independent Asylum Commission 2008; Künnecke 2007; Sonnino and Denozza 2005; UNHCR 2005).
- Socio-cultural-legal context, particularly in relation to SOGI. There still exist significant differences in relation to social perceptions of sexual behaviour and gender roles across Europe as well as in protection provided by law (Gerhards

---

[2] A common definition of quantitative/qualitative method is, as McConville and Chui (2007, p. 48) describe: 'Quantitative research deals with numbers, statistics of hard data whereas qualitative data are mostly in the form of words.'

2005; Giordano 2001; Philips 2001; Waaldijk 2006). By comparing three countries that reflect different approaches to sexuality and gender identity, we were able to explore the influence of these differences on asylum adjudication.

While intersectionality is key as a theoretical concept underpinning this research (Chap. 3), it also guides our methodology. By applying intersectionality as methodology, we follow Matsuda's approach in that we 'ask the other question' (Matsuda 1991). Using an intersectional approach was vital for exploring the socio-legal experiences of SOGI claimants and guided how we developed the different methods we used for the data collection across the three case study countries and at EU and CoE levels.

2.2 Methods

In order to achieve an analysis that offers both breadth and in-depth understanding, we used a mixed-methods approach (Blanck 1993; Epstein and King 2002; Travers 1999; Travers and Manzo 1997). Data was collected using the following methods:[3]

- 143 interviews with SOGI asylum claimants and refugees, NGOs, policy-makers, decision-makers, members of the judiciary, legal representatives, and other professionals;
- 16 focus groups with SOGI asylum claimants and refugees;
- 24 non-participant contextual observations of court hearings;
- Two online surveys for SOGI asylum claimants and refugees and professionals working with SOGI asylum claimants and refugees;
- Documentary analysis of international, European and domestic case law, policy documents, NGO reports, case files, etc.;
- Freedom of Information (FOI) requests.

All of the above covered Germany, Italy and the UK, as well as the EU and CoE. A range of qualitative research methods were used (Bertaux 1981; Morgan 1998; Seal 2004; Seale et al. 2004). While the online surveys produced some numerical data, qualitative interviews and focus groups offered more in-depth accounts of the legal treatment of the participants' claims and the impact on their social experience and well-being. Our ontological and epistemological standpoint is that asylum claimants and refugees are experts on the refugee experience. Hearing their knowledge and experience is essential to gain unique insights into those experiences and to verify whether international, European and domestic legal frameworks in place address appropriately their claims (Hynes 2003, p. 13). In total, 157 asylum claimants and refugees participated in the semi-structured interviews and focus groups (64 in semi-structured interviews and 93 in focus groups).

---
[3] All fieldwork materials are available on the SOGICA website: www.sogica.org/en/fieldwork/.

As we aimed to include a range of perspectives in our project, when recruiting participants, we looked for a diverse sample in terms of sexual orientation, sex, gender identity, country of origin and other factors such as ethnicity, religion, age and social class. We also tried to reach participants in different regions and nations (with regard to the UK) within our three countries, recognising the importance of place in terms of both where participants came from and where they settled or resided in the host country. To make our research as accessible as possible, we provided translations of the project flyer, information sheets and consent forms not only in German and Italian, but also in Arabic, Farsi, French, Turkish and Urdu.[4] Many of the asylum claimant and refugee participants were found through contacts with local, national and international NGOs offering support to asylum claimants, legal practitioners, or through contacts with other claimants. A European-wide network of SOGICA Project Friends that we had launched at the beginning of our research and that consisted of people with experience and expertise on SOGI asylum issues, supported us in recruiting participants for our research by cascading information to their contacts and networks.

In order to be able to base findings on a heterogeneous sample, it was important not to rely solely on gatekeepers,[5] but use other recruitment strategies. Gatekeepers often fear that their clients are 'too vulnerable' and traumatised to participate in research projects and, as we have also experienced, may, with the best of intentions, close the door to researchers. In addition, NGOs might only refer participants who they see as the 'ideal' sample (for example, for the reputation of the organisation; Hynes 2003, p. 14).[6] In light of these factors, to recruit participants, we used a wide range of means such as publishing the call for participants in newsletters, mailing lists, relevant publications, and on social media – our own and those of other individuals and organisations. We also distributed flyers about the research through NGOs, community groups and LGBTIQ+ cafés and bars (although this was the least successful method). Many of the participants were found through snowballing (that is, a participant suggested another participant) and direct contacts.

We are aware that, even though we adopted different recruitment strategies, we may have not reached the most isolated SOGI claimants, for instance LGBTIQ+ people who are dispersed to remote areas where they have no possibility at all to access support groups, or who have to live in concealment because of their living arrangements (living with their family, for instance).

We also noticed some differences with regard to recruiting participants in the three countries due to different structures and political and policy cultures. For instance, in contrast to the UK, where support groups for SOGI claimants have existed for at least a decade, in Italy and Germany the existence of these groups has

---

[4] http://www.sogica.org/en/fieldwork/.

[5] In this context, individuals usually working in NGOs or law firms, acting as intermediaries between researchers and potential research participants.

[6] When gatekeepers are involved, it is important to make sure that potential research participants understand that the service provision they receive from that organisation is not affected by their decision to participate in the research or not (Clark-Kazak 2017, p. 12).

2.2 Methods

been a fairly recent phenomenon. In Germany and Italy, most of the support organisations and groups that now exist were set up in or since 2015. Because of the more established nature of organisations in the UK, there has also been more (positive) media interest in SOGI claims and there is also a policy culture and established principles of consultation and transparency between policy-makers and 'stakeholders' – at least on paper. And while decision-makers in Germany and the UK were recruited through official means (judicial authorities, government departmental channels, etc.), in Italy this was to a large extent only possible through personal contacts. In general, our participants were self-selecting. Consequently, it is likely that the lawyers and decision-makers (but also NGO and other professionals) we interviewed, and on whose accounts we draw in Chaps. 4, 5, 6, 7, 8, 9 and 10, are committed to addressing failings in the SOGI asylum system, perhaps to a greater degree than a random sample of stakeholders would be.

Furthermore, there were some striking differences in the demographics of the SOGI claimants who participated in individual interviews and focus groups, especially with regard to their country of origin. Many of the Italian participants came from French-speaking countries and all of them came from Africa; in Germany, participants came from Africa, the Middle East, Asia, Eastern Europe and the Caribbean; and in the UK, participants came from Africa, Asia, the Middle East, the Caribbean and Central America. In addition, in Italy it was more difficult to find lesbian participants and cases based on gender identity. This may be also due to the different paths of arrival followed by many transgender people (for example, people from South America who have been living in Italy for many years) (Chap. 5). The different arrival paths might also be the reason why participants in Italy were younger (in the UK, for instance, more people claim 'sur place'[7]).

It needs to be said that not all of the different identifiers included in LGBTIQ+ are represented in our study. Our sample does not include any intersex claimant and only three claimants who identified as bisexual. Therefore, it needs to be kept in mind that 'questions of access and recruitment can be central to understanding the "outcomes" of the research' (Rapley 2007, p. 17). Nevertheless, as the demographics of our asylum claimant and refugee participants summarised in Tables 2 and 3 below demonstrate, we managed to recruit a diverse sample for our research. In Germany and the UK, we were able to recruit almost equal numbers of women and men for individual interviews and more women for the focus groups. Some other differences between the participants of the three countries emerged: the educational level of individual interview participants in Germany was higher than in Italy and the UK (which also seemed the case for focus group participants, but data is missing here; see table below). Also to note is that in the UK a wider range of legal avenues are available to claimants (Chap. 4), with some of our participants waiting for the outcome of a judicial review or fresh claim. Not reflected in the tables below is the

---

[7] A sur place refugee is 'a person granted refugee status based on international protection needs which arose sur place, that is, on account of events which took place after they left their country of origin' (https://ec.europa.eu/home-affairs/what-we-do/networks/european_migration_network/glossary_search/refugee-sur-place_en).

claimants' family status and number of children, as we did not collect information from all the participants about that matter. From the information we have, the majority of participants were single and in each country five of the individual interview participants had children (in Germany about 40% of the focus group participants had children).

All of the interview and focus group audio files were transcribed, mainly by professional transcribers who had signed our confidentiality agreement, although a small number were transcribed by members of the project team. We then uploaded the transcripts, as well as the court hearing observation notes, onto the software programme NVivo. This data analysis software is mainly used for qualitative data analysis and allows for comparative analysis. We coded the interview, focus group and observation files according to a coding framework that we developed after a coding pilot exercise involving a small number of interviews. The software then enabled us to pull out the relevant codes (or nodes, as termed in NVivo) for the analysis and writing up of our results.

In the following, we explain the different methods used.

2.2.1 Semi-structured Interviews

Most of the 143 semi-structured interviews carried out were one-to-one interviews, but 12 interviews were held with two people: either couples, friends or professional colleagues.[8] We conducted interviews in a wide range of locations in Germany, Italy, the UK and Brussels to gain understanding of regional and national differences.[9] The overall number of participants interviewed in each category of participants is summarised in Table 1:

These in-depth interviews were semi-structured, that is, we followed an interview guide but remained flexible in terms of the wording and the order of the questions, and left space for discussion of matters not raised by our questions. The purpose of the guide was to provide direction, ensuring that the interviews focused on the crucial topics we aimed to explore. In contrast to structured interviews, which consist mainly of closed-ended questions, semi-structured interviews allow the interviewer to find out about feelings and perceptions of participants that do not fit into pre-chosen options. Furthermore, too much standardisation can inhibit building

---

[8] In Italy, 42 interviews were conducted, three of which were with two interviewees; in the UK 52 interviews were conducted, five of which were with two interviewees; in Germany 41 interviews were conducted, four of which were with two interviewees; at the European level eight individual interviews were conducted.

[9] In Italy, interviews were conducted in 13 locations (across ten regions); in Germany, interviews also took place in 13 different locations (across eight federal states: Hesse, Lower Saxony, Saxony, Berlin, North Rhine-Westphalia, Rhineland-Palatinate, Saarland and Bavaria); in the UK, interviews were conducted in ten different cities, one of which was in Scotland, one in Northern Ireland (by telephone), and all the others in England.

2.2 Methods

Table 1 Number of participants

Participants	UK	Germany	Italy	European level
Asylum claimants and refugees	25	21 (3 of which also worked in NGOs)	18 (2 of which also worked in NGOs)	–
NGOs	16	14	11	2
Lawyers	6	5	6	-
Decision-makers	8	2	7	-
Policy-makers	1	1	–	3
Other professionals	1	2	3	3
Total	**57**	**45**	**45**	**8**

Many thanks to our placement student Alba Trabandt (University of Sussex/Freie Universität Berlin), who assisted us in creating the first draft of the tables used in this chapter

Table 2 Demographics of interview participants – asylum claimants and refugees

	Germany (21)	Italy (18)	UK (25)
Sex	10 female	3 female	13 female
	11 male	15 male	10 male
			2 identify as neither
Gender Identity	7 women	2 women	12 women
	9 men	15 men	9 men
	1 woman (trans)	1 trans (FtM)	1 transwoman
	1 man (trans)		1 transman
	1 female born identified as male		2 not answered
	1 trans ('female inside, male outside')		
	1 S/he ('gender not important to me')		
Sexual Orientation	9 lesbian	2 lesbian	9 lesbian
	8 gay	14 gay	8 gay
	1 hetero	1 heteroromantic asexual	2 heterosexual
	3 queer	1 not sure	1 bisexual
			1 pansexual
			1 transsexual
			3 not answered
Age range	24–48	17–36	24–47
Asylum status	1 Dublin case (church asylum)	3 no decision yet	4 no first decision yet
	8 refused and in the appeal process	7 refused and in the appeal process	2 waiting for decision on fresh claim

(continued)

Table 2 (continued)

	Germany (21)	Italy (18)	UK (25)
	12 international protection granted	6 international protection granted	3 refused and in appeal process
		2 not answered	3 refused and in the process of submitting fresh claim
			1 judicial review pending
			5 international protection granted
			7 not answered
Country of Origin	1 Egypt	3 Cameroon	2 Bangladesh
	2 Iran	3 Gambia	1 Benin
	2 Jamaica	2 Ivory Coast	3 Cameroon
	2 Lebanon	1 Libya	2 Egypt
	2 Morocco	1 Mali	1 Guatemala
	1 Nigeria	7 Nigeria	2 Kenya
	1 Oman	1 Senegal	1 Kyrgyzstan
	2 Russia		1 Libya
	2 Syria		2 Malawi
	1 Tanzania		1 Malaysia
	1 Turkmenistan		1 Nigeria
	4 Uganda		2 Pakistan
			1 South Africa
			1 Tanzania
			2 Trinidad
			1 Uganda
			1 Zimbabwe
Educational background	8 secondary school education	2 primary school education	1 primary school education
	11 further and higher education	5 secondary school education	8 secondary school education
	2 not answered	6 further and higher education	8 further and higher education
		5 not answered	8 not answered
Religion	3 Atheist	1 Atheist	1 Agnostic
	6 Christian	6 Christian	8 Christian
	1 Humanist	5 Muslim	1 Muslim
	1 Jewish	6 not answered	6 religious, but not specified
	2 Muslim		4 no religion
	1 Orthodox (not specified)		5 not answered
	3 no religion		
	4 not answered		

The descriptions and terms used in this table are largely those that were chosen by the participants, which is why there are a variety of identifiers in this table, especially with regard to gender identity and sexual orientation

2.2 Methods

Table 3 Demographics of focus groups participants

	Germany	Italy	UK
Number of focus groups	6	5	5
Participants	35	32	26
Sex	23 female	2 female	17 female
	12 male	30 male	9 male
Gender Identity	22 women	2 women	17 women
	11 men	30 men	9 men
	1 trans woman		
	1 gender fluid		
Sexual Orientation	21 lesbian	2 lesbian	15 lesbian
	11 gay	21 gay	4 gay
	2 bisexual	2 bisexual	7 not answered
	1 not answered	7 not answered	
Age range	21–48	17–39	23–57
Asylum status	3 waiting for decision	4 waiting for decision	20 pending decision or waiting for appeal
	20 refused and in the appeal process	4 refused	2 refused
	2 international protection granted	9 in appeal process	4 refugee status
	10 not answered	6 international protection granted	
		9 not answered	
Country of Origin	2 Iraq	6 Cameroon	1 Bangladesh
	4 Jamaica	3 Gambia	1 Cameroon
	1 Morocco	3 Ghana	1 Iraq
	5 Nigeria	1 Guinea Conakry	1 Jamaica
	1 Syria	2 Ivory Coast	1 Kenya
	21 Uganda	16 Nigeria	2 Malawi
	1 not answered	1 Togo	1 Namibia
			1 Nigeria
			3 Pakistan
			1 Tanzania
			2 Uganda
			1 Zimbabwe
			10 not answered
Educational background	2 no school	1 no school	1 secondary school education
	1 primary school education	3 primary school education	3 further and higher education
	12 secondary school education	4 secondary school education	22 not answered
	14 further and higher education	6 further and higher education	
	6 not answered	18 not answered	

(continued)

Table 3 (continued)

	Germany	Italy	UK
Religion	1 Atheist	12 Christian	2 Christian
	27 Christian	5 Muslim	3 religious but not specified 1 no religion
	6 Muslim	1 no religion	20 not answered
	1 religious but not specified	14 not answered	

trust and rapport (Burns 1994, p. 278). Semi-structured interviews focus on the participant's perspective rather than the researcher's and allow participants to use their own language to describe their experiences and social reality.

These are some of the advantages to a semi-structured and more flexible interviewing approach. However, a corollary is that coding becomes more difficult and the interview data is less comparable than it would be with structured interviews (Burns 1994, pp. 278–279). Entirely open-ended interviews, on the other hand, would have been too loosely structured for our purposes (Burns 1994, pp. 279–280). We followed some of Burns' advice for questioning techniques, for instance, in reflecting back to the participants what they had said, and in using descriptive questions (for example, describing people and events) and probing questions such as 'Can you tell me more?' We started interviews in a friendly and supportive way, allowing participants to be in control of the flow of the information (Burns 1994, p. 281). It was important to follow what our participants said, rather than impose a predetermined agenda in order to get sufficient detail and depth of data (Rapley 2007, p. 18).

Our approach recognises the interactive nature of data collection, and rests on the assumption that an interview is always a joint production of accounts (Rapley 2007). We followed the approach Rapley (2007, p. 26, original emphasis) calls '"*engaged, active* or *collaborative*" interviewing'. It was vital to us to respect participants' privacy by not asking overly personal questions. Furthermore, being honest and encouraging dialogue about what our study could achieve and what the limitations were, were essential, in our view, to building a trusting relationship (Krause 2017). We engaged with our participants' discourse by also bringing in our own perspectives (we thus question the 'neutrality' of the researcher – see more on our positionality in Sect. 2.3).

As Krause (2017) suggests, especially when conducting research with refugees who have experienced human rights violations, it is vital to enable participants to speak about the issues that are important to them. Krause thus argues that '[c]rucially, when participants can speak out about issues that are relevant for them, they are not treated as "data sources" but as persons' (Krause 2017, p. 20). This issue is also important from an intersectional perspective. For this reason, even though our research focused on sexuality, gender identity and 'refugeeness', we also asked participants questions addressing other identifiers such as 'race' and religion. We 'tested' the interview guides with several pilot interviews, asking the participants how they felt about particular questions (Burns 1994, p. 281), and amended the guide according to the feedback that we received.

2.2   Methods   33

SOGI asylum claimants and refugees were asked open questions about their social and legal experiences with regard to their asylum claims. In order to minimise the levels of stress, we tried to keep the interview length to an hour. We made participants aware that they could stop the interview at any time or choose not to answer particular questions. The semi-structured interviews with policy-makers, decision-makers, members of the judiciary, lawyers and NGO workers explored these actors' positive and negative practical experiences with SOGI asylum claims. As Chaps. 4, 5, 6, 7, 8, 9 and 10 will demonstrate, these interviews provided in-depth data. Most participants gave permission for their interviews to be audio recorded and transcribed. In a few cases where participants did not give permission, notes were taken. The interviews (and the focus groups) were conducted in semi-public places (for example, spaces in universities or quiet cafés) or in places familiar to the participant (local LGBTIQ+, refugee and migrant organisation venues or the offices of law firms).

2.2.2   *Focus Groups*

We conducted 16 focus groups with 93 SOGI asylum claimants and refugees in Germany (six focus groups), Italy (five focus groups) and the UK (five focus groups). Focus groups offer an opportunity for sharing and comparing views in a way that individual interviews do not. Questions in the focus groups concentrated on opinions about the asylum process for SOGI claimants, life in the respective countries and support services available.

In Germany five focus groups were held in English and one in German; in the UK, all five focus groups were conducted in English; in Italy three were conducted in English, one in French and one in a mixture of English and French. In our pilot focus groups we found that smaller groups worked better and were more interactive. Matters of sensitivity and confidentiality are also more manageable in a small group. Consequently, we decided to keep the groups fairly small (each focus group had six participants on average). Most focus groups were recruited through NGOs, thus participants often knew each other. This had the advantage of participants feeling more relaxed with each other; a disadvantage, however, was that they may not have articulated specific points which they assumed everybody already knew, and conversely, differences in opinion may not have been expressed for fear of alienating peers (Macnaghten and Myers 2007, 70).

In line with ethical standards – guided by the University of Sussex, academic and professional bodies and also our own principles – we tried to make our information sheets and consent forms as detailed as possible (Sect. 2.3). Nonetheless, this meant that going through these documents with a group of participants and making sure that every participant understood what participation involved, was challenging. Some participants found the information sheet and the consent form too bureaucratic, and some participants were illiterate or nearly illiterate, so we allowed time to explain everything carefully and in detail. All participants signed the consent form, but we also made sure that we received consent verbally. In a few focus groups (in Italy) assistants helped with translation, filling out forms and taking notes. We moderated the focus groups and endeavoured to encourage all participants to speak using appropriate strategies. For example, where one participant tended to dominate the conversation, the interviewer would look away from that person and turn their body towards somebody who had contributed less (Macnaghten and Myers 2007). Sometimes participants asked us to use simpler and more basic language, and we also discovered that descriptors such as 'men loving other men' and 'women loving other women' were sometimes preferable to 'being gay or lesbian', as some participants did not identify that way (even if in relation to demographic questions, participants mostly adapted to those categories). In the pilot carried out in Italy, we also discovered that the original opening question we had set seemed to require a 'capacity of abstraction' that made some people uncomfortable from the outset.[10] Therefore, we changed it to a question asking more specifically about the arrival in the host country.[11]

We had some ethical concerns about conducting focus groups with asylum claimants and refugees (Sect. 2.3), based on the potential re-traumatisation participants might experience when listening to other participants' stories. Yet, according to the feedback we received from participants, these focus group discussions were largely positive experiences. The focus groups offered participants a way to reflect on particular issues within a group setting, sometimes for the first time, and to become aware that other people faced similar issues. Often there were passionate discussions in the groups, especially when participants discussed the decision-making process and how to prove their sexual orientation.

2.2.3 Observations in Courts

We conducted 24 non-participant contextual observations of court hearings of asylum appeals in Germany (ten), Italy (three) and the UK (11) between February 2018 and April 2019.[12] Using a guide, these observations focused on how the different actors involved dealt with asylum claimants' SOGI and related aspects of their claims.[13] As Burns (1994, p. 265) points out, 'the functional distinction between participant and non-participant observation is ambiguous as it is impossible to avoid

---

[10] 'With regard to your sexual orientation or gender identity, what would you say, how is life in the UK/Italy/Germany different to life in your country of origin?'

[11] 'Would you like to tell me something about your arrival in this country?'

[12] The 11 court hearings in the UK were conducted between February and November 2018 in the First Tier Tribunal and Upper Tribunal. The ten court hearings in Germany were conducted in administrative courts between March 2018 and April 2019. In Italy, we tried to gain access to 10 court hearings between March 2018 and February 2019, and only effectively observed three out of these.

[13] http://www.sogica.org/wp-content/uploads/2019/12/Court-Observation-guide-.pdf.

2.2 Methods

interactions in social situations. The aim of non-participant observation is to observe unobtrusively by minimising interactions with participants. The hearings we observed in Germany and the UK were open to the public and no authorisation was required, however, we needed assistance from lawyers and NGO workers/volunteers to identify forthcoming SOGI asylum appeals, as the detail and nature of appeals is not published. In Italy, we could only observe two tribunal hearings directly, and one indirectly via an interpreter and a lawyer, whom we interviewed when the hearing ended. Hearings are not public and in seven cases the relevant judges did not authorise the attendance of third parties. In these cases, we were denied access despite the claimants' consent and sometimes despite our presence at the venue of the hearing.

While we tried to observe unobtrusively, to respect and avoid distracting the claimants, at times we made our presence as researchers known to the judges. In all three countries, lawyers and NGO workers fed back to us that they thought our presence made a difference as to how the hearings were conducted and their outcome.[14] When we refer to the court hearings we observed, we specify the court, the broad geographical location and the year the hearing took place, but omit further details to protect the anonymity of the claimants.

2.2.4 Online Surveys

Between August 2018 and March 2019, SOGI asylum claimants and refugees in Europe, and those supporting them, were invited to complete an online questionnaire about their experiences with SOGI asylum procedures and wider social experiences. Although these volumes focus on a comparison between the three country case studies – Germany, Italy and UK – the online survey included participants from across Europe, contributing to a broader understanding of the situation of SOGI claimants in Europe. There were two separate surveys: one for claimants and one for people who work with or support them.[15] These surveys had the following aims: to provide some quantitative data and further qualitative material across Europe to complement the detailed fieldwork described above and inform the project's policy recommendations; to provide complete anonymity to people who did not feel comfortable participating in interviews or focus groups, but wanted the chance to have their voices included in the research; to broaden the opportunities for contributing to the research to the many individuals who expressed an interest in the project and

---

[14] For example, in Germany, out of the ten appeal hearings we observed, four were rejected, five accepted and one received subsidiary protection (instead of refugee status). In the UK, out of the 11 appeal hearings observed, seven of the appeals have been accepted, two were refused, and two were still pending. From the 10 court appeals in Italy that we tried to access between March 2018 and February 2019, three were granted refugee status, two were granted humanitarian protection and five were still pending at the time of writing.

[15] The surveys can be found on our website http://www.sogica.org/en/fieldwork/.

could not be accommodated throughout the fieldwork, both in the case study countries and in other countries.

We developed the questionnaires according to what is described in the literature as 'model questionnaire' (Burns 1994, p. 349), including an introduction, body of survey and demographic questions. The (numbered) questions were grouped into logical sections with a smooth transition between them, and some 'lighter' questions at the end (Burns 1994, pp. 349–358). Most of these questions were 'closed questions', in other words, participants were able to choose from a range of options, but with the option to provide additional responses in free text form. Some questions had a sliding scale from one to ten (for instance, 'how easy/difficult is it…'). The surveys were made available in different languages[16], and participants were offered a document with a range of answers to potential queries they could have on the surveys.[17]

Information about our research and links to the online survey was distributed through our website, social media, SOGICA's quarterly newsletters, Project Friends, LGBTIQ+ and refugee mailing lists, and our professional networks. In total, 157 supporters and 82 claimants filled in the online surveys, but not everyone answered all the questions. As the survey was based on a non-representative sample and received a relatively low response rate, we treat the quantitative aspects of the data with care in the subsequent chapters. We use the European-wide quantitative data to provide some background to particular issues, while we use the surveys' qualitative data to complement our fieldwork in Germany, Italy and the UK. A full analysis of the results of the survey can be found elsewhere.[18] Here, we provide a summary of the demographics of survey respondents.

Perhaps unsurprisingly, the majority of the 82 SOGI claimants who answered the survey were claiming asylum in the three SOGICA case countries, as it was here where we had the most contacts (Fig. 1). It is likely that some of the SOGICA claimants we interviewed also participated in the survey. However, we also reached respondents in many other European countries. Seventeen percent of the respondents were claiming asylum in Austria, Belgium, Denmark, Greece, Hungary, Ireland, Portugal, Spain, Sweden, Switzerland and the Netherlands. Unfortunately, we do not know where 29% of the respondents claimed asylum, as these respondents did not disclose that information.

In terms of countries of origin, the survey reached a sample slightly different from our interview and focus group participants (Tables 2 and 3). As in our qualitative research sample, a high percentage of survey respondents were from Uganda (16%), Nigeria (7%) and Jamaica (4%), however our survey reached more SOGI claimants from Syria (9%). Twenty-eight percent of survey respondents came from other countries, including some that were not represented in our other methods'

---

[16] http://www.sogica.org/wp-content/uploads/2019/12/Qualtrics-survey_information.pdf.

[17] The survey for claimants was available in Arabic, German, English, Italian, French, Spanish and the survey for supporters was available in English, German, Italian and Spanish. Translation was offered through Google Translate (owing to limited resources).

[18] http://www.sogica.org/en/publications/.

2.2 Methods

sample, such as Algeria, Armenia, El Salvador, North Macedonia, Sierra Leone and Turkey.[19]

Regarding gender, gender identity and sexual orientation, the survey respondents' self-identification was fairly similar to our interviewees' and group participants' self-identification: 34% described their gender or gender identity as male, 23% as female, 7% as trans, 5% as queer, and 1% as 'other' (for sexuality, see Fig. 2).[20]

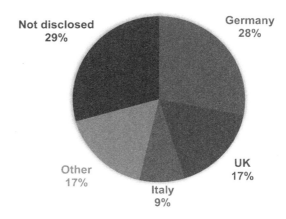

Fig. 1 In what country are you claiming asylum?

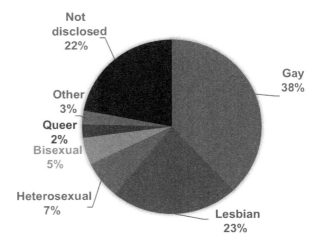

Fig. 2 How would you describe your sexuality?

---

[19] The other countries of origin were Bangladesh, Cameroon, Egypt, Iran, Lebanon, Libya, Malaysia, Morocco, Oman, Pakistan, Russia, South Africa and Zimbabwe. Thirty-six per cent of respondents did not disclose from which country they were from.

[20] Thirty per cent of respondents preferred not to disclose their gender or gender identity, or did not answer this question.

In terms of religious identity, age and educational background, the survey respondents' demographics matched those of our interviewees (Tables 2 and 3). The majority were Christian (Fig. 3), between 25 and 34 years old (45%, Fig. 4), and their highest level of education completed was further or higher education (38%, Fig. 5).

From the 157 people who answered the 'survey for people who work with or support LGBTIQ+ people claiming asylum', the majority (41%) were working or volunteering with an LGBTIQ+ organisation or with an organisation providing legal advice and/or representation (19%) (Fig. 6).

Also here, perhaps unsurprisingly, the majority of respondents were working in the UK (39%), Italy (17%), and Germany (9%), and it is likely that some of our interviewees participated in the survey. Other countries where respondents were working (34%) were Austria, Belgium, Cyprus, Denmark, France, Greece, Ireland, Malta, Norway, Portugal, Slovenia, Spain, Sweden, Switzerland, and the Netherlands.

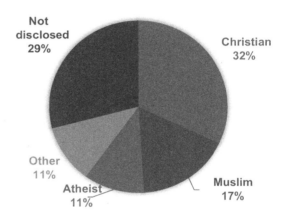

Fig. 3 How would you describe your religious or non-religious identity?

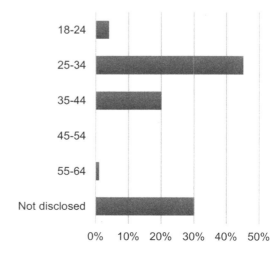

Fig. 4 How old are you?

2.2 Methods

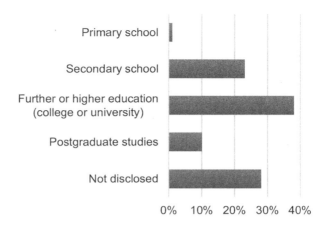

Fig. 5 What is the highest level of education that you have completed?

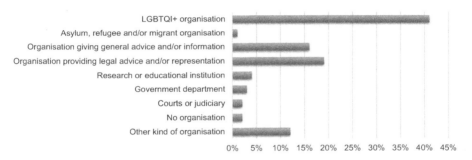

Fig. 6 What kind of organisation do you work or volunteer with?

The data of the surveys, which were created using Qualtrics Survey Software, was analysed using the statistical software package SPSS. However, we did not carry out any bivariate and multivariate analysis or statistical tests to measure the correlation between variables (McConville and Chui 2007, p. 62). For our purposes, univariate analysis (looking at only one variable at a time) was sufficient. When we refer to survey respondents in this publication, we use codes: C corresponding to claimants and S to supporters.

2.2.5 Documentary Analysis

During the course of our research, we analysed a variety of documents: international treaties and international courts' and committees' decisions, European and domestic legislation, case law, policy documents, NGO reports, case files, etc. These documents were available through publicly accessible sources (for example, Refworld) and provided by the research participants. This material was used to support the analysis of the fieldwork primary data in the chapters that follow. We also produced four case law tables for European, German, Italian and UK case law, which contributed to our analysis.[21]

2.2.6 Freedom of Information Requests

In order to gain more official information about SOGI asylum statistics, training offered to interviewers and decision-makers, etc., we submitted freedom of information (FOI) requests to the relevant authorities in Germany, Italy and the UK.[22] Freedom of information laws are the means by which members of the public or NGOs are entitled to ask for and receive information held by national governments. Legislation varies from one European country to another.[23]

FOI is 'a relatively new research innovation in academia' (Walby and Luscombe 2018, p. 10). In recent years, it has been recognised that FOI 'is a powerful tool available to researchers' (Savage and Hyde 2014, p. 315), with more and more researchers using it (Walby and Luscombe 2018, p. 2), although, as some authors argue, researchers are still not making sufficient use of it (Bunt 2018; Savage and Hyde 2014; Turnbull 2015; Walby and Luscombe 2017).

FOI requests can be seen as 'an innovative research technique for qualitative researchers' (Turnbull 2015), and are especially useful when combined with other methods (Savage and Hyde 2014), but like all methods of data collection, they have advantages and disadvantages. The main advantage of FOI requests is that '[b]y providing a way to access information produced and/or assembled by public authorities, freedom of information requests allow data to be accessed that otherwise could not be, at least without lengthy negotiations with public authorities' (Savage and Hyde 2014, p. 308). FOI allow researchers to gain access to information and documents that are not publicly available, especially valuable in situations where it is difficult to gain access to gatekeepers, as was the case in Germany where we could not gain access to BAMF staff.

However, there are also disadvantages, as we discovered. Making FOI requests can be time-consuming when public authorities do not provide the information

---

[21] http://www.sogica.org/en/case-studies/.

[22] http://www.sogica.org/en/fieldwork/.

[23] In Germany, there is the Federal Act Governing Access to Information held by the Federal Government (Freedom of Information Act) of 5 September 2005 (Federal Law Gazette [BGBl.] Part I, p. 2722), last amended by Article 2 (6) of the Act of 7 August 2013 (Federal Law Gazette I, p. 3154) (http://www.gesetze-im-internet.de/englisch_ifg/index.html). In Italy, the right of access to administrative documents was reaffirmed and further expanded by the legislative decree 25 May 2016, no. 97 (https://www.gazzettaufficiale.it/eli/id/2016/06/08/16G00108/sg), but the implementation of these new provisions is still problematic. In the UK, the Freedom of Information Act 2000 provides public access to information held by public authorities in England, Wales and Northern Ireland, and in Scotland for UK-wide public bodies (https://www.legislation.gov.uk/ukpga/2000/36/contents).

2.2 Methods

needed and the researcher is 'fishing around for information' (Turnbull 2015). The path that researchers need to take to gain the required information is unpredictable and dependent on the person who coordinates the request (Walby and Luscombe 2018, p. 10).

Our FOI requests were drafted in consultation with relevant stakeholders (in Germany, the LSVD; in Italy the UNHCR Italy; in the UK, the UKLGIG and Asylum Research Consultancy). We had different experiences with how public authorities responded to our FOI requests and, more generally, our research.

In Germany, we tried several times to gain access to interviewers and decision-makers, but the BAMF rejected our request on each occasion.[24] In order to gain the information we needed, we prepared comprehensive FOI requests containing 30 questions. As these questions were addressed to different public authorities, we liaised with the party 'Die Linke', who submitted these questions as a parliamentary request ('Kleine Anfrage'). The government responded to the request within 4 weeks.[25] Nonetheless, the government's response was not comprehensive and some of the information requested could not be provided due the country's federal structure. For instance, in its response, the government stated that individual federal states are responsible for reception and that the government did not have information about how federal states respond to vulnerabilities. The government also stated that they did not have information about specific accommodation for SOGI claimants, or what happens if claimants ask to be moved from their accommodation centre. Furthermore, no statistical information about SOGI claims exists (Chap. 4).

In Italy, the process of gaining access to information was more difficult. In February 2019, the FOI request was sent to the National Commission for the Right of Asylum ('Commissione Nazionale Asilo') and the Minister of Internal Affairs (Department for civil liberties and immigrants). We received no confirmation that they had received the FOI request and they did not respond to the request, nor to reminders sent in May 2019. In fact, all the participants in our fieldwork in Italy, including decision-makers, were found through personal contacts after attempts to make contact at an institutional level failed. It is rare for Italian public administrative bodies to respond to such information requests from citizens, although they are formally obliged to do so 'in a reasonable time'. We then sent a complaint to an opposition party's member of Parliament, including a request to submit, through him, a parliamentary question ('interrogazione parlamentare'). However, we did not receive a reply. As context, the political climate in Italy throughout 2017 and 2018 became tense, which our analysis of the asylum reforms highlights (Chap. 6).

---

[24] Between November 2017 and November 2018, we contacted BAMF staff on more than five occasions and by email, telephone and post. These communications were made to: a special officer for SOGI claims; the BAMF press office; BAMF arrival centres; and branch offices. Where we received a reply to our request, it was that participation in our study was not possible 'for reasons of capacity'.

[25] 'Kleine Anfrage der Abgeordneten Ulla Jelpke u.a. und der Fraktion DIE LINKE. Situation von LSBTI-Geflüchteten', BT-Drucksache 19/1030, 04.06.2019 (questions were sent by SOGICA to Die Linke on 10 April 2019 and sent by them to the parliament on 8 May 2019).

In the UK, the process was also far from quick or transparent. Three FOI requests were submitted in January 2019: one to the Ministry of Justice and two to the Home Office.[26] The FOI request to the Ministry of Justice as well as the one to the Home Office regarding detention were answered but elicited no new information, largely on the basis that neither department held the information we were requesting. With regard to the third FOI request, which was the most detailed, covering decision-making, we only received a full answer to our request in June 2019 (FOI reference 52467), thus much later than the specified 20 working days, despite further emails and complaints on our part to both the Information Commissioner's Office and to the Home Office.[27] Nonetheless, much of the information provided was either not relevant or did not directly answer the questions posed in our FOI request. In addition, the Home Office stated that it was withholding information regarding the decision-making process on 'public interest' grounds:

> Regarding your request for information and the questions used to identify the basis for an asylum claim, we do hold the information, but have decided to exempt this information under section 31 of the FOIA 2000. Section 31(1)(e) allows us to exempt information if its disclosure would or would be likely to prejudice Law Enforcement – the operation of immigration controls. This exemption requires us to consider whether, in every respect the public interest in maintaining the exemption stated above, outweighs the public interest in disclosing the information. Arguments for and against disclosure in terms of the public interest are set out in the attached Annex 1. (p. 3)

In short, the way the FOI requests in Italy and the UK were handled raises important concerns regarding democratic accountability of officials and transparency in public policy, not only in relation to the substance of the responses we received, but also in terms of procedural failures that make freedom of information a right that in some cases exists only on paper.

2.3 Ethical Implications: Doing Research with SOGI Refugees

It might be said that fulfilling ethical standards is important for any project. However, due to the particular situation in which SOGI asylum claimants find themselves, considering ethical implications when conducting research with this group of participants was particularly important (Held 2019). Before we started the research,

---

[26] The FOI request to the Ministry of Justice as well as the request to the Home Office regarding decision-making were submitted directly by SOGICA. The other request to the HO regarding LGBTIQ+ detainees and their treatment in immigration detention centres was submitted by the Asylum Research Centre on behalf of us.

[27] It also appears to be Home Office practice to send emails and letters as PDF attachments in the name of non-existent employees: when we telephoned the Home Office switchboard in June 2019 and asked to speak to any one of the three individuals that were signatories in the correspondence, we were told that no-one with those names worked in the team in question.

several ethical issues were identified and ethical approval from the University of Sussex' Ethics Committee obtained.[28]

The interviews and focus groups with asylum claimants and refugees invariably involved individuals who had gone through difficult life experiences. Depression, PTSD and anxiety are common in the refugee population (Chap. 9). Therefore, the retelling of traumatic events can have a considerable impact on research participants' mental health. If their SOGI was the basis for the harm inflicted on them, then talking about these aspects of themselves, and their experiences in this regard, may be re-traumatising. Yet, as Stevenson and Willott (2006) point out, we may not always have the right understanding of what topics will be sensitive for a participant.[29] There may be other intersecting aspects of SOGI claimants' identities that are more difficult to talk about and foresee. Furthermore, policy-makers, members of the judiciary, legal representatives, and NGO workers interviewed delved into intimate aspects of the lives and experiences of SOGI claimants, which also risked causing them some distress and anxiety about their and their clients' confidentiality.

It was important to us not to cause psychological harm by asking questions in an insensitive way or probing too much about experiences that might have caused distress to the participant (Krause 2017). We tried to minimise risks to asylum claimant and refugee participants by offering to refer them to agencies and services (where available) capable of dealing professionally and in a supportive way with any mental or physical health issues. We also provided a list of support services available in the relevant countries.[30] Nonetheless, we were also aware that listening to participants' potential disclosures of (sexual) violence and trauma might be distressing for us and impact on our well-being (Krause 2017, p. 4). Therefore, before going into the field, we received training on 'vicarious trauma' from Freedom from Torture, to learn about the signs of vicarious trauma and how to practice self-care in the course of our fieldwork.

We obtained informed consent from all research participants, who were given comprehensive information about the project. This consisted of a clear and honest discussion with the researchers, alongside an information pack (in their preferred language where possible), which explained the project aims, purpose of the data collection, methods, data storage, information on how to withdraw consent and contact information for further enquiries.[31] This information allowed individuals to consciously decide whether they felt emotionally and mentally prepared to share and discuss their experiences. Participants were given time to reflect and ask questions on the information given. Consent forms included questions about consent to audio-record interviews, with information on how all data would be anonymised for

---

[28] Certificate of approval for Ethical Review ER/NH285/1.

[29] For instance, researchers need to be careful not to bring up potential guilt for having left family members behind by probing about family members/partners (Hynes 2003, p. 14).

[30] http://www.sogica.org/wp-content/uploads/2019/12/Organisations-to-signpost-to.pdf.

[31] http://www.sogica.org/wp-content/uploads/2019/12/Information-sheet.pdf.

publication.[32] With regard to the self-completed surveys, submitting a response to the survey implied consent (this was stated on the information sheet preceding the survey).[33] Participants were given the opportunity to withdraw consent, and request the destruction of any data relating to them, at any time up to the publication of an outcome, without giving any reason, and without repercussion or penalty for the participant. This was explained clearly by both the researcher and on the information sheet provided to each participant.

Many of our participants would typically be seen as 'vulnerable'. Yet, the issue of 'vulnerability' is complex (Krause 2017). As further discussed in Chap. 4, asylum claimants and refugees might in some circumstances be officially defined as 'vulnerable', – for example 'transsexual and intersex people' for the purposes of immigration detention in the UK (Home Office 2018), and they might also in some sense be 'vulnerable' because they are more likely to be exposed to human rights violations (Chap. 3). Nonetheless, not all asylum claimants and refugees are vulnerable or would like to be identified as such in the everyday sense of the word, which can have infantilising connotations; most individuals seeking protection have needed to be immensely strong and resourceful, and might not consider themselves vulnerable (Stevenson and Willott 2006). In fact, we might think of asylum systems as not addressing pre-existing vulnerabilities but actually imposing vulnerability. In addition, vulnerability has also been described as a term that is 'overused' (James 2020, p. 33). Taking intersectionality seriously means that when assessing vulnerability, we 'need to consider both the individual circumstances of each research participant, rather than see them as a homogenous group' (Stevenson and Willott 2006, p. 383). By focusing on hardship and using victimising notions, people seeking asylum are often portrayed as having similar experiences including the shared experience of vulnerability (Krause 2017), but they may find this label patronising. Instead of homogenising SOGI claimants as a 'vulnerable group', the intersecting characteristics of each person need to be taken into account when assessing individual vulnerability. It is also important to highlight asylum claimants' and refugees' agency. For instance, many are themselves involved in establishing networks, support groups, and other forms of refugee activism (Bhimji 2016). In this respect, while it might be crucial to anonymise data to avoid risks, it is also important to grant participants the autonomy to decide for themselves whether they want their accounts to be anonymised or not (Clark-Kazak 2017; Krause 2017). In our research, about a quarter of the SOGI claimants and refugee participants chose to be named, while the other three-quarters chose to be anonymised (some provided a pseudonym, for others we chose one), or did not mind either way. To be consistent, we refer to all participants only by first name, including professionals. Occasionally, when we refer to very sensitive matters, we use neither a real name nor a pseudonym.

It has been highlighted that the uniqueness of the refugee experience brings high levels of distrust with it – because of mistreatment in countries of origin, but also

---

[32] http://www.sogica.org/wp-content/uploads/2019/12/Consent-form_individual-interview.pdf.

[33] http://www.sogica.org/wp-content/uploads/2019/12/Qualtrics-survey_information.pdf.

mistreatment during the asylum process (Hynes 2003, p. 13). SOGI claimants in particular might have had experiences of not being able to trust people and 'be out' with regard to their SOGI. In the host country they might have had negative experiences with government officials, housing and other social service providers, and the discrimination they experience adds to their levels of mistrust. This will be compounded by the power differentials between researchers and researched and the fact that researchers often treat research participants solely as 'data source' and not as active subjects with rights, dignity and agency (Krause 2017).[34] The asylum system disempowers SOGI claimants, and often they have internalised disempowering messages. Traditional approaches to research can make asylum claimants and refugees feel exploited (Cochrane 2015).

The three researchers who conducted interviews with SOGI claimants are all cisgendered (one male, two female) – one gay, one lesbian and one heterosexual – and White academics with considerable social, economic and cultural capital. Consequently, power inequalities between us and our participants were likely to exist on grounds of 'refugeeness', gender, 'race', socio-economic status and political rights. For instance, one of the participants in a focus group in Italy complained about the fact that we were White researchers, stating that 'we cannot understand' in full depth their stories and feelings, and that researchers are not necessarily aware of the pain they go through (focus group no. 1, northern Italy). In the interactive process of data collection, power differentials (real or assumed) need to be addressed, while acknowledging that power is relative and exists in all relationships, in other words, it can shift and change. It was thus important to not only consider the intersecting identities of participants, but also those of the researchers. Our gender, sexuality, 'race' and nationality will necessarily have had an impact on how open participants felt to talk about their experiences. For instance, one NGO volunteer we interviewed (Thomas, Germany) felt that LGBTIQ+ asylum claimants and refugees might not tell him about their experiences with discrimination 'out of politeness and hospitality'.

While we were aware that power differentials could not be eliminated, we aimed to conduct research that brought reciprocal benefits, and established 'ethical relationships between researchers and participants that are responsive to the needs, concerns and values of participants' (Mackenzie et al. 2007, p. 307). Our aim was to do research *with* refugees instead of *for* or *on* refugees (Hynes 2003, p. 14) and to work collaboratively as much as possible. Even in so doing, however, power imbalances were unavoidable: three years into the research and having developed ongoing relationships with a number of our participants, we sometimes found ourselves in situations where journalists or event organisers contacted us asking if we knew of any

---

[34] For instance, during the 7-year involvement of one of us with the Lesbian Immigration Support Group in the UK, it often happened that after access to participants had been gained, trust won, and women been interviewed, researchers failed to follow up or contact the group again. Such conduct contributes to SOGI claimants' frustration and mistrust of researchers, but it also denies claimants the opportunity to use any research findings for their own causes (Krause 2017; Mackenzie et al. 2007).

individuals claiming asylum on SOGI grounds who might wish to speak at a conference or appear in a programme. We had to decide which of our many participants to contact about such opportunities, which might not only be enjoyable experiences for the individual in question, but also constitute 'evidence' to include in an appeal bundle. While we always stressed the advantages and disadvantages of such public engagement opportunities to individuals, the underlying power differential remained in place.

In order to achieve our collaborative objectives so far as possible, we established an Advisory Board consisting of five members with expertise in socio-legal research and SOGI asylum claims, including two beneficiaries of international protection, who oversaw the methodological and ethical soundness of the research, as well as offered advice on any aspect of the activities carried out to achieve our aims and objectives. In the spirit of knowledge exchange, we were keen to collaborate with research participants and stakeholders throughout the project, and tried to make this a genuinely two-way process so that we could also give something in return. All researchers were engaged with local NGOs and gave presentations and workshops for LGBTIQ+, refugee and migrant organisations and offered various forms of support to individual and NGO participants, in light of occasional requests. We provided letters for participants confirming that they had participated in our study, which they could use as part of their claims and appeals. We kept in contact with many participants throughout the project and offered emotional and practical support. We invited participants to attend and speak at conferences and events we organised, and connected them with other people and groups, which often helped in breaking down isolation. We sent out a regular newsletter to participants (and increasingly to other people who subscribed to it – a total of more than 1,200 individuals by January 2020) to provide updates on the project.[35] We also created a database of resources for use by SOGI claimants, practitioners and researchers alike.[36]

While there is a risk that interviews can re-traumatise participants, the potential therapeutic effect of telling their story in a safe environment has also been pointed out (Harrell-Bond and Voutira 2007). In particular, the focus groups, which provided a space for open discussions, seemed to have had cathartic effects on participants (Giulio, referring to focus groups no. 1 and 2, northern Italy). As Rosette, who for the first time visited LeTRa when we had the focus group (no. 3, Bavaria, Germany), described her feelings: 'Yeah. I can talk and express myself, and at least listen to people, how other people really feel'. Inspired by the same focus group, Ayeta said 'I feel that we should be always... we have to select some few days that we can be together and talk about issues and everybody's issues'. People were excited about and committed to participating in the study. As Kennedy (Italy) explained: 'and that is the reason why I am so happy, you know, in doing these

---

[35] http://www.sogica.org/en/the-project/activities-plan/.
[36] http://www.sogica.org/en/sogica-database/.

interviews, for us to pass a message across to the governments, not just Nigeria, to Africa, governments, to Africa leaders'.

We tried to avoid raising any expectations on the part of participants that participating in this research would enhance outstanding asylum applications, but very often participants were keen to take part in order to make their voices heard, and above all to help improve the lives and experiences of SOGI refugees in the future (see also Venturi 2017). For instance, Winifred, who participated in focus group no. 4 in Bavaria, Germany, and who is a researcher herself, said:

> We really appreciate taking part in this interview. We really appreciate it. It is a very big opportunity, even though we don't know what will come out. Or we know it will help us in the future, but we really appreciate it. Maybe by then, those people who will be in our shoes now, they will have a better future, they will be given different opportunities. So we really appreciate being part of this interview.

In the following chapters, we hope we succeed in making the voices of our participants heard.

References

Anderson, J., Hollaus, J., Lindsay, A., & Williamson, C. (2014). *The culture of disbelief. An ethnographic approach to understanding an under-theorised concept in the UK asylum system.* Refugee Studies Centre. http://rsc.socsci.ox.ac.uk/files/publications/working-paper-series/wp102-culture-of-disbelief-2014.pdf

Bertaux, D. (Ed.). (1981). *Biography and society: The life history approach in the social sciences.* Beverly Hills: Sage.

Bhimji, F. (2016). Visibilities and the politics of space: Refugee activism in Berlin. *Journal of Immigrant & Refugee Studies, 14*(4), 432–450. https://doi.org/10.1080/15562948.2016.1145777.

Blanck, P. D. (1993). *Interpersonal expectations.* Cambridge: CUP.

Bunt, A. J. (2018, October 15). Freedom of information requests as a tool for social science research. *Methods Blog.* https://walesdtp.ac.uk/methodsblog/2018/10/15/freedom-of-information-requests-as-a-tool-for-social-science-research/

Burns, R. B. (1994). *Introduction to research methods* (2nd ed.). Melbourne: Longman.

Clark-Kazak, C. (2017). Ethical considerations: Research with people in situations of forced migration. *Refuge: Canada's Journal on Refugees, 33*(2), 11–17.

Cochrane, C. (2015). *Sharing knowledge; Sharing power – What we learned.* CSEL. https://csel.org.uk/assets/images/resources/SKSP-event-short-report.pdf

Committee on Migration, Refugees and Population. (2009). *Improving the quality and consistency of asylum decisions in the council of Europe member states.* http://assembly.coe.int/nw/xml/XRef/Xref-XML2HTML-en.asp?fileid=12271&lang=en

El-Enany, N. (2008). Who is the new European refugee? *European Law Review, 33*(3), 313–335.

Epstein, L., & King, G. (2002). The rules of interference. *The University of Chicago Law Review, 69*(1), 1–134.

EUROSTAT. (2019). *Asylum statistics—Statistics Explained.* https://ec.europa.eu/eurostat/statistics-explained/index.php/Asylum_statistics

Ferreira, N., & Kostakopoulou, D. (Eds.). (2016). *The human face of the European Union: Are EU law and policy humane enough?* Cambridge University Press. http://www.cambridge.org/gb/academic/subjects/law/european-law/human-face-european-union-are-eu-law-and-policy-humane-enough

FRA – European Union Agency for Fundamental Rights. (2010a). *Access to effective remedies: The asylum-seeker perspective.* http://fra.europa.eu/sites/default/files/fra_uploads/1691-report-access-remedies_EN.pdf

FRA – European Union Agency for Fundamental Rights. (2010b). *The duty to inform applicants about asylum procedures: The asylum-seeker perspective.* http://fra.europa.eu/sites/default/files/report-asylum-seeker-perspective_en.pdf

Gerhards, J. (2005). *Kulturelle Unterschiede in der Europäischen Union: Ein Vergleich zwischen Mitgliedsländern, Beitrittskandidaten und der Türkei.* VS Verlag für Sozialwissenschaften.

Giordano, C. (2001). Europe: Sociocultural aspects. In *International encyclopaedia of the social & behavioural sciences* (pp. 4917–4923). New York: Elsevier.

Güler, A., Shevtsova, M., & Venturi, D. (Eds.). (2019). *LGBTI asylum seekers and refugees from a legal and political perspective: Persecution, asylum and integration.* Springer. https://www.springer.com/us/book/9783319919041.

Harrell-Bond, B., & Voutira, E. (2007). In search of 'invisible' actors: Barriers to access in refugee research. *Journal of Refugee Studies, 20*(2), 281–298. https://doi.org/10.1093/jrs/fem015.

Held, N. (2019). Sexual orientations and gender identity claims of asylum in Germany. In C. Kueppers & Bundesstiftung Magnus Hirschfeld (Eds.), *Refugees & Queers: Forschung und Bildung an der Schnittstelle von LSBTTIQ, Fluchtmigration und Emanzipationspolitiken* (pp. 53–80).

Home Office. (2018). *Immigration Act 2016: Guidance on adults at risk in immigration detention.* https://assets.publishing.service.gov.uk/government/uploads/system/uploads/attachment_data/file/721237/Adults_at_risk_in_immigration_detention_-_statutory_guidance__2_.pdf

Hynes, T. (2003). *The issue of 'trust' or 'mistrust' in research with refugees: Choices, caveats and considerations for researchers.* UNHCR – UN High Commissioner for Refugees. http://www.unhcr.org/research/working/3fcb5cee1/issue-trust-mistrust-research-refugees-choices-caveats-considerations-researchers.html

Independent Asylum Commission. (2008). *Fit for purpose yet? The Independent Asylum Commission's Interim Findings. A nationwide review of the UK asylum system in association with the Citizen Organising Foundation.* http://www.independentasylumcommission.org.uk/

James, F. (2020). *Refugee protection. United Kingdom country report. Multilevel governance of mass migration in Europe and beyond project (#770564, Horizon2020) report series.* file:///Users/md468/Downloads/Refugee_Protection_United_Kingdom_Countr.pdf

Khan, T. (2016). *Investigating the British asylum system for lesbian, gay and bisexual asylum-seekers: Theoretical and empirical perspectives on fairness.* PhD thesis, University of Liverpool.

Krause, U. (2017). *Researching forced migration: Critical reflections on research ethics during fieldwork* (RSC Working Paper Series, 123). Refugee Studies Centre.

Künnecke, M. (2007). *Tradition and change in administrative law: An Anglo-German comparison.* Berlin: Springer.

Lomba, S. D. (2004). *The right to seek refugee status in the European Union.* Antwerp: Intersentia.

Lukac, E., & Eriksson, H. (2017). *LGBT asylum seekers in Sweden: Conceptualising queer migration beyond the concept of "Safe third country"* (p. 29). Oxford Research.

Mackenzie, C., McDowell, C., & Pittaway, E. (2007). Beyond 'Do no harm': The challenge of constructing ethical relationships in refugee research. *Journal of Refugee Studies, 20*(2), 299–319. https://doi.org/10.1093/jrs/fem008.

Macnaghten, P., & Myers, G. (2007). Focus groups. In C. Seale, G. Gobo, J. F. Gubrium, & D. Silverman (Eds.), *Qualitative research practice* (pp. 65–79). London: SAGE.

Matsuda, M. J. (1991). Beside my sister, facing the enemy: Legal theory out of coalition. *Stanford Law Review, 43*(6), 1183–1192.

McConville, M., & Chui, W. H. (Eds.). (2007). *Research methods for law.* Edinburgh: Edinburgh University Press.

Morgan, D. L. (1998). *The focus group guidebook.* Thousand Oaks: Sage Publications.

Philips, S. U. (2001). Gender ideology: Cross-cultural aspects. In *International encyclopaedia of the social & behavioural sciences* (pp. 6016–6020). New York: Elsevier.

References

Rapley, T. (2007). Interviews. In C. Seale, G. Gobo, J. F. Gubrium, & D. Silverman (Eds.), *Qualitative research practice*. Sage.

Savage, A., & Hyde, R. (2014). Using freedom of information requests to facilitate research. *International Journal of Social Research Methodology, 17*(3), 303–317. https://doi.org/10.1080/13645579.2012.742280.

Seal, C. (Ed.). (2004). *Social research methods: A reader*. Routledge.

Seale, C., Gobo, G., Gubrium, J. F., & Silverman, D. (Eds.). (2004). *Qualitative research practice*. Los Angeles: Sage.

Sonnino, S., & Denozza, M. (2005). *Linee Guida per la Valutazione delle Richieste di Riconoscimento dello Status di Rifugiato*. Ministero dell'Interno – Commissione Nazionale per il Diritto d'Asilo. http://www.cestim.it/argomenti/28rifugiati/linee-guida-commissione-2005.doc

Stevenson, J., & Willott, J. (2006). *Cultural influences in data collection and analysis: Issues in conducting research with refugees*. Leeds Metropolitan University.

Travers, M. (1999). *The British immigration courts: A study of law and politics*. New York: The Policy Press.

Travers, M., & Manzo, J. F. (Eds.). (1997). *Law in action: Ethnomethodological and conversation analytic approaches to law*. Aldershot: Ashgate.

Turnbull, S. (2015, April 6). Using access to information requests to gather qualitative data. *Oxford Law Faculty*. https://www.law.ox.ac.uk/centres-institutes/centre-criminology/blog/2015/04/using-access-information-requests-gather

UNHCR – UN High Commissioner for Refugees. (2005). *UNHCR Provisional comments on the proposal for a council directive on minimum standards on procedures in member states for granting and withdrawing refugee status* (Council Document 14203/04, Asile 64, of 9 November 2004). http://www.unhcr.org/43661ea42.pdf

Venturi, D. (2017). Reflections on empirical research with LGBTI refugees—A legal scholar's perspective. *Oxford Monitor of Forced Migration, 6*(2), 20–23.

Waaldijk, C. (2006). General situation with respect to sexual orientation discrimination at the national level. In C. Waaldijk & M. Bonini-Baraldi (Eds.), *Sexual orientation discrimination in the European Union: National laws and the employment equality directive* (pp. 61–85). The Hague: T.M.C. Asser Press.

Walby, K., & Luscombe, A. (2017). Criteria for quality in qualitative research and use of freedom of information requests in the social sciences. *Qualitative Research, 17*(5), 537–553. https://doi.org/10.1177/1468794116679726.

Walby, K., & Luscombe, A. (2018). Ethics review and freedom of information requests in qualitative research. *Research Ethics, 14*(4), 1–15. https://doi.org/10.1177/1747016117750208.

Whittaker, D. (2006). *Asylum seekers and refugees in the contemporary world*. London: Routledge.

Open Access This chapter is licensed under the terms of the Creative Commons Attribution 4.0 International License (http://creativecommons.org/licenses/by/4.0/), which permits use, sharing, adaptation, distribution and reproduction in any medium or format, as long as you give appropriate credit to the original author(s) and the source, provide a link to the Creative Commons license and indicate if changes were made.

The images or other third party material in this chapter are included in the chapter's Creative Commons license, unless indicated otherwise in a credit line to the material. If material is not included in the chapter's Creative Commons license and your intended use is not permitted by statutory regulation or exceeds the permitted use, you will need to obtain permission directly from the copyright holder.

Chapter 3
A Theoretical Framework: A Human Rights Reading of SOGI Asylum Based on Feminist and Queer Studies

With my gender… it's like… why don't they stop, I don't think it's important to ask. What I'll be, I'll be. It's important I'm queer and I'm here.

(Prince Emrah, Germany)

The notion of vulnerability does not reflect the whole life experience of an individual (…) so talking about specific needs may also help to expand the range of beneficiaries.

(Cristina, UNHCR Italy)

… men, they have got all the say on women, on how we, we grow up. It makes me like very, very angry and like, why?

(Meggs, UK)

3.1 Introduction

Since SOGI considerations have started to inform the interpretation and the implementation of the Refugee Convention (Chap. 1), a broad range of scholars from different disciplines have explored how questions of sexual orientation and gender identity can be effectively addressed within international, supranational and domestic asylum systems. The debate around aspects of RSD and beyond generated by this theoretical exchange within the same discipline and between different research areas has contributed to the (ongoing) normative movement towards a more inclusive Refugee Convention framework. In an attempt to nurture this continuous debate, we outline the theoretical and analytical frameworks that shape the subsequent analysis. We take advantage of the authors' diverse experience in different academic fields to apply an interdisciplinary approach, addressing our subject from various perspectives. We start from the recognition that a detailed understanding and application of the Refugee Convention is vital as the floor for addressing SOGI asylum claims, but not in itself sufficient to ensure that these are fairly treated. Section 3.2 therefore looks to human rights to show how interweaving human rights frameworks with refugee law heightens understanding in this field of asylum. To

© The Author(s) 2021
C. Danisi et al., *Queering Asylum in Europe*, IMISCOE Research Series,
https://doi.org/10.1007/978-3-030-69441-8_3

this end, the main body of this chapter develops an approach that addresses the failings from the perspective of international human rights law (IHRL), both alone and in interaction with international refugee law (IRL). However, we then argue that, without explicitly recognising the gendered and sexualised nature of SOGI asylum, IHRL is only part of the solution. In Sects. 3.3 and 3.4 below, we claim that feminist and queer theories, and particular threads of debate within these broad disciplines, can help to understand the experiences of SOGI minorities fleeing persecution and, importantly, to explain why, despite improvements to the law and guidance that recognise the right to protection on this basis, there has been insufficient progress on the ground. In this way, combining a human rights-based approach that is largely legal with political and sociological contributions from feminism and queer theories facilitates a more holistic analysis.

3.2 A Human Rights Approach to SOGI Asylum: What Role for Rights?

The theoretical debate over the application of the Refugee Convention through a 'human rights paradigm' is not new (Anker 2002; Cantor 2016; Storey 2015). Yet, what this 'paradigm' means for SOGI asylum claims, and how to interpret the concepts at play within this context, remains largely unexplored. In her seminal study of the role of human rights in sexual orientation asylum claims, Jenni Millbank showed that 'the lack of a human rights framework, in general, combined with an underdeveloped analysis of sexual orientation as a human rights issue' can lead to 'extremely regressive refugee determinations' (Millbank 2004, p. 194). She demonstrates how different framings of SOGI minorities as human rights holders potentially restrict or expand protection under the Refugee Convention. She also makes it clear that the lack of a human rights framework in the field of asylum cannot simply be addressed by referring to international human rights standards, that is, those emerging from the international human rights treaties binding upon the European countries explored in our study. These include, at minimum, the European Convention on Human Rights (ECHR) and the Charter of Fundamental Rights of the European Union (CFR), which also binds the European Union.[1]

Millbank's work does not provide a fully expounded theoretical model for the basis of a human rights 'paradigm' for SOGI asylum.[2] Nevertheless, her contribution provides a good starting point for the aim of this section: to construct a human

---

[1] Council of Europe, *European Convention for the Protection of Human Rights and Fundamental Freedoms, as amended by Protocols Nos. 11 and 14*, 4 November 1950; European Union: Council of the European Union, *Charter of Fundamental Rights of the European Union (2007/C 303/01)*, 14 December 2007, C 303/1.

[2] Although she only addressed sexual orientation asylum claims, her findings apply equally to gender identity, as the denial of human rights enjoyment is common to all members of SOGI minorities (Muntarbhorn 2017; Ramón Mendos 2019).

rights approach to SOGI asylum. To this end, and applying a multi-layered approach following Millbank, we focus on three interrelated aspects of the potential role played by human rights: a) the status of SOGI *within* human rights law; b) the general relation *between* human rights and refugee law when SOGI is in play; and c) the possibility of reading human rights law *in parallel* with the international refugee system based on the Refugee Convention to protect SOGI within and beyond asylum.

The reason for such a threefold investigation lies in the very foundations of the idea of human rights, based on 'the recognition of the inherent dignity and equal and inalienable rights of all members of the human family'.[3] Yet, as Paul Johnson, Martha Nussbaum and Robert Wintemute demonstrate (Johnson 2013a; Nussbaum 2010; Wintemute 1996), when SOGI minorities are the subject, inherent dignity is not always a guarantor of equal rights. 'Inclusiveness' remains the ideal culmination of an evolutionary process for IHRL, rather than a category of interpretation when these minorities claim 'to have rights'. Using the lens of Arendt's work, SOGI minorities should be protected as members of their countries' 'political communities'. Instead, along with stateless and refugee people[4] – that is, political communities' outsiders – SOGI minorities may find themselves recognised as humans but 'with no effective citizenship and no place in the world' (Arendt 1973, p. 296). As a result, people who are both members of SOGI minorities and asylum claimants may face extreme difficulties in accessing international legal protection.

It is true that, for some critics, 'the idea of human rights as a project (…) is already affected by – and overtly and covertly implicated in – structures of power, laying bare the fallacy of human rights as linked to an external, optimistic pursuit of freedom' (Kapur 2018, p. 2). Equally, human rights advocacy has not always led to the transformation of power relations or to meaningful freedoms for people in need of international protection (Bhabha 2002). Yet, inspired by Arendt's assertion of the primordial 'right to have rights' (Arendt 1973) and while avoiding defining freedom for SOGI claimants as simply 'an accumulation of rights' (Kapur 2018, p. 6), we intend to reconsider IHRL in light of its underlying inclusionary rationale in the asylum context. In fact, while IRL is driven by an exclusionary rationale, leading to a kind of 'in or out' process depending upon whether the specific conditions required by the 'refugee' definition are met, IHRL remains the more inclusive international legal regime. Yet, simply framing IRL as a 'surrogate human rights protection system' (Cantor 2016, p. 357) does not provide any solid ground for our approach. Instead, by recognising that these two international systems are interrelated while remaining distinct (Chetail 2014, p. 24), we need to reframe how human rights should be embedded in IRL to effectively address the challenges that SOGI claimants experience in practice, thus showing how the intersection between these legal fields is potentially beneficial.

---

[3] UN General Assembly, *Universal Declaration of Human Rights*, Resolution 217(III), 10 December 1948.
[4] As Mann explained, the categories of refugee and stateless people 'were interchangeable for Arendt, but came to be understood as distinct' (Mann 2017, p. 9).

To this end, this section elaborates a human rights approach to SOGI asylum by exploring three claims, which ultimately relate to the enjoyment of rights regardless of one's citizenship or of state's consent. First, human rights are essential to qualify SOGI as core aspects of identity and to verify how these should be protected as such (Sect. 3.2.1). Second, human rights in light of SOGI provide a tool for interpreting the Refugee Convention, thus questioning the interaction to date between IHRL and IRL (Sect. 3.2.2). Third, besides helping us elaborate procedural guarantees for people in need of international protection, a human rights approach to SOGI asylum also contributes to substantial developments in terms of autonomous means of protection when refugee law does not offer any or sufficient guarantees to people fleeing homophobia and transphobia (Sect. 3.2.3).

3.2.1 Human Rights and SOGI: Reconsidering Personhood Through a SOGI and Anti-stereotyping Lens

In attempting to (re)affirm the recognition of the inherent dignity of every person, IHRL has provided a fertile environment for setting the conditions to, at a minimum, promote individual autonomy and self-determination.[5] In this context, SOGI are increasingly framed as categories subject to international law protection for the fundamental role they play in defining and expressing personhood[6] (or 'humanity', as Muntarbhorn states it: 2017, p. 2). Despite not being expressly included in universal and regional core human rights treaties prior to their partial inclusion in the CFR, the recognition that human rights violations could be motivated by individuals' or groups' SOGI has led to a twofold process.

On the one hand, within international and regional human rights systems, there has been a movement towards a gradual 'definition' of SOGI as universal concepts, as opposed to 'invented' Western categories (Chase 2016, p. 704; Lee 2016). Similarly to the development of the notion of refugee within IRL as apparent in the Refugee Convention (Hathaway 1991, p. 136), this process has identified generalised categories of protection rather than naming marginalised groups in need of protection. That is why, in IHRL, sexual orientation has increasingly been addressed as an 'inherent'[7] and 'most intimate',[8] aspect of human personality, as a basis on

---

[5] Given the purpose of these volumes, the doctrinal foundations of human rights cannot be explored. It is, nonetheless, evident that we conceive human rights as 'given', rather than 'agreed upon' (Dembour 2010).

[6] This term is used here in order to stress the complexity of identities of people in need of international protection, including SOGI claimants, which requires a more complex analysis of individual situations than a focus on a particular aspect of one's identity for asylum purposes (Firth and Mauthe 2013).

[7] Inter-American Court of Human Rights, *Identidad de Género, e Igualdad y No Discriminación a Parejas del Mismo Sexo*, Opinión Consultiva OC-24/17, 24 November 2017, para. 40.

[8] ECtHR, *Dudgeon v. United Kingdom*, Application no. 7525/76, 22 October 1981, para. 52.

which marginalised people are entitled to ask for and obtain protection.[9] That is also why, in supporting what may be a human rights reading of refugee law in the search for a PSG, the CJEU found that 'a common ground' exists in that 'a person's sexual orientation is a characteristic so fundamental to his identity that he should not be forced to renounce it'.[10] The same is true of gender identity, considering that the freedom to name one's gender identity has been framed in the human rights context as 'one of the most basic essentials of self-determination'.[11]

This evolution in understanding has not escaped criticism. For instance, Gross affirmed that 'in societies where men have sex with men regardless of any specific sexual identity, defining people as having a sexual orientation that is integral to their humanity constitutes an exportation of the "Western" model of sexual orientation identity and its categorisation of this orientation as a distinct and autonomous feature of the self' (Gross 2013, p. 127; Sect. 3.4). Yet, for our purposes, human rights have created the necessary framework for self-identification, in the sense that SOGI should be protected as such when people choose to refer to these traits in order to express or determine their personhood. In fact, SOGI may correspond to a variety of human rights and freedoms with concrete consequences – as will emerge below – in terms of determination of refugee status.[12] As such, adopting a human rights approach in relation to SOGI asylum supports the protection of the infinite range of ways in which these core characteristics find expression.

In this respect, it is worth noting that common concepts in IRL have already been reconsidered to take into account such developments in IHRL. For instance, the concept of 'exogenous' harm has been questioned for advancing the idea of 'endogenous' harm (Hathaway and Pobjoy 2012), which better expresses SOGI minorities' well-founded fear of persecution. Equally, this understanding of SOGI as the most intimate characteristics of personhood rules out the infamous behaviour/identity dichotomy explored by scholars in the field of asylum (Wessels 2016). As a consequence, our analysis considers any position by countries of origin or host countries supporting a denial or a restriction of an individual's SOGI through human rights violations to be unlawful and intolerable.

On the other hand, a more refined – although not always consistent – clarification of states' obligations under IHRL has materialised in order to protect individuals whose SOGI is at odds with societal norms (Muntarbhorn 2017, p. 2). While it is

---

[9] The same is true at domestic level. For instance, in one of the leading cases of SOGI asylum in the UK, sexual identity was accepted as being 'a fundamental characteristic and an integral part of human freedom': *HJ (Iran) and HT (Cameroon) v Secretary of State for the Home Department* [2010] UKSC 31, para. 33.

[10] Joined Cases C-199/12, C-200/12 and C-201/12, *X, Y and Z v Minister voor Immigratie, Integratie en Asiel*, 7 November 2013, ECLI:EU:C:2013:720, para. 70.

[11] ECtHR, *Van Kuck v. Germany*, Application no. 35968/97, 12 June 2003, para. 73.

[12] By embracing such an approach, we are not suggesting any normative content for SOGI. Instead, to avoid imposing particular notions on SOGI minorities, these human rights principles will be read through queer and feminist lenses (Sects. 3.3 and 3.4) to assess how fair European asylum systems are towards SOGI claimants.

true that, in relation to human rights treaties, 'States gave their consent to a notion of human rights that had certain types of violations in mind, and not others that did not exist at the time',[13] this evolutionary trend does not depend on states' consent but on the ability to read human rights in light of their potential ultimate scope. In other words, human rights bodies have increasingly called upon states to apply the principle of equality and non-discrimination, enshrined in all universal and regional human rights treaties, to more and more freedoms and rights as meaningful expressions of people's dignity, and so one's SOGI. Here, two interrelated consequences are fundamental for SOGI minorities.

First, by bringing to the fore the distinction between negative and positive obligations as two sides of the same coin, the protection of SOGI minorities is now recognised as requiring a proactive role from national authorities, one that addresses the social marginalisation deriving from past discrimination. In light of the complexity of SOGI, this proactive role entails a strong anti-stereotyping approach. By exploring developments aimed at eradicating structural disadvantage and discrimination against certain groups, such as women and ethnic minorities,[14] Eva Brems and Alexandra Timmer advocate a 'legal methodology' consisting of 'naming' and 'contesting' widely accepted beliefs that impair the recognition of the equal dignity and personal autonomy of all individuals (Brems and Timmer 2016; Timmer 2011, 2015). When applied to SOGI minorities, an anti-stereotyping approach translates into contesting 'ready-made opinions' and 'preconceived ideas that lead to bias' (Timmer 2011, p. 713) and perpetuate discrimination. Such an approach has, for example, allowed the UN Human Rights Council (HRC), the ECtHR and the CJEU to eradicate 'traditional' ideas about the ability of members of SOGI minorities to establish a family life worthy of protection, thus ensuring in some circumstances the same treatment already provided to members of the heterosexual majority.[15] Considering that stereotypes tie SOGI minorities to a particular identity by placing 'a certain mould on individuals, independent of what they are capable of, experience or desire' (Timmer 2011: 715), this anti-stereotyping 'legal methodology' is instrumental in the asylum context. It supports the need to fight against the structural disadvantages from which SOGI claimants suffer by avoiding a default judgment of the individual on account of assumed group characteristics. It requires us, as will be particularly apparent in Chaps. 6 and 7, to name and contest mechanisms connected to asylum adjudicators' mental processes by which, for example, SOGI are consciously or unconsciously defined in terms of societal roles, of 'openness' or appearance/expression in Western terms (Millbank 2009; Spijkerboer 2013, 2018).

---

[13] Inter-American Court of Human Rights, *Atala Riffo and Others v. Chile*, 24 February 2012, para. 74.

[14] In relation to gender, Holtmaat states: 'Stereotypes tend to fixate gender identities and gender roles and make them appear as real, universal, eternal, natural, essential and/or unchangeable. (…) stereotypes often serve to maintain existing power relationships; they are control mechanisms' (Holtmaat and Naber 2011, p. 57).

[15] For instance, ECtHR, *Schalk and Kopf v. Austria*, Application no. 30141/04, 24 June 2010, para. 99.

3.2 A Human Rights Approach to SOGI Asylum: What Role for Rights?

It also requires that we question asylum systems as heteronormatively framed, thus giving rise to a process of 'contestation' of the assumed heterosexual nature of claimants' personhood in every phase of asylum.[16]

Second, the range of SOGI-related scenarios identified as human rights violations is growing. What were previously accepted as 'permissible' treatments or attitudes towards SOGI minorities are increasingly recognised as breaching IHRL. While these developments are often framed simply in terms of prohibited discrimination, there are more progressive readings of IHRL, with positive implications for SOGI asylum, though still unrealised in some cases. Two examples illustrate this point. On a positive note, the Inter-American Court of Human Rights has asserted that 'the discrimination suffered by [SOGI minorities] is also highly harmful of [their] right to physical integrity'.[17] This is because the process of SOGI self-perception often occurs in a hostile environment, where prejudices are widespread within the family itself. In terms of improved readings of the notion of persecution and of agents of persecution, as well as recognition of lack of protection by the state and/or family, this development is valuable for SOGI claimants. Less positively, the prohibition or the lack of legal recognition of same-sex relationships (in the form of marriage or civil partnerships) irrespective of SOGI is still not seen as a human rights violation under IHRL. Although some fear that this would lead to human rights being used as a vehicle for reinforcing 'homonormativity in the form of marriage of same-sex couples at the expense of giving equal value to diverse forms of living' (Gross 2013, pp. 123–124), this development would enhance the scope and extent of asylum protection in SOGI claims via the notion of persecution.

This evolution has a significant impact on IRL. It is worth noting that, although the general prohibition on discrimination is enshrined in the Refugee Convention (Article 3), the meaning of discrimination in IRL remains distinct, that is, more restrictive, if compared to the interpretation of this concept in IHRL (Dowd 2011, p. 28). As a result, when evaluating asylum claims, decision-makers may find it hard to consider the impact of discrimination on the individual's ability to live a dignified life, including family life, to the same extent that they would in a human rights claim. This has led, in practice, to an arbitrary selection of which human rights count as relevant to asylum claims, something we question throughout our study. For this reason, in light of the fact that IHRL demands protection of SOGI, a reconsideration of the role of IHRL as an interpretative tool of IRL is needed to frame the appropriate human rights approach for SOGI asylum.

---

[16] See how this approach was successfully applied by the ECtHR in relation to gender stereotyping, for instance, in *Carvalho Pinto De Sousa Morais v. Portugal*, Application no. 17484/15, 25 July 2017, paras. 52–55.

[17] Inter-American Court of Human Rights, *Identidad de Género, e Igualdad y No Discriminación a Parejas del Mismo Sexo*, Opinión Consultiva OC-24/17, 24 November 2017, para. 48.

3.2.2 Human Rights and the Refugee Convention: Establishing the Right Relationship

Like IHRL, refugee law developed at a time when SOGI minorities were barely recognised on the international rights agenda. There is no evidence suggesting such issues were discussed during the preparatory work of the Refugee Convention (UNHCR 1990, p. 36), a deplorable omission given the targeting of SOGI minorities in the violence that led to the Refugee Convention (McAdam 2014; Plant 1987). Yet, despite the differences in aims and scope of application, IHRL and IRL interact and, sometimes, converge when SOGI asylum is considered (Houle and Allister 2017).[18] When the content of these international law areas coincides, this interaction has the potential to create a more inclusive international refugee system. In principle, this may happen where the prohibition on discrimination and the principle of non-refoulement are concerned, as both rights are enshrined in the Refugee Convention as well as in IHRL. That is why both scholars and the UNHCR have stressed that the Refugee Convention should be read through the prism of human rights (Foster and Hathaway 2014; Hathaway 1991; UNHCR 2002, paras 5, 9, 2011, pp. 1, 8, 14, 16, 36, 81, 2012, paras 5–7). Beyond this, it remains unclear precisely how human rights should inform IRL. A human rights approach to SOGI asylum needs to define the extent of this interaction in light of the implications for SOGI protection.

From a general point of view, this interaction should not come as a surprise if we consider the general rules on interpretation of international law as codified in the 1969 Vienna Convention on the Law of the Treaties (VCLT). According to Article 31 of this Convention, 'a treaty shall be interpreted in good faith in accordance with the ordinary meaning to be given to the terms of the treaty in their context and in the light of its object and purpose' (para. 1), and 'there shall be taken into account, together with the context (…) any relevant rules of international law applicable in the relations between the parties' (para. 3, c). This means that, while human rights cannot be the only element used to interpret the Refugee Convention, IHRL occupies a primary position among these other international rules when this Convention has to be interpreted and applied.[19] In line with the previous sub-section, we may argue that, in order to respect these rules on interpretation, the Refugee Convention should be read through the ordinary meaning that its terms – for example, discrimination, persecution, well-founded fear – have acquired in today's society and, where SOGI asylum is concerned, taking into account SOGI-specific features. Equally, these rules of interpretation require an interaction between IRL and IHRL that is based on an understanding of human rights that looks at the reasons why international

---

[18] For example, in relation to the Canadian experience. Interestingly, if we consider Millbank's comparative study involving UK, Australia and Canada, only the Canadian refugee system allowed such a convergence, because it was ultimately based on a non-discriminatory understanding of sexual orientation as a human rights issue (Millbank 2005).

[19] See also para. 1 of the Preamble and Article 3 of the Refugee Convention.

protection is due to SOGI minorities under international law. In other words, only when this interpretation is grounded in the idea of human rights in light of the ideal category of 'inclusiveness' and through an anti-stereotyping approach, can the continuing marginalisation and inequality affecting SOGI minorities be avoided in the refugee context. While our human rights approach for SOGI asylum embraces this model of interaction for the application of IRL, and consequently of European asylum law, the appropriateness of other 'models' already advanced or in use to this day requires further consideration. These come into play, first, from a general point of view and, second, from a more specific SOGI perspective.

Having regard to the general relation between IHRL and IRL, the model of refugee law as surrogate human rights protection based on early Hathaway's writings (Hathaway 1991) deserves attention. Whether or not it has been extensively embraced in theory and in practice (Cantor 2016, p. 378 ff), his model has supported a 'normative reading' of the Refugee Convention by using human rights to provide objective standards on the basis of which asylum adjudicators can read notions that the authors of that Convention intentionally left open. In so doing, it stresses the failure of the state in the claimant's country of origin to respect basic international duties in human rights terms, thus favouring the identification of a selection of rights that, when denied or restricted in the country of origin, may trigger the surrogate protection of IRL (Hathaway 1991, pp. 108–112). Nonetheless, this reasoning has more to do with the scope of application of IHRL and states' obligation to avoid human rights violations abroad, than it has to do with the primary aim of the Refugee Convention (Goodwin-Gill and McAdam 2007). An immediate consequence is indeed a conflation of the individual well-founded fear of persecution with the lack of protection due to that failure – a conflation of two separate concepts of the Convention's definition of refugee. Applying Hathaway's approach, based in practice on a selection of rights rather than looking at human rights as a whole, interpreters of the Refugee Convention act in conflict with the very foundation of human rights as an indivisible catalogue, as well as in an arbitrary way limiting the object of IHRL's protection.

When applied more specifically to SOGI, the inconsistencies in this approach are evident. By focusing on the failure of the country of origin to provide protection,[20] asylum adjudicators concentrate on the lack of guarantees for the enjoyment of non-derogable rights. In doing so, however, they disregard the effect of violating the full, interdependent, range of human rights in generating a well-founded fear of persecution in people who identify as belonging to SOGI minorities. Moreover, in practice, this model reinforces some negative trends in the protection of SOGI under IHRL, which connect these core characteristics to only certain human rights and, stereotypically, to certain aspects of life (Johnson 2013a; McGoldrick 2016). In the SOGI

---

[20] According to Spijkerboer, SOGI claimants have exploited this model by overstating specific human rights violations and, in turn, reinforcing the European/non-European dichotomy regarding States' friendliness towards SOGI minorities. However, whether this collateral consequence really takes place remains to be shown, also on the basis of our fieldwork, as analysed in subsequent chapters (Spijkerboer 2018, p. 22).

asylum context, a good example can be taken from the case law of the CJEU. When it was called upon to read EU asylum law in light of the wide EU's human rights framework in a ruling related to claims based on sexual orientation, the CJEU referred directly to the right to respect for private life as 'naturally' connected to sexual orientation, something that is incompatible with the indivisibility of human rights.[21]

Considering the specific features of SOGI in the context of asylum, the UNHCR's interpretative activity also needs to be reconsidered. While the UNHCR has supported a human rights reading of the Refugee Convention since the first publication of its 'Handbook on Procedures and Criteria for Determining Refugee Status', a coherent explanation of how IHRL and IRL interact has not been developed (also Cantor 2016, pp. 352–353). This is evident when SOGI claims are involved, as the UNHCR 2012 SOGI Guidelines show (UNHCR 2012). By referring to the Universal Declaration of Human Rights as the cornerstone of IHRL, the Guidelines state that 'all people, *including* LGBTI individuals, are entitled to enjoy the protection provided for by international human rights law on the basis of equality and non-discrimination' (UNHCR 2012, para. 5, our emphasis). While they stress that 'respect for fundamental rights as well as the principle of non-discrimination are core aspects of the 1951 Convention', setting the ground for an interaction in line with Article 31 VCLT, the Guidelines then limit their potential scope in at least two ways. First, they refer only to the refugee definition as one that needs to be interpreted through a human rights lens; however, such an interpretative interaction should inform the application of the entire Refugee Convention (see Articles 2-34), even if IHRL may provide independent, and broader, protection beyond the refugee definition, as we discuss below. Second, the Guidelines explicitly refer to the 2007 'Yogyakarta Principles on the Application of International Human Rights Law in relation to Sexual Orientation and Gender Identity' as a privileged instrument for identifying the human rights protection framework applicable in the context of SOGI (UNHCR 2012, para. 7).[22] Yet, despite their positive impact on the evolution of IHRL and their diffusion within universal human rights bodies (Thoreson 2009), these Principles only reflect 'well-established' principles of IHRL (UNHCR 2012, para. 7). Given that the aim of the Principles is to ensure universal visibility to 'already binding' SOGI-related human rights obligations, they do not go as far as they should in defining how IHRL should be read on the basis of the overarching principles of equality and non-discrimination.[23] As a result, one cannot exclude the possibility that the UNHRC SOGI Guidelines may generate ambiguous interpretations of the Refugee Convention if applied without a sufficiently encompassing understanding of IHRL and SOGI.

---

[21] Joined Cases C-199/12, C-200/12 and C-201/12, *X, Y and Z v Minister voor Immigratie, Integratie en Asiel*, 7 November 2013, ECLI:EU:C:2013:720.

[22] See the update version of these Principles: Various 2017.

[23] Interestingly, Gross (2013, pp. 126–128) also criticises these Principles for their definitions of SOGI, for example, '[s]exual orientation defined as such is a feature of modern "Western" societies but not necessarily a feature of all humanity'.

In order to avoid such pitfalls, we suggest a more principled approach to the interaction between IHRL and IRL as a part of a human rights approach to SOGI asylum. Following the legal and theoretical developments explored above (Sect. 3.2.1), a framework for interpreting the Refugee Convention through a human rights lens should be based on two essential features: (1) the principle of equality and non-discrimination, as the major point of intersection between IRL and IHRL, including in terms of positive obligations and an anti-stereotyping approach; and (2) recognition of SOGI as core aspects of individual personhood needing protection. This approach would enable an evaluation of the impact of denying or restricting human rights in terms of an individual's SOGI and their ability to express their personhood. By 'measuring' how serious a human rights violation is for particular individuals, the approach suggested here would also question and avoid rigid categorisations of rights when defining a refugee under the Refugee Convention. Equally, while having regard to the VCLT, this approach eliminates the likelihood of a selective or limited application of IHRL that results in the continuation of 'permissible persecution' of SOGI minorities through refugee law (Johnson 2007, p. 99). In addition, a positive collateral effect of this approach would be to finally clarify what protection is really achievable through IRL when interpreted in the light of IHRL and what autonomous role IHRL can additionally play, owing to the impossibility of stretching the interpretation of IRL in a way that goes well beyond its ordinary meaning. Considering the range of experiences faced by SOGI claimants before, during and after the asylum process, IHRL may further complement the Refugee Convention, both procedurally and substantively, as we will now discuss.

3.2.3 Human Rights as an Independent Basis for Protection in SOGI Asylum: From Procedural Guarantees to Substantive Fairness

As Bhabha states, people in need of international protection appear to be 'a temporary and increasingly disenfranchised category of non-citizens' who need to wait until their status is settled to enjoy the prospect of long-term safety and, at least to a certain extent, non-discriminatory treatment (Bhabha 2002, p. 115). Although the Refugee Convention (Articles 3-34) provides a framework of guarantees that binds state parties, these are not based on the requirement that refugees should be treated equally to citizens in the host states, nor are they framed in terms of human rights (Cantor 2016; Chetail 2014). As scholars in this field have explored, the process faced by asylum claimants underlines, in particular, two different situations where IHRL provides an independent basis for protection: the evaluation of the asylum request and the life in the host countries during and after the asylum process. In contrast to the period of departure and travel towards a 'safe haven', where the question of jurisdiction under relevant human rights treaties is also still debatable in terms of obligations to issue humanitarian visas (Danisi 2019; Moreno-Lax 2018;

Chaps. 4 and 5), human rights obligations certainly apply when people in need of international protection submit an asylum request. It is at this precise moment that the risk of an 'intersection of borders of inequality' (Peroni 2018) emerges strongly for SOGI claimants, but also when human rights may concretely shape a fair system for the evaluation of their applications, their reception and integration (Chaps. 6, 7, 8 and 9).

While IHRL does not encompass a right to receive asylum, universal and regional human rights bodies have defined the conditions for facilitating the right to claim asylum, thus sowing the seeds for defining the concept of fairness in the asylum context. First, in light of the principle of non-refoulement, reaffirmed in the European context by Article 19 CFR as the corner stone of the protection to be granted to everyone, a thorough individual evaluation of each asylum request is due. Even when a third country qualifies as 'safe' (Chap. 6), for example as a consequence of international agreements for facilitating readmission or transferal, the evolution of IHRL binds national authorities to verify whether or not, for personal circumstances or characteristics or for lack of procedural guarantees in the country of destination, a person risks being exposed to torture or inhuman or degrading treatment.[24] The fairness of any asylum system thus depends on the national authority's ability to take into account the specific situation of people claiming asylum, through the lenses proposed in this chapter, in order to promote a dignified treatment.[25] This principle applies well beyond non-refoulement, spreading its potential effect to the entire human rights catalogue when applied to the situation of people in need of international protection. To use the words of the ECtHR, the ultimate aim is always 'to avoid situations which may reproduce the plight that forced these persons to flee in the first place'.[26]

When these general guarantees, aiming – at a minimum – to ensure individual assessment and effective access to an asylum procedure, are applied to people requesting asylum on SOGI grounds, they result in an individualised procedure that, among other things, considers the specific needs of the claimant and avoids stereotyping. This individualised approach is evident in the context of reception at European and universal level,[27] as a result of the interpretation of the right to liberty and security in light of the need of people belonging to SOGI minorities to avoid being placed with people having the same socio-cultural and/or religious background of their persecutors. An anti-stereotyping approach has, in turn, found application in the assessment of asylum requests. Here, a fair approach precludes

---

[24] The case law of the ECtHR is a remarkable example of this trend: among others, ECtHR, *M.A. and Others v. Lithuania*, Application no. 59793/17, 11 December 2018.

[25] For a seminal case in the European context, see ECtHR, Grand Chamber, *M.S.S. v. Belgium and Greece*, Application no. 30696/09, 21 January 2011.

[26] ECtHR, *O.M. v. Hungary*, Application no. 9912/15, 5 July 2016, para. 53.

[27] At European level, ECtHR, *O.M. v. Hungary*, Application no. 9912/15, 5 July 2016, para. 53. At universal level, see the UN Working Group on Arbitrary Detention 2018, where SOGI migrants have been identified within the group of 'vulnerable people and/or at risk', whose detention 'must not take place'. See also Various 2017, Principle 23, E.

questioning that is detrimental to the dignity of SOGI claimants or that relies exclusively on stereotypical ideas of sexual minorities.[28]

This human rights approach to SOGI asylum includes some of the benchmarks against which we will assess the fairness of European asylum systems. In an attempt to deliver a fair system, national authorities often identify particular people, such as women claimants, as 'vulnerable' or members of 'vulnerable' groups. Scholars such as Martha Fineman, and Timmer and Lourdes Peroni (Fineman 2008; Peroni and Timmer 2013) have emphasised the negative consequences of such identification, including the stigmatisation of some individuals and groups in a way that risks perpetuating stereotypes. Yet, from a purely legal perspective, 'vulnerability' seems to underline, as a matter of principle, a higher risk of being exposed to human rights violations. This risk may be due to personal characteristics, the claimant's history of past discrimination, or measures adopted by transit or host countries against migrants, including people claiming asylum. In this way, in the asylum context, the attribution of vulnerability may simply increase visibility of the need for support for specific claimants and, without creating new human rights obligations, may focus attention on the human rights positive duties of national authorities (Ippolito 2018). For example, in some cases, the qualification as 'vulnerable' could result in lowering the threshold for finding degrading or discriminatory treatment for the purpose of recognising refugee status (Brandl and Czech 2015). Overall, however, when vulnerability emerges as a group-centred concept, it seems in tension with an approach such as ours that resists stereotypes and highlights intersectionality (also Chap. 2). As such, 'compounded vulnerability' (Timmer 2013) seems to be the only definition that should be applied to SOGI claimants as a group. Following Timmer's approach, 'compounded vulnerability' can be defined as the higher risk SOGI claimants run of being exposed to human rights violations owing to the intersection of multiple 'endogenous' traits defining their individual personhood (like SOGI, gender, disability, refugeness, etc.) with 'exogenous' contexts (like reception conditions or asylum interview). In fact, while rejecting an application of vulnerability as an exclusionary tool,[29] we can accept a strategic use of vulnerability as framed here to underline a temporary condition of human rights deprivation to be specifically addressed through structural and individual solutions required from states.

The same applies in the context of integration. While the Refugee Convention does not include SOGI in its non-discrimination provisions, a human rights approach requires that these claimants be able to enjoy the full catalogue of human rights and freedoms, that is, at least the rights and freedoms that emerge from international human rights treaties binding host states, irrespective of their SOGI, asylum background and/or their status as non-citizens. Equal access to employment, healthcare or education, to name a few examples (Chap. 9), will not address all claimants'

---

[28] See CJEU, Joined Cases C-148/13 to C-150/13, *A, B and C v Staatssecretaris van Veiligheid en Justitie*, 2 December 2014, ECLI:EU:C:2014:2406.

[29] See the exclusionary effect of the 'vulnerability' label in ECtHR, Grand Chamber, *Ilias and Ahmed v. Hungary*, Application no. 47287/15, 21 November 2019.

needs and rights (ORAM 2010, pp. 27–35). Under IHRL, states are also required to enable SOGI minorities to express their SOGI in every dimension of life, including family relationships.[30] They must also identify and address the intersection of different grounds of discrimination when these emerge as an obstacle to integration (Muntarbhorn 2017, p. 12), in line with the intersectional lenses proposed in the next Section. Nonetheless, the current protection of SOGI minorities in some host countries fails to respect all rights that SOGI minorities should enjoy. This hampers the necessary improvements needed for a truly fair SOGI asylum. For instance, it would be difficult to justify a finding of persecution for denial of recognition of same-sex unions in claimants' countries of origin while in many European states such unions are still not legally recognised.

The prevailing standards in human rights protection of SOGI minorities in some European states may also prevent the use of alternatives to asylum to protect people who are forced to flee their countries on SOGI grounds. Here, human rights may provide the autonomous framework for looking beyond asylum to offer protection. For example, a human rights-based approach may require states to ensure the right to family reunification irrespective of SOGI, to issue humanitarian visas, or to promote the rights of SOGI minorities in international relations with countries of origin of SOGI refugees.[31]

In sum, in the first part of this chapter, we have laid out a human rights approach to SOGI asylum demonstrating what a genuine interaction between IRL and IHRL entails, as the basis for identifying individualised procedures and solutions for people in need of international protection in general and SOGI claimants in particular. However, we posit that addressing SOGI asylum only through this human rights approach cannot create the necessary improvements both within and outside asylum procedures without an understanding of the larger context within which these claims exist. That is why, to understand the socio-legal experiences of SOGI asylum claimants we need to complement the above analysis with some brief inroads into feminism and queer theories.

3.3 A Feminist Approach to SOGI Asylum

In this section we ask what feminist analysis brings to an understanding of SOGI asylum. We start by explaining why it is useful to look to feminism when seeking to understand and improve the experiences of SOGI minorities claiming asylum in Europe. While our two other underpinning bodies of literature – human rights

---

[30] For example, ECtHR, *Oliari and Others v. Italy*, Applications nos. 18,766/11 and 36,030/11, 21 July 2015.

[31] The latter can also be meant as an obligation to not cooperate with these countries if the economic or other kinds of cooperation contribute, even indirectly, to human rights abuses against SOGI minorities. See International Law Commission (2001), especially Article 16 if the conditions included therein are satisfied.

scholarship and queer theories – have an obvious link to research addressing SOGI asylum as a European human rights challenge, the connection to feminism may be less obvious. Our reasoning is that it is impossible to fully understand any global forms of injustice and abuse, including the injustice and abuse that drives some people to claim asylum, without feminism; that feminism is an essential tool of analysis for any project with a social justice goal, not only in its underpinning aims, but also in the debates that it has generated. Furthermore, there are fundamental intersections between gender and SOGI persecution, and the way that IRL and domestic policy addresses both that make feminism of particular relevance here, as we show below.

Feminism is not, of course, a unified theory (nor is queer theory or human rights scholarship) and there are many different 'feminisms'. It is conceptualised here (rather than defined) in its very broadest sense as a body of scholarship and activism that recognises gender and/or sex as a critical factor in explaining and combatting societal and global inequality, that is, a social force for change embracing theory and activism. This encompasses activities from lobbying the UN to empower women through the Millennium Development Goals, to seeking to increase the proportion of women on company boards in the UK, to demonstrating for women's right to enter temples in India. Furthermore, there are many scholars and activists who come within this understanding of feminism but who would reject that label because of its association with Western/White women's scholarship, in favour of another term. Most obviously, Alice Walker coined the term 'Womanist' for 'A black feminist or feminist of color' (Walker 2004, p. xi).

Our starting point is the recognition that women and SOGI minorities experience high levels of discrimination and abuse around the world on the basis of their SOGI, and that these experiences sometimes force them to flee their homes and countries of origin. We illustrate this with a quote from Lord Hope taken from a landmark case for women claiming asylum in the UK, because it highlights what is distinctive about women's persecution: 'The reason why the appellants fear persecution is not just because they are women. It is because they are women in a society which discriminates against women'.[32] Lord Hope's words could equally be rewritten as: 'The reason why the appellants fear persecution is not just because they are LGBTIQ+. It is because they are LGBTIQ+ people in a society which discriminates against LGBTIQ+ people'.

This goes to the heart of what is distinctive about gender and SOGI persecution. The archetypal refugee is an *individual* fleeing a time-specific and space-bound form of political persecution – defectors from North Korea or perceived collaborators in Iraq, to give two examples (Home Office 2016, 2019). The oppression and marginalisation of women, in contrast, has been shown through feminism to be a

---

[32] Lord Hope, *Islam v. Secretary of State for the Home Department and R. v. Immigration Appeal Tribunal and Secretary of State for the Home Department, ex parte Shah*, UK House of Lords, [1999] 2 WLR 1015, p. 22. There are a number of analogies made with sexual orientation in the ruling, and Lord Millett explicitly states (para. 20): 'Thus I would accept that homosexuals form a distinct social group.'

phenomenon that is as diverse as it is universal (as queer theories have shown in relation to SOGI minorities). As Verdirame points out, '[t]he recognition of a political dissident as a refugee may expose the wrongdoing of a government, but the grant of refugee status to women fleeing gender-based persecution or gay men escaping homophobia will often also expose the wrongdoing of a society' (Verdirame 2012, pp. 559–560). The abuse of women and SOGI minorities is generally ongoing, systematic and is a phenomenon of both 'refugee-producing' and 'refugee-receiving' countries.[33]

Despite this seeming incongruence between gender and SOGI-based persecution, on the one hand, and the premise of refugee law, on the other, 'refugee-receiving countries' have, since the late twentieth century, come to recognise gender and SOGI-based asylum claims, generally by using the category of PSG in this context. In the UK, the 1999 case of *Shah and Islam*, from which Lord Hope's words are taken, was the catalyst for this. Yet, this deployment also causes problems in classification: if one adopts a universalising theory of women's oppression, as some Western second wave feminism may be viewed as doing (such as de Beauvoir 1997; Daly 1979; Millett 1977),[34] then any woman who is outside the country of her nationality should be able to claim asylum but no state would be positioned to provide it because of the global nature of women's persecution. Of course, this is not the case for many reasons relating to IRL and its domestic application, but this oversimplification highlights the potential difficulty faced by advocates for women and SOGI minorities claiming asylum, and which we explore further in the debates we highlight below. Several complex facts need to be reconciled here: (a) women and SOGI minorities are indeed in need of refuge because of their experiences as women and SOGI minorities; (b) those experiences are not universal but, on the contrary, highly diverse to the extent that the very categories of women and SOGI minorities (and its many variations) are increasingly contested, raising the question of what, if anything, is the shared basis for being defined and self-defining as a woman or member of a SOGI minority; (c) broadly speaking, feminist and queer activists, lawyers and scholars share a commitment to using refugee law to protect women and SOGI minorities from persecution; (d) the most expedient way to promote the interests of women and SOGI asylum claimants within the flawed but existing paradigm of 'refugee-producing' and 'refugee-receiving' countries may be to depict the former as misogynistic, homophobic and transphobic regimes and the latter as havens characterised by freedom and democracy.

In the confines of a few pages, what is the best way to 'use' feminism, given its breadth, to address these difficulties? There are some obvious points of entry when

---

[33] See, for example, ONS figures for domestic abuse in England and Wales 2018. https://www.ons.gov.uk/peoplepopulationandcommunity/crimeandjustice/bulletins/domesticabuseinenglandandwales/yearendingmarch2018#prevalence-of-domestic-abuse

[34] Recognising the problematic universalising elements to these works should not detract from recognition that all of these writers made significant contributions to second wave feminism and establishing gender as the critical site of activism, theory and debate that it now is globally.

approaching SOGI asylum from a feminist perspective. One would be to take a practitioner-based, bottom-up approach building on the similarities in concrete terms between claims based on gender and SOGI persecution: the fact that persecution is often carried out by private actors, that evidence is therefore more difficult to secure, that shame and stigma may contribute to claimants' experiences, and that sexual violence is often a cause of flight. Alternatively, one could take a top-down approach, starting with the abstract concept of a refugee in international law and then considering how that maps onto the experiences of women and SOGI minorities (recognising that many women also identify as members of a SOGI minority). Taking either of these starting points, one could look to a wealth of gender-focused writing on asylum that challenges the core paradigm of the Refugee Convention and its failure to meet the needs of women. Feminist refugee scholars have shown, first, how IRL was created to address the persecution of the male, individual, human rights-bearing subject and, second, how women have been shoe-horned into the PSG category to address this (Crawley 2001; Firth and Mauthe 2013; Greatbatch 1989; Kneebone 2005; Macklin 1995; Oxford 2005).[35] Much of this theory would apply to SOGI asylum and shed light on why SOGI claims often fail, and various writers have addressed women's and SOGI asylum together (Lewis 2014; Neilson 2005).

We feel that either of those approaches, while of interest, would provide little more than a literature review. Instead, in this section we take a different approach, one we feel is more original and therefore more productive: we look beyond the refugee literature to specific debates within feminism as a broader body of scholarship. These debates – dating back half a century – analyse gender inequality through the lenses of culture, identity and difference in a way that sheds new light on SOGI-based asylum claims.

3.3.1 Feminism and Multiculturalism

Our starting point is a debate that speaks directly to the question above concerning how, within the prevalent paradigm of 'refugee-producing' and 'refugee-receiving' countries, it is possible to promote the interests of women and SOGI asylum claimants without affirming cultural binaries of oppressive and saviour states. In 1999, there was an academic and public discussion about whether Western democratic states are more advanced than non-Western regimes in terms of women's rights, sparked by the question posed by Susan Moller Okin: 'Is multiculturalism bad for women?' in her publication under that name. She went on to ask: 'What should be done when the claims of minority cultures or religions clash with the norm of

---

[35] For more discussion of PSG in application to SOGI claims see Dustin and Held (2018) and Chap. 7.

gender equality that is at least formally endorsed by liberal states (however much they continue to violate it in their practices)?'(Okin 1999).

While Okin recognised that all societies are characterised by gender inequality, she believed that Western democracies have moved further away from their patriarchal pasts than other types of society. She asked: '[w]hen a woman from a more patriarchal culture comes to the United States (or some other Western, basically liberal, state), why should she be less protected from male violence than other women are?'(Okin 1999, p. 20). Okin was not writing about asylum. However, this is an argument that is often used by advocates and activists for refugee women and SOGI minorities: for example, women in the UK are protected from Female Genital Mutilation (FGM); we should extend that protection to women from other countries (Singer 2012). Women from countries that either allow FGM or fail to protect women from FGM, and who are able to escape, should be entitled to claim asylum and the mechanism for doing so is generally their membership of a PSG. Similar arguments are made in relation to SOGI: '[the gay man's] country of nationality is therefore not affording him the necessary level of protection. So the receiving country should'.[36]

Applying Okin's reasoning to the field of asylum, we find what is in fact the present reality: here, the world is divided into 'refugee-producing countries' (countries where women are oppressed through 'practices' such as FGM) and 'refugee-receiving countries' (countries where women are liberated and that liberation is expressed in ways that may include genitoplasty among other forms of cosmetic surgery, but which are not oppressive because they are perceived as being freely chosen). One could argue that Okin both explains and solves the problem of gender equality: the values and gender equality standards of Western societies are more progressive than those in other parts of the world; they simply need to be applied systematically and universally. If this is true in the context of gender-based asylum claims, it is equally true for SOGI minorities seeking protection. The problem is not one of analysis or understanding, but simply of application.

We reject this position and do so by approaching it through a number of other feminist-based analyses deriving from intersectionality, Black and post-colonial perspectives and interrogations of 'cultural identities'. Most of the writers cited are not responding to Okin directly, but their work undermines her arguments from various perspectives in ways that are useful to understanding SOGI-based asylum.

3.3.2 Intersectional Feminist Writing

The binary categories that Okin's work depends upon are disrupted when we introduce the notion of intersectionality. Intersectionality is generally attributed to USA legal scholar and civil rights activist Kimberlé Crenshaw, who is credited with

---

[36] *HJ (Iran) and HT (Cameroon) v. Secretary of State for the Home Department,* [2010] UKSC 31, 7 July 2010, para. 65.

3.3 A Feminist Approach to SOGI Asylum

coining the term, but the concept dates back to at least the late 1970s with the work of the Combahee River Collective:

> The most general statement of our politics at the present time would be that we are actively committed to struggling against racial, sexual, heterosexual, and class oppression and see as our particular task the development of integrated analysis and practice based upon the fact that the major systems of oppression are interlocking (Combahee River Collective 1977, p. 13).

A decade later, Crenshaw developed intersectionality as an anti-discrimination tool to explain and combat Black women's experiences of inequality by showing that these experiences are not only distinct from White women's and Black men's, but also cannot be explained by simply adding recognition of racism to recognition of gender oppression (Brah and Phoenix 2004; Crenshaw 1991; Hill Collins and Bilge 2016; Phoenix and Pattynama 2006). As she argued: 'Because the intersectional experience is greater than the sum of racism and sexism, any analysis that does not take intersectionality into account cannot sufficiently address the particular manner in which Black women are subordinated' (Crenshaw 1989, p. 140).

Intersectionality has subsequently developed into a large body of scholarship, including work that critiques the value of the concept itself (Anthias 2013; Firth and Mauthe 2013; Grabham et al. 2008; Nash 2008). It has an obvious application to the issues discussed here. Davis, for example, argues that applying an understanding of intersectionality will lead to legal redress for human rights abuses that is better able to address the realities of women's experiences, with application to asylum and furthermore to SOGI asylum (Davis 2015). However, two things are striking in considering it as an explanatory tool when approaching asylum from the perspective of gender and SOGI. Firstly, the ubiquity of the concept of intersectionality in academia but also beyond: bodies such as CEDAW, for example, routinely reference it in statements such as 'discrimination against women based on sex and/or gender is often inextricably linked with and compounded by other factors that affect women, such as "race", ethnicity, religion or belief, health, age, class, caste, being lesbian, bisexual or transgender and other status' (CEDAW 2014, para. 6). In some ways, intersectionality has become a victim of its own success, a value that is universally espoused, mainstreamed to the point of being taken for granted, and assumed to be now fully entrenched beyond feminist discourse.[37] Secondly, at the same time and paradoxically, it is startling to see how little impact it has as an applied concept in law or policy – certainly in relation to asylum where, as we will see in subsequent chapters, decision-makers appear unable to recognise that lesbian women claiming asylum have been persecuted on the basis of both their gender and their sexuality.

---

[37] Both the Inter-American Court of Human Rights and the UN independent expert on SOGI have stressed the need for an intersectional approach with such other grounds to capture the harmful effect of discriminatory treatment on individuals in question. So, sex, ethnic origin, age, religion, socio-economic factors including poverty, and/or armed conflicts may exacerbate discrimination on SOGI grounds: Inter-American Court of Human Rights, *Identidad de Género, e Igualdad y No Discriminación a Parejas del Mismo Sexo*, Opinión Consultiva OC-24/17, 24 November 2017, para. 48; Muntarbhorn 2017, p. 5.

And we see the failure to apply any grasp of intersectionality at even a basic level in the assumptions about religious, age and class-based identity that are prevalent in asylum decision-making.

Moreover, this plays out beyond the legal asylum machinery in terms of the support structures available to people seeking asylum, who often end up choosing between LGBTIQ+ or migrant support groups rather than groups that can address the totality of their experiences. Intersectional analyses can be of tangible value here in undermining such tunnel-vision thinking. Patricia Hill Collins, for example, points to the way a 'queer of colour critique' uses intersectionality to both draw from and critique 'critical race theory', feminism and queer theories. This can highlight gaps in political agendas: an LGBTIQ+ focus on workplace and marriage equality does not address the high rates of violence and murder experienced by Black trans people (Hill Collins 2019, pp. 106–107). In the next section, we look to queer intersectionality theories to support our analysis.

An intersectional approach is critical to our analysis, yet it has drawbacks. It can be used on multiple levels, simplistically, or with different meanings (Phoenix and Pattynama 2006). Moreover, following Floya Anthias (2013), we argue that its deconstructionist project may have limitations when applied to law and policy. The risk is that intersectionality alone may simply create and affirm a larger number of categories than previously without enhancing understanding or the means to address inequality. Additionally, it may entrench an identity-based approach at the expense of socio-economic analysis. None of these flaws are inherent in the discourse and many scholars have developed intersectionality-based approaches to improve it, which is why we defend intersectionality as a key notion to inform our analysis in subsequent chapters. We are also guided by Hill Collins in recognising intersectionality as 'a metaphor of social transformation (…) It arrived in the midst of ongoing struggles to resist social inequalities brought about by racism, sexism, colonialism, capitalism, and similar systems of power' (Hill Collins 2019, p. 27). In this way, as much as a theory, it is a problem-solving tool that can support scholars bridging the gap between theory and practice in the area of refugee studies in a holistic way that few other theoretical approaches are able to do. Moreover, it complements the Black and post-colonial scholarship considered in the next section.

3.3.3 Anti-essentialism

Critiques of 'Is multiculturalism bad for women?' build on and foreshadow a large body of writing by feminists and those who would reject the label but who share a common recognition that feminism, as it developed through its first and second waves in the West, had little to say to or to offer Black or minoritised women, partly because of a tendency to homogenise and extrapolate the experiences of all women based on those of White women and partly because of its failure to acknowledge historical contexts, specifically histories of colonialism, racism and slavery. This has implications for those writing and active in the field of asylum, which we go on to explore, considering some of the gender-focused, Black and post-colonial scholarship that challenges essentialist notions of culture and identity and effectively complements intersectionality.

Discourses that contrast a free Western and westernised female subject with a subjugated Other – frequently embodied in the form of the veiled Muslim woman – have been interrogated over several decades, although often not with a focus on refugee law. Writing in the 1980s, Chandra Talpade Mohanty contrasted the 'truncated' life the average 'Third World' woman is assumed to lead with the '(implicit) self-representation of Western women as educated, as modern, as having control over their own bodies and sexualities, and the freedom to make their own decisions' (Mohanty 1988, p. 337). And in 1991, Isabelle R Gunning used the term 'arrogant perception' for Western descriptions of other 'cultural practices' such as FGM, suggesting that Western feminists' 'articulations of concern over the contemporary practice of genital surgery in third world nations are often perceived as only thinly disguised expressions of racial and cultural superiority and imperialism' (Gunning 1991, p. 212). From post-colonialism and subaltern studies, and in an earlier women-focused articulation of the homonationalism discussed in Sect. 3.4, Gayatri Chakravorty Spivak demonstrates how 'the protection of women (today the "third-world woman") becomes a signifier for the establishment of a *good* society' (Spivak 1988, p. 94). Her most famous quote could be rewritten to describe European asylum as '[straight] White men [and White women] are saving brown women [and queer people] from brown men' (Spivak 1988, p. 92).

Writers who approach gender through an analysis of culture challenge the portrayal of women as victims of their cultures and of cultures as unchanging monoliths. As Avtar Brah points out, we should conceive cultures 'less in terms of reified artefacts and rather more as processes' (Brah 1991, p. 174). Uma Narayan has highlighted how early feminist condemnations of Sati as an Indian practice reinforced portrayals of unchanging non-Western cultures, in which 'Indian women seem to go up in flames – on the funeral pyres of their husbands and in the "kitchen accidents" that are the characteristic mode of dowry-murder – without historical pause' (Narayan 1997, p. 48). Narayan draws attention to the way colonial condemnation of Sati was politically motivated:

> Thus liberty and equality could be represented as paradigmatic "Western values," hallmarks of its civilizational superiority, at the very moment when Western nations were engaged in slavery, colonization, expropriation, and the denial of liberty and equality not only to the colonized but to large segments of Western subjects, including women (Narayan 2000, pp. 83–84).

She calls for a commitment to 'antiessentialism' both in relation to women and culture, resisting the reification of cultures that prevails (Narayan 2000, p. 98). In the current context and a climate of terrorism and Islamophobia, the archetypal Other has become further entrenched as the veiled Muslim woman – as has been widely recognised and written about by feminists and women writers (Abu-lughod 2015; Farris 2017). The challenge to essentialist thinking is particularly relevant to research with LGBTIQ+ refugees subject to compartmentalisation based on narrow understandings of the experiences of just a few individuals.

Move to the context of refugee law and this illustrates a problem that Audrey Macklin starts to identify when she points out:

> If the United States, or Canada, or Australia are refugee-acceptors, it follows that whatever they do cannot constitute persecution, because that would make them potential refugee-producers (…) The practical consequence of this effacement will be that gender persecution will be most visible and identifiable as such when it is committed by a cultural Other. So the commonality of gender oppression and homophobia is disguised by attributing abuse to culture (Macklin 1995, p. 271).

Or, as Razack points out:

> racial and cultural othering, as an important part of how [a woman's asylum] claim is presented, arise initially from the need for a refugee claimant to establish that she has a well-founded fear of persecution from which her own state will not or cannot protect her. The simplest and most effective means of doing so is to activate in the panel members an old imperial formula of the barbaric and chaotic Third World and by implication, a more civilized First World (Razack 1995, p. 69).

This analysis is highly relevant to a research project with policy-related as well as scholarly ambitions. The most promising way of supporting women's asylum claims in the courts is usually to argue that the claimant is fleeing from an oppressively patriarchal regime to seek refuge in the liberal West, reinforcing a simplified 'us' and 'them' concept of culture in which the individual woman can appear to be a pathetic victim. This is illustrated well in relation to FGM. In 2006, in the UK, the House of Lords granted asylum to a woman from Sierra Leone fleeing FGM stating that: 'Even the lower classes of Sierra Leonean society regard uninitiated [non-FGM] indigenous women as an abomination fit only for the worst sort of sexual exploitation'.[38] The implication is that, in contrast to rational Western individuals, Sierra Leoneans are bound to act in certain ways by their culture. In this example, the interests of the claimant are best served by reinforcing stereotypes of backward cultures. It would be difficult for an advocate to bring in the kind of contextual factors that would lead to a less simplistic portrayal of cultures and, at the same time, pursue the best interests of the client in these cases.

Leti Volpp shows how narratives such as this have been developed and deployed in the name of women's protection: 'colonialist and imperialist discourse which opposes tradition (East) and modernity (West), and which associates East with ancient ritual, despotism, and barbarity, and West with progress, democracy and enlightenment' (Volpp 1996, pp. 1588–1589). Sexual and gender violence is only 'cultural' when it happens in a non-Western country or within a minority community in the West. Feminist theory has interrogated cultural relativism and the use of a cultural defence in courts to defend men who abuse women (Coleman 1998; Nussbaum 2000, pp. 48–50; Phillips 2003; Volpp 1996). Yet, here we have a

---

[38] *Secretary of State for the Home Department (Respondent) v. K (FC) (Appellant) Fornah (FC) (Appellant) v. Secretary of State for the Home Department (Respondent)* [2006] UKHL 46, para. 7.

situation where cultural stereotypes can work to the advantage of groups of individuals seeking protection in the face of a hostile immigration climate and in need of all the strategies and tools that are available.

This presents a problem for advocates and legal representatives in such cases: they can 'buy into' cultural stereotypes when these seem likely to work to their client's advantage in leading to a grant of international protection, or they can reject such strategies as reinforcing gendered cultural stereotypes and risk acting against their client's immediate interests. The dilemma has been articulated by Volpp, writing about the use of cultural defences in criminal cases in North America:

> The first issue we face is the strong tension between helping an individual person and the broader effects of employing stereotypes. (…) What do we do then if we want to help an individual woman? Do we want to say that her horrific barbaric culture that condones these practices from which she has absolutely no escape, led to these bad acts or led to her being trapped, or led to her not fleeing? Are we using racism to get rid of sexism? Is there a way in which we are relying on certain kinds of problematic descriptions that buy into already existing preconceptions about our communities to help individual women? We know there are broader stereotypes out there and that is why we think they work and that is why we might use them. We need to consider these implications (Volpp 2002, p. 4).

Volpp is concerned by the strategy of deploying cultural stereotypes to help individual women. Nonetheless, for the refugee paradigm to function effectively for women, the USA (or UK, Germany or Italy) has to be presumed to be a site of liberation. Women's claims will be best served by depicting them as victims not only of abuse that is equivalent to persecution, but also abuse that is different to the regular day-to-day violence against women that occurs in Western 'refugee-receiving countries'. This argument is equally applicable to SOGI asylum: in the case of a lesbian woman from an African country, particularly a country where same-sex relations are illegal but the law is not enforced, it would be a reckless or overly confident advocate who did not deploy the ideal narrative of an individual who comes to realise how different she is to her fellow intolerant homophobic citizens and embraces European values and freedoms as an alternative. In seeking to undermine cultural stereotypes without damaging the asylum claims of women and sexual and gender minorities, feminist scholarship on agency and choice is a useful resource and is the subject of the next section.

3.3.4 Recognising Agency

We have argued that, while intersectionality will be critical to understanding the experiences that are the focus of this work, it needs to be accompanied by an analysis that interrogates prevalent understandings of culture and cultural identity. What these discourses share is a recognition of context and agency. They illustrate how successfully patriarchal, capitalist and neo-liberal forces have diverted attention from the gender and 'race' oppression and exploitation of the West by focusing on the extreme abuses of women at the hands of non-Western state and non-state actors, at the expense of a focus on their own misdeeds. The writers we discussed disrupt the simple story of illiberal regimes perpetuating illiberal practices against SOGI minorities. They also draw attention to the way that gender and cultural or ethnic affiliations come together to deny agency to women and a range of minorities – a phenomenon that is nowhere truer than in the field of asylum, where we are presented with the 'vulnerable' (or thus rendered) displaced woman seeking Western protection (ICIBI 2018, p. 40). The danger is in the attribution of a cultural group identity to the 'other'. What is lost is the agency of both victim and perpetrators of 'cultural practices' and that has implications on various levels for asylum, as we discuss in subsequent chapters.

Elsewhere, feminism has both prioritised and problematised choice. Marilyn Friedman develops the concept of autonomy in connection with a specific definition of identity based on the perspectives, values, wants and commitments that matter to her. To live autonomously is to live in accordance with those priorities. However, Friedman draws attention to the constraints within which agency is exercised in a way that is particularly relevant to SOGI claimants, arguing that even lives of suffering can afford opportunities to exercise agency: 'A valiant, noble, inspiring sort of autonomy emerges when someone stubbornly preserves or pursues what she deeply cares about during a time of suffering or tragedy and against hostile opposition' (Friedman 2003, p. 26). We can apply this conceptualisation of autonomy to understand the decisions made by, for example, a lesbian woman who is unable to live openly in her home country and 'chooses' to leave to seek asylum in Europe, even though this means separation from her children. Martha Nussbaum, writing to address the 'unequal human capabilities of women', attributes it to the failure to see women as 'ends' in themselves (Nussbaum 2000, pp. 1–2) and develops a political approach to gender justice based on 'capabilities' – 'what people are actually able to do and to be' – while also questioning the conditions in which choices are made. Finally, feminism has been instrumental in challenging definitions of Western subjects as individuals, making life choices in contrast with non-Western subjects lacking in agency (Madhok et al. 2013). This is particularly valuable in considering how to extend asylum protection to groups including women and SOGI minorities without framing them as eternal victims (Henry 2013).

In this section, using Okin's work as a launch pad, we have identified discourses that explicitly or implicitly critique her analysis in ways that are helpful to an understanding of SOGI asylum. These volumes are not only an academic contribution, but also seek to make recommendations for improving asylum for SOGI minorities in Europe. That leads us to ask how the intellectual and practical work of exposing neo-colonial discourses can coexist with the ongoing imperative of protecting women and SOGI minorities from abuse. One could argue that deploying cultural stereotypes is a necessary evil in the case of asylum claims by women and SOGI minorities. However this argument is flawed, not only because of the wider damage of what Narayan has called 'the package picture of cultures', but also in individual asylum cases (Narayan 2000). First, not everyone who is fleeing sexual or gender-based violence is able to conform to cultural stereotypes. Second, if successful asylum claims for women and SOGI minorities rely on extreme contrasts between conditions for these groups in the host country and the country of origin, then people seeking asylum and those who support them will have an interest in seeing 'refugee-producing countries' maintain the harshest, most misogynistic, most homophobic and most transphobic laws and regimes. Third, the intersection of a gender and group-based identity to deny agency perpetuates the binaries of a Western individual subject with agency and a non-Western 'other' without agency.

In terms of solutions, feminist approaches to dismantling homogenising portrayals of the cultural woman 'other' often rely on enhanced voice and agency for women from different cultures, as have campaigners in relation to SOGI minorities. We discuss feminist writers' analysis of choice and agency above. However, in the area of asylum law these strategies are probably the hardest to apply, because they come into conflict with the fixed categories of victim and saviour, generally relied upon by decision-makers, even if only implicitly. One of the challenges we face here is to make recommendations for improving asylum processes for SOGI claimants that do not rely on deploying a 'package picture of cultures' that persecute their SOGI minorities. While this debate neither solves gender inequality nor provides a solution to SOGI asylum, it does identify themes to shape what follows: essentialism, difference, culture, agency.

3.4 Queer Theoretical Approaches to SOGI Asylum

Moving to our third body of work, queer theoretical approaches have an obvious bearing on the subject of SOGI asylum. Sexual orientation and gender identity are two categories that are often either problematically conflated or treated as separate entities of identification and experience. As we show in this section, a queer theoretical approach can help us to understand how sex, gender, and sexuality are intrinsically linked. As we will demonstrate, the light that queer theories shed on these categories, as well as their theoretical framing of 'identity', can help understand the legal and social experiences of SOGI claimants. In addition, these approaches can be productively used to pursue (fairer) decision-making. The intersections of sexuality with 'race', gender and class alone do not fully explain the particular experiences of these SOGI minorities who lack protection, go through the asylum process – where they have to prove their SOGI – and are seen and perceived by other people as 'asylum seekers' (and the particular connotations and stereotypes that come with it). Therefore, in order to acknowledge the particular experiences of SOGI claimants, intersectional queer approaches need to include 'refugeeness' as a category in their analyses. As we argue, not only does 'refugeeness' need to be added to intersectional analysis, but also 'space', as space shapes these intersectional experiences in particular ways and is co-constitutive of sexuality (and other categories). Our analysis in the subsequent chapters will be led by these theoretical approaches, and in turn will add new understandings to queer theories in general, and queer geographies in particular.

Queer theories emerged as a body of literature in diverse fields of studies in the early 1990s (feminist theories and lesbian and gay studies have been crucial in this development) and has since then been influential in many different academic disciplines and areas of research. Here, we do not aim to give a comprehensive overview of published work in the field of queer theories; instead, we will focus on those approaches that we consider most helpful and relevant for our analysis, and in particular for understanding the legal and social experiences of SOGI claimants.

We begin with a short overview of queer theories' main ideas with regard to the relationship between sex, gender, and sexuality and the conceptualisation of identity. We then look at queer theoretical approaches that bring in intersectional thinking – building on the intersectional feminist writing discussed above (Sect. 3.3.2). Here, we will we argue that queer studies not only need to be intersectional, but also need to include the experience of being a queer asylum claimant in their analysis and production of theoretical and analytical frameworks. The same counts for the field of 'queer geography', which offers useful approaches for analysing the social experiences of queer refugees, which we discuss in Sect. 3.4.3. This field explores 'the ways in which space is sexed and sex is spaced, or in other words, the ways in which the spatial and the sexual constitute each other' (Taylor 1997, p. 3). While work published in this area will be useful for our analysis, with our particular focus on how queer refugees experience certain spaces and how their identities are shaped by these spaces, our research adds a new understanding to this field. We show that the relationship between queer refugee identities and spaces are shaped by 'refugeeness'. We argue that both 'space' and 'refugeeness' are categories that need to be included in intersectional analyses. Finally, we summarise how these understandings of sex, gender, sexuality, identity, intersectionality and space may be used for decision-making processes and social policies.

3.4.1 Queer Theoretical Understanding of Sex, Gender, Sexuality and Identity

Since the 1990s, queer theorists have offered new ways of thinking the relationship between sex, gender, and sexuality. These poststructuralist theorists consider these categories and the relationship between them not as natural or biologically determined, but as socially, legally and historically produced. Queer theorists conceptualise sexuality as the product of social processes, as regulated and produced, and as constantly changing (see, for instance, Butler 1990; Sedgwick 2008; Warner 1993). Furthermore, they define sexuality as institutionalised in the ways in which 'in the everyday political terrain, contests over sexuality and its regulation are generally linked to views of social institutions and norms of the most basic sort' (Warner 1993, p. xiii). As Chaps. 4 onwards suggest, the institutionalisation of sexuality is also seen in the asylum process.

3.4 Queer Theoretical Approaches to SOGI Asylum

By drawing on the ground-breaking work of Michel Foucault, especially his first volume of the *History of Sexuality* (1990), queer theorists challenge the idea of thinking of sexuality in terms of fixed identities. As Foucault showed, this Western understanding of fixed sexual identities has its roots in the late nineteenth century, when psychiatric, legal, moral, religious and medical discourses emerged that categorised people into different sexual human beings and produced sexual subjects:

> The nineteenth-century homosexual became a personage, a past, a case history, and a childhood, in addition to being a type of life, a life form, and a morphology, with an indiscreet anatomy and possibly a mysterious physiology. Nothing that went into his total composition was unaffected by his sexuality (Foucault 1990, p. 43).

During that time, 'the homosexual' came into being as a distinct 'species', one that is deviant and 'abnormal'. Whereas prior to that time the main concern was about sexual practices (such as sodomy), in the late nineteenth century a distinct sexual identity ('the homosexual') was created. Consequently, as Foucault's work demonstrates, Western understandings of sexuality are based on the concept of identity. This distinction between practice or behaviour and identity is one that has a particular significance in relation to SOGI asylum as highlighted throughout this work, and in particular in Chap. 10.

Queer theorists draw on Foucault, but take his ideas further by demonstrating that the fixedness of sexual identities is based on polarisations including hetero/homo, male/female and masculine/feminine. They challenge the idea that these categories are based on fixed binaries and are 'naturally' linked (Butler 1990; Jagose 1996; Sedgwick 2008; Warner 1993). Queer theorists destabilise these binaries by decoupling sex, gender and sexual desire, and by conceptualising gender and sexuality as a constant work-in-progress (Warner 1993, p. xiii).

In her book *Gender Trouble* (1990), the most prominent queer theorist, Judith Butler, explains the relationship between sex, gender and sexuality as follows: 'The heterosexualisation of desire requires and institutes the production of discrete and asymmetrical oppositions between "feminine" and "masculine," where these are understood as expressive attributes of "male" and "female"' (Butler 1990, p. 23). The 'natural order' of heterosexuality is maintained through a fixed binary system of sex and gender, and this binarism is necessary for compulsory heterosexuality. In other words, we have an underlying assumption that someone is born as either male or female, then presents themselves through either a masculine or feminine gender, and is attracted to the opposite sex. Butler argues that there is a link between gender and (hetero)sexuality in the ways in which 'under conditions of normative heterosexuality, policing gender is sometimes used as a way of securing heterosexuality' (Butler 1999, p. xii). But what we take as the internal essence of gender is manufactured through repetitive gendered stylisation of the body. In that sense, gender is performative; it is not a noun but a verb. There is no pre-existing gender. Gender is performatively produced through the repetitive, compulsory citation of gendered norms: 'There is no gender identity behind the expressions of gender; that identity is performatively constituted by the very "expressions" that are said to be its results' (Butler 1999, p. 33). The ways in which gender is policed and enforced affects everyone, 'but has particularly dangerous outcomes for trans people' (Spade 2015, p. 9). This becomes most obvious when looking at the murder rates of trans people worldwide but is also evident in everyday experiences of non-binary and trans people in a binary gendered world, such as when using a public bathroom, for instance, when verbal and physical harassment is often experienced (Spade 2015).

These theoretical ideas are useful for the analysis of the legal and social experience of SOGI claimants in several ways. First, it needs to be recognised that Western concepts and labels may not capture the ways in which SOGI claimants understand and express their sexual orientation and gender identity (Lee and Brotman 2011). As Calogero Giametta (2014, p. 587) points out, Western understandings of sexuality are often problematic for asylum claimants, who 'negotiate their sexual and gender identities across cultural constructions of gender liminality and sexual identity that do not match the repertoires of Western LGBTI identifications and lifestyles'. Sexuality is often lived in much more fluid ways, without the need to conform to fixed identity labels as it is common in Western societies (see, for instance, Wekker's 2006, fascinating study of a women's community in Surinam). This can be problematic, if decision-makers make decisions on SOGI claims through the lens of Western conceptualisations of gender and sexuality. Furthermore, queer theorists show that sexual identity is fluid and subject to change during the course of a lifetime (Jagose 1996; Seidman 1993), which may be helpful to asylum decision-making, by challenging the simplistic categorising imperative that characterises asylum procedures as the basis for determining whether an individual should be granted protection or not.

Second, the Western model of sexuality takes gay identity and homosexual conduct as interchangeable and 'presumes clarity of boundaries between heterosexual and homosexual identity and requires public expression of private and sexual behaviour' (Morgan 2006, pp. 151–152). This can lead to the conflation of sexual conduct and sexual identity in decision-making, and a failure to recognise the complexities of sexual identity (O'Leary 2008). SOGI claimants may then be expected to be 'out and proud' and conform to Western stereotypes of what it means to be LGBTIQ+ (for example, visiting gay bars, participating in lesbian and gay groups and Gay Prides, etc.) (Bennett and Thomas 2013; Morgan 2006). These expectations of conformity to Western notions of homosexual behaviour make it more difficult for SOGI asylum claimants to 'demonstrate' and 'prove' their SOGI.

Third, persecution on grounds of sexuality is often linked to how gender is performed, demonstrating the links between gender and sexuality that Butler has so powerfully demonstrated (see above). As Nora Markard argues:

> Gender doesn't simply differentiate between "men" and "women", to the exclusion of inter* bodies and certain trans* and inter* identities. It is also fundamentally heteronormative, predetermining the acceptable sexual preference and the specific way in which to "do gender". (…) An intersectional approach can make these dimensions visible in a more differentiated manner (Markard 2016, p. 56).

Understanding the co-constitution of gender and sexuality can improve decision-making, especially in terms of how persecution is assessed, but there are also intersections with other categories that need to be taken into account.

3.4.2 Intersectional Queer Approaches

Focusing on gender and sexuality as the main categories of analysis, the early queer theoretical approaches were criticised for the lack of discussion of intersections with other categories. While above we discussed intersectionality as it developed in relation to feminism and 'race', there is now an extensive body of work that brings in an intersectional approach to queer theories (see, for instance, Taylor et al. 2010), and looks specifically at the intersections of sexuality with socio-economic class (McDermott 2010; Penney 2015; Taylor 2007), disability (Inckle 2010), 'race' (Kuntsman and Miyake 2008; Mercer and Julien 1988; Somerville 2000; Stoler 1995) and religion (Bakshi et al. 2016; Giametta 2014; Puar 2007). There has also been work specifically on bisexuality, long under-represented, invisible and marginalised in sexualities and queer scholarship (Klesse 2018; Monro et al. 2017). As Surya Monro, Sally Hines and Antony Osborne (2017, p. 671) argue, especially 'the peak years of queer theory – the mid to late 1990s – was a period in which scholars were particularly silent about bisexuality'. This is surprising, as the category of bisexuality 'raises important critical questions about the intersections of sexuality and gender, and the epistemologies of these categories' (Monro et al. 2017, p. 675). These questions help us understand the assessment of bisexual people's asylum claims in subsequent chapters, and also why bisexual asylum claimants are rendered invisible by the asylum system.

There has also been an increasing interest in the relationship between sexuality and 'race', or the 'raciality' of queerness. As Adi Kuntsman and Esperanza Miyake (2008, p. 5) argue:

> We believe that "raciality" and "queerness" should always be interrogated together as queerness/raciality in order to hear the invisible, to see the inaudible. How and/or what are the ways in which "raciality" becomes silent and/or silenced within the queer discourse and practice? What do these silences do and how can they be conceptualised?

Black and Asian queer theorists have challenged the White male and Western focus of queer theories (see, for instance, Eng et al. 2005; Ferguson 2004; Gopinath 2005; Johnson and Henderson 2005). Some scholars have extended Foucault's analysis and shown that the formation of sexual subjects cannot be separated from the formation of racial subjects, that racism and ideologies of sexual morality actually work together (Mercer and Julien 1988; Somerville 2000; Stoler 1995). In this context, Kobena Mercer and Isaac Julien argue that 'the prevailing Western concept of sexuality... *already contains racism.* Historically the European construction of sexuality coincides with the epoch of imperialism and the two inter-connect' (Mercer and Julien 1988, p. 106, original emphasis).

Others have explored the relationship between normative constructions of gender, sexuality and 'race' in the context of nations and borders, or *queer diasporas* (Gopinath 2005; Manalansan 2006). These scholars also encourage us to think about sexual identities from a postcolonial perspective (Manalansan 2006; Badruddoja Rahman 2006) and decolonise queer studies by bringing in transnational perspectives on the studies of sexuality, to show how sexuality, 'race', gender and religion intersect transnationally (Bakshi et al. 2016).

To adopt a transnational perspective when looking at these intersections is particularly important when considering how 'homonationalist' discourses shape the asylum process and the legal and social experiences of queer refugees. In *Terrorist Assemblages*, Jasbir Puar develops the conceptual frame of 'homonationalism' for understanding the complexities of 'how "acceptance" and "tolerance" for gay and lesbian subjects have become a barometer by which the right to and capacity for national sovereignty is evaluated' (Puar 2013, p. 33). Puar is critical of the narrative of progression of LGBTIQ+ rights, which includes some individuals while excluding others. As she argues, these rights are used to reinforce boundaries between a 'civilised' and 'uncivilised world', with religious values in particular constructed as 'backward'. In this way, LGBTIQ+ human rights discourses play a critical role in defining a racialised Other whose lack of progress is proved by their rejection of sexual and gay equality.

Puar argues that, in our times, 'an exceptional form of national heteronormativity is now joined by an exceptional form of national homonormativity'[39] (Puar 2007, p. 2), and some homosexual bodies are now 'worthy of protection by nation states' (Puar 2013, p. 337). Homonationalist discourses produce the idea of Western nations as 'LGBTIQ+ tolerant' in contrast to non-Western 'LGBTIQ+ intolerant' nations. This discourse is shaped by neoliberal capitalist structures, for instance, the tourist industry that defines gay-friendly and not-gay-friendly destinations, and recognition by the economic market of the consumer-value of SOGI minorities and the 'pink pound'. As Puar points out, these definitions are coupled with religion, in that Muslim-majority states are perceived as being particularly intolerant of SOGI minorities. The consequence of this is that the 'liberal' Western gay subject is defined in contrast with the 'oppressed' and/or homophobic non-Western subject (Hubbard and Wilkinson 2015, p. 605). The intersections of sexuality, 'race' and religion become visible here in the ways in which 'Muslim' and 'gay' are seen as incompatible identities, and the conflation of 'race' and religion leads to a discourse

---

[39] Heteronormativity is a concept coined by Michael Warner (1991) and describes the ways in which heterosexuality functions as the 'norm', as a given, the 'default'. The concept is gendered and based on (fixed) gender roles/expectations. Homonormativity is a concept coined by Lisa Duggan and describes 'a politics that does not contest dominant heteronormative assumptions and institutions — such as marriage, and its call for monogamy and reproduction — but upholds and sustains them while promising the possibility of a demobilized gay constituency and a privatized, depoliticized gay culture anchored in domesticity and consumption' (Duggan 2002, p. 179).

that constructs Islam as a homophobic religion (Haritaworn et al. 2008; Puar 2007), failing to recognise the voices within often small and under-resourced organisations around the world interpreting faith in LGBTIQ+ friendly ways.[40] In that respect, an apparent intolerance towards SOGI minorities is often used as justification for Islamophobia (Hubbard and Wilkinson 2015).

As we will dissect further in later chapters, these discourses have an effect on the asylum process that SOGI claimants go through, as well as on their lived experiences. With regard to the asylum process, the perceived incompatibility between 'Muslim' and 'gay' affiliations makes it particularly difficult for LGBTIQ+ Muslim individuals to secure international protection due to the expectation that they either reject their religion to be truly LGBTIQ+ or refrain from being LGBTIQ+ to be truly religious. As Giametta's (2014) research shows, being openly religious can undermine someone's asylum claim. Decision-makers often perceive religion, non-Western religions in particular, as patriarchal and homophobic, and religious believers are therefore viewed as backward, irrational and bound by tradition. Asylum claimants are expected to embrace progress and separate themselves from the 'backward non-West'. Claimants, as well as lawyers and supporters, might co-create these homonationalist discourses by presenting a narrative of 'suffering' in the 'backward' homophobic country of origin.

In terms of social experiences, these volumes look at how gender, sexuality, 'race' and religion intersect, including the ways in which SOGI claimants experience sexism, transphobia, homophobia, racism and Islamophobia. The intersectional queer approaches that we have outlined here are useful, not only for understanding the relationship between sex, gender and sexuality, but also how other categories intersect with them, or are co-constitutive of them. Yet, what is missing in intersectional approaches is the particular experience of being a 'refugee', an experience which may include but is not fully covered by an analysis of 'race' or nationality. As our analysis demonstrates, the experiences of SOGI refugees are shaped by the many different identities and identifiers that they choose or which are imposed on them, as is true for any individual, but also by their unique experiences within the asylum process. In the next section, we argue that it is also important to bring in the notion of 'space' when looking at the intersectional experiences of SOGI refugees.

3.4.3 *Queer Geographies*

The relationship between sexuality and space in the lives of queer refugees is particularly interesting. To analyse the social experiences of queer refugees, we draw on concepts and theories developed in the field of 'queer geographies'. As Kath Browne, Jason Lim and Gavin Brown (Browne et al. 2009, p. 4) argue:

---

[40] Such as Imaan in the UK or Al-Fitrah Foundation in South Africa.

Sexuality – its regulation, norms, institutions, pleasures and desires – cannot be understood without understanding the spaces through which it is constituted, practiced and lived. Sexuality manifests itself through relations that are specific to particular spaces and through the space-specific practices by which these relations become enacted.

Queer refugees have to leave what is often the only location they have known, their country of origin, because of their sexuality and, when arriving in the host country, asylum spaces, such as refugee camps or dispersal accommodation, again shape the ways in which they can experience and live out their sexuality. The implications of this are further explored in Chaps. 5, 8 and 10.

Studies in the field of sexual geographies have proliferated since the mid-1990s, demonstrating the relationship between sexuality and space; how spaces are sexually structured and how space is constitutive in shaping sexuality (see, for instance, Bell and Valentine 1995; Browne et al. 2009; Doan 2015; Hubbard 2012; Johnston and Longhurst 2009). They have demonstrated the ways in which sexuality is made in mundane interactions in certain places and how those interactions sexualise space. In particular, they have shown how everyday spaces (such as the street, the home, the workplace) are constituted as heterosexual through repetitive heterosexual performances (Bell and Valentine 1995; Johnston and Valentine 1995; Valentine 1993, 1996). This literature is helpful for analysing the experiences of SOGI refugees, and how they experience everyday spaces as sexualised such as the heterosexualisation of accommodation centres.

Since the early 2000s, these studies have also increasingly looked at processes of inclusion and exclusion in LGBTIQ+ spaces, especially 'gay villages' all over the world, particularly in the UK, North America, Australia, Singapore and South Africa (see, for instance, Andersson 2015; Binnie and Skeggs 2004; Caluya 2008; Han 2015; Held 2017; Nero 2005; Tan 2015; Tucker 2009; Visser 2003, 2013). In this literature, sexual geographers have shown that, within these spaces, exclusions are produced on grounds of identifiers other than sexuality. In this respect, it has been argued that particular lesbian and gay identities are constructed in LGBTIQ+ spaces that exclude differences on grounds of class (Rooke 2007; Taylor 2007), 'race', (dis)ability, sexual desires, and gender (appearance) (Casey 2004; Skeggs 1999), and produce normativities and a certain form of homonormativity (Bell and Binnie 2004; Brown 2014). These studies have also revealed that 'gay villages' focus on an able-bodied, White, middle-class, young clientele and are male dominated.

While there have been interesting studies conducted on the racialisation of LGBTIQ+ spaces in Australia (Caluya 2008), the USA (Andersson 2015; Han 2015; Nero 2005), South Africa (Livermon 2014; Tucker 2009; Visser 2003, 2013) and the UK (Bassi 2006; Held 2017; Kawale 2003, 2004), none of these studies have explicitly taken the experiences of SOGI refugees in these spaces into account. These studies are revealing, however, in the ways in which they demonstrate exclusionary and discriminatory practices based on 'race' (for example, clubs' door policies), and how sexual desires are shaped by 'race' through fetishisations, exoticisations, or dislike.

Queer geographies have not only shown how the spaces we inhabit are made through our repetitive actions, but also how these spaces shape us; the way that we do what we are supposed to do, what is perceived to be common sense, in any given place. Space is not simply an empty entity or container that can be filled with things or people. It is not dead and fixed, but alive, active, fluid and always under construction. Space is active and always 'in process' (Crang and Thrift 2000, p. 3). Building on this understanding informs our recognition of how queer refugee subjectivities are shaped by space, especially asylum spaces such as refugee accommodation centres (Chap. 8).

Asylum spaces are shaped by 'refugeeness' and shape 'refugeeness', in particular through the ways in which people feel 'out of place', or as 'space invaders' (Puwar 2004). As Nirmal Puwar (2004, p. 8) describes the relationship between bodies and space:

> Some bodies are deemed as having the right to belong, while others are marked out as trespassers, who are, in accordance with how both spaces and bodies are imagined (politically, historically and conceptually), circumscribed as being "out of place". Not being the somatic norm, they are space invaders.

As it will become clear in our analysis, certain spaces are marked as 'refugee spaces', whereas others are marked as 'LGBTIQ+ spaces', often leaving SOGI refugees feeling out of place in most spaces.

In sum, Queer theoretical approaches provide a frame of analysis for understanding, on one hand, how the concepts of gender and sexuality are utilised in decision-making processes and, on the other, how they shape the experiences of SOGI refugees and people seeking asylum and their sense of themselves. Bringing in an intersectional approach to queer theories is important, as it gives us a tool to analyse how gender and sexuality are co-constituted by other social categories such as 'race', class and religion. Taking intersectional approaches seriously means to 'ask the other question' (Matsuda 1991); for instance, in accounts on sexuality, we need to ask 'where is gender here?', in accounts on gender we need to ask 'where is "race" here?', and so forth. This is vital for exploring the socio-legal experiences of SOGI claimants. We suggest that intersectional queer theories can be productively used in SOGI asylum cases to analyse whether there is a Western bias in decision-making and how credibility assessments might draw on racialised sexual stereotypes. Our study looks at how asylum law and policies play a role in producing these categories, but also how they might be shaped and reconstructed by SOGI claimants themselves (Berger 2009). Importantly, we argue that in order to acknowledge the particular experiences of SOGI claimants, queer intersectional approaches need to include 'refugeeness' as a category in their analyses. Finally, from queer geographies we take the interrogation of space and the way that space shapes these intersecting experiences in particular ways and is co-constitutive of sexuality (and other categories).

3.5 Concluding Remarks

Various themes have emerged in this chapter, including dignity, essentialism, cultural differences, space, agency, equality, and above all identity or personhood – the concept underpinning all asylum claims in relation to credibility and the question: Are you *really* gay (or lesbian, bisexual, transgender)? Identification of these themes helps us to understand that, while SOGI asylum claimants have much in common and are often homogenised as a group, they have individual, distinct experiences and perspectives that cannot be overlooked. So, while necessarily identifying commonalities in our work based on the shared characteristics that people possess, and which are the focus for the protection they claim as well as the discrimination they undergo, we return to identity and identities throughout these volumes as a way of humanising the 'queer refugee'.

To conclude, the theoretical mix of human rights, feminism and queer theories constitutes the lens through which we will analyse our fieldwork and the parameters against which we will assess the asylum systems under comparison, including the following specific insights:

- Human rights are critical in facilitating an interpretation of the Refugee Convention that is grounded in the idea of human rights in light of the ideal category of 'inclusiveness' and through an anti-stereotyping approach, which requires individualised assessment and solutions to avoid the continuing marginalisation and inequality affecting SOGI minorities in the refugee context.
- From feminism, we take a recognition of 'culture' as a problematic term in its current usage. We critique essentialist frameworks that fail to recognise the different facets of asylum claimants' identities and we also interrogate agency, the individual agency and potential for agency, of all 'actors' in the SOGI asylum field.
- Queer theories inform our understanding of the fluidity of sexuality and gender (and by implication, of other identities such as 'refugee'), and from queer geography we take our questioning of location and space in its broadest sense as critical to LGBTIQ+ asylum experiences, ensuring asylum systems recognise the fluidity of sexuality and gender, and are mindful of how refugeeness affects people's legal and social experiences.

As a necessary caveat, we recognise that it would be naïve to argue that blending aspects of human rights, feminism and queer theories can fully explain and address the injustices of SOGI asylum in Europe. Indeed, it might be argued that it takes us down a narrow neoliberal path that 'solves' SOGI asylum only for those willing and able to transform themselves to fit the Western individual consumer-citizen model, or its LGBTIQ+ alter ego. Writers such as Kapur and Otto (Kapur 2018; Otto 2017) address whether feminist and queer politics benefit from deploying human rights or rather lose their radical, questioning and liberatory edge. Put simply, does extending human rights to women and gay people merely extend patriarchal and heteronormative entitlements and values to some Others – putting women in the boardroom, letting lesbians marry, granting asylum to the right kind of 'gay' – while leaving racism, misogyny, heteronormativity and neoliberalism fundamentally intact? Our answer is both theoretical and practical: a single-lens approach to the 'problem' of SOGI asylum leaves many questions unanswered and, more importantly, is not able to address the injustices in current European approaches to SOGI claims. Our argument is that, without dismantling existing asylum frameworks, there are incremental improvements to be made for SOGI minorities by looking to a wider range of knowledge sources, of which human rights, feminism and queer theories appear to us as the most helpful.

We will return to these critical parameters and lenses throughout these volumes and in particular in Chaps. 10 and 11, where we consider how they help (theoretically) to improve our understanding of the European SOGI asylum panorama and (practically) to inform our recommendations.

References

Abu-lughod, L. (2015). *Do muslim women need saving?* (Reprint ed.). Harvard University Press.

Andersson, J. (2015). "Wilding" in the West Village: Queer space, racism and Jane Jacobs hagiography. *International Journal of Urban and Regional Research*, 39(2), 265–283. https://doi.org/10.1111/1468-2427.12188

Anker, D. E. (2002). Boundaries in the field of human rights: Refugee law, gender, and the human rights paradigm. *Harvard Human Rights Journal*, 15, 133–317.

Anthias, F. (2013). Intersectional what? Social divisions, intersectionality and levels of analysis. *Ethnicities*, 13(1), 3–19. https://doi.org/10.1177/1468796812463547

Arendt, H. (1973). *The origins of totalitarianism* (New ed.). New York: Harcourt Brace Jovanovich.

Badruddoja Rahman, R. (2006). *Queer spaces, places, and gender the tropology of Rupa*. http://www.suedasien.info/analysen/1680.html

Bakshi, S., Jivraj, S., & Posocco, S. (2016). *Decolonizing sexualities: Transnational perspectives, critical interventions*. Oxford: Counterpress.

Bassi, C. (2006). Riding the dialectical waves of gay political economy: A story from Birmingham's commercial gay scene. *Antipode*, 38(2), 213–235. https://doi.org/10.1111/j.1467-8330.2006.00577.x

Bell, D., & Binnie, J. (2004). Authenticating queer space: Citizenship, urbanism and governance. *Urban Studies*, 41(9), 1807–1820. https://doi.org/10.1080/0042098042000243165

Bell, D., & Valentine, G. (Eds.). (1995). *Mapping desire: Geographies of sexualities*. Psychology Press.

Bennett, C., & Thomas, F. (2013). Seeking asylum in the UK: Lesbian perspectives. *Forced Migration Review*, 42, 25.

Berger, S. (2009). Production and reproduction of gender and sexuality in legal discourses of asylum in the United States. *Signs: Journal of Women in Culture and Society*, 34(3), 659–685. https://doi.org/10.1086/593380

Bhabha, J. (2002). Internationalist gatekeepers: The tension between asylum advocacy and human rights. *Harvard Human Rights Journal*, 15, 155.

Binnie, J., & Skeggs, B. (2004). Cosmopolitan knowledge and the production and consumption of sexualized space: Manchester's Gay Village. *The Sociological Review*, 52(1), 39–61. https://doi.org/10.1111/j.1467-954X.2004.00441.x

Brah, A. (1991). Difference, diversity, differentiation. *International Review of Sociology*, 2(2), 53–71. https://doi.org/10.1080/03906701.1991.9971087

Brah, A., & Phoenix, A. (2004). Ain't I A woman? Revisiting intersectionality. *Journal of International Women's Studies*, 5, 75–86.

Brandl, U., & Czech, P. (2015). General and specific vulnerability of protection-seekers in the EU: Is there an adequate response to their needs. In F. Ippolito & S. Iglesias Sánchez (Eds.), *Protecting vulnerable groups. The European human rights framework* (pp. 247–270). Oxford: Oxford University Press.

Brems, E., & Timmer, A. (2016). *Stereotypes and human rights law*. Cambridge: Intersentia.

Brown, M. (2014). Gender and sexuality II: There goes the gayborhood? *Progress in Human Geography*, 38(3), 457–465. https://doi.org/10.1177/0309132513484215

Browne, K., Lim, J., & Brown, G. (2009). *Geographies of sexualities: Theory, practices and politics*. Farnham: Ashgate.

Butler, J. (1990). *Gender trouble: Feminism and the subversion of identity*. London: Routledge.

Butler, J. (1999). *Gender trouble: Tenth anniversary edition*. Abingdon: Taylor & Francis.

Caluya, G. (2008). 'The Rice Steamer': Race, desire and affect in Sydney's gay scene. *Australian Geographer*, 39(3), 283–292. https://doi.org/10.1080/00049180802270481

Cantor, D. J. (2016). Defining refugees: Persecution, surrogacy and the human rights paradigm. In B. Burson & D. J. Cantor (Eds.), *Human rights and the refugee definition* (pp. 349–395). Leiden: Brill.

Casey, M. (2004). De-dyking queer space(s): Heterosexual female visibility in gay and lesbian spaces. *Sexualities*, 7(4), 446–461. https://doi.org/10.1177/1363460704047062

CEDAW – Committee on the Elimination of Discrimination against Women. (2014). *General recommendation No. 32 on the gender-related dimensions of refugee status, asylum, nationality and statelessness of women*, UN doc. CEDAW/C/GC/32. https://documents-dds-ny.un.org/doc/UNDOC/GEN/N14/627/90/PDF/N1462790.pdf?OpenElement

Chase, A. T. (2016). Human rights contestations: Sexual orientation and gender identity. *The International Journal of Human Rights*, 20(6), 703–723. https://doi.org/10.1080/13642987.2016.1147432

Chetail, V. (2014). Are refugee rights human rights? An unorthodox questioning of the relations between refugee law and human rights law. In R. Rubio-Marín (Ed.), *Human rights and immigration*. Oxford: Oxford University Press.

Coleman, D. L. (1998). The seattle compromise: Multicultural sensitivity and Americanization. *Duke Law Journal*, 47(4), 717–783. https://doi.org/10.2307/1372912

Combahee River Collective. (1977). *A black feminist statement*.

Crang, M., & Thrift, N. (2000). Introduction. In M. Crang & N. Thrift (Eds.), *Thinking space* (pp. 1–30). London: Routledge.

Crawley, H. (2001). *Refugees and gender: Law and process*. Bristol: Jordan Publishing.

Crenshaw, K. (1989). Demarginalizing the intersection of race and sex: A black feminist critique of antidiscrimination doctrine, feminist theory and antiracist politics. *University of Chicago Legal Forum*, 139–168.

Crenshaw, K. (1991). Mapping the margins: Intersectionality, identity politics, and violence against women of color. *Stanford Law Review*, 43(6), 1241–1299. https://doi.org/10.2307/1229039

Daly, M. (1979). *Gyn/ecology: Metaethics of radical feminism* (New ed.). London: The Women's Press.

Danisi, C. (2019). Crossing Borders between international refugee law and international human rights law in the European context: Can human rights enhance protection against persecution based on sexual orientation (and beyond)? *Netherlands Quarterly of Human Rights*, 37(4), 359–378.

Davis, A. N. (2015). Intersectionality and international law: Recognizing complex identities on the global stage. *Harvard Human Rights Journal*, 28, 205–242.

de Beauvoir, S. (1997). *The second sex* (New ed.). London: Vintage Classics.

References

Dembour, M.-B. (2010). What are human rights? Four schools of thought. *Human Rights Quarterly*, 32(1), 1–20. https://doi.org/10.1353/hrq.0.0130

Doan, P. L. (2015). *Planning and LGBTQ communities: The need for inclusive queer spaces*. New York: Routledge.

Dowd, R. (2011). Dissecting discrimination in refugee law: An analysis of its meaning and its cumulative effect. *International Journal of Refugee Law*, 23, 28–53. https://doi.org/10.1093/ijrl/eeq043

Duggan, L. (2002). The new homonormativity: The sexual politics of neoliberalism. In D. Nelson & R. Castronovo (Eds.), *Materializing democracy: Toward a revitalized cultural politics*. Durham: Duke University Press.

Dustin, M., & Held, N. (2018). In or out? A queer intersectional approach to 'particular social group' membership and credibility in SOGI asylum claims in Germany and the UK. *GenIUS – Rivista di studi giuridici sull'orientamento sessuale e l'identità di genere*, 5(2), 74–87.

Eng, D. L., Halberstam, J., & Muñoz, J. E. (2005). Introduction. *Social Text*, 23(3–4), 1–17. https://doi.org/10.1215/01642472-3-3-4_84-85-1

Farris, S. R. (2017). *In the name of womem's rights: The rise of femonationalism*. Durham: Duke University Press.

Ferguson, R. A. (2004). *Aberrations in black: Toward a queer of color critique*. Minneapolis: University of Minnesota Press.

Fineman, M. A. (2008). The vulnerable subject: Anchoring equality in the human condition. *Yale Journal of Law and Feminism*, 20(1), 1–23.

Firth, G., & Mauthe, B. (2013). Refugee law, gender and the concept of personhood. *International Journal of Refugee Law*, 25(3), 470–501. https://doi.org/10.1093/ijrl/eet034

Foster, M., & Hathaway, J. C. (2014). *The law of refugee status* (2nd ed.). Cambridge: Cambridge University Press.

Foucault, M. (1990). *The history of sexuality. Volume 1*. Harmondsworth: Penguin Books.

Friedman, M. (2003). *Autonomy, gender, politics*. Oxford: Oxford University Press.

Giametta, C. (2014). 'Rescued' subjects: The question of religiosity for non-heteronormative asylum seekers in the UK. *Sexualities*, 17(5–6), 583–599. https://doi.org/10.1177/1363460714526130

Goodwin-Gill, G. S., & McAdam, J. (2007). *The refugee in international law* (3rd ed.). Oxford: Oxford University Press.

Gopinath, G. (2005). *Impossible desires: Queer diasporas and South Asian public cultures*. Durham: Duke University Press.

Grabham, E., Cooper, D., Krishnadas, J., & Herman, D. (Eds.). (2008). *Intersectionality and Beyond: Law, Power and the Politics of Location* (1st ed.). London: Routledge.

Greatbatch, J. (1989). The gender difference: Feminist critiques of refugee discourse. *International Journal of Refugee Law*, 1(4), 518–527.

Gross, A. (2013). Post/colonial queer globalisation and international human rights: Images of LGBT rights. *Jindal Global Law Review*, 4(2), 33.

Gunning, I. R. (1991). Arrogant perception, world-travelling and multicultural feminism: The case of female genital surgeries. *Columbia Human Rights Law Review*, 23, 189–248.

Han, W. C. (2015). *Geisha of a different kind: Race and sexuality in gaysian America*. New York: New York University Press.

Haritaworn, J., Tauquir, T., Erdem, E., & Miyake, E. (2008). Gay imperialism: Gender and sexuality discourse in the 'war on terror'. In A. Kuntsman (Ed.), *Out of place: Interrogating silences in queerness/raciality* (pp. 71–95). York: Raw Nerve Books Ltd.

Hathaway, J. (1991). *The law of refugee status*. Toronto: Butterworths.

Hathaway, J. C., & Pobjoy, J. (2012). Queer cases make bad law. *New York University Journal of International Law and Politics*, 44, 315–389.

Held, N. (2017). 'They look at you like an insect that wants to be squashed': An ethnographic account of the racialized sexual spaces of Manchester's Gay Village. *Sexualities*, 20(5–6), 535–557. https://doi.org/10.1177/1363460716676988

Henry, M. (2013). Sexual exploitation and abuse in UN peacekeeping missions: Problematising current responses. In S. Madhok, A. Phillips, & K. Wilson (Eds.), *Gender, agency, and coercion* (pp. 122–142). London: Palgrave Macmillan. https://doi.org/10.1057/9781137295613_8

Hill Collins, P. (2019). *Intersectionality as critical social theory*. Durham: Duke University Press.

Hill Collins, P., & Bilge, S. (2016). *Intersectionality* (1st ed.). Cambridge: Polity Press.

Holtmaat, R., & Naber, J. (2011). *Women's human rights and culture: From deadlock to dialogue*. Cambridge: Intersentia.

Home Office. (2016, October). *Country information and guidance. North Korea: Opposition to the Regime. Version 2.0*. https://assets.publishing.service.gov.uk/government/uploads/system/uploads/attachment_data/file/566215/CIG_North_Korea_Opposition_to_the_Regime.pdf

Home Office. (2019, February). *Country policy and information note. Iraq: Perceived collaborators. Version 2.0*. https://assets.publishing.service.gov.uk/government/uploads/system/uploads/attachment_data/file/778003/Iraq_-_external___perceived_collaborators_-_CPIN_-_v.2.0__Feb_2019_.pdf

Houle, F., & Allister, K. M. (2017). Quand le droit international des droits de l'Homme et le droit canadien des réfugiés LGBTQ+ convergent. *Canadian Journal of Women and the Law, 29*(2), 317–342.

Hubbard, P. (2012). *Cities and sexualities*. London: Routledge.

Hubbard, P., & Wilkinson, E. (2015). Welcoming the world? Hospitality, homonationalism, and the London 2012 Olympics. *Antipode, 47*(3), 598–615. https://doi.org/10.1111/anti.12082

ICIBI - Independent Chief Inspector of Borders and Immigration. (2018). *An inspection of the vulnerable persons resettlement scheme. August 2017 – January 2018*. https://assets.publishing.service.gov.uk/government/uploads/system/uploads/attachment_data/file/705155/VPRS_Final_Artwork_revised.pdf

Inckle, K. (2010). Bent: Non-normative embodiment as lived intersectionality. In Y. Taylor, S. Hines, & M. Casey (Eds.), *Theorizing intersectionality and sexuality* (pp. 255–273). Basingstoke: Palgrave Macmillan.

International Law Commission. (2001). *Draft Articles on Responsibility of States for Internationally Wrongful Acts* (Yearbook of the International Law Commission, vol. II). UN.

Ippolito, F. (2018). La vulnerabilità come criterio emergente per una maggiore tutela del migrante nel contenzioso internazionale. *Rivista di Diritto Internazionale*.

Jagose, A. (1996). *Queer theory: An introduction*. New York: New York University Press.

Johnson, T. (2007). Flamers, flaunting and permissible persecution. *Feminist Legal Studies, 15*(1), 99–111. https://doi.org/10.1007/s10691-006-9053-7

Johnson, P. (2013a). *Homosexuality and the European court of human rights* (1st ed.). Abingdon: Routledge.

Johnson, E. P., & Henderson, M. (2005). *Black queer studies: A critical anthology*. Durham: Duke University Press.

Johnston, L., & Longhurst, R. (2009). *Space, place, and sex: Geographies of sexualities*. Lanham: Rowman & Littlefield.

Johnston, L., & Valentine, G. (1995). Wherever I lay my girlfriend, that's my home: The performance and surveillance of lesbian identities in domestic environments. In D. Bell & G. Valentine (Eds.), *Mapping desire: Geographies of sexualities* (pp. 99–113). London: Routledge.

Kapur, R. (2018). *Gender, alterity and human rights: Freedom in a fishbowl*. Cheltenham: Elgar.

Kawale, R. (2003). Kiss is Just a Kiss…Or is it? South Asian Lesbian and bisexual women and the construction of space. In N. Puwar & P. Raghuram (Eds.), *South Asian women in the diaspora* (pp. 181–199). Oxford: Berg.

Kawale, R. (2004). Inequalities of the heart: The performance of emotion work by lesbian and bisexual women in London, England. *Social & Cultural Geography, 5*(4), 565–581. https://doi.org/10.1080/1464936042000317703

Klesse, C. (2018). On the government of bisexual bodies: Asylum case law and the biopolitics of bisexual erasure. In H. Richter (Ed.), *Biopolitical governance: Race, gender and economy* (pp. 163–190). Lanham: Rowman & Littlefield International.

References

Kneebone, S. (2005). Women within the refugee construct: 'Exclusionary inclusion' in policy and practice — The Australian experience. *International Journal of Refugee Law*, 17(1), 7–42. https://doi.org/10.1093/ijrl/eei002

Kuntsman, A., & Miyake, E. (2008). Introduction. In A. Kuntsman & E. Miyake (Eds.), *Out of place: Interrogating silences in queerness/raciality* (pp. 5–9). York: Raw Nerve Books.

Lee, P.-H. (2016). LGBT rights versus Asian values: De/re-constructing the universality of human rights. *The International Journal of Human Rights*, 20(7), 978–992. https://doi.org/10.1080/13642987.2016.1192537

Lee, E. O. J., & Brotman, S. (2011). Identity, refugeeness, belonging: Experiences of sexual minority refugees in Canada. *Canadian Review of Sociology / Revue Canadienne de Sociologie*, 48(3), 241–274. https://doi.org/10.1111/j.1755-618X.2011.01265.x

Lewis, R. A. (2014). "Gay? Prove it": The politics of queer anti-deportation activism. *Sexualities*, 17(8), 958–975.

Livermon, X. (2014). Soweto nights: Making black queer space in post-apartheid South Africa. *Gender, Place & Culture*, 21(4), 508–525. https://doi.org/10.1080/0966369X.2013.786687

Macklin, A. (1995). Refugee women and the imperative of categories. *Human Rights Quarterly*, 17(2), 213–277.

Madhok, S., Phillips, A., Wilson, K., & Hemmings, C. (2013). *Gender, agency, and coercion*. London: Palgrave Macmillan.

Manalansan, M. F. (2006). Queer intersections: Sexuality and gender in migration studies. *International Migration Review*, 40(1), 224–249. https://doi.org/10.1111/j.1747-7379.2006.00009.x

Mann, I. (2017). *Humanity at sea*. Oxford: Oxford University Press.

Markard, N. (2016). Persecution for reasons of membership of a particular social group: Intersectionality avant la lettre? *Sociologia del Diritto*, 45–63. https://doi.org/10.3280/SD2016-002004

Matsuda, M. J. (1991). Beside my sister, facing the enemy: Legal theory out of coalition. *Stanford Law Review*, 43(6), 1183–1192.

McAdam, J. (2014). Rethinking the origins of 'persecution' in refugee law. *International Journal of Refugee Law*, 25(4), 667–692.

McDermott, E. (2010). Multiplex methodologies: Researching young people's well-being at the intersections of class, sexuality, gender and age. In Y. Taylor, S. Hines, & M. Casey (Eds.), *Theorizing intersectionality and sexuality* (pp. 235–254). London: Palgrave Macmillan.

McGoldrick, D. (2016). The development and status of sexual orientation discrimination under international human rights law. *Human Rights Law Review*, 16(4), 613–668. https://doi.org/10.1093/hrlr/ngw030

Mercer, K., & Julien, I. (1988). Race, sexual politics, and black masculinity: A Dossier. In R. Chapman & J. Rutherford (Eds.), *Male order: Unwrapping masculinity* (pp. 97–164). London: Lawrence & Wishart.

Millbank, J. (2004). The role of rights in asylum claims based on sexual orientation. *Human Rights Law Review*, 4(2), 193–228.

Millbank, J. (2005). A preoccupation with perversion: The British response to refugee claims on the basis of sexual orientation, 1989-2003. *Social & Legal Studies*, 14(1), 115–138. https://doi.org/10.1177/0964663905049528

Millbank, J. (2009). From discretion to disbelief: Recent trends in refugee determinations on the basis of sexual orientation in Australia and the United Kingdom. *The International Journal of Human Rights*, 13(2–3), 391–414. https://doi.org/10.1080/13642980902758218

Millett, K. (1977). *Sexual politics* (New ed.). London: Virago.

Mohanty, C. T. (1988). Under Western eyes: Feminist scholarship and colonial discourses. *Feminist Review*, 30(1), 61–88. https://doi.org/10.1057/fr.1988.42

Monro, S., Hines, S., & Osborne, A. (2017). Is bisexuality invisible? A review of sexualities scholarship 1970–2015. *The Sociological Review*, 65(4), 663–681.

Moreno-Lax, V. (2018). *Accessing asylum in Europe*. Oxford: Oxford University Press.

Morgan, D. A. (2006). Not gay enough for the government: Racial and sexual stereotypes in sexual orientation asylum cases. *Law & Sexuality*, 15, 135–175.

Muntarbhorn, V. (2017). Report of the Independent Expert on protection against violence and discrimination based on sexual orientation and gender identity, 35th Session of the Human Rights Council, UN doc. A/HRC/35/36. https://documents-dds-ny.un.org/doc/UNDOC/GEN/G17/095/53/PDF/G1709553.pdf?OpenElement

Narayan, U. (1997). *Dislocating cultures: Identities, traditions, and third-world feminism* (1st ed.). New York: Routledge.

Narayan, U. (2000). Undoing the 'package picture' of cultures. *Signs*, 25(4), 1083–1086.

Nash, J. C. (2008). Re-thinking intersectionality. *Feminist Review*, 89(1), 1–15.

Neilson, V. (2005). Homosexual or female? Applying gender-based asylum jurisprudence to lesbian asylum claims. *Stanford Law & Policy Review*, 16(2), 417.

Nero, C. (2005). Why are the gay ghettos white? In E. P. Johnson & M. Henderson (Eds.), *Black queer studies: A critical anthology* (pp. 228–245). Durham: Duke University Press.

Nussbaum, M. C. (2000). *Women and human development: The capabilities approach* (1st ed.). Cambridge: Cambridge University Press.

Nussbaum, M. (2010). *From disgust to humanity*. Oxford: Oxford University Press.

O'Leary, B. (2008). "We cannot claim any particular knowledge of the ways of homosexuals, still less of iranian homosexuals ...": The particular problems facing those who seek asylum on the basis of their sexual identity. *Feminist Legal Studies*, 16, 87–95.

Okin, S. M. (1999). *Is multiculturalism bad for women?* (J. Cohen, M. Howard, & M. C. Nussbaum, Eds., 1st ed.). Princeton: Princeton University Press.

ORAM - Organization for Refuge, Asylum and Migration. (2010). *Rights and Protection of Lesbian, Gay, Bisexual, Transgender and Intersex Refugees and Asylum Seekers under the Yogyakarta Principles*. ORAM.

Otto, D. (Ed.). (2017). *Queering international law: Possibilities, alliances, complicities, risks*. London: Routledge.

Oxford, C. G. (2005). Protectors and victims in the gender regime of asylum. *NWSA Journal*, 17(3), 18–38.

Penney, J. (2015). *After queer theory: The limits of sexual politics*. London: Pluto Press.

Peroni, L. (2018). The borders that disadvantage migrant women in enjoying human rights. *Netherlands Quarterly of Human Rights*, 36(2), 93–110. https://doi.org/10.1177/0924051918771229

Peroni, L., & Timmer, A. (2013). Vulnerable groups: The promise of an emerging concept in European Human Rights Convention law. *International Journal of Constitutional Law*, 11(4), 1056–1085. https://doi.org/10.1093/icon/mot042

Phillips, A. (2003). When culture means gender: Issues of cultural defence in the English courts. *Modern Law Review*, 66, 510–531.

Phoenix, A., & Pattynama, P. (2006). Intersectionality. *European Journal of Women's Studies*, 13(3), 187–192. https://doi.org/10.1177/1350506806065751

Plant, R. (1987). *The pink triangle: The Nazi war against homosexuals*. Edinburgh: Mainstream.

Puar, J. K. (2007). *Terrorist assemblages: Homonationalism in queer times*. Durham: Duke University Press. https://doi.org/10.1215/9780822390442

Puar, J. (2013). Rethinking homonationalism. *International Journal of Middle East Studies*, 45(2), 336–339. https://doi.org/10.1017/S002074381300007X

Puwar, N. (2004). *Space invaders: Race, gender and bodies out of place*. Oxford: Berg.

Ramón Mendos, L. (2019). *State-sponsored homophobia 2019: Global legislation overview update*. ILGA. https://ilga.org/downloads/ILGA_World_State_Sponsored_Homophobia_report_global_legislation_overview_update_December_2019.pdf

Razack, S. (1995). Domestic violence as gender persecution: Policing the Borders of nation, race, and gender. *Canadian Journal of Women and the Law*, 8, 45.

References

Rooke, A. (2007). Navigating embodied lesbian cultural space: Toward a lesbian habitus. *Space and Culture*, 10(2), 231–252. https://doi.org/10.1177/1206331206298790

Sedgwick, E. K. (2008). *Epistemology of the closet (updated with a new preface)*. Oakland: University of California Press.

Seidman, S. (1993). Identity and politics in a "postmodern" gay culture: Some historical and conceptual notes. In M. Warner (Ed.), *Fear of a queer planet: Queer politics and social theory* (pp. 105–142). Minneapolis: University of Minnesota Press.

Singer, D. (2012). Women seeking Asylum: Failed twice over. In H. Rehman, L. Kelly & H. Siddiqui (Eds.) *Moving in the shadows: Violence in the lives of minority women and children* (pp. 225–243). London: Ashgate.

Skeggs, B. (1999). Matter out of place: Visibility and sexualities in leisure spaces. *Leisure Studies*, 18(3), 213–232. https://doi.org/10.1080/026143699374934

Somerville, S. B. (2000). *Queering the color line: Race and the invention of homosexuality in American culture*. Durham: Duke University Press.

Spade, D. (2015). *Normal life: Administrative violence, critical trans politics, and the limits of law*. Durham: Duke University Press.

Spijkerboer, T. (Ed.). (2013). *Fleeing homophobia: Sexual orientation, gender identity and asylum*. London: Routledge.

Spijkerboer, T. (2018). Gender, sexuality, asylum and European human rights. *Law and Critique*, 29, 221–239.

Spivak, G. C. (1988). Can the subaltern speak? In C. Nelson & L. Grossberg (Eds.) *Marxism and the interpretation of culture* (pp. 271–313). London: Macmillan Education.

Stoler, A. L. (1995). *Race and the education of desire: Foucault's history of sexuality and the colonial order of things*. Durham: Duke University Press.

Storey, H. (2015). The law of refugee status: Paradigm lost? *International Journal of Refugee Law*, 27(2), 348–360.

Tan, C. K. (2015). Rainbow belt: Singapore's gay Chinatown as a Lefebvrian space. *Urban Studies*, 52(12), 2203–2218. https://doi.org/10.1177/0042098014544761

Taylor, A. (1997). A queer geography. In A. Medhurst & S. Munt (Eds.), *Lesbian and gay studies: A critical introduction* (pp. 3–19). London: Cassel.

Taylor, Y. (2007). *Working class lesbian life: Classed outsiders*. Basingstoke: Palgrave Macmillan.

Taylor, Y., Hines, S., & Casey, M. (2010). *Theorizing intersectionality and sexuality*. London: Palgrave Macmillan.

Thoreson, R. R. (2009). Queering human rights: The Yogyakarta principles and the norm that dare not speak its name. *Journal of Human Rights*, 8(4), 323–339. https://doi.org/10.1080/14754830903324746

Timmer, A. (2011). Toward an anti-stereotyping approach for the European Court of Human Rights. *Human Rights Law Review*, 11(4), 707–738. https://doi.org/10.1093/hrlr/ngr036

Timmer, A. (2013). A quiet revolution: Vulnerability in the European Court of Human Rights. In M. Freeman (Ed.) *Vulnerability: Reflections on a new ethical foundation for law and politics* (pp. 147–170). London: Ashgate.

Timmer, A. (2015). Judging stereotypes: What the European Court of Human Rights can borrow from American and Canadian equal protection law. *American Journal of Comparative Law*, 63(1), 239–284. https://doi.org/10.5131/AJCL.2015.0007

Tucker, A. (2009). Framing exclusion in Cape Town's gay village: The discursive and material perpetuation of inequitable queer subjects 1. *Area*, 41(2), 186–197. https://doi.org/10.1111/j.1475-4762.2008.00852.x

UN Working Group on Arbitrary Detention. (2018). *Revised deliberation no. 5 on deprivation of liberty of migrants*. UN working group on arbitrary detention. https://www.refworld.org/docid/5a903b514.html

UNHCR - UN High Commissioner for Refugees. (1990). *The Refugee Convention, 1951: The Travaux préparatoires analysed with a Commentary by Dr. Paul Weis*. UNHCR - UN High Commissioner for Refugees.

UNHCR - UN High Commissioner for Refugees. (2002). *Guidelines on international protection: Gender-related persecution within the context of Article 1A(2) of the 1951 convention and/ or its 1967 protocol relating to the status of refugees*. UNHCR - UN High Commissioner for Refugees.

UNHCR - UN High Commissioner for Refugees. (2011). *Handbook on Procedures and Criteria for Determining Refugee Status under the 1951 Convention and the 1967 Protocol relating to the status of refugees*. UNHCR - UN High Commissioner for Refugees. http://www.unhcr.org/uk/publications/legal/3d58e13b4/handbook-procedures-criteria-determining-refugee-status-under-1951-convention.html

UNHCR - UN High Commissioner for Refugees. (2012). *Guidelines on international protection no. 9: Claims to refugee status based on sexual orientation and/or gender identity within the context of Article 1A(2) of the 1951 convention and/or its 1967 protocol relating to the status of refugees (HCR/GIP/12/09)*. UNHCR - UN High Commissioner for Refugees. http://www.unhcr.org/509136ca9.pdf

Valentine, G. (1993). Negotiating and managing multiple sexual identities: Lesbian time-space strategies. *Transactions of the Institute of British Geographers*, 18(2), 237–248. https://doi.org/10.2307/622365

Valentine, G. (1996). (Re)negotiating the 'heterosexual street. In N. Duncan (Ed.), *BodySpace: Destabilizing geographies of gender and sexuality* (pp. 146–155). London: Routledge.

Various. (2017). *The Yogyakarta principles plus 10 (YP+10): The application of international human rights law in relation to sexual orientation and gender identity*. ICJ - International Commission of Jurists. https://yogyakartaprinciples.org/

Verdirame, G. (2012). A friendly act of socio-cultural contestation: Asylum and the big cultural divide. *New York University Journal of International Law & Politics*, 44(2), 559–572.

Visser, G. (2003). Gay men, leisure space and South African cities: The case of Cape Town. *Geoforum*, 34(1), 123–137. https://doi.org/10.1016/S0016-7185(02)00079-9

Visser, G. (2013). Challenging the gay ghetto in South Africa: Time to move on? *Geoforum*, 49, 268–274. https://doi.org/10.1016/j.geoforum.2012.12.013

Volpp, L. (1996). Talking culture: Gender, race, nation, and the politics of multiculturalism. *Columbia Law Review*, 96, 1573.

Volpp, L. (2002). *Cultural Defenses in the criminal legal system*. Berkley: Bepress. https://works.bepress.com/leti_volpp/72/

Walker, A. (2004). *In search of our mothers' gardens: Womanist prose* (Reprint ed.). Boston: Houghton Mifflin Harcourt USA.

Warner, M. (1991). Introduction: Fear of a queer planet. *Social Text*, 29, 3–17.

Warner, M. (Ed.). (1993). *Fear of a queer planet: Queer politics and social theory*. Minneapolis: University of Minnesota Press.

Wekker, G. (2006). *The politics of passion: Women's sexual culture in the Afro-Surinamese diaspora*. New York: Columbia University Press.

Wessels, J. (2016). "Discretion", persecution and the act/identity dichotomy. *Vrije University Migration Law Series*, 12. https://rechten.vu.nl/en/Images/Wessels_Migration_Law_Series_No_12_jw_tcm248-760198.pdf

Wintemute, R. (1996). *Sexual orientation and human rights*. Oxford: Clarendon Press.

References

Open Access This chapter is licensed under the terms of the Creative Commons Attribution 4.0 International License (http://creativecommons.org/licenses/by/4.0/), which permits use, sharing, adaptation, distribution and reproduction in any medium or format, as long as you give appropriate credit to the original author(s) and the source, provide a link to the Creative Commons license and indicate if changes were made.

The images or other third party material in this chapter are included in the chapter's Creative Commons license, unless indicated otherwise in a credit line to the material. If material is not included in the chapter's Creative Commons license and your intended use is not permitted by statutory regulation or exceeds the permitted use, you will need to obtain permission directly from the copyright holder.

Part II
The Legal and Social Experiences of SOGI Asylum Claimants and Refugees

Chapter 4
The Policy and Guidance

> ...*rather dead here than a deportation....*
>
> (Zouhair, Germany)
>
> ...*i only knew i could live freely in Europe as a Gay person but i didnt know how different country operate on the basis of their LGBT right. so, when i first got here. that was when i was told that i have to apply for asylum.*
>
> (C63, claimant, Italy)
>
> ...*winning an asylum claim is like running up an escalator backwards, it is possible but you need to try really hard.*
>
> (Deirdre, lawyer, UK)

4.1 Introduction

The contours of international protection in EU member states are mainly determined by three elements: the 1951 Refugee Convention and the EU Common European Asylum System (CEAS), alongside international human rights law, including the 1950 ECHR (Chap. 3). While Germany and Italy are bound by the CEAS recast instruments,[1] the UK has remained only bound by the 2003 Reception Directive, 2004 Qualification Directive and 2005 Procedures Directive.[2] Yet, this and other type of legislative options do not, in themselves, necessarily produce considerable variations across the EU (Querton 2019), as many other factors contribute to different degrees of policy variation between EU member states. Amongst these

---

[1] Especially Directive 2011/95/EU (Qualification Directive), Directive 2013/32/EU (Procedures Directive) and Directive 2013/33/EU (Reception Conditions).

[2] Council Directive 2003/9/EC, Council Directive 2004/83/EC and Council Directive 2005/85/EC respectively. At the time, the UK government stated, for example, that it had 'grave concerns about the way in which the provisions in the amended Reception Directive would allow asylum seekers to work after 6 months if a decision at first instance has not been reached and would place stringent restrictions on Member States' ability to detain asylum seekers in exceptional circumstances' (UK Government 2011). While Denmark obtained an 'opt-out' from the recast CEAS instruments, Ireland and the UK have negotiated an optional 'opt-in'.

© The Author(s) 2021
C. Danisi et al., *Queering Asylum in Europe*, IMISCOE Research Series, https://doi.org/10.1007/978-3-030-69441-8_4

factors, it is worth considering in particular geographical location, political context and internal governance structure, further contextualised by the statistics available.

First, geographical location influences to a considerable degree how countries choose to design their asylum legal and policy framework. Italy, being one of the EU frontline member states, is under pressure – internally and externally – to adhere to minimum standard solutions and to adopt a 'closed door policy' towards non-EU citizens. Together with Greece and Spain, Italy is the place of arrival of migrants headed to Europe by sea and the country where the EU 'hotspot' system has been established (Anci et al. 2016; European Commission 2015).[3] The main consequence of continuous arrivals is a permanent emergency situation, where people in need of international protection risk seeing their specific needs disregarded. The policy of the Lega Nord / M5S Italian government of closing Italy's harbours to the NGO-managed boats rescuing people from the Mediterranean hampered continuous arrivals in Italy, but with the consequence of raising the number of deaths at sea and increasing the suffering of people prevented from reaching a 'safe harbour' as soon as possible (Danisi 2018; UNHCR 2019).

Second, the political context also plays a key role in shaping countries' asylum systems. An obvious example is Germany, which has taken a leading role in what is often referred to as Europe's 'refugee crisis', processing more asylum claims than any of the other 27 EU member states and receiving 1.3 million refugees between 2015 and 2017 alone (Deutsche Welle 2017). In September 2015, Angela Merkel, the Chancellor of Germany and leader of the CDU at the time,[4] made a decision that will be remembered for years to come: she decided against protecting the country's border with Austria and preventing hundreds of thousands of refugees from coming into the country, and instead insisted on 'letting them in' (Merkel 2016). Merkel's 'generous' asylum politics were met with an increase in anti-immigrant sentiments, led by the far-right party Alternative for Germany (Alternative für Deutschland, AfD), with a far-right political movement playing a key role in German politics for the first time since the Nazi movement in the 1930s (Die Welt 2016). In the 2017 general election, the AfD gained 12.6% of the votes and 94 seats in the Bundestag (German Federal Parliament) (Der Bundeswahlleiter 2017). In 2018, the AfD managed for the first time to have seats in all of the parliaments of the 16 federal states (Die Welt 2018). People seeking asylum and refugees in Germany thus find themselves in a country full of contradictions: a (one-time) generous border politics and welcome culture ('Willkommenskultur'), but also an increasingly hostile

---

[3] Hotspot centres can be defined as 'locations in which irregularly arriving refugees and migrants could quickly be identified, primarily through obligatory fingerprinting, screened to identify any protection needs, and subsequently filtered for the purposes of the processing of asylum applications or return to their countries of origin' (Amnesty International 2016). SOGI asylum claimants and, more generally, members of vulnerable groups are not excluded from this process, and no adequate specific procedures apply. NGOs and associations have also highlighted the lack of respect for human rights standards in the new hotspot centres (Oxfam, ASGI & A Buon Diritto 2015).

[4] Christlich Demokratische Union Deutschlands – Christian Democratic Union of Germany.

4.1 Introduction

environment. In Italy, as well, the political environment has become increasingly hostile towards refugees and migrants. Instances of racism have increasingly been reported in the media, including murders (Catozzella 2018), with the UN High Commissioner for Human Rights, Michelle Bachelet, denouncing this trend and pointing to the need for a UN task force in Italy to monitor this phenomenon (Corriere della Sera 2018). This is likely to be driven by the government's anti-immigration policies, which have had significant consequences on the general asylum system of the country.

Similarly, migration debates in the UK have been marked by the then Home Secretary Theresa May's comment in 2012 that the government wished to 'create here in Britain a really hostile environment for illegal migration' (Kirkup and Winnett 2012). This led the Council of Europe's Commissioner for Human Rights to express concern about the effect of negative public rhetoric towards migrants, particularly irregular migrants, and state that '[f]or many years now there has been a dominant political debate in the UK characterised by alarmism' (Commissioner for Human Rights 2016). This alarmism, it is fair to say, persists to this day, even if there are also some signs that public attitudes have changed on the theme of immigration (The Economist 2019). In the light of its centrality in public debates, the UK asylum and immigration processes have been subjected to frequent scrutiny by public bodies and officials in recent years, including through the Parliament (Home Affairs Committee 2019a, b; House of Commons Home Affairs Committee 2013a), the Independent Chief Inspector of Borders and Immigration (ICIBI 2014, 2016), and civil society organisations (Quertel 2012; Stonewall and UKLGIG 2016). This bleak scenario was compounded by the result in the 2016 EU referendum, with a spike in racist and homo/transphobic hate crime discernable at the time and since (Marsh et al. 2019). These developments across the three countries under comparison suggest that increasing right wing populism in Europe targets *all* marginalised groups – including SOGI minorities and SOGI claimants – and suggests that individuals who are minoritised on more than one basis, such as SOGI claimants, will be particularly disadvantaged. The symbiosis between homophobia, transphobia, racism and xenophobia is all too apparent in this context.

Third, internal governance structures shape to a large extent variations within a single country. All countries under comparison are illustrative in this regard, as they have strong municipality variations (in the case of Italy), a federal structure (in the case of Germany) or even countries that benefit from devolved powers (in the case of the UK). To use Germany as an example of these internal variations, the administration of asylum is not homogeneous across the country, despite Germany adhering to all CEAS instruments. Bavaria, in particular, is often cited as 'the trial balloon for all these bad things that are happening now, such as deportation camps and AnkER [asylum reception] centres' (Sofia and Emma, NGO workers). Conversely, in the UK, Scotland was particularly supportive of Syrian refugees, taking 40% of those received by the UK before Christmas 2015 (Scottish Government News 2016), reflecting differences between the four nations that make up the UK. Following dispersal of people seeking asylum throughout the UK to ease pressure on the South East of England (Chap. 8), Glasgow, Scotland's biggest city, was estimated to be home to 10% of the UK's asylum claimant population (Scottish Government 2013) and the inequitable distribution of asylum claimants through the UK's dispersal policy is recognised (Home Affairs Committee 2018), with the poorest regions receiving most asylum claimants (Lyons and Duncan 2017). The municipal, federal or devolved structure of political systems influences how asylum policies are implemented, and differences in implementation exist between different municipalities/states/countries, as will be explored throughout subsequent chapters.

A better understanding of the role of geographical location, political context and internal governance structures is given by also looking at domestic statistics, as these are instructive in uncovering the range of differences and similarities across and within EU member states' asylum policy. According to the German Federal Office for Migration and Refugees (Bundesamt für Migration und Flüchtlinge, BAMF), in 2016 Germany received the highest number of applications in its history: 745,545 (BAMF 2016). In fact, Germany received and processed more asylum requests in the first 9 months of 2016 than the rest of the EU combined, and produced 420,000 decisions (Deutsche Welle 2017). By 2018, and in the sequence of the EU-Turkey migration deal,[5] the numbers of asylum applications had gone down to 185,853 (BAMF 2018a). The top five countries of origin in 2018 included Syria, Iraq, Iran, Nigeria and Turkey (BAMF 2018a), all countries with poor records of treatment of SOGI minorities (Ramón Mendos 2019). In 2018, BAMF granted international protection to 35% of the claimants, the refusal rate thus being 65% (BAMF 2018a). The BAMF does not produce statistics with regard to SOGI claims, recording only age, gender, religion and, for Syrian and Afghan claimants, also ethnicity (BAMF 2018b).

In Italy, according to the Italian Minister of Internal Affairs, 53,596 international protection claims were lodged in 2018. Pakistan, Nigeria and Senegal were amongst the top four countries of origin, all countries where same-sex conduct is criminally punished (Ramón Mendos 2019). Despite various positive elements in the Italian asylum system that will be explored throughout this chapter and the rest of these volumes, the rate of successful applications is only 33%, with 7% of claimants granted refugee status in 2018 and 67% refused any form of international protection (Dipartimento Libertà Civili e Immigrazione 2019).

Although UK officials and leaders frequently emphasise the country's proud history of supporting refugees and commitment to continuing to do so (Home Office 2017b; May 2015, 2016), in practice, even within Europe, the UK takes a relatively small number of people claiming asylum (Sturge 2019, p. 3). While having a much smaller number of asylum applications in 2018 (29,380) than other countries, the rate of refusal of initial claims in the UK was 67% – exactly the same as in Italy and close to the one in Germany (Sturge 2019). Similarly to Italy, the top four countries from which asylum claimants originated in 2017 – Iran, Iraq, Eritrea and Pakistan – are jurisdictions where same-sex conduct is criminalised (Ramón Mendos 2019; Sturge 2019). In response to the crisis in Syria, and rather than participating in a

---

[5] https://www.consilium.europa.eu/en/press/press-releases/2016/03/18/eu-turkey-statement/pdf.

common EU initiative to accept more refugees, the UK government launched the Syrian Vulnerable Persons Resettlement Scheme, to take people identified as vulnerable by the UNHCR (including persons at risk due to their SOGI), and which was expanded to resettle 20,000 Syrians by 2020 (Home Office 2017c).

Against this background, in this chapter we explore key aspects of policy and guidance in place in Germany, Italy and the UK in relation to SOGI, asylum, and SOGI asylum, thus setting the context for the subsequent chapters in which we explore our findings relating to a range of aspects of SOGI asylum. A country's SOGI asylum policy does not exist in a vacuum. In fact, it is developed in the context of broader SOGI and asylum policies, and these may operate in ways that reinforce each other or foster tensions. The choice of the countries under comparison, as explored in Chap. 2, is informed by the need to research how those broader SOGI and asylum policies influence – or not – a country's approach to SOGI asylum. Consequently, we proceed in Sect. 4.2 by discussing social and legal dimensions of SOGI, offering a broad picture of the protection of SOGI-related rights and the social environment in this context. In Sect. 4.3, we offer an outline of the national asylum systems, including the domestic overall policy frameworks and key political developments. In Sect. 4.4 the focus shifts to the domestic SOGI asylum systems, including consideration of statutory instruments, guidance and degree of compliance with international and supranational obligations. Finally, in Sect. 4.5 we look at how policy shapes the life of claimants after the granting or denial of international protection, and conclude in Sect. 4.6 with some final remarks.

4.2 Social and Legal Dimensions of SOGI

The manner in which SOGI are (legally) regulated and (socially) experienced varies considerably from country to country and within each country. Despite globalising trends and international and supranational developments, the identities and lived realities of non-heterosexual and non-cisgender people across Europe are still considerably dependent on where they grow up and live, constrained by a range of legal and socio-cultural factors.

One obvious, albeit generic, starting point to this discussion is ILGA-Europe's European Rainbow Map, an index that attempts to measure the legal protection and social climate affecting SOGI minorities in Europe by using a scale between 0% (gross violations of human rights and discrimination) and 100% (respect for human rights and full equality) (ILGA-Europe 2019). While Italy has scored 27% in this exercise, Germany has scored 59% and the UK has scored 81%. EU-wide comparative research has confirmed that stark differences subsist between countries in relation to: SOGI-related discrimination in employment and other areas; access to and legal recognition of one's preferred gender; and freedom of assembly and expression; abuse, hatred and violence (FRA 2015). It is important, however, to zoom in, and see how the specific context of the countries on which we are focussing has developed in recent times.

Discrimination on grounds of SOGI in the field of employment is prohibited across all EU member states, in the light of the EU Framework Employment Directive,[6] and jurisprudence developed by the CJEU throughout decades on sex discrimination, including people who have undergone sex reassignment (Ellis and Watson 2015). In the UK, for example, the Employment Equality (Sexual Orientation) Regulations 2003 extended workplace equality rights to cover sexual orientation. The Equality Act 2010 then extended protection from discrimination to several fields and on an extensive range of grounds, including SOGI, and required public bodies to promote equality on the same range of grounds – a level of anti-discrimination legislation that does not find a parallel in Germany or Italy.

In relation to family-related rights, the scenario is more fragmented, with each EU member state retaining widely different legal frameworks. The UK, for example, introduced civil partnership for same-sex couples in 2005 through the Civil Partnership Act 2004, and same-sex marriage through the Marriage (Same Sex Couples) Act 2013 (in England, Wales and Scotland) and the Northern Ireland (Executive Formation etc) Act 2019 (in Northern Ireland). Equal adoption rights were also granted in England and Wales through the Adoption and Children Act 2002. Germany has also for a long period only recognised same-sex registered life partnerships,[7] but introduced same-sex marriage and adoption rights in 2017.[8] Despite still lagging behind most other Western European countries, Italy eventually also adopted an act on same-sex civil unions in 2016.[9] The legislator carefully avoided equating same-sex civil unions with opposite-sex marriage, and civil unions afford the bare minimum of the rights necessary to respect the right to respect for family life as enshrined in Article 8 ECHR. Interestingly, significant regional differences have emerged in respect of the use made of this legal status, with same-sex couples in the north of Italy making considerably more use of it than in the south (AGI 2018), which reinforces the idea of the south of Italy as a social environment less open or friendly towards SOGI minorities. Child adoption and surrogacy by same-sex couples remain outside the boundaries of legality, with judicial bodies filling the legislative gap by ruling on a case-by-case basis on grounds of the principle of the best interests of the child.[10]

Similarly, in relation to gender identity one sees wide variations in the legal framework across the three countries under comparison. In the UK, transgender rights have been a particular focus for policy since the early 2000s, and the Gender Recognition Act in 2004 recognised people's right to change their gender. Subsequently, the government launched an Action Plan in 2011 (Government Equalities Office 2011), there was a parliamentary inquiry in 2016 (House of

---

[6] Council Directive 2000/78/EC of 27 November 2000 establishing a general framework for equal treatment in employment and occupation, OJ L 303, 2.12.2000, p. 16–22.
[7] Act on Registered Life Partnerships, 16 February 2001, Federal Law Gazette I p. 266.
[8] Act to Allow Persons of the Same Sex to Marry, 20 July 2017, Federal Law Gazette I p. 2787.
[9] Law no. 76, 20 May 2016.
[10] See, among others, Supreme Court, judgment of 26 May 2016, No. 12962.

4.2 Social and Legal Dimensions of SOGI

Commons Women and Equalities Committee 2016), and a consultation on the Reform of the Gender Recognition Act was carried out in 2018 (Government Equalities Office 2018b). In Italy, however, it took judicial intervention to ensure that transgender individuals could amend their personal data without having to undergo sex reassignment surgery,[11] and could remain married when choosing to undergo sex reassignment surgery.[12] Germany again stands somewhere in the middle, with the rights of people undergoing sex reassignment being regulated since 1980,[13] but framed in very restrictive terms that had to be gradually challenged in courts and amended by the legislature. Crucially, German law now recognises non-binary gender, by allowing people to choose 'diverse gender' or no gender marker at all, both at birth and throughout life.[14]

While no particular issues arise in relation to freedom of assembly or reunion in any of these countries (for example, in relation to having the right to hold Pride events), not all of them consider homophobia or transphobia an aggravating circumstance in criminal conduct. While in the UK and Germany the law recognises the concept of 'hate crime' and 'hate speech' for homophobia and transphobia-motivated criminal acts,[15] there is no equivalent in Italy. Considering the significant number of homophobic and transphobic attacks reported by the media (Bovo 2018) and the recurrence of statements against SOGI minorities, even from key figures in the government (Arachi 2018), the social environment appears increasingly less friendly towards SOGI minorities in Italy.

Although SOGI are clearly recognised and protected to some extent by the law in all three countries under comparison, including at constitutional level,[16] the levels of protection are often insufficient and inadequate, most strikingly in Italy. Even in the UK, where the legal framework appears to be robust, people from SOGI minorities continue to face discrimination, harassment, disadvantage and inequality in a number of different policy areas. In education, for example, homophobic, biphobic and transphobic bullying, harassment and language remain a major problem (Hudson-Sharp and Metcalf 2016, p. 11). Furthermore, SOGI minorities in the UK are still at greater risk of being victim of hate crime compared to heterosexual and cis-gendered people, with recorded incidences increasing over time (Home Affairs Committee 2016). Mainstream services also often remain inaccessible to SOGI minorities because of heteronormative assumptions and the fear of discrimination (Hudson-Sharp and Metcalf 2016, p. 64). All of this takes place in the context of

---

[11] See, among others, Tribunal of Rovereto, judgment no. 194, 3 May 2013.

[12] Constitutional Court, judgment no. 170, 11 June 2014.

[13] Act on the change of first name and determination of gender identity in special cases (Transsexual law – TSG), 10 September 1980, Federal Law Gazette I p. 1654.

[14] Act on Change of Information in Birth Certificate, 21 December 2018, Federal Law Gazette I, no. 48, p. 2635.

[15] UK Criminal Justice and Immigration Act 2008 and UK Legal Aid, Sentencing and Punishment of Offenders Act 2012; Section 46 of the German 1998 Criminal Code, as amended in 2015.

[16] See, for example, Italian Constitutional Court, judgment no. 138, 14 April 2010, regarding sexual orientation, and judgment no. 170, 11 June 2014, regarding gender identity.

'austerity' measures, cuts in public spending and obstacles in access to justice that have been recognised as increasing poverty and inequality in the UK for many people, including SOGI minorities, asylum claimants and – of course – SOGI claimants (EHRC 2018; Special Rapporteur on extreme poverty and human rights 2019). This points to the need for feminist, intersectional, queer and human rights approaches in this field, along the lines explored in Chap. 3.

These insufficient levels of legal protection and social respect have potential implications for the adjudication of SOGI asylum claims and how broader asylum policy issues affect these claimants. In Italy, for example, most of our participants, including claimants of international protection, connected issues of social integration with the lack of equal rights for SOGI minorities, compounded by an increasingly negative social attitude towards migrants and widespread hate crime and speech on ethnic origin grounds. Even when good work is being carried out in the field of SOGI and social justice, those involved in such initiatives and policies are often unable to influence decisions and developments in the field of asylum and refugees, owing to structural and organisational divides (Finn, representative of a municipality, Germany). Yet, as subsequent chapters will reveal, these different standards do not prevent the rise of good practices in SOGI asylum where the legal and social protection of SOGI minorities remains problematic.

We will turn to specific issues affecting SOGI asylum claimants in Sect. 4.4 and subsequent chapters. Before we do that, it is necessary to understand better how the asylum legal and policy framework operates in Germany, Italy and the UK.

4.3 The National Asylum Systems

4.3.1 *The Key Legal Instruments and Actors*

All three countries under analysis are signatories of the Refugee Convention and members of the CEAS, making it natural to start our analysis of these countries' asylum systems with an overview of the types of international protection that the Refugee Convention and the Qualification Directive offer. Under the Refugee Convention, people seeking international protection can claim refugee status (Chap. 1). This is a status that, depending on each country signatory to the Convention, can be determined by either domestic authorities or the UNHCR itself. In the case of Germany, Italy and the UK, it is the role of domestic authorities to adjudicate asylum claims internally. Where the requirements to grant refugee status are not met, domestic authorities in EU member states can instead grant subsidiary protection, a legal status recognised by the EU Qualification Directive and defined in its Article 2 as a form of protection for a:

> third-country national or a stateless person who does not qualify as a refugee but in respect of whom substantial grounds have been shown for believing that the person concerned, if returned to his or her country of origin, or in the case of a stateless person, to his or her country of former habitual residence, would face a real risk of suffering serious harm as

defined in Article 15, and to whom Article 17(1) and (2) does not apply, and is unable, or, owing to such risk, unwilling to avail himself or herself of the protection of that country.

Finally, and as a 'residual' form of protection left to the discretion of states, domestic authorities can also grant humanitarian protection when a person does not fulfil the criteria either for refugee status or subsidiarity protection. This is a form of protection that is mainly suitable for those claimants who, in order to respect the principle of non-refoulement and Article 3 ECHR, cannot be deported. Yet, it is not regulated at EU level, but solely at national level. It generally entails less comprehensive protection than refugee status or subsidiary protection, and it ceases once the situation of danger leading to the protection comes to an end. Despite all three countries under comparison having a history of making this range of forms of international protection available to claimants and possessing many other similarities owing to the CEAS standards, each national asylum system has developed in starkly different ways.

In both Germany and Italy, the right to asylum has constitutional standing. In Germany, it is enshrined in Article 16a(1) of the Basic Law (Grundgesetz, GG). Although this norm only refers to 'political persecution', German courts have assumed that this norm conforms to the Refugee Convention and have therefore used it to decide on any asylum claim (Markard 2015). Still, refugee status in accordance with the Refugee Convention is now more commonly granted under §3(1) of the Asylum Act (Asylgesetz, AsylG).[17] Furthermore, subsidiary protection is granted under §4(1) of the Asylum Act, and a prohibition of deportation ('Abschiebungsverbot', akin to what is generally understood as humanitarian protection) can be granted under §60(5)(7) of the Residence Act (Aufenthaltsgesetz, AufenthG). A wide-ranging legal reform came into force in August 2019, mainly affecting the quality of legal advice and representation, extending the length of stay in initial reception centres, further regulating the access to employment, limiting access to social benefits, and facilitating the deportation of claimants to countries of origin (including by using pre-removal detention) (AIDA and ECRE 2019). The wish to make the German asylum system more restrictive is clear.

In Italy, the right to asylum has also been enshrined constitutionally, in Article 10(3) of the Constitution, which provides that foreigners 'who see denied the enjoyment of democratic freedoms granted by the Constitution' should be given protection in Italy. This provision has a broad potential application, being more generous than the Refugee Convention's definition of refugee or than EU asylum provisions, as 'the denial of the enjoyment of fundamental freedoms' could be sufficient for the recognition of asylum, the reason for persecution, for instance, being irrelevant (Benvenuti 2010, p. 36; Bonetti 2011, p. 35). However, although courts have asserted that asylum can be granted directly on the basis of this constitutional norm,[18] it has

---

[17] An English version of the Asylum Act is available online: https://www.gesetze-im-internet.de/englisch_asylvfg/index.html.
[18] Supreme Court, judgments no. 11441, 18 June 2004; no. 8423, 4 May 2004; and no. 4674, 26 May 1997.

generally not been applied in such broad terms, with external sources (EU law and other international obligations) playing the key role in the field of asylum. Legislative decree no. 251/2007 constitutes the key asylum statute in Italy, but attempts to regulate migration flows have translated into significant and restrictive legislative reforms in 2017 and 2018.[19]

Conversely, in the UK, the right to asylum does not have constitutional standing. Asylum is a part of broader immigration policy, and asylum and immigration are often conflated (Casey 2016). UK legislation includes the Immigration and Asylum Act 1999, the Nationality, Immigration and Asylum Act 2002, and the Immigration Acts 2014 and 2016. The details of asylum policy are contained in section 11 of the Immigration Rules.[20] New legislation and continuous updating of the immigration rules have made this area increasingly complex and at points impenetrable (Singer 2019).

The institutional framework that implements the asylum statutory framework also varies considerably across the three countries under comparison. In Germany, the Federal Office for Migration and Refugees (BAMF) is the body responsible for the implementation of asylum procedures and refugee protection, as well as migration research and the nationwide promotion of integration.[21] The BAMF thus decides whether asylum claimants are entitled to constitutional asylum, refugee status or any other form of protection such as subsidiary protection or prohibition of deportation. Decision-making practices by the BAMF have been scrutinised since the 'BAMF scandal' in 2018, where the regional BAMF office in Bremen was accused of fraud and granting people status who did not have genuine claims, but this could not be proved as no systematic irregularities were found (NDR 2019).

The model adopted in Italy is radically different. The Italian authorities responsible for adjudicating asylum claims are the 'territorial commissions' ('commissioni territoriali'), which carry out the individual interview and individual assessment for each claim.[22] Until 2018, these commissions comprised: one representative of the local municipality/authority; two representatives of the central government / Ministry of Internal Affairs, including a (local) police officer; and one representative of the UNHCR. The representatives of the UNHCR seem to enjoy particular respect and professional esteem in this context, owing to their expertise and full-time commitment to refugee matters (Titti, decision-maker). If we exclude the UNCHR staff, before 2018, asylum requests were evaluated by people who were

---

[19] Decree Law no. 13/2017 (converted into Law no. 46, 13 April 2017), so-called 'Decreto Minniti'; Decree Law no. 113/2018 (converted into Law no. 132, 1 December 2018), so-called 'Decreto Salvini'. On the latter, see CILD (2018).
[20] https://www.gov.uk/guidance/immigration-rules.
[21] http://www.bamf.de.
[22] Law No. 189/2002 (Modifica alla normativa in materia di immigrazione e di asilo); Presidential Decree (Regolamento relativo alle procedure per il riconoscimento dello status di rifugiato) [Regulation on the functioning of the asylum system]. A short history of the Italian system is also available here: www.interno.gov.it/it/ministero/dipartimenti/dipartimento-liberta-civili-e-limmigrazione/commissione-nazionale-diritto-asilo.

4.3 The National Asylum Systems

not experts in the field of asylum or migration. Furthermore, the fact that most commissions' members were nominated by local authorities had consequences:

> they are a reflection of the best and the worst of the territories. So, in my experience, if I had to tell you about the police officers of the South, they usually tend to be much less racist than the northern police headquarters, maybe because they have more experience in the fight against organised crime, in a police force that does not just deal with small drug trafficking, petty crime sometimes related to immigrant youth, so they have a different notion of safety (Roberto, decision-maker).

The need for professional staff with expertise in asylum was recognised by the 2018 reform, which changed the composition of the territorial commissions to: one representative of the central government, with the role of president; two professional officers with a higher education degree, who have substituted the police officers and the representatives of municipalities / local authorities; and a representative of the UNHCR.[23] This change has been generally evaluated positively by our participants, on the basis that more qualified staff might lead to fairer evaluations and better-founded decisions (Silvana and Maurizio, judges). This positive assessment also relates to the relatively young age of the new staff, which some participants hope will translate into more 'open minds' and fewer prejudices about specific groups of claimants. These opinions are also based on the idea that the new staff replaced police officers and local authorities' representatives who, irrespective of their background, were mainly perceived as pursuing security or locally-based interests and, often, as being the members of the territorial commissions most influenced by bias and prejudices (Maria Grazia, decision-maker). The fact that the UNHCR remains represented in these commissions is a unique feature of the Italian system, setting it apart in the European context (Chap. 6). While generally seen as a positive feature, for some of our participants the involvement of the UNHCR should not be seen as entirely positive, because a 'EU-based national asylum system' may also have interests independent from the UNHCR and which may not always correspond to the UNHCR vision (Daniele, decision-maker). These local territorial commissions are coordinated by the National Commission for the Right to Asylum (Chap. 6).

Finally, in the UK, asylum is the responsibility of the Home Office, with the Home Secretary being the responsible minister. The department responsible for immigration and asylum has had a troubled history: in 2006 it was declared 'not fit for purpose' by its own minister and a large backlog of outstanding asylum claims was identified (House of Commons Home Affairs Committee 2013b). Within the Home Office, asylum applications are now managed by UK Visas and Immigration (UKVI). Prior to 2013, this was the task of the UK Border Agency (UKBA), but this agency was split up by the Home Secretary to end its 'closed, secretive and defensive culture' (Barrett 2013). Problems are far from having been completely solved (Hill 2019). The Home Office is still considered to be 'extremely flawed (…) just faceless. And, extremely elusive and you will be on the phone for hours and you

---

[23] The professional dynamics within territorial commissions are further explored in Chaps. 6 and 7.

won't get anywhere and they only write letters and put fake names at the end of it' (Chloe, NGO worker) (Chap. 2). One Home Office staff member also asserted that the Home Office is:

> very cynical as an organisation (…) [it has a] culture of cynicism as opposed to outright disbelief (…) I think the decision-making in the Home Office the last two to three years has… gone a lot worse. I don't think I have seen in my 12 years decisions as poor as this, across the board, asylum and non-asylum (Bilal, presenting officer).

At the same time it was suggested that there are serious issues of lack of communication, poor team work and insufficient learning strategies amongst the Home Office staff:

> there was a disconnect [between first decision-makers and presenting officers, representing the Home Office in judicial appeals] and there wasn't really that sort of learning sort of loop that you might expect. And, you know, there has been attempts to try to bring it together a bit more, but there was still too much of a gap between the people who were managing the case, the litigation cases, and the sort of first line decision-makers. And the same was true I think of the, of the country of origin information, too much of a gap between the people producing it, and the people who were using it (Daniel, official).

The UK has an Independent Chief Inspector of Borders and Immigration, a post established to monitor and inform Home Office borders and immigration work (ICIBI 2019), which is also informed by stakeholders gathered in a Refugee and Asylum Forum, and an Independent Advisory Group on Country Information (IAGCI), which consists of a panel of experts and practitioners that supports the work of the Independent Chief Inspector, a system lauded for its transparency and merit by one panel member (Wilf, independent advisor). The substance and detail of Home Office asylum activity is therefore regularly and independently scrutinised. Asylum and immigration policy is reviewed and challenged by civil society, through the work of NGOs such as the Refugee Council and legal forums such as the Immigration Law Practitioners Association's Refugee Working Group. Yet, despite these mechanisms, reform and improvements are frustratingly slow:

> [even] when there has been an acceptance that the change that I have recommended should be made (…) nothing seems to have happened. And it is not always obvious why; whether it has got to ministers and there is pushback or whether it has been overtaken by something else which is a higher priority. There is not always clarity about why things are taking such a long time (David, official).

The overall assessment of the Home Office is thus quite critical, as one of our survey participants explained:

> There often appears to be inconsistency, and a wide variation in the quality of HO decisions and refusal letters. These documents can be incoherent, badly written, non-sensical and contradictory. The entire system often gives the impression of being driven by targets, by racism and by the need to placate misplaced public hysteria about immigration. For LGBT people these deep flaws are exacerbated by the fact that many decision makers seem to be unable to comprehend the realities of homophobia, internalised homophobia and discrimination – both in the UK and elsewhere (S110, NGO volunteer, UK).

4.3 The National Asylum Systems

After this brief discussion, and in anticipation of many discussions in subsequent chapters, one question requires consideration: in general, can the asylum systems of the three countries under comparison be considered consistent with international and European law and policy?

4.3.2 Degree of Compliance with Supranational and International Obligations

While superficially it may appear that the protection offered by these countries to asylum claimants is in line with their international (including Refugee Convention, the ECHR and relevant UN human rights treaties) and EU law obligations, a more detailed consideration raises serious doubts.

It is clear that EU law is much more influential than international law in these domestic asylum systems. This is mostly due to the supranational nature of EU law and the principle of supremacy of EU Law (Avbelj 2011). Participation in the EU framework seems to push these countries to adhere to 'minimum standard solutions'. In other words, the necessity to comply with EU standards in the field of asylum has progressively meant setting aside other possible solutions, more respectful of the rights of asylum claimants and refugees. The consequences of this can be felt not only in relation to the rules that apply to reception conditions or the applicable procedures, where EU standards influence considerably the domestic legal frameworks, but also in relation to aspects of the RSD process. Yet, not even EU standardisation efforts are fully effective, as national and even regional standards and practices have considerable influence as well. In the words of Terry, member of the European Parliament:

> there was a resistance to, you know, having any kind of functioning system, for asylum, in place altogether. So, I mean, that's kind of what we are up against at the moment, an absolute resistance to make anything work. And it is not about taking in… a couple of hundred refugees; it is a very ideological fight that is happening right now (…) And that is why there is so much resistance and so many problems actually implementing legislation that we already have. Because in some fields, I mean, I think in some fields we really need to work legislatively, but in some things we also already have decent legislation and if it was properly implemented and enforced, the situation of many people would improve massively, but it is just not being enforced.

Thomas, a German NGO volunteer, also expressed this idea by saying:

> My experience is that, no matter what the laws are, in the administrative implementation by [German] federal states the differences are so great that the influence of European legislation would not be so great now. Because we are experiencing that many things that are normal in all other federal states are not going on in Bavaria, just because a Minister of the Interior simply instructs his authorities to do things one way or another. No matter what the laws are.

And the same problem presents itself in Italy:

> On the subject of international protection, the lack of homogeneity of the decisions taken by the [territorial] commissions and the courts is a very serious problem. If it is serious at the level of the European Union, since it has directives but then the [recognition] rates vary between 10 and 90% according to the country that examines the claim (…). Something similar, not at those levels, exists between [territorial] commissions and courts. Not only regarding how some questions are analysed, but also regarding certain countries [of origin] (…) the relevance of social integration for the purpose of issuing humanitarian permits, for example, is a very big problem of lack of homogeneity (Livio, lawyer).

This lack of homogeneity and adherence to legislative standards across Europe may well worsen with 'Brexit'. While UK governments have not questioned the UK's membership of the UN and related commitments (Braithwaite 2016), the UK's relationship with European bodies is uncertain. The decision by the UK government in 2016 to leave the EU following the referendum did not lead to any immediate withdrawal from EU asylum instruments and the UK is already not bound by some EU-wide measures: the UK is not part of the Schengen Zone, has not opted into the recast 2011 Qualification Directive or 2013 Reception Directive, and has said it will not opt into the proposed Dublin IV Regulation (Goodwill 2016). However, it is unclear the extent to which leaving the EU will reduce protection for people claiming asylum in the UK. On the one hand, '[m]ost proposals for further reform both within the UK and at an EU level have been largely regressive and are expected to become more so, as pressure to deal with the migrant crisis increases'; against that, 'without a commitment to a shared European System, in the current environment, a race to further reduce protection to a lowest common denominator of standards could ensue' (Patrick 2016). At any rate, some UK decision-makers already discount the relevance of any European jurisprudence: 'Strasbourg court doesn't bind us, it is only guidance. The only decisions that bind us in this [SOGI asylum] area are the Supreme Court['s], it is not an area that the CJEU, which is in Luxembourg, really deals with' (Adrian, judge). This is despite the fact that both the Strasbourg and Luxembourg Courts do have a significant bearing on SOGI asylum matters at a domestic level (Danisi et al. 2019; Ferreira 2021).

Even more worrying is the simultaneous likelihood that the UK government will seek 'opt-outs' from the ECHR, thus allowing it to ignore a range of human rights obligations of the ECHR system – a proposal that goes much further than the commitment to repeal the UK's Human Rights Act 1998 under the previous Prime Minister David Cameron (BBC News 2017). It is true that UK courts are not the keenest followers of Strasbourg jurisprudence (Ferreira 2015), but leaving the ECHR would mean asylum claimants in the UK would no longer benefit from the decisions of the Strasbourg Court, no matter how insufficiently or reluctantly applied they may be at times. If the UK were also not bound by decisions of the CJEU, there would be far greater scope for arbitrary decision-making in the UK in response to political and media pressures to control borders.

The UN framework, however, plays a role as well. The UNHCR, specifically, is influential in Italy, owing to its role in contributing to the decision-making in the administrative asylum adjudication bodies. This is something unique in comparison to other countries in Europe, where the UNHCR does not have this primary role owing to domestic asylum authorities controlling the RSD process themselves. Yet, the UNHCR representative is only one of the four members of these bodies, so the final decision on granting asylum is a collective one. Still, the UNHCR representative may influence the decision-making positively, considering that their mission is to protect claimants (while the state's primary aim is patently to protect its borders). It may therefore be important to retain this role for the UNHCR in the Italian context, ensuring its power and resources.

A final point is in order: the alleged existence of 'refusal quotas' or 'deportation rates'. Indeed, in relation to Germany, we were told that:

> the immigration office that is dealing with a client of ours, they recently again told me and the lawyer that they just get pressure from the government of Upper Bavaria, because they do not meet the deportation quota. (…) that fits with what Seehofer [Bavaria's internal affairs minister] so proudly said, on his 69th birthday 69 people were deported. And so, well, I think, it's also things that are partly unknown to the public, but I have the feeling that some things really happen there, at the level of immigration offices and district offices, where other forms of pressure are exerted because the political wind is changing (Sofia and Emma, NGO workers).

In the context of the UK, we were also told that 'the Home Office has targets of numbers of refusals expected (I believe this is currently around 80%). These quotas mean that the scales are heavily weighted against those seeking asylum' (S130, NGO volunteer, UK). Whether such quotas are official or mythical, enforced or indicative, they remain ingrained in people's consciences, and do nothing to enhance people's trust in the asylum system. Moreover, they run against international refugee law, which relies on humanitarian and human rights requirements (Chap. 3), and cannot depend on quotas or numerical thresholds.

Bearing in mind the concerns discussed in this section, we are now better able to understand the key aspects of the SOGI dimension of the asylum systems in Germany, Italy and UK.

4.4 SOGI Dimensions of Domestic Asylum Systems

The domestic treatment of asylum claimants – including SOGI claimants – is plagued by complex internal webs of factors that supersede EU harmonisation efforts. In some countries, such as the UK, some decision-makers are convinced that SOGI asylum adjudication 'is not an issue':

> things have moved on so much… I think that there will always be homophobia in the system, whether that is in the Home Office, or even amongst certain judges, but I think that the ethos overall in the Home Office and here [judiciary] actually is such that no one would ever, ever… express that [homophobia] or… in their work or in their speech without something happening (…). And someone would be immediately pulled up because it is so unusual (Harry, senior judge).

Yet, Amanda, an NGO worker in Brussels, also highlights how SOGI asylum domestic adjudication seems to be to some extent resistant to European developments:

> interesting how the French case law and Italian case law has stuck to the grounds [for persecution] or to their own interpretation even when CJEU case law has come along and said "no, criminalisation [is not enough for persecution to be found], legislative measures criminalising sexual orientation needs to actually be implemented and for it to be persecutory". So, so there is kind of like a stubbornness in certain countries for the better (…) in other countries (…) eastern European countries, it is still an issue and for example in Bulgaria after *X, Y and Z* and *A, B and C*, there were still flagrant violations of human dignity and not taken on board what the Court had said in *X, Y and Z* and a lack of transparency as to how decision-makers and judges were processing SOGI claims.

Often, member states make an effort to follow legally binding developments, but may lack resources and quality control mechanisms, as pointed out by Helena, an EASO staff member. Here, we explore the main SOGI dimensions of the German, Italian and UK asylum systems, with a focus on particular milestones and the use of the notion of vulnerability.[24]

4.4.1 Milestones in Policy and Guidance

In all three countries under comparison, it is currently accepted that SOGI asylum claims fall within the remit of domestic refugee law. In Germany, that has been clear since a landmark decision of the Federal Administrative Court (Bundesverwaltungsgericht) in 1988,[25] where it was decided that persecution on grounds of sexual orientation could fall under the right to asylum for political persecution ('asylerheblichen Merkmals'), enshrined in Article 16a of the Basic Law. The Federal Administrative Court decided that, under specific circumstances, the persecution of gay men in Iran could be accepted as 'political persecution'. However, this judgment, which still stands today in relation to constitutional asylum, was based on a problematic understanding of homosexuality. As Hübner (2016) argues, considering when the decision was made, in some ways it was progressive, as it drew on an understanding of sexuality as *not* 'curable', but as 'irreversible', 'inescapable' and 'fateful'. However, the Court's decision pathologised gay men in other ways, namely as not being able to control their sexual urges ('triebhaft'). Moreover, criminalisation of same-sex sexual activities was not sufficient for granting asylum, and the Court specified that criminalisation was not a sufficient ground if such norms existed to protect 'public morality' (Hübner 2016; Kalkmann 2010). In the

---

[24] For a succinct comparative overview of the SOGI asylum systems in Germany, Italy and the UK, refer to the table at http://www.sogica.org/en/case-studies/.
[25] BVerwGE, 15 March 1988, C 278.86.

case of Iran, however, the Court found that the death penalty was a very harsh punishment and disproportional to keeping public morality.[26]

This decision, on which many others have subsequently been based, introduced a distinction between homosexuals whose sexual orientation was 'irreversible' and those whose sexual orientation was only 'latent' (and who were therefore able to choose whether to be gay or not). For the latter, it implicitly denied one's right to live one's sexual orientation openly, and forced them to live 'in the closet' (Markard 2013, p. 75). The consequence of this decision was that, up to 2012, some courts based their decisions on an assessment of the 'intensity' of the irreversibility of homosexuality, and often commissioned medical and sexual 'scientific' reports to assess this (Hempel 2014, p. 42). This led to rather obscure decisions in the administrative courts (Chap. 7).[27]

The path to legal recognition of SOGI asylum claimants in Italy took a different course. Despite its potential application, Article 10(3) of the Italian Constitution has never been used in SOGI asylum cases. A joint reading of Articles 3 (on the right to equality) and 10 of the Constitution could provide for a sufficient basis to use the Constitution to grant asylum to SOGI claimants. Nonetheless, territorial commissions and judges have never adopted such an approach and, instead, have awaited statutory recognition of SOGI asylum claims, as we will discuss below.[28] In the UK, it was neither a constitutional text nor a statute that offered legal standing to SOGI asylum claims. Instead, it was the House of Lords that recognised that women in Pakistan constituted a particular social group,[29] with the same approach subsequently being applied to SOGI asylum claims.[30]

Statutory recognition of the legal standing of SOGI asylum claims across the board (as opposed to a constitutionally protected form of political asylum) can now be found in all three countries under comparison. In Germany, the granting of refugee status on the Refugee Convention ground of PSG is a fairly recent phenomenon and only took place in 2005, when Article 10(1) of the 2004 Qualification Directive was transposed into German law through the Residence Act. This also established a sounder foundation for the recognition of claims of persecution on grounds of SOGI, a move held to be 'very important' by German lawyers to overcome asylum being seen as merely connected to 'race', religion and political opinion (Gisela,

---

[26] It is worth noting that West Germany had also criminalised homosexuality for over 20 years and legalised it only in 1969 (it was decriminalised in East Germany in 1968). Moreover, in West Germany, it was argued that these laws were in place to protect morality and judgments by the Federal Administrative Court contributed to maintaining this. So, in this judgment the Court might have tried to defend its own previous jurisprudence (Hempel 2014, p. 47).

[27] For a table of SOGI asylum case law in Germany, see http://www.sogica.org/database/held-sogica-table-of-german-sogi-case-law-1988-2018-september-2018/.

[28] For a table of SOGI asylum case law in Italy, see http://www.sogica.org/database/danisi-italian-sogica-case-law-table-2019/.

[29] *Shah and Islam v Secretary of State for the Home Department*, House of Lords, 2 A.C. 629, 1999.

[30] See The Refugee or Person in Need of International Protection (Qualification) Regulations 2006, 6(e), and UKVI 2011, p. 11. For a table of SOGI asylum case law in the UK, see http://www.sogica.org/database/9513/.

lawyer). Since then, the fear of persecution by non-state actors has also been accepted in refugee claims (Hempel 2014; Kalkmann 2010). Statutory reference to SOGI in asylum law in Italy was also a consequence of the transposition of CEAS instruments, which increased considerably the 'legal consciousness' of the notion of PSG including SOGI claims (Livio, lawyer).[31] In relation to both sexual orientation and gender identity, the Italian legislator simply copied the content of the EU Qualification Directives, affirming that SOGI may be relevant for the identification of a PSG under the Refugee Convention. Finally, UK statutes also recognise the notion of PSG as enshrined in EU instruments, including a specific reference to sexual orientation.[32]

Asylum adjudication authorities sometimes develop guidelines to strengthen their decision-making in relation to certain types of claims (Sect. 4.5). Gender-related asylum guidelines were generally the precursor for SOGI-related ones. Initially developed in Canada (Aberman 2014, p. 61) and then in other countries and at UNHCR level (UNHCR 2002), gender-related asylum guidelines have thus played an important role in the absence of SOGI-specific asylum guidelines, for example, in terms of the role of private actors in persecution and social norms in the constitution of a PSG, and are still believed to be of relevance for SOGI claims, especially those made by women claimants (Neilson 2005). SOGI-specific asylum guidelines have, however, increasingly made their appearance in the international arena, and can now be found at domestic level, for example, in Canada (Dustin and Ferreira 2017) and at an international level, developed by the UNHCR (UNHCR 2012).

Neither in Germany nor in Italy is there domestic policy guidance regarding SOGI claims specifically, making international and/or gender-related asylum guidelines – where available – of value. Germany does not have any guidelines for assessing SOGI claims (BMI 2019, p. 7) and has also not generally 'implemented any gender guidelines for assessing and considering refugee claims' (Center for Gender & Refugee Studies 2014, p. 30). However, the BAMF has 'internal instructions on asylum procedure – persecution on grounds of belonging to a particular social group' (BAMF 2017). Perhaps to compensate for the lack of guidelines, the BAMF has officers who specialise in SOGI claims (Mariya, NGO worker). In Italy, despite the absence of SOGI-specific guidance, the involvement in territorial commissions of UNHCR representatives with decision-making powers seems, in practice, to have increased the application of the UNHCR SOGI guidelines. UNHCR Italy does, indeed, dedicate much attention to these claims, giving rise to good practices in some territorial commissions and organising specific trainings on this topic on behalf of the National Commission of Asylum (Chap. 6). This does not in itself afford any special protection to SOGI claims, but ensures a certain visibility to SOGI claimants in Italy. This may explain why criminalisation of same-sex conduct

---

[31] Sexual orientation was introduced by Article 8 of Legislative decree no. 251/2007 and gender identity was introduce by Article 1(f) of Legislative decree no. 18/2014 (Balboni 2012, Chapter III).
[32] Section 6, The Refugee or Person in Need of International Protection (Qualification) Regulations 2006.

in countries of origin has been seen as persecution in itself (Chap. 7). To complement UNHCR standards, Italian lawyers and decision-makers follow closely CJEU jurisprudence on SOGI asylum (Daniele, decision-maker).

Conversely, the UK Home Office has produced guidance specific to SOGI claims, consisting of the 2011 guidance on gender identity and 2016 guidance on sexual orientation (Home Office 2011, 2016a). In addition, there is a growing number of SOGI-specific Country Policy Information Notes.[33] Both sets of documents tend to show a high degree of sensitivity to the particular issues likely to affect SOGI claimants. The sexual orientation guidance, in particular, has been found to be concise, clear and sensitive (ICIBI 2014), as well as appreciated more generally: 'I quite like the guidance. In terms of [what] it does, it has actually made me learn things' (Umar, legal advisor). Admittedly, some concerns subsist with these guidance documents, such as the problematic application of 'discretion logic' (Chap. 7), the lack of a clear obligation to record SOGI asylum claims as such, and insufficient understanding of the internal nature of gender identity (Bach 2013, p. 35; ICIBI 2014, p. 11). Nonetheless, if the Home Office guidance – on SOGI and all aspects of asylum – were applied consistently to SOGI claims, in particular in light of the low threshold of proof, it is unlikely that there would be the numbers and kinds of refusals that have been reported by campaigners, journalists and advocates (APPG on Global LGBT Rights 2016, p. 54; UKLGIG 2018). This suggests a gap between Home Office guidance and its implementation by caseworkers (ICIBI 2014). On a positive note, the production of Home Office guidance is a relatively transparent process, with officials consulting on both new Asylum Policy Instructions and Country Policy Information Notes, as well as coordinating stakeholder groups with senior members of NGOs working on asylum and LGBTIQ+ protection and rights. Furthermore, lawyers make use of the UNHCR SOGI guidelines, including in the context of appeals (Upper Tier tribunal observation, London 2018).

Against this background, we will now consider how the domestic asylum systems under comparison have dealt with the notion of 'vulnerability' in the context of SOGI claims.

4.4.2 Vulnerability and SOGI Asylum

The way asylum claimants are treated throughout the asylum process depends to a great extent on whether they meet the (variable) definition of a 'vulnerable person', something we started exploring in Chap. 2. Article 21 of the Reception Directive does not offer an abstract definition of 'vulnerability', but clarifies that it includes individuals:

such as minors, unaccompanied minors, disabled people, elderly people, pregnant women, single parents with minor children, victims of human trafficking, persons with serious ill-

---

[33] https://www.gov.uk/government/collections/country-policy-and-information-notes.

nesses, persons with mental disorders and persons who have been subjected to torture, rape or other serious forms of psychological, physical or sexual violence, such as victims of female genital mutilation.[34]

Although SOGI asylum claimants are not expressly mentioned in this provision, they will fall within its remit at least when – as it is often the case – they have been victims of human trafficking, have serious illnesses or mental disorders, or have been subjected to torture, rape or other serious forms of psychological, physical or sexual violence. A doctor who provides medico-legal reports in asylum cases in the UK involving torture or abuse, estimated that 90% of the women and more than 50% of the men he saw had been raped in circumstances connected to the basis of their asylum claim; he also estimated that 25% of his clients were LGBTIQ+ (Carl, doctor with an organisation providing medico-legal reports, UK).

The reform of the CEAS instruments has prompted a discussion about replacing the notion of 'vulnerability' with that of 'specific needs', thus avoiding the risk of being perceived as 'favouring' certain claimants and focusing on tailoring the asylum system to individual needs (Ferreira 2018). This was explained by Alfred, a European Parliament member of staff, as follows:

> I think the whole notion of vulnerability is a bit left behind, because it wasn't appropriate for what we are talking about. It is about vulnerability, but it is about… it is individual assessment and sometimes you need to take a closer look at stuff.

For the time being, however, 'vulnerability' is still the legal notion used.

In Germany, apart from unaccompanied children, there is no 'requirement in law or mechanism in place to systematically identify vulnerable persons in the asylum procedure' (ECRE et al. 2019, p. 49). A medical examination takes place in the reception centres and medical staff might inform the BAMF of symptoms of trauma, but there is no specific screening and systematic procedure in place with regard to vulnerabilities. Although in 2016 the Asylum Act was amended to include the identification of vulnerability, it still fails to adequately transpose the Procedures Directive, as it only requires the BAMF to carry out the interview in an appropriate manner but not to provide specific support throughout the asylum procedure (AIDA 2017, p. 42). As there is no systematic process, it is down to the federal states to decide how they deal with the identification of vulnerabilities, and also how they define vulnerable groups. Some federal states, such as Berlin for instance, have introduced pilot schemes for the identification of vulnerabilities, so that vulnerable claimants are referred to specialised institutions (AIDA 2017, p. 43). According to information from our participants, Berlin and Mainz include SOGI claimants in the group of vulnerable claimants (Joachim, NGO worker; Frank S., legal advisor). There is no comprehensive information available on which federal states have specific procedures with regard to the identification of vulnerabilities and which include SOGI claimants (BMI 2019). Only the federal state of Rhineland-Palatinate has procedures and guidelines in place that conform to EU legislation with regard to

---

[34] This definition is repeated in Article 20(3) of the Qualification Directive (further discussion of 'vulnerability' in the context of the CEAS can be found in Brandl and Czech 2015; ECRE 2017).

4.4 SOGI Dimensions of Domestic Asylum Systems

identification and housing of vulnerable claimants (ECRE et al. 2019, p. 50). Yet, the BAMF does have some guidance in place to handle certain cases in a particularly sensitive manner, if necessary by especially trained decision-makers (Chap. 6). This includes unaccompanied children, victims of torture and traumatised asylum claimants, and victims of gender-specific persecution, which includes SOGI claimants. In a response to a parliamentary request, the government stated that the BAMF has implemented 'a concept for the identification of vulnerable persons in the asylum procedure' since 2015; however, it is not clear what this entails, apart from the fact that the 'concept serves to identify particular needs during the entire asylum procedure by all employees of the BAMF who come into contact with applicants' (BMI 2019).

In Italy, statutory norms have transposed the recast CEAS directives mentioned above, but have not gone beyond them. This means that SOGI asylum claimants are not comprehensively identified and treated as members of a vulnerable group, except if, upon individual assessment, they are recognised as victims of torture, rape or serious violence. A careful individual assessment is, however, not done systematically, owing to the large number of individuals arriving to Italy, as we heard from several participants (Chap. 5).

In the UK, the notion of vulnerability is particularly evident in relation to the Syrian Vulnerable Persons Resettlement scheme, which prioritises vulnerable people on the basis of the UN vulnerability criteria (Home Office 2017c). These include women and girls at risk, but not explicitly SOGI minorities. However, the government confirmed that '[p]ersons who are at risk due to their sexual orientation or gender identity are usually referred for resettlement using the category "Legal and Physical Protection Needs"' (Home Office 2016b).

Vulnerability, as a label, is also relevant in relation to detention. The UN Working Group on Arbitrary Detention has stated that '[d]etention of migrants in other situations of vulnerability or at risk, such as pregnant women, breastfeeding mothers, elderly persons, persons with disabilities, *lesbian, gay, bisexual, transgender and intersex persons*, or survivors of trafficking, torture and/or other serious violent crimes, must not take place' (UN Working Group on Arbitrary Detention 2018, our emphasis). Yet, there are clear violations of this guidance in the European context. While Germany and Italy are bound by the current Reception Directive, which restricts the use of detention, the UK is only bound by the original Reception Directive, which does not refer to detention.

In Germany, although detention rates have been traditionally low, there are no statistics available on detention of asylum claimants, as federal states do not disaggregate data for detained foreigners and claimants for international protection (ECRE et al. 2019, pp. 96–97).

In Italy, asylum claimants are generally not detained, but their liberty may be restricted if, on the basis of an individual assessment, it is believed that there is a risk of escape from Italy.[35] Yet, this seems to happen rarely: none of the SOGI

---

[35] Article 6(d) of Legislative decree no. 142, 18 August 2015.

claimants we interviewed had been detained and none of our other participants mentioned cases of detention. Moreover, emergency situations due to the flow of people arriving to Italy have led to rethinking some aspects of the Italian reception system, with the establishment of a number of centres of identification and expulsion.[36] In line with the 2015 EU 'European Agenda on Migration' (European Commission 2015), the aim has been to accelerate as much as possible returns of 'irregular immigrants', as well as of those people whose request for international protection is rejected. The 2018 Italian reform increased the maximum period of deprivation of liberty allowed for immigrants in repatriation centres from 90 to 180 days. Running the risk of violating Italy's international human rights obligations, this reform also introduced the possibility of detaining people claiming asylum in 'hotspots' for 30 days, in order to ascertain their identity and nationality.

Finally, the UK does detain migrants and asylum claimants, and currently stands out as the only EU member state to detain migrants indefinitely, something which is the focus of campaigning by asylum and human rights advocates.[37] The UK has one of the largest networks of detention centres – or Immigration Removal Centres – in Europe and, within them, people claiming or who have claimed asylum are the largest group of detainees (Singer 2019, pp. 6–7). The government-commissioned, but independent, Shaw Report found that '[t]he time that many people spend in detention remains deeply troubling' (Shaw 2016, p. viii). The Parliamentary Joint Committee on Human Rights recommended the introduction of a 28-day time limit 'to end the trauma of indefinite detention' (Joint Committee on Human Rights 2019, p. 3), but the Home Office rejected this recommendation by arguing that 'an immigration detention time limit of 28 days would severely constrain the ability to maintain balanced and effective immigration control, potentially incentivise significant abuse of the system, and put the public at risk' (Nokes 2019).

Following the Shaw Report, transgender and intersex – but not LGB – people were identified as being 'particularly vulnerable to harm in detention' (Home Office 2018a; UKVI 2016). As the Home Office points out in its policy on the processing of asylum claims in detention, the High Court 'did not find sexual orientation or those with claims based on sexual orientation to be unsuitable for detention or for asylum consideration in detention' (Home Office 2017d, sec. 3.8.3). Against this, the Equal Treatment Bench Book states that '[t]here is substantial evidence that LGB asylum seekers are particularly vulnerable while held in detention, experiencing discrimination, harassment and violence from other detainees and members of staff' (Judicial College 2018, p. 223). The report on asylum accommodation by the Independent Chief Inspector in 2018 also identified LGBTIQ+ people as 'particularly vulnerable' and on that basis recommended that the government keep data on them and review the appropriateness of providing 'no choice' accommodation and

---

[36] The plan has been announced under the motto 'zero tolerance' for irregular third-country nationals (Tgcom24 2016).

[37] For example, campaigns by Liberty (https://www.libertyhumanrights.org.uk/campaigning/oppose-indefinite-detention) and Detention Action (https://detentionaction.org.uk/get-involved/end-indefinite-detention/).

4.5 Refugee Status Determination (RSD) Outcomes and Life After the Decision...   119

forced bedroom-sharing (ICIBI 2018, p. 14). In its response, the Home Office accepted all these recommendations (Home Office 2018c, p. 6), but in 2019 a parliamentary committee inquiry into immigration detention again identified particular concerns for LGB people in detention who are not recognised as 'adults at risk' and urged the government to do more in implementing Equality/LGBTIQ+ Officers in detention centres:

> We recommend that the Government should recognise that LGBTQI+ people are vulnerable in immigration detention, thereby extending the recognition that it already affords to trans and intersex people to all LGBTQI+ individuals. Secondly, the Home Office should monitor and publish statistics on the number of LGBTQI+ people it detains (House of Commons Home Affairs Committee 2019, pp. 20–21).

However, in a report published the following year, the Independent Chief Inspector found 'inconsistencies across the Home Office in understanding vulnerability and the impact on certain groups, particularly LGBTQI+ detainees' (Bolt 2020, p. 31). The same report noted the creation in 2016 of the Detention Gatekeeper function, which included protecting 'potentially vulnerable individuals from being detained when it is not appropriate to do so', while also stating that that data on the number of LGBTIQ+ persons detained was not centrally recorded on Home Office systems (Bolt 2020, pp. 34 and 40). This shows firstly a lack of clarity about which individuals within the LGBTIQ+ group are defined as vulnerable and should therefore not be detained, and secondly a failure to record the information that would make it possible to apply any such criteria.

Despite these efforts, striking differences between the countries under comparison are patent, as it will be explored in Chap. 8. Striking differences can also be observed in the life of claimants after the RSD process is concluded, as we will now consider.

4.5 Refugee Status Determination (RSD) Outcomes and Life After the Decision on a SOGI Asylum Claim

The standards adopted in substantive decision-making are strikingly different between and within the countries under comparison. A more detailed analysis of these differences is given in Chap. 7. Here, we explore more generally the different potential outcomes of the RSD process, as well as whether guidance is available to decision-makers in reaching those outcomes.

In terms of outcomes of the asylum claim, it is worth noting from the outset that, although Germany, Italy and the UK have a history of granting refugee status, subsidiary protection or humanitarian protection ('prohibition of deportation' in Germany) to claimants, this triad is under threat. Humanitarian protection in Italy constituted a domestic form of international protection meant as a residual possibility at authorities' disposal to offer a 'permit to stay' ('permesso di soggiorno') to those claimants who could not satisfy the requirements to be granted refugee status or subsidiary protection. It was granted to foreign citizens who showed 'serious reasons, in particular of a humanitarian nature or resulting from constitutional or international obligations of Italy',[38] and it allowed for a permit between 6 months and 2 years (usually a 1 year, renewable permit). The Italian 2018 reform removed the possibility of granting humanitarian protection, and this is in potential violation of the asylum constitutional norm (Curi 2019).[39] The 2018 reform has, nonetheless, introduced a special residence permit for specific cases based on similar humanitarian considerations (for those in need of medical care, victims of domestic violence or serious labour exploitation, those coming from a country that is in a temporary situation of disaster and those who have performed acts of 'high civil value').

The triad of refugee status / subsidiary protection / humanitarian protection still holds, however, in other EU member states. In the UK, for example, positive determinations by UKVI will either consist of refugee status, humanitarian protection (generally under Articles 3 or 8 ECHR), discretionary or other leave to remain. As an alternative to refugee status, humanitarian protection may be granted in situations where refugee protection is refused, but it would be unsafe to return claimants to their country of origin. This effectively covers subsidiary protection as well, and is less common (Home Office 2017a).

Differences between the asylum systems in the countries under comparison are also obvious in terms of the existence and use of policy guidance, produced and used to reach RSD decisions. The UK Home Office, for example, has developed a range of policy documents that guide decision-making in relation to a range of 'categories' of claimants and countries of origin. Although these Home Office policy documents are generally perceived as being of good quality, including by decision-makers in other countries, in fact:

> … you have these products which, are often quite sort of complex and nuanced and… then you have within those products something which says policy, and so you have a relatively junior, relatively inexperienced caseworker trying to make a decision usually under time pressure, and they come across this thing which says "policy", which effectively pares down to the basics a much more complex set of issues, and, essentially, in many instances, [it] is an argument for safe return. So… so the caseworker goes straight to that and thinks "ok, it is obviously safe to return." (David, official)

On the other hand, some countries, like Italy, do not produce any such policy guidance. Somewhere in-between, as in relation to many other matters explored above, in Germany the BAMF does produce some internal instructions. Importantly, these take intersectionality into account to a certain extent, by explaining that

---

[38] Article 19, Testo Unico Immigrazione – Law 25 July 1998, no. 286. There is no exact definition of the circumstances that may lead to the recognition of this protection, but it should be viewed as a 'remedial solution' for asylum claimants who, despite not satisfying the criteria for the recognition of refugee status or subsidiary protection, are nonetheless in a vulnerable position (for example, HIV-positive asylum claimants, or people arriving from seriously unstable countries or with serious human rights violations).

[39] This reform cannot, however, be applied retrospectively, so any asylum claim lodged before the entry into force of this reform can still benefit from humanitarian protection: Supreme Court, judgment no. 4890, 23 January 2019.

asylum decisions should take 'into account the individual situation as well as the personal circumstances of the applicant, including factors such as family and social background, gender and age' (BAMF 2017).

From the three countries where we focused our research, the UK was the first (and so far the only one) to produce statistics on the number of SOGI asylum applications, grants and refusals. Following pressure to do so dating back to 2009 (Bell and Hansen 2009, p. 65), in 2011 Home Office staff were instructed to flag claims based on sexual orientation (not gender identity) on the Home Office database, but the Vine report in 2014 found a 'woefully poor level of compliance' in this matter, with only 36% of the 116 sexual orientation asylum cases identified by John Vine, the Chief Inspector of Borders and Immigration, flagged as such (ICIBI 2014, p. 43). Based on the gap between the number of sexual orientation cases flagged by the Home Office and the number identified by the Vine report research, the Chief Inspector estimated in 2014 that 3.9% of asylum claims may be on sexual orientation grounds – three times higher than the 1.4% suggested by the Home Office (ICIBI 2014, p. 43). The Home Office first published 'experimental' statistics for asylum claims based on sexual orientation – but not gender identity – in November 2017 and again a year later (Home Office 2018b). Although these statistics do not show whether sexual orientation was the sole basis of an application or indicate whether sexual orientation had any bearing on the final determination, these figures are illuminating. First, they show the countries with the highest number of applications where sexual orientation was raised as a factor, namely Pakistan, Nigeria and Bangladesh, thus again countries where same-sex conduct is criminalised (Ramón Mendos 2019). Second, they show fluctuations, with a significant drop in the number of sexual orientation based grants of international protection compared to other asylum claims: from 39% to 22% during the 3-year period (2015–2017), while the overall fall in grants was proportionately less, from 40% to 32%. This period also saw an increase in claims with a sexual orientation component from 5.4% to 7.3% of all claims.

Despite their weaknesses, these 'experimental' statistics for the first time provide legal practitioners, advisors and academics with a baseline for assessing discrepancies in decision-making in cases involving claimants' sexual orientation and show the need to publish similar statistics for gender identity-based claims.

Despite the lack of statistics, it is clear that in Germany and Italy there is a significant number of SOGI asylum claimants as well, something clearly suggested by the overall number of participants in our own fieldwork (Chap. 2) and their testimonies explored throughout these volumes. In Germany, we were told that a survey of 150 asylum claimants in 2017 indicated that 40% received a positive decision from the BAMF, that is, at the administrative level (Leon, LGBTIQ+ community project staff). Other participants also estimated that about around a quarter of lesbian asylum claimants they assist obtain some form of international protection (Sofia and Emma, NGO workers). In Italy, participants also offered some estimates, namely that two out of ten asylum appeals relate to sexual orientation (Silvana, Judge), and that 50% of SOGI asylum claims are successful at appeal level (Nazarena, lawyer).

Even in the absence of reliable statistics, it is evident that a number of SOGI asylum claimants will be successful and a number will not. It is apposite to look briefly here at the kinds of international protection that SOGI asylum claimants tend to receive and what kind of rights are connected to these, as well as to what happens when all avenues are exhausted and claimants are left without any protective legal status.

If the outcome of an asylum claim is eventually positive, the decision may lead to the recognition of refugee status or what materially are subsidiarity protection or humanitarian protection (in the case of Italy post-2018 reform, special residence permit, and in the case of the UK, also discretionary or other leave to remain).

In Germany, when granted international protection, SOGI claimants seem to be mostly granted refugee status. Nonetheless, even if claimants are granted refugee status, that status initially only lasts for 3 years, which – compared to Italy and the UK – fosters greater instability. In the UK, as previously stated, there is no official data on gender identity-based applications and the 'experimental statistics' for LGB decisions give no breakdown of the form of protection granted, distinguishing only between 'grants' and 'refusals'. However, in the UK, overall the vast majority of positive decisions of all asylum claims are grants of refugee status, generally entailing leave to remain for 5 years initially, before then leading to indefinite leave. A smaller proportion of claimants are granted humanitarian protection and an even smaller proportion granted discretionary leave to remain.[40]

In Italy, despite an overall rate of recognition of refugee status of only 7% (Sect. 4.1), the legal status that seems to be most commonly granted to SOGI claimants is also refugee status. Moreover, even if of dubious legal correctness, subsidiary protection seems to be favoured in cases of reduced credibility of claimants from countries where there is homo/transphobic legislation (Maurizio, judge; Mara, lawyer). Humanitarian protection seems to be favoured for SOGI claimants by some territorial commissions (Nicola and Giulio, LGBTIQ+ group volunteers), in particular regarding trans claimants from Latin American (where legislation often protects SOGI minorities, but rates of violence against them are high), who have worked in Italy as sex workers for several years (Roberto, decision-maker; Valentina, social worker). In these ways, rather than being doctrinal and uniform, international protection decisions in Italy seem to be entirely contextual (Mara, lawyer). With the 2018 reform and removal of humanitarian protection, decisions are likely to become even less favourable and more contextual.

Some pre-2018 reform asylum decisions in Italy did grant humanitarian protection to SOGI claimants, perhaps as a compromise – when in doubt – between offering full-fledged refugee protection and returning SOGI claimants to their countries of origin. In the case of refugee status, and in line with the rights already provided by the Refugee Convention, the Italian legislation grants to refugees a broad

---

[40] In 2018, 33% of initial decisions were positive, of which 26% were refugee status and the other 7% were for humanitarian protection, discretionary or other leave to remain; 67% of decisions were refusals (Refugee Council 2019).

protection, which is wider when vulnerable people are involved.[41] This entails (even if only on paper, as we will see in Chaps. 8 and 10): a renewable 5-year permit to stay; the right to work without discrimination in comparison to Italian citizens; the right to access the education system, and the social and health care systems without discrimination of any kind; and the right to family reunification.

From a social integration perspective, some strides have been made in the countries under comparison, but far from enough. In Germany, the Integration Act was introduced in 2016,[42] 'which on the one hand promotes the integration of people into society and the labour market and on the other hand commits them to their own integration efforts ("promote and demand")' (BMWi 2019). The Act aims to give refugees better training opportunities and a clearer framework, and facilitates companies that want to train and employ refugees. It includes the '3 + 2' regulation, which gives claimants who only have a 'Duldung' ('tolerated stay') the opportunity to do a 3-year apprenticeship and are allowed two more years of stay if they stay in the same occupation. When claimants obtain refugee status, they are entitled to full benefits and are obliged to find their own accommodation (however, they can usually stay in the asylum accommodation until they have found a place). The Integration Act also introduced the 'Wohnsitzauflage' (residence regulations), which require refugees to live in a particular federal state, and even in a particular area for 3 years if they, or their spouse, are not in training, working or studying (Deutscher Bundestag 2019). With this regulation, the federal government in fact takes away freedom from refugees and further increases their social isolation. This can be particularly negative for SOGI claimants, for whom social isolation is often a significant problem, as they have to live in very remote areas without any access to LGBTIQ+ communities and groups (Chap. 8).

In Italy, life after being granted international protection is very often no easier than before. Support can be very limited, and the accommodation enjoyed as asylum claimant may no longer be available. Refugee integration policies are of limited reach, and do not specifically address SOGI refugees. Only in 2007 was there a serious attempt to introduce a refugee integration strategy.[43] Italian authorities are now obliged to produce, at least every 2 years, a National Plan with guidelines for interventions in areas where refugee integration measures have greater chances of success. These interventions should include specific programmes for access to employment, health services, housing and education, as well as for improving knowledge of Italian language and combating discrimination that refugees may suffer. Representatives of the UNHCR and of the Italian Equal Opportunities Office are involved in these new initiatives, with the prospect of significant developments benefitting SOGI refugees. Yet, no strategic plan has yet been drawn up. This lack of strategic plan may also have contributed to private actors playing a significant role in this area. Although Catholic-led entities are generally dominant in refugee sup-

---

[41] At least on paper: Article 19, Legislative decree no. 251, 27 November 2007.
[42] 5 August 2016, Federal Law Gazette I, no. 39, p. 1939.
[43] Article 29, Legislative decree no. 251, 27 November 2007.

port, LGBTIQ+ associations are also increasingly involved in the development of specific projects aimed at helping SOGI refugees in the post-RSD stage (Chaps. 8 and 9).

Similarly, in the UK, once claimants are granted refugee status or some form of leave to remain, they are often confronted with entirely new problems. Newly recognised refugees have a 'move on' or grace period of only 28 days before their asylum support ends, at which point many become homeless and have to turn to friends and family – something which may be harder for SOGI minorities, leaving them more dependent on food banks and charities (Basedow and Doyle 2016; House of Commons Home Affairs Committee 2017, p. 43). Integration is the point at which policy differences across the UK are clearest. The UK consists of England, Scotland, Wales and Northern Ireland. Asylum and immigration policy is reserved – meaning it is the responsibility of the UK government and the application and decision-making process is the same across the UK.[44] However, the Scottish, Welsh and Northern Irish legislatures and executives have responsibility for integration. There is no data on where claimants granted international protection eventually settle, nor on individuals whose applications are refused but do not leave the UK. Nor is there any overarching UK refugee integration strategy, except for those accepted as part of the Syrian Vulnerable Persons Resettlement Scheme (Doyle 2014, pp. 6 and 10). The UNHCR has called for a national strategy for refugee integration (UNHCR 2017, p. 27), regardless of how individuals arrive in the UK, as has the All Party Parliamentary Group on Refugees, which also called for the post of 'Minister for Refugees' to be created (APPG on Refugees 2017, p. 56). A government-commissioned report on integration in general in 2016 did discuss asylum and immigration. However, this was not in relation to how new people can be supported in integrating, but rather viewing them as a factor relevant to the *lack* of integration in British society, with asylum claimants' accommodation through dispersal in poorer areas cited in relation to the increase in 'local feelings of unfairness over pressure on housing and other resources and can exacerbate community tensions' (Casey 2016, p. 35). Moreover, the Home Affairs Committee has pointed to the discrepancy between people's treatment depending on whether they arrive through the Syrian Vulnerable Persons Resettlement Scheme or not:

> The introduction of the Syrian Vulnerable Persons Resettlement Programme means that the UK now has a system which differentiates between refugees in terms of the services they receive based on the country of origin and the process through which they arrived in the country. We believe that this is inappropriate and that the same support should be available for refugees who transfer from the asylum system as those who arrive under a resettlement programme (House of Commons Home Affairs Committee 2017, p. 44).

In contrast to the UK overall or England, both the Welsh and Scottish governments have introduced refugee integration strategies or policies. The Welsh plan makes no mention of SOGI refugees, but it has a commitment to support survivors

---

[44] With minor differences – for example, the Court of Session in Scotland replaces the Court of Appeal in England and Wales.

4.5 Refugee Status Determination (RSD) Outcomes and Life After the Decision...

of sexual violence (Welsh Government 2019). The Scottish strategy identifies concerns in relation to SOGI claimants and makes a commitment to '[s]tart dialogue with LGBTI organisations in regard to particular issues faced by LGBTI refugees and asylum seekers, and raised through the New Scots engagement process in relation to accommodation and issues of safety' (Scottish Government 2013, p. 42). Scotland has also played a leading role in welcoming Syrian refugees. In Northern Ireland, a Refugee Integration Strategy – separate to Northern Ireland's Race Equality Scheme – was recommended and a draft for consultation was reported to be in development (Office of the First Minister and Deputy First Minister 2015, p. 15). However, no strategy has been published and integration is seen to be a particular challenge in Northern Ireland in light of its history as a divided society (Potter 2014, p. 14).

A priority for claimants granted international protection is often bringing family members to join them, using their right to family reunification. Although often neglected – and even detrimental to their claims (Chap. 7) – SOGI claimants often have (same- or opposite-sex) partners and children, with whom they wish to reunite. EU CEAS instruments recognise the right to family reunification with 'family members'.[45] 'Family members' categorically include spouses and (unmarried and 'under age') children, but only include unmarried partners 'in a duly attested stable long-term relationship' and registered partners upon member states' discretion.[46] This degree of discretion translates into different legal rights for SOGI asylum claimants in different EU member states and a disadvantaged position compared with heterosexual and cis-gender asylum claimants. This is the case even if it is recognised that EU member states must ensure the maintenance of family unity and must therefore give residence permits to family members (de Schutter 2009, p. 94). The current legal framework has thus been considered inadequate, because it relies on the nuclear, heteronormative model of families, and children are the proof of a stable relationship in many member states, which may be less applicable for same-sex relationships (Helena, EASO staff member). In any case, there is no clear data on whether and to what extent the right to family reunification is enjoyed by SOGI refugees.

In Germany, family reunification rights have been restricted in the case of subsidiary protection, which is the status most commonly granted to Syrian refugees (Nina, legal advisor). Family reunification for beneficiaries of subsidiary protection was suspended between March 2016 and July 2018 and then curtailed to 1000 visas a month to be decided on humanitarian grounds (AIDA 2017, pp. 22 and 100). In Italy too, the right to family reunification is respected, entailing the possibility for family members to obtain a permit to stay, but the limited recognition of same-sex relationships compared to other EU member states clearly translates into a more precarious position of SOGI claimants in relation to heterosexual and cis-gender

---

[45] Articles 9 ff, Council Directive 2003/86/EC of 22 September 2003 on the right to family reunification, OJ L 251, 03/10/2003 P. 0012–0018 (Family Reunification Directive).

[46] Articles 4 and 10 of the Family Reunification Directive.

asylum claimants (Giuseppe, lawyer). Conversely, the UK, possessing the broadest legal framework for SOGI minorities of the three countries under comparison, also frames the right to family reunification in broader terms. That means that the UK government allows same-sex spouses to join individuals granted refugee status (but not subsidiary protection), and allows the same right to same-sex partners when they are civil partners or have lived together in a relationship akin to marriage or a civil partnership for two or more years.[47] Yet, given that most SOGI asylum claims are made because an individual was not or would not be able to establish a durable same-sex relationship in the country of origin, SOGI minorities are invariably treated less favourably than heterosexual and cis-gender asylum claimants in relation to family reunification. To address this to some extent, Home Office guidance states that when the standard requirements for family reunification are not met, the application must be refused, but:

> [c]onsideration must then be given to the family exceptional circumstance guidance or any compassionate factors which may warrant a grant of leave outside the rules, including whether the requirement to live together would have put a same-sex or unmarried couple in danger (Home Office 2019, p. 16).

Despite this statement, none of our participants had been granted refugee status and subsequently been given family reunion with a partner. Securing family reunification rights has, in any case, been made more difficult by the removal of legal aid from family reunion cases (APPG on Refugees 2017, p. 56). The Refugees (Family Reunion) Bill [HL] introduced in 2018 includes a 'civil or unmarried partner' in the definition of family member, but without addressing the particular evidentiary problems that exist in establishing such family relations for SOGI refugees.

For individuals who have been denied any form of international protection and reached the end of the legal road, individual experiences vary and are also enormously difficult to research. Claimants may be detained – in particular in the UK – and returned to their country of origin. Or, if substantial grounds exist for believing that they may be at risk of torture or ill-treatment in their country of origin, they may be given some form of leave to remain, in light of the jurisprudence of the Strasbourg Court on Article 3 ECHR and the principle of non-refoulement (Ferreira 2021), and domestic constitutional provisions (Salerno 2010). In none of the countries under comparison are there figures giving a breakdown of the number or proportion of SOGI asylum claims that exhaust their legal avenues or information about what happens to people in that situation – whether they remain in the country supported by friends, family or community organisations, become destitute, try to reach another European country or are returned.

---

[47] Part 11, paragraph 352A, of the Immigration Rules HC 395.

4.6 From Policy to Law, from Law to Practice

This chapter has allowed us to map out the key instruments and guidelines that affect SOGI asylum claimants, including in the fields of general SOGI, general asylum and specific SOGI asylum matters. A good degree of similarity was expected, in light of the EU CEAS, but against this expectation, we found significant and striking differences. Governmental policies have translated into different legal frameworks, and law and policy options are implemented in different ways, out of political choice and/or resource limitations. The next chapters will bring out in stark ways how practice differs from country to country (regardless of similarities on 'paper') and even within the same country (depending on the governance system, actors involved and a range of other circumstances).

The insufficient human and material resources invested in the asylum system play a key role in this debate. Asylum systems tend to be massively under-resourced at all levels (Noah, NGO social worker, Germany). The incredible pressures on asylum systems prompt some participants to suggest that many claimants in the system should be re-directed to other paths, such as work permits, educational visas, etc. (Filippo, senior judge). Such suggestions – no matter how sensible – would undoubtedly be met by many policy-makers across Europe with strong resistance, for fear of creating 'pull factors'.

The situation is further complicated by the ongoing Brexit process. While this may represent an opportunity for CEAS to be strengthened without the reluctant presence of the UK, it may also translate into the loss of an ally of SOGI rights. As Terry, member of the European Parliament, told us:

> on the one side Britain has actually been a very problematic… player in the whole question of… asylum policies, so has been very hesitant to adopt any kind of progressive asylum policies, not really wanting to be part of the whole system to start with (…) and not really wanting any common European standards that are, you know, founded on human rights, for example. (…) but when it comes to SOGI and when it comes to, you know, a more broader discussion about sexual orientation and gender identity, I have the impression that (…) many of the [UK European Parliament] members are more progressive than the average. So when it comes, for example, [to] pushing for giving special status for people because of sexual orientation and gender identity… we have met a lot of support (…) And that's why now with Brexit (…) this might actually impact… also the power division in the Parliament, and I guess in the Council, as well, on this kind of questions, which has positive and negative impacts…

This resonates with what scholars have argued (Danisi et al. 2019). Jean, also member of the European Parliament, was of a similar view, stating that:

> I am worried that the UK asylum policy will become more restrictive (…) That said, I mean, I know there is quite a degree of criticism about the way in which the UK's system has worked on SOGI claims, but I do think that it's moved further forward than a number of other EU member states, and because I think the UK (…) are actually quite willing to stand up for rights in that area. I think they are also quite important in the European asylum system as a whole. (…) there is quite an important sort of progressive voice there, which is potentially going to be missing from the European asylum discussion generally and that, I think, is worrying.

What is also clear is that Brexit may bring about the end of the involvement of the UK with the Dublin system (Chap. 6).[48] As suggested by a European Commission staff member we interviewed, leaving the Dublin system would make it more difficult for the UK to limit the overall number of asylum claimants reaching its territory. This may also translate into more SOGI asylum claimants reaching the UK, which may play in their favour, if for a particular reason they favour presenting their claim in the UK as opposed to another EU member state.

While administrative asylum backlogs seem to be diminishing owing to reduced arrival of claimants in Europe, there is a high number of appeals against negative decisions, which increases courts' and tribunals' backlogs; additionally, the high rate of successful appeals seem to indicate poor decision-making standards (AIDA 2017, p. 11). Some will counter-argue, in the case of the UK, for example, that:

> the Home Office, the sort of knee jerk response from the Home Office in relation to the success rates is that essentially the majority are all about new evidence. So, it is not that we made a mistake or we made a misjudgement in the process, everything along the way was correct at the time that it was decided, and then at the last minute somebody chucks something else in and that is what turns the decision. (…) I don't know whether it is true or not, but I don't think the department does either, because I don't think there is any real analysis going on with that to, to get, to take comfort from that being the case (Daniel, official).

Importantly, decision-making standards are ever-changing. For example, as Barbara (lawyer, Germany) shared with us, while CJEU jurisprudence may have initially prompted a more responsive and generous approach to SOGI claims in Germany, the BAMF soon started to worry that there might be too many claims, so they changed their approach again to focus on 'asylum relevance'.

More generally, local conditions remain powerful determinants of SOGI asylum adjudication, influenced by different degrees of societal tolerance, awareness of the authorities and domestic policies on SOGI matters. As Alfred, staff member of the European Parliament, put it, 'we feel that among Western European member states… there is much less of a problem with this [protection of SOGI asylum claimants in CEAS] than some Eastern European member states'. Although the overall picture may be more complex, this points to significant differences within the EU on this matter:

> if you have a group of member states that doesn't even want to acknowledge the fact that there is something in the notion of gender, it is very hard to push a progressive agenda when it comes to sexual orientation and gender identity (Terry, member of the European Parliament).

In some cases, xenophobia, misogyny and homo/bi/transphobia also combine with toxic results:

---

[48] Regulation (EU) No 604/2013 of the European Parliament and of the Council of 26 June 2013 establishing the criteria and mechanisms for determining the Member State responsible for examining an application for international protection lodged in one of the Member States by a third-country national or a stateless person, OJ L 180, 29.6.2013, p. 31–59.

some of the member states which are more resistant to actually having a more welcoming policy towards asylum seekers… will also be the ones that may tend to be more resistant as well to the whole, the whole gender and sexual orientation sort of dimension too (Jean, member of the European Parliament).

Rising populism and political extremism across Europe have rendered the experiences of people seeking asylum more and more difficult, affecting SOGI claimants in particular ways, for example, when translated into homophobic and transphobic crimes. There are some attempts to address this increasing hostility: the UK government's 2018 LGBT Action Plan included a commitment to 'continue our work to ensure that the needs of all LGBT claimants are met in the asylum process, regardless of whether their claim was lodged on this basis' (Government Equalities Office 2018a, p. 17). There is, however, no reference to SOGI asylum claimants in the 2019 annual progress report (Government Equalities Office 2019), which was published in the context of charges of hypocrisy against the Home Office for publicly supporting Pride while deporting a gay rugby player to a country where he faced an extensive prison sentence.[49] Moreover, this 'LGBT-friendly' rhetoric does not tally with policies hostile to migrants and refugees:

because of Brexit, you know most people don't want to think about migration, asylum seekers, do they. So, I think there is a lot of hostility, because they can say "well, we are representing popular opinion". Governments will chase the poll… (Gary and Debbie, NGO workers, UK)

More generally, there is still (and perhaps increasingly) a divide between the treatment offered to SOGI asylum claimants and 'native' SOGI minorities, leaving us very far from an asylum system informed by the human rights, feminist, queer and intersectional approaches delineated in Chap. 3. The overlaps between the fights for rights by these two groups are barely acknowledged, and alliances are still the exception, which leaves many synergies unexplored. As the remaining chapters in these volumes show, this leaves SOGI claimants exposed to abuse and injustice, perpetrated both by public and private actors across Europe. The fact that humanitarian visas – allowing people to flee for safety by travelling documented, for example, through 'humanitarian corridors' facilitated by the Community of Sant'Egidio (Valentina, social worker, Italy) – are not regulated at a European level or generally issued by domestic authorities, makes people's journeys to Europe all the more perilous. To this we now turn in Chap. 5.

References

Aberman, T. (2014). Gendered perspectives on refugee determination in Canada. *Refuge: Canada's Journal on Refugees,* 30(2), 57–66.

AGI. (2018). *Quante unioni civili sono state celebrate da quando la legge è in vigore.* AGI. https://www.agi.it/cronaca/unioni_civili_celebrate-3889453/news/2018-05-12/

---

[49] http://www.sogica.org/en/life_stories/kens-story-when-my-asylum-application-was-denied-i-felt-cold-and-hopeless-as-though-my-life-were-over/.

AIDA – Asylum Information Database. (2017). *Country report: Germany*. AIDA – Asylum Information Database. http://www.asylumineurope.org/sites/default/files/report-download/aida_de_2017update.pdf

AIDA – Asylum Information Database, & ECRE – European Council on Refugees and Exiles. (2019). *Germany: A controversial law package passes the Parliament*. AIDA – Asylum Information Database. https://www.asylumineurope.org/news/14-06-2019/germany-controversial-law-package-passes-parliament-1

Amnesty International. (2016). *Hotspot Italy: How EU's Flagship Approach Leads to Violations of Refugee and Migrant Rights*. Amnesty International. https://www.amnesty.org/en/documents/eur30/5004/2016/en/

Anci, Caritas, Cittalia, Fondazione Caritas Migrantes, & UNHCR. (2016). *Rapporto sulla protezione internazionale in Italia*. www.anci.it/Contenuti/Allegati/Rapporto%20protezione%20internazionale%202016.pdf

APPG on Global LGBT Rights. (2016). *The UK's stance on international breaches of LGBT rights*. http://www.lgbtconsortium.org.uk/files/lgbt/downloads/APPG%20LGBT%20Report.pdf

APPG on Refugees. (2017). *Refugees welcome? The experience of new refugees in the UK*. Refugee Council. https://www.refugeecouncil.org.uk/information/resources/refugees-welcome-the-experience-of-new-refugees-in-the-uk/

Arachi, A. (2018). *Il ministro Fontana: 'Le famiglie gay? Non esistono'*. Corriere della Sera. https://www.corriere.it/politica/18_giugno_02/lorenzo-fontana-famiglie-gay-non-esistono-ora-piu-bambini-meno-aborti-abc3cae2-65d4-11e8-b063-cd4146153181.shtml

Avbelj, M. (2011). Supremacy or primacy of EU law: (Why) does it matter? *European Law Journal, 17*(6), 744–763.

Bach, J. (2013). Assessing transgender asylum claims. *Forced Migration Review, 42*, 34–36.

Balboni, M. (2012). *La protezione internazionale in ragione del genere, dell'orientamento sessuale e dell'identità di genere*. Torino: Giappichelli.

BAMF – Bundesamt für Migration und Flüchtlinge. (2016). *Asylgeschäftsbericht 12/2016*. http://www.bamf.de/SharedDocs/Anlagen/DE/Downloads/Infothek/Statistik/Asyl/201612-statistik-anlage-asyl-geschaeftsbericht.html

BAMF – Bundesamt für Migration und Flüchtlinge. (2017). *Dienstanweisung Asylverfahren – Verfolgung wegen Zugehörigkeit zu einer bestimmten sozialen Gruppe, DA-Asyl Stand*. https://www.proasyl.de/wp-content/uploads/2015/12/DA-Asyl-April-2017.pdf

BAMF – Bundesamt für Migration und Flüchtlinge. (2018a). *Asylgeschäftsbericht 12/2018*. http://www.bamf.de/SharedDocs/Anlagen/DE/Downloads/Infothek/Statistik/Asyl/201812-statistik-anlage-asyl-geschaeftsbericht.html

BAMF – Bundesamt für Migration und Flüchtlinge. (2018b). *Das Bundesamt in Zahlen 2017*. http://www.bamf.de/SharedDocs/Anlagen/DE/Publikationen/Broschueren/bundesamt-in-zahlen-2017.html

Barrett, D. (2013). *Theresa May splits border agency to end 'secretive and defensive' culture*. https://www.telegraph.co.uk/news/uknews/immigration/9954974/Theresa-May-splits-border-agency-to-end-secretive-and-defensive-culture.html

Basedow, J., & Doyle, L. (2016). *England's forgotten refugees: Out of the fire and into the frying pan*. London: Refugee Council.

BBC News. (2017). *Human rights won't stop terror fight—May*. https://www.bbc.com/news/election-2017-40181444

Bell, M., & Hansen, C. (2009). *Over not out. The housing and homelessness issues specific to lesbian, gay, bisexual and transgender asylum seekers*. London: Metropolitan Support Trust.

Benvenuti, M. (2010). Andata e ritorno per il diritto di asilo costituzionale. *Diritto, Immigrazione, Cittadinanza* XII, February: 36–58.

BMI – Bundesministerium des Innern, für Bau und Heimat. (2019). *Kleine Anfrage der Abgeordneten Ulla Jelpke u.a. Und der Fraktion DIE LINKE: Situation von LSBTI-Geflüchteten (BT-Drucksache19/10308)*. https://www.ulla-jelpke.de/wp-content/uploads/2019/06/19_10308-LSBTI-Gefl%C3%BCchtete.pdf

References

BMWi – Bundesministerium für Wirtschaft und Energie. (2019). *Geflüchtete Menschen erfolgreich integrieren: Maßnahmen und Initiativen*. https://www.bmwi.de/Redaktion/DE/Artikel/Wirtschaft/fluechtlingspolitik.html

Bolt, D. (2020). *Annual inspection of 'Adults at Risk in Immigration Detention' (2018–19)*. Independent Chief Inspector of Borders and Immigration. https://www.gov.uk/government/publications/annual-inspection-of-adults-at-risk-in-immigration-detention-2018-19

Bonetti, P. (2011). Il diritto di asilo nella costituzione italiana. In C. Favilli (Ed.), *Procedure e garanzie del diritto di asilo*. Padova: CEDAM.

Bovo, A. (2018). *Le aggressioni omofobe verbali e fisiche di un terribile 2018*. Gay.it. https://www.gay.it/gay-life/news/le-aggressioni-omofobe-verbali-e-fisiche-di-un-terribile-2018

Braithwaite, J. (2016). *UK statement delivered to the UNHCR Executive Committee in Geneva, 4 October 2016*. GOV.UK. https://www.gov.uk/government/news/uk-statement-delivered-to-the-unhcr-executive-committee-in-geneva-4-october-2016

Brandl, U., & Czech, P. (2015). General and specific vulnerability of protection-seekers in the EU: Is there an adequate response to their needs. In F. Ippolito & S. Iglesias Sánchez (Eds.), *Protecting vulnerable groups. The European human rights framework* (p. 247). Oxford: Oxford University Press.

Casey, L. (2016). *The Casey review: A review into opportunity and integration*. GOV.UK. https://www.gov.uk/government/publications/the-casey-review-a-review-into-opportunity-and-integration

Catozzella, G. (2018). *Il razzismo è diventato la normalità in Italia*. L'Espresso. http://espresso.repubblica.it/visioni/2018/12/18/news/razzismo-italia-1.329768

Center for Gender & Refugee Studies. (2014). *Review of gender, child, and LGBTI asylum guidelines and case law in foreign jurisdictions: A resource for U.S. Attorneys*. University of California Hastings College of the Law. https://cgrs,uchastings.edu/sites/default/files/Review_Foreign_Gender_Guidelines_Caselaw_0.pdf

CILD – Italian Coalition for Civil Liberties and Rights. (2018). The Salvini Decree has been approved: Legislative changes on immigration. *Cild.Eu*. https://cild.eu/en/2018/09/25/the-salvini-decree-has-been-approved-legislative-changes-on-immigration/

Commissioner for Human Rights. (2016). *Memorandum on the human rights of asylum seekers and immigrants in the United Kingdom, 22 March 2016, CommDH(2016)17*. Council of Europe. https://papers.ssrn.com/sol3/papers.cfm?abstract_id=2759269

Corriere della Sera. (2018). *Onu-Salvini, è polemica: «In Italia razzismo», «Prevenuti, non accettiamo lezioni»*. Corriere della Sera. https://www.corriere.it/cronache/18_settembre_10/onu-in-italia-violenza-razzismo-invieremo-team-valutare-situazione-4c6fa08c-b4dc-11e8-9795-182d8d9833a0.shtml

Curi, F. (2019). *Immigrazione e sicurezza. Commento al d.l. 4 ottobre 2018, n. 113, conv. con mod. in legge 1 dicembre 2018, n. 132*. Ospedaletto: Pacini.

Danisi, C. (2018). What 'safe harbours' are there for people seeking international protection on sexual orientation and gender identity grounds? A human rights reading of international law of the sea and refugee law. *GenIUS – Rivista di studi giuridici sull'orientamento sessuale e l'identità di genere (Special Issue on SOGI Asylum)*, 5(2), 9–24.

Danisi, C., Dustin, M., & Ferreira, N. (2019). Queering Brexit: What's in Brexit for sexual and gender minorities? In M. Dustin, N. Ferreira, & S. Millns (Eds.), *Gender and queer perspectives on Brexit* (pp. 239–272). Cham: Springer International Publishing. https://doi.org/10.1007/978-3-030-03122-0_10.

de Schutter, O. (2009). *Homophobia and discrimination on grounds of sexual orientation in the EU member states: Part I – Legal analysis*. Wien: FRA – European Union Agency for Fundamental Rights.

Der Bundeswahlleiter. (2017). *Bundestagswahl 2017: Endgültiges Ergebnis*. https://www.bundeswahlleiter.de/info/presse/mitteilungen/bundestagswahl-2017/34_17_endgueltiges_ergebnis.html

Deutsche Welle. (2017). *More asylum requests processed in Germany than rest of EU combined*. DW.COM. https://www.dw.com/en/more-asylum-requests-processed-in-germany-than-rest-of-eu-combined-reports/a-36984339

Deutscher Bundestag. (2019). *Zustimmung zur Entfristung der Wohnsitzauflage für Asylberechtigte*. Deutscher Bundestag. https://www.bundestag.de/dokumente/textarchiv/2019/kw20-pa-inneres-wohnsitz-641764

Die Welt. (2016, December 21). Anschlag in Berlin: Internationale Presse spricht Angela Merkel Mut zu. *Die Welt*. https://www.welt.de/politik/ausland/article160485455/Fuer-Merkel-ist-der-Terroranschlag-eine-Heimsuchung.html

Die Welt. (2018, October 28). Hessen-Wahl 2018: Das Ende einer beispiellosen AfD-Serie. *Die Welt*. https://www.welt.de/politik/deutschland/article182892676/Hessen-Wahl-2018-Das-Ende-einer-beispiellosen-AfD-Serie.html

Dipartimento Libertà Civili e Immigrazione. (2019). *Dati asilo 2017–2018*. http://www.libertaciviliimmigrazione.dlci.interno.gov.it/sites/default/files/allegati/riepilogo_anno_2018.pdf

Doyle, L. (2014). *28 days later: Experiences of new refugees in the UK*. Refugee Council. http://www.refugeecouncil.org.uk/assets/0003/1769/28_days_later.pdf

Dustin, M., & Ferreira, N. (2017). Canada's Guideline 9: Improving SOGIE claims assessment? *Forced Migration Review, 56*(October), 80–83.

ECRE – European Council on Refugees and Exiles. (2017). *The concept of vulnerability in European asylum procedures*. http://www.asylumineurope.org/sites/default/files/shadow-reports/aida_vulnerability_in_asylum_procedures.pdf

ECRE – European Council on Refugees and Exiles, AIDA – Asylum Information Database, & Asyl und Migration. (2019). *National country report: Germany, 2018 update*. ECRE – European Council on Refugees and Exiles. https://www.asylumineurope.org/sites/default/files/report-download/aida_de_2018update.pdf

EHRC – Equality and Human Rights Commission. (2018). *The cumulative impact of tax and welfare reforms*. EHRC – Equality and Human Rights Commission. https://www.equalityhumanrights.com/en/publication-download/cumulative-impact-tax-and-welfare-reforms

Ellis, E., & Watson, P. (2015). *EU anti-discrimination law* (2nd ed.). Oxford: Oxford University Press.

European Commission. (2015). *Communication from the Commission to the European Parliament, the Council, the European Economic and Social Committee and the Committee of the Regions: A European Agenda on Migration (Brussels, 13.5.2015 COM(2015) 240 final)*. https://ec.europa.eu/home-affairs/sites/homeaffairs/files/what-we-do/policies/european-agenda-migration/background-information/docs/communication_on_the_european_agenda_on_migration_en.pdf

Ferreira, N. (2015). The Supreme Court in a final push to go beyond Strasbourg. *Public Law, 3*, 367–375.

Ferreira, N. (2018). Reforming the Common European Asylum System: Enough rainbow for queer asylum seekers? *GenIUS – Rivista di studi giuridici sull'orientamento sessuale e l'identità di genere (Special Issue on SOGI Asylum), 5*(2), 25–42.

Ferreira, N. (2021). An exercise in detachment: The Strasbourg Court and sexual minority refugees. In R. Mole (Ed.), *Queer migration and asylum in Europe* (pp. 78-108). London: UCL.

FRA – European Union Agency for Fundamental Rights. (2015). *Protection against discrimination on grounds of sexual orientation, gender identity and sex characteristics in the EU – Comparative legal analysis – Update 2015*. Publications Office of the European Union. http://fra.europa.eu/en/publication/2015/lgbti-comparative-legal-update-2015

Goodwill, R. (2016). *European Union opt in decision: Dublin IV Regulation: Written statement – HCWS370*. UK Parliament. https://www.parliament.uk/business/publications/written-questions-answers-statements/written-statement/Commons/2016-12-16/HCWS370

Government Equalities Office. (2011). *Advancing transgender equality: A plan for action*. HM Government. https://www.gov.uk/government/publications/transgender-action-plan

References

Government Equalities Office. (2018a). *LGBT action plan*. Her Majesty's Stationery Office. https://assets.publishing.service.gov.uk/government/uploads/system/uploads/attachment_data/file/721367/GEO-LGBT-Action-Plan.pdf

Government Equalities Office. (2018b). *Reform of the Gender Recognition Act 2004*. GOV.UK. https://www.gov.uk/government/consultations/reform-of-the-gender-recognition-act-2004

Government Equalities Office. (2019). *LGBT action plan: Annual progress report 2018 to 2019*. Her Majesty's Stationery Office. https://assets.publishing.service.gov.uk/government/uploads/system/uploads/attachment_data/file/814579/20190702__LGBT_Action_Plan__Annual_Report__WESC.pdf

Hempel, J. J. (2014). *Sexuelle Orientierung als Asylgrund: Entwicklungen der europäischen Asylrechtspraxis am Beispiel Deutschlands* [Diplomarbeit]. Universitaet Wien.

Hill, A. (2019). Home Office chaos and incompetence lead to unlawful detentions, claim whistleblowers. *The Guardian*. https://www.theguardian.com/uk-news/2019/apr/28/home-office-chaos-and-incompetence-leads-to-unlawful-detentions-claim-whistleblowers

Home Affairs Committee. (2016). *Oral evidence: Hate crime and its violent consequences, HC 609*. http://data.parliament.uk/writtenevidence/committeeevidence.svc/evidencedocument/home-affairs-committee/hate-crime-and-its-violent-consequences/oral/43388.pdf

Home Affairs Committee. (2018). *Asylum accommodation: Replacing COMPASS*. House of Commons. https://publications.parliament.uk/pa/cm201719/cmselect/cmhaff/1758/175807.htm#_idTextAnchor059

Home Affairs Committee. (2019a). *'Cavalier' Home Office failing in its responsibility for immigration detention—News from Parliament*. UK Parliament. https://www.parliament.uk/business/committees/committees-a-z/commons-select/home-affairs-committee/news-parliament-2017/immigration-detention-report-published-17-19/

Home Affairs Committee. (2019b). *Settlement scheme risks repeat of Windrush Scandal, Committee warns*. UK Parliament. https://www.parliament.uk/business/committees/committees-a-z/commons-select/home-affairs-committee/news-parliament-2017/eu-settlement-scheme-report-published-17-19/

Home Office. (2011). *Gender identity issues in the asylum claim: Transgender*. GOV.UK. https://www.gov.uk/government/publications/dealing-with-gender-identity-issues-in-the-asylum-claim-process

Home Office. (2016a). *Asylum policy instruction. Sexual orientation in asylum claims. Version 6.0*. GOV.UK. https://assets.publishing.service.gov.uk/government/uploads/system/uploads/attachment_data/file/543882/Sexual-orientation-in-asylum-claims-v6.pdf

Home Office. (2016b). *Refugees: Syria: Written question - HL3787*. UK Parliament. https://www.parliament.uk/business/publications/written-questions-answers-statements/written-question/Lords/2016-12-02/HL3787

Home Office. (2017a). *National statistics: How many people do we grant asylum or protection to?* GOV.UK. https://www.gov.uk/government/publications/immigration-statistics-january-to-march-2017/how-many-people-do-we-grant-asylum-or-protection-to

Home Office. (2017b). *Refugee leave – Version 4.0*. Statewatch. http://www.statewatch.org/news/2017/mar/uk-home-office-refugee-settlement-limits-policy-3-17.pdf

Home Office. (2017c). *Syrian Vulnerable Persons Resettlement Scheme (VPRS) guidance for local authorities and partners*. GOV.UK. https://assets.publishing.service.gov.uk/government/uploads/system/uploads/attachment_data/file/631369/170711_Syrian_Resettlement_Updated_Fact_Sheet_final.pdf

Home Office. (2017d). *Asylum claims in detention: Policy equality statement*. GOV.UK. https://www.gov.uk/government/uploads/system/uploads/attachment_data/file/667250/Home_Office_PES_-_Processing_asylum_claims_in_detention_-_September_2017.pdf

Home Office. (2018a). *Immigration Act 2016: Guidance on adults at risk in immigration detention*. GOV.UK. https://assets.publishing.service.gov.uk/government/uploads/system/uploads/attachment_data/file/721237/Adults_at_risk_in_immigration_detention_-_statutory_guidance__2_.pdf

Home Office. (2018b). *National statistics – Experimental statistics: Asylum claims on the basis of sexual orientation.* GOV.UK. https://www.gov.uk/government/publications/immigration-statistics-year-ending-september-2018/experimental-statistics-asylum-claims-on-the-basis-of-sexual-orientation

Home Office. (2018c). *The Home Office response to the Independent Chief Inspector of Borders and Immigration's report: An inspection of the Home Office's management of asylum accommodation provision.* GOV.UK. https://assets.publishing.service.gov.uk/government/uploads/system/uploads/attachment_data/file/757725/Formal_Response_Asylum_Accommodation.pdf

Home Office. (2019). *Family reunion: For refugees and those with humanitarian protection. Version 3.0.* GOV.UK. https://assets.publishing.service.gov.uk/government/uploads/system/uploads/attachment_data/file/787275/family-reunion-guidance-v3.0ext.pdf

House of Commons Home Affairs Committee. (2013a). *Asylum. Seventh report of session 2013–14. Volume I.* House of Commons. https://publications.parliament.uk/pa/cm201314/cmselect/cmhaff/71/71.pdf

House of Commons Home Affairs Committee. (2013b). *The work of the UK Border Agency (October–December 2012).* House of Commons. https://publications.parliament.uk/pa/cm201314/cmselect/cmhaff/486/48602.htm

House of Commons Home Affairs Committee. (2017). *Asylum accommodation. Twelfth report of session 2016–17.* House of Commons. https://www.publications.parliament.uk/pa/cm201617/cmselect/cmhaff/637/63702.htm

House of Commons Home Affairs Committee. (2019). *Immigration detention. Fourteenth report of session 2017–19 (HC 913).* House of Commons. https://publications.parliament.uk/pa/cm201719/cmselect/cmhaff/913/913.pdf

House of Commons Women and Equalities Committee. (2016). *Transgender equality: First report of session 2015–16.* UK Parliament. https://www.parliament.uk/business/committees/committees-a-z/commons-select/women-and-equalities-committee/inquiries/parliament-2015/transgender-equality/

Hübner, K. (2016). Fluchtgrund sexuelle Orientierung und Geschlechtsidentität: Auswirkungen von heteronormativem Wissen auf die Asylverfahren LGBTI-Geflüchteter. *Feministische Studien, 34*(2), 242. https://doi.org/10.1515/fs-2016-0005.

Hudson-Sharp, N., & Metcalf, H. (2016). *Inequality among lesbian, gay bisexual and transgender groups in the UK: A review of evidence.* National Institute of Economic and Social Research. http://www.niesr.ac.uk/sites/default/files/publications/160719_REPORT_LGBT_evidence_review_NIESR_FINALPDF.pdf

ICIBI – Independent Chief Inspector of Borders and Immigration. (2014). *An investigation into the Home Office's handling of asylum claims made on the grounds of sexual orientation March–June 2014.* GOV.UK. https://assets.publishing.service.gov.uk/government/uploads/system/uploads/attachment_data/file/547330/Investigation-into-the-Handling-of-Asylum-Claims_Oct_2014.pdf

ICIBI – Independent Chief Inspector of Borders and Immigration. (2016). *An inspection of asylum casework. March – July 2015.* http://icinspector.independent.gov.uk/2016/02/04/the-independent-chief-inspector-of-borders-and-immigrations-inspection-of-asylum-casework-march-july-2015/

ICIBI – Independent Chief Inspector of Borders and Immigration. (2018). *An inspection of the Home Office's management of asylum accommodation provision.* GOV.UK. https://assets.publishing.service.gov.uk/government/uploads/system/uploads/attachment_data/file/757285/ICIBI_An_inspection_of_the_HO_management_of_asylum_accommodation.pdf

ICIBI – Independent Chief Inspector of Borders and Immigration. (2019). *Independent Chief Inspector of Borders and Immigration: About us.* GOV.UK. https://www.gov.uk/government/organisations/independent-chief-inspector-of-borders-and-immigration/about

ILGA-Europe. (2019). *Rainbow Europe.* https://rainbow-europe.org/

Joint Committee on Human Rights. (2019). *Immigration detention: Sixteenth report of session 2017–19.* https://publications.parliament.uk/pa/jt201719/jtselect/jtrights/1484/1484.pdf.

References

Judicial College. (2018). *Equal Treatment Bench Book*. https://www.judiciary.uk/publications/new-edition-of-the-equal-treatment-bench-book-launched/

Kalkmann, M. (2010). German Report. *Fleeing Homophobia, Seeking Safety in Europe: Best Practices on the (Legal) Position of LGBT Asylum Seekers in the EU Member States*. https://www.yumpu.com/en/document/view/21133881/draft-questionnaire

Kirkup, J., & Winnett, R. (2012). Theresa May interview: 'We're going to give illegal migrants a really hostile reception'. *The Telegraph*. https://www.telegraph.co.uk/news/uknews/immigration/9291483/Theresa-May-interview-Were-going-to-give-illegal-migrants-a-really-hostile-reception.html

Lyons, K., & Duncan, P. (2017, April 9). 'It's a shambles': Data shows most asylum seekers put in poorest parts of Britain. *The Guardian*. https://www.theguardian.com/world/2017/apr/09/its-a-shambles-data-shows-most-asylum-seekers-put-in-poorest-parts-of-britain

Markard, N. (2013). EuGH zur sexuellen Orientierung als Fluchtgrund: Zur Entscheidung „X, Y und Z gegen Minister vor Immigratie en Asiel" vom 7.11.2013. *Asylmagazin*, 12, 402–408. https://www.asyl.net/fileadmin/user_upload/beitraege_asylmagazin/Beitraege_AM_2013/AM2013-12_beitragmarkard.pdf

Markard, N. (2015). Wer gilt als Flüchtling—Und wer nicht?: Rechtliche Grundlagen. *Sozial Extra*, 39(4), 24–27. https://doi.org/10.1007/s12054-015-0055-z.

Marsh, S., Mohdin, A., & McIntyre, N. (2019). Homophobic and transphobic hate crimes surge in England and Wales. *The Guardian*. https://www.theguardian.com/world/2019/jun/14/homophobic-and-transphobic-hate-crimes-surge-in-england-and-wales

May, T. (2015). *Theresa May's speech to the Conservative Party Conference – In full*. The Independent. http://www.independent.co.uk/news/uk/politics/theresa-may-s-speech-to-the-conservative-party-conference-in-full-a6681901.html

May, T. (2016). *Oral statement to parliament—G20 Summit: PM Commons statement*. GOV.UK. https://www.gov.uk/government/speeches/g20-summit-pm-commons-statement-7-september-2016

Merkel, A. (2016). *Sommerpressekonferenz von Bundeskanzlerin Merkel*. Startseite. https://www.bundesregierung.de/breg-de/aktuelles/pressekonferenzen/sommerpressekonferenz-von-bundeskanzlerin-merkel-848300

NDR. (2019). *BAMF-"Skandal" wird immer kleiner*. https://daserste.ndr.de/panorama/archiv/2019/BAMF-Skandal-wird-immer-kleiner,bamf204.html

Neilson, V. (2005). Homosexual or female—Applying gender-based asylum jurisprudence to lesbian asylum claims. *Stanford Law & Policy Review*, 16(2), 417.

Nokes, C. (2019). *Letter to Harriet Harman QC MP*. https://www.parliament.uk/documents/joint-committees/human-rights/correspondence/2017-19/Immigration_detention_Government_response.pdf

Office of the First Minister and Deputy First Minister. (2015). *Racial Equality Strategy 2015–2025*. The Executive Office. https://www.executiveoffice-ni.gov.uk/sites/default/files/publications/ofmdfm/racial-equality-strategy-2015-2025.pdf

Oxfam, ASGI, & A Buon Diritto. (2015). *Negli hotspots gravi violazioni dei diritti dei migranti*. ASGI. https://www.asgi.it/notizie/oxfam-asgi-a-buon-diritto-hotspots-gravi-violazioni-diritti-migranti/

Patrick, A. (2016). *Mapping the great repeal: European Union law and the protection of human rights*. Thomas Paine Initiative at Global Dialogue. https://global-dialogue.org/mapping-the-great-repeal-eu-law-and-the-protection-of-human-rights/

Potter, M. (2014). *Refugees and asylum seekers in Northern Ireland. Research and information service research paper. NIAR 348-14*. Northern Ireland Assembly. http://www.niassembly.gov.uk/globalassets/documents/ofmdfm/motions/motions/community-relations-refugee-week/refugees-and-asylum-seekers.pdf

Quertel, C. (2012). *I feel as a woman I'm not welcome*. Asylum Aid. http://www.asylumaid.org.uk/wp-content/uploads/2013/02/ifeelasawoman_report_web_.pdf

Querton, C. (2019). The impact of Brexit on gender and asylum law in the UK. In M. Dustin, N. Ferreira, & S. Millns (Eds.), *Gender and queer perspectives on Brexit* (pp. 209–238). Cham: Springer International Publishing. https://doi.org/10.1007/978-3-030-03122-0_9.

Ramón Mendos, L. (2019). *State-sponsored homophobia 2019: Global legislation overview update.* ILGA. https://ilga.org/downloads/ILGA_World_State_Sponsored_Homophobia_report_global_legislation_overview_update_December_2019.pdf

Refugee Council. (2019). *Asylum statistics. Annual Trends.* https://www.refugeecouncil.org.uk/wp-content/uploads/2019/03/Asylum_Statistics_Annual_Trends_Mar_2019.pdf

Salerno, F. (2010). L'obbligo internazionale di non-refoulement dei richiedenti asilo. *Diritti Umani e Diritto Internazionale, 4*, 487–515.

Scottish Government. (2013). *New Scots: Integrating refugees in Scotland's Communities 2014–2017.* Scottish Government. http://www.gov.scot/Resource/0043/00439604.pdf

Scottish Government News. (2016). *Syrian Resettlement Programme.* https://beta.gov.scot/news/scotland-welcomes-refugees/

Shaw, S. (2016). *Review into the welfare in detention of vulnerable persons.* Home Office. https://www.gov.uk/government/publications/review-into-the-welfare-in-detention-of-vulnerable-persons

Singer, S. (2019). 'Desert Island' detention: Detainees' understandings of 'law' in the UK's immigration detention system. *Refugee Survey Quarterly, 38*(1), 1–29. https://doi.org/10.1093/rsq/hdy020

Special Rapporteur on extreme poverty and human rights. (2019). *Visit to the United Kingdom of Great Britain and Northern Ireland: Report of the Special Rapporteur on extreme poverty and human rights (Human Rights Council, Forty-first session, A/HRC/41/39/Add.1).* United Nations General Assembly. https://undocs.org/A/HRC/41/39/Add.1

Stonewall, & UKLGIG – UK Lesbian and Gay Immigration Group. (2016). *No safe refuge. Experiences of LGBT asylum seekers in detention.* http://www.stonewall.org.uk/resources/no-safe-refuge-2016

Sturge, G. (2019). *House of Commons library briefing paper number SN01403.* https://researchbriefings.parliament.uk/ResearchBriefing/Summary/SN01403

Tgcom24. (2016). *Migranti, il piano di Minniti: Aprire un Cie in ogni regione e raddoppiare espulsioni.* Tgcom24. http://www.tgcom24.mediaset.it/cronaca/notizia_3048882201602a.shtml

The Economist. (2019). *Britons are warming to immigration. Will their next prime minister?* The Economist. https://www.economist.com/britain/2019/07/11/britons-are-warming-to-immigration-will-their-next-prime-minister

UK Government. (2011). *Written statement to Parliament. European Union opt-in decision: Amended asylum procedures and reception conditions directives.* GOV.UK. https://www.gov.uk/government/speeches/european-union-opt-in-decision-amended-asylum-procedures-and-reception-conditions-directives

UKLGIG – UK Lesbian and Gay Immigration Group. (2018). *EU/EEA & Brexit.* UKLGIG. https://uklgig.org.uk/?page_id=2272

UKVI – UK Visas and Immigration. (2011). *Transgender identity issues in asylum claims.* UK Visas and Immigration. https://www.gov.uk/government/publications/dealing-with-gender-identity-issues-in-the-asylum-claim-process

UKVI – UK Visas and Immigration. (2016). *Policy paper. Adults at risk in immigration detention.* UKVI – UK Visas and Immigration. https://www.gov.uk/government/uploads/system/uploads/attachment_data/file/547519/Adults_at_Risk_August_2016.pdf

UN Working Group on Arbitrary Detention. (2018). *Revised deliberation no. 5 on deprivation of liberty of migrants.* UN Working Group on Arbitrary Detention. https://www.refworld.org/docid/5a903b514.html

UNHCR – UN High Commissioner for Refugees. (2002). *Guidelines on international protection no. 1: Gender-related persecution within the context of Article 1A(2) of the 1951 Convention and/or its 1967 Protocol relating to the Status of Refugees (HCR/GIP/02/01).* UNHCR –

References

UN High Commissioner for Refugees. http://www.unhcr.org/publications/legal/3d58ddef4/guidelines-international-protection-1-gender-related-persecution-context.html

UNHCR – UN High Commissioner for Refugees. (2012). *Guidelines on international protection no. 9: Claims to refugee status based on sexual orientation and/or gender identity within the context of Article 1A(2) of the 1951 Convention and/or its 1967 Protocol relating to the Status of Refugees (HCR/GIP/12/09)*. UNHCR – UN High Commissioner for Refugees. http://www.unhcr.org/509136ca9.pdf

UNHCR – UN High Commissioner for Refugees. (2017). *Towards Integration. The Syrian Vulnerable Persons Resettlement Scheme in the United Kingdom*. UNHCR – UN High Commissioner for Refugees. https://www.unhcr.org/uk/protection/basic/5a0ae9e84/towards-integration-the-syrian-vulnerable-persons-resettlement-scheme-in.html

UNHCR – UN High Commissioner for Refugees. (2019). *Desperate journeys. Refugees and migrants arriving in Europe and at Europe's borders (January–December 2018)*. Geneva: UNHCR.

Welsh Government. (2019). *Nation of sanctuary – Refugee and asylum seeker plan*. https://gov.wales/docs/dsjlg/publications/equality/190128-refugee-and-asylum-seeker-plan-en.pdf

Open Access This chapter is licensed under the terms of the Creative Commons Attribution 4.0 International License (http://creativecommons.org/licenses/by/4.0/), which permits use, sharing, adaptation, distribution and reproduction in any medium or format, as long as you give appropriate credit to the original author(s) and the source, provide a link to the Creative Commons license and indicate if changes were made.

The images or other third party material in this chapter are included in the chapter's Creative Commons license, unless indicated otherwise in a credit line to the material. If material is not included in the chapter's Creative Commons license and your intended use is not permitted by statutory regulation or exceeds the permitted use, you will need to obtain permission directly from the copyright holder.

Chapter 5
Life in the Countries of Origin, Departure and Travel Towards Europe

> *I was living but not really living, I had no taste of anything. I had no life.*
> (Sandra, Germany)
>
> *We should help these people to create a vocabulary, their vocabulary. They have never narrated themselves.*
> (Valentina, social worker, Italy)
>
> *When I was in my own country, I don't know about asylum but the intention is to be free, to be safe.*
> (Ophelie, focus group no. 2, Glasgow, UK)

5.1 Introduction

According to the United Nations (UN), at least 258 million people are moving across countries around the globe, consciously or unconsciously, in search of a safe and dignified life (IOM 2019; UN 2017). The international attempt to regulate these movements through the so-called Compacts seems unlikely to provide effective solutions.[1] Often criticised as being non-binding instruments but with great potential in shaping states' future behaviour (Türk 2018), the Compacts are not explicit in including SOGI minorities in the measures to be adopted through international cooperation for improving the management of migration and refugee flows, while respecting their human rights. It is noticeable that objective no. 7 ('Address and reduce vulnerabilities in migration') of the Global Compact related to migration refers to 'victims of violence, including sexual and gender-based violence (…) [and] persons who are discriminated against on any basis' as examples of

---

[1] UN General Assembly, *Global Compact for Safe Orderly and Regular Migration*, adopted at the seventy-third session, 19 December 2018; *Global Compact on Refugees*, adopted at the seventy-third session, 17 December 2018, A/RES/73/151. The Compacts follow the adoption of the *New York Declaration for Refugees and Migrants*, adopted at the seventy-first session, 19 September 2016, A/RES/71/1.

vulnerable groups and, more generally, advances the development of gender-responsive migration policies (Atak et al. 2018). Equally, the Global Compact on Refugees pays attention in all fields to 'sexual and gender-based violence', while calling upon states to strengthen international efforts to prevent and combat it (paras. 5, 13, 51, 57, 59, 72 and 75). Yet, although this wording may be inclusive of SOGI, the Compacts avoided any specific reference or commitment in relation either to migrants who identify themselves as LGBTIQ+ or to SOGI claimants, perhaps owing to the need for the widest possible consensus among UN member states to secure the Compacts' adoption. This represents a missed opportunity to raise awareness of SOGI asylum claimants' needs at the universal level and speed up multilateral solutions to the movements across countries of people fleeing homophobia and transphobia.

Yet, as Victor Madrigal-Borloz stated, for many SOGI claimants 'the trauma and persecution start well before their actual flight to safety', while 'the journey to safety can prove particularly treacherous [because these claimants] continue to face prejudice and violence in countries of transit and host countries' (UN Independent Expert on protection against violence and discrimination based on sexual orientation and gender identity 2019). Therefore, he called upon states to grant 'safe settings' well before the asylum process starts in the receiving country, in order to cover also their often long-term travels and stays in transit countries. This opinion is also shared by some European policy-makers. As Terry, a member of the European Parliament, explained:

> Very often we start looking at a process of fleeing when the person arrives in the European Union but, actually (…) there is a long process before that. And the question would be, how can we actually make sure that people get legal entry ways that don't include (…) being on the road for weeks or even months in very vulnerable situations?

Significantly, SOGI claimants also perceive us to be experiencing a particular historical moment. According to Diana (Germany), 'the refugee concept has changed a bit from seven years ago (…) we did not have a refugee crisis like now'.

For these reasons, this chapter aims to analyse the complex situation faced by SOGI claimants before they leave their countries of origin, during their travel to, and arrival in Europe. Considering the paucity of studies in this specific area of SOGI asylum (Danisi 2018; Piwowarczyk et al. 2017; Winton 2019), and the fact that these are often country specific (Munir 2019; Odlum 2019) rather than addressing the multinational journeys that occur, this chapter also explores the implications of these journeys for SOGI claimants' experiences with the asylum process. As Chiara, a psychotherapist who works with migrants arriving in Italy through the Mediterranean Sea, explained, the experiences of SOGI asylum claimants are complex, and besides the abuses suffered in their home countries, their travels are also 'a synonym of violence and ill-treatment'. The reception systems in Europe, which should provide appropriate support at arrival, are instead the cause of additional trauma.

As context for understanding SOGI claimants' subsequent experiences in Germany, Italy and UK, this chapter first looks at their lives in their countries of origin, including their social experiences and family relations, and, through these lenses, at the treatment reserved to SOGI minorities in those countries (Sect. 5.2). Recognition of the importance of these aspects of life in countries of origin may facilitate subsequent analysis of how SOGI asylum claims are assessed and whether or not claimants' personhood is respected by European decision-makers (Chap. 7). Second, by questioning the lack of alternatives to asylum, including the possibility of obtaining humanitarian visas under IRL and IHRL, this chapter considers whether SOGI claimants are aware of the possibility of claiming international protection in Europe on the basis of their fear of persecution on SOGI grounds and whether their travel routes are consciously chosen. The travel experience is also investigated, in an attempt to analyse whether and how it influences the subsequent asylum application and wellbeing in host countries. Third, by exploring the procedures upon arrival in Europe, this chapter verifies whether or not host countries provide the 'safe settings' advocated by the UN SOGI Independent Expert (Sect. 5.3). These settings include, at the very least, the existence of effective means for informing claimants about the possibility of seeking asylum on SOGI grounds, as well as an assessment of the protection needs of each individual (Sect. 5.4). Some provisional concluding remarks are provided in Sect. 5.5.

5.2 Life in the Countries of Origin

While often disregarded in SOGI asylum analyses, understanding the life experiences of people claiming asylum on SOGI grounds *beyond* persecution is essential to the intersectional and integrated approach advanced in our theoretical and analytical frameworks (Chap. 3). Focussing attention only on episode(s) potentially amounting to persecution risks ignoring not only fundamental aspects of claimants' personhood but, also, relevant data that may contribute to shaping fair asylum decision-making.

For this reason, we investigate: how SOGI claimants saw their lives before being forced to flee; what their social experiences were, including activism for SOGI equality; and what their perception was of how SOGI minorities are treated in their countries of origin. While a number of NGOs and international organisations have reported on the legal treatment of SOGI minorities (Ramón Mendos 2019), the insights of our participants on the social environment that determines the life experiences of SOGI claimants shed light on a largely unexplored area. Here, we offer, through SOGI claimants' lenses, an analysis of these pre-departure experiences.

5.2.1 'Ordinary' Lives

It is often assumed that SOGI claimants left a life of absolute misery for a life of absolute freedom. Yet, such an assumption reflects an over-simplistic paradigm of persecutory and protective countries. In fact, experiences are far more nuanced.

One of the recurrent feelings shared by people claiming asylum on SOGI grounds appears to be the sense of frustration at having been forced to leave their 'ordinary lives', including everything they had built up over the course of their lifetime. This includes family, social and love relationships, as well as employment, all aspects of one's private and public life protected by IHRL (for example, Article 17 ICCPR or Article 8 ECHR). As a result, against all sort of related stereotypes still popular among decision-makers (Chaps. 6 and 7), SOGI claimants do not always show a total rejection of their countries of origin (Giametta 2016, p. 68). At the same time, feelings of disempowerment may shape their individual experiences after arriving in Europe, as we will see across these volumes.

The case of Alphaeus (Germany) is illustrative: 'I was an engineer before in my country. I had my own company, a construction company. And unfortunately that all ended like that'. A similar experience was shared by Sandra (Germany):

> In my country I worked, before everything went bad, I worked, so I had my own place, my own space. Yes, I understand people flee for different reasons. Some lose their parents, some lose their families but, at the end of the day, you lose something. I had all this (…) I had plans for my life, I had goals to achieve, and things were really going the way that I had planned. And I was there and seeing my friends, being happy (…) in my country we buy land, pieces of land and build houses. [Now] I'm like… I felt like a failure.

Kamel (Italy) shared similar feelings: 'I left a family, my job, my house, my friends, my lover... I left many things. I left a country'. Equally, Kennedy (Italy) stressed: 'If they can amend the laws tomorrow, I will be among the first person to… voluntarily to go, because before I left, I was still having a life'. As Ibrahim (Germany) reiterated: 'Despite the stress, I did have a structure and community and I didn't want to leave all of this behind'. Alphaeus concluded: 'If I'm told Uganda is better [in terms of LGBTIQ+ rights], I go back to my country because I had a life'.

This sense of loss and disempowerment, which has clear consequences also for integration in the host country (Chaps. 8 and 9), is expressed well by Marhoon:

> I've worked in Oman for ten years, so that the retirement money that I've paid from my own money has been lost. Ten years! I will not have it here in Germany. (…) Are they going to employ someone who's 24 or someone who's like me [much older]? Will I have a senior position like I used to have in Oman? (…) I have all these questions and all this confusion.

The only solution remains the one indicated by Milad (Germany): 'I had to start from scratch. Building zero. It was really difficult'.

These accounts of positive experiences, relationships and achievements in claimants' lives in their countries of origin need to be balanced by experiences of discrimination, abuse and forced concealment of their SOGI. In this respect, Ibrahim (Germany) remembered:

5.2 Life in the Countries of Origin

> I stayed in a Lebanon jail for five years. (...) My family had an idea – if we put him in jail away, jail makes boys into men and people will forget his issues, that he is a sissy boy (...). And they made for me a case of drugs, just to put me away.

Bella (Italy) also evoked how her life changed when some people found her with another woman:

> They started blackmailing me to bring money (...) so that they will not take you to the police. (...) Before escaping, I was paying but I could not [do it anymore] because I was the one taking care of my child.

Similarly, Lutfor (UK) explained:

> I tried my best, to stay in Bangladesh. (...) It is your country, you can speak to them and (...) I had a very good result [in] school, college so, if I could hide my sexuality, if I didn't come out, I could go [to a] top level job, government job. I had to give up.

In these environments, the ability to express one's personhood is seriously restricted. In this respect, Marhoon (Germany) explained his experience as an exception:

> I was very comfortable with my sexuality since I was 19, so even on dating apps I would use my face, which was very rare in Oman. Most people don't use... I didn't lead a double life, I didn't have a wife or kids. Most guys did in Oman.

Equally, according to Milad (Germany):

> We met in some secret places that we only know each other. We also had the apps (...). But was not public. Was always private. (...) with friends drinking tea, drinking coffee, talk, go for a walk (...) to the cinema. [But] I was always careful.

Kennedy (Italy) recalled how having a relationship is nevertheless possible in these difficult circumstances:

> We fell in love, year 2008. So we were together, although it was secret, strictly secret, nobody knows about our relationship. But the reason why we have the greatest opportunity [is] that I have my own house, so he normally comes, he comes, he sleeps any time he likes.

Yet, an ambivalence between a desire for the lost country and the realisation of things SOGI claimants can enjoy in Europe also emerges powerfully, especially when religion plays a key role in shaping oppressive social environments. As the experience of Meggs (UK) shows:

> Zimbabwe is a very Christian country, so homosexuality is just a sin. (...) you grew up knowing that (...) you are not supposed to do it and you are still trying to find yourself (...) and say "this is who I am". (...) Regardless of the economy and everything (...) sometimes I wish I was home. I love, I love Zimbabwe (...) I am only seeing it now that it was really bad. But, I just grew up knowing that if I have got tea morning, if I have lunch and I have dinner in the evening, that is all, so to me that is how it used to work and it never used to bother me.

This does not mean that SOGI claimants are always able to exercise greater freedom after they arrive in Europe. As Fares explained in relation to his fellow nationals:

> I don't have a lot of friends from Syria here in Germany. Not all the Syrian gays came out and say that we are gays, they're still in the closet. Here in Germany, there are a lot of

people from Syria, so we cannot come out directly. [But] You should be proud of yourself, because every time when I was in the closet, I was thinking "oh my God, I'm ashamed, I'm something bad", [and] I prayed to God to change my life, or to be straight.

People who were involved in activism before fleeing their country experienced additional difficulties. In fact, despite the restrictions they faced in their countries of origin, many people fleeing homophobia and transphobia described their activism in Nigeria, Malaysia, Oman, Egypt and Zimbabwe, to give a few examples. Interestingly, the term 'activism' acquires a broad meaning in similar contexts, because it is not restricted to the political dimension.

For Marhoon (Germany), activism meant 'gather[ing] people in private spaces (…) because [Oman is] a segregated society (…) and [I] like[d] to build a community'. Most of the time, the willingness to campaign for certain social issues was hampered by the fear of making one's SOGI public. In fact, Kennedy (Italy) reported:

We [were] thinking what could we do to stop the massive killing (...) of the homosexual people in Nigeria? [We wanted] to sensitise the people (...) we came out not to say "we are gay", but we [came] out, you know, to tell the public that they should stop killing.

Besides the fact that open activism in relation to LGBTIQ+ issues was rare, attempts to register or formally establish associations often failed. Amber (UK), fleeing Malaysia, said:

We can't explicitly say we are campaigning for LGBT rights, otherwise we will get into trouble. [We tried] to register our organisation with the Home Ministry (…) but we were never granted status, even after appealing. So our resources are limited with no funding.

As Ximena (UK) also confirmed, the price to pay for carrying out such activities extends from threats to one's safety to the need to flee the country.

This kind of involvement with SOGI activism may have a positive impact on asylum decision-making. As Louis, a volunteer from Rainbow Refugees Frankfurt in Germany, suggests, experiences of activism in the country of origin may speed up the evaluation process, while in their absence 'it takes much longer'. Moreover, according to Roberto, a decision-maker in Italy, activism in fields other than LGBTIQ+ campaigns may also be relevant for granting refugee status on SOGI grounds if the activities attract 'a certain visibility'. This is also relevant for countries where no laws criminalising same-sex acts are in force, such as Eastern European countries, where 'social' persecution may, nevertheless, be prevalent, as well as for the use of other grounds beyond PSG during the evaluation of the asylum request. While we will return to this matter in Chap. 7, data related to the treatment of SOGI minorities in countries of origin are particularly rich and deserve specific investigation.

5.2.2 Treatment of SOGI Minorities in Countries of Origin

To this day, approximately 75 countries still have in force legislation criminalising non-heterosexual and non-cisgender identities and/or behaviours (Ramón Mendos 2019). This information alone, however, does not reflect what living in one of these countries means to SOGI claimants. The effect of such a legislation on claimants' lives may vary to a significant extent. To use the words of Ibrahim (Germany), fleeing Lebanon:

> I have my scars, I have hospital reports, I have everything with me, that I faced violence, discrimination and so on. But not all LGBT people face violence. Maybe, people just flee because they want to live a decent life, they want to live life with love, to love what they want, to live their true identity.

With this in mind, the perspectives on the social environment in their countries of origin that SOGI claimants shared were enlightening. To illustrate the range of treatment suffered by SOGI minorities worldwide, an analysis per country of origin, which is connected by claimants' experiences, is appropriate at this point.

Starting with participants from Africa, Rosette (Germany), fleeing Uganda, explained how pervasive homophobia is across different life spheres in her country of origin:

> We were disqualified from that school [after I was found being intimate with another girl] and then my parents were really mad about me and (…) I was transferred to my uncle's place. (…) My mother said that she doesn't want to know what I am, who I am, whatever. She didn't even take time for me to explain how I feel. (…) But when the [uncle's] wife also realised why I was disqualified from school, then he [the uncle] also turned blue, he really did not want me to associate with (…) their kids. (…) One day my mother came and said "now we have to go back to town". I was happy [but] what I didn't know was that she was going to force me to marry. (…) I was so frustrated, very frustrated, and I felt like dying but I could not kill myself. (…) All that time I stayed together with that man, it was as if he was raping me. I was married for 18 years. (…) In Uganda you can't survive. (…) They will say no, how? Why? You have a demon, they believe that if they put a sword on you and cut, bleeding you, that the demon is getting out, that's what they believe.

Alphaeus (Germany), also fleeing Uganda, confirmed this by stating that '[t]he time I left, it was a terrible time where many gay people were castrated, many gay people were being beaten badly'. William (Germany) had a similar view:

> Uganda is a country where the police and the government and the law are so strict and they cannot allow it. Then you talk about the people and their culture. [They] cannot allow that to happen. Never. Never! You cannot even talk about it.

According to Aisha (Germany), in Uganda:

> We are not taken as people who understand. Many people, they think we are mad, we are crazy (…) when they found out that I'm that, they take you like you are not a human being, you are not supposed to be with them together. They take you like they have to stone you to death.

Referring to Nigeria, Nelo (Italy) stated: 'They look [at you] like an animal, so they describe this thing [like] you are an abomination to the land'. Patti (UK), fleeing the same country, stressed:

> When you talk about it, some of the family, they kill the person because they think that that is a shame to the family, if other people got to know about it. Or, one demon has possessed this family, or they are a cursed family (...) and no one will want to associate with the person. Even me, as a hair stylist, and I am going to let people know about it, some of them won't want me to touch their hair. They think "oh, she is possessed". (...) So, I don't know when that is going to come off from Black people's head, it is like, no go area.

Silver (Italy), who explicitly refused to hide in Nigeria ('I can't say I'm not gay. I was born this way'), recalled that a friend suggested to him 'If they see you, they understand that you are gay, so stay at home. (...) You can't live in Abuja, because if they find who you are, you will be dead'.

Similar perceptions of the Nigerian social and cultural environment were shared by Tina (Germany), Kennedy (Italy) and Bella (Italy), among others. As Kennedy put it, '[if] you are gay or homosexual, lesbian, you are enemy to the state, and to the members of your family, to the members of the society'. Bella further explained:

> Even if I am not a lesbian (...) they will say "no, she is a lesbian, you see her (...) she is following girls". (...) Without seeing you as a lesbian, without maybe catching you doing it (...) everybody will hate you. Everybody will discriminate you, you know, look as if you are alone.

This degree of rejection may reach the level described by Momo (Italy), fleeing Senegal:

> When they knew that I'm not a simple man, that I'm gay, no one wanted to see me again (...). Mums love their children. When children are gay, many mums try to protect them, but many others don't. Some mums may even kill you in your room when they discover that you are gay.

Diarra (Italy), an asylum claimant from Mali, explained that, in his country, even for his mother life could become unbearable if people found out about his sexual orientation:

> When they know that you are gay, they beat you with a cane to death. People say that our country is a Muslim country and homosexuals do not exist. They do not want [to] even hear that word. (...) Change these people's mind, it is not easy.

Siri (Italy), from the Ivory Coast, explained in turn that in his country:

> If people get to know that you are gay, you can be killed, because you can be stoned by some or be beaten with sticks by others, you'll be struck, they will beat you up, while other[s] will film you for uploading your picture onto social networks, your face on social media.

Dev and Fred (Italy), who fled Cameroon, also referred to 'popular justice': 'Homosexuality (...) is punished with a one year prison sentence by Cameroonian law and, above all, even with a condemnation to death by popular justice'. As Irma, who arrived in Germany from Cameroon, further explained:

5.2 Life in the Countries of Origin

> Where I come from, they are looking at it, taboo. That you break the culture, you have given a shame to your whole family. (...) They will call the chiefs (...) of the village, they will follow protocol, kill you or send you to prison. Before then they can even isolate you from the village.

Alain A. (Italy), also fleeing Cameroon, stressed that homophobia is a cultural problem:

> These people are treated like animals, they are treated like they are not human beings. (...) And you are an outcast in the society because first you lose your family, then you lose all the friends you have, and then everywhere you go in the society you are being haunted by the people because of your sexual orientation. So, at times so many people don't even get the chance to experience their life or to try to, like, discover who they really are because of the society. So, being homosexual or having sexual orientation problem in Africa in general, and again my country, is very, very, very, very horrible. (...) And if somebody kills you because you are homosexual, the person is not penalised. (...) It is not about the government accepting, it is about the population. The government can say "yes, we support same-sex marriage", but you will still face torment and the people don't want, the problem is the people, cultural, Africa is like so hooked up to culture and religion.

Finally, according to Martin (UK), the Cameroonian police takes a particular and negative approach towards SOGI minorities:

> They look at it like it is abnormal, it is a witchcraft, you are just like practising something, you know what I mean, you are in a cult which you do that to kill other people, so they look at you like a threat for them. (...) You might be rescued by the police. But they will take you to prison, and you have no right to a lawyer to talk to, you have no right to people to talk to, and the police themselves they are part of the population. They have the same feeling, they have the same belief, the people who are supposed to protect you, they will be the one basically hitting you, oh my God, I don't want to talk about it, hopefully you don't get raped there.

In contrast, Amadin (UK) reported some differences between the behaviours of the authorities and the population in Benin:

> The law punishes when you act. (...) As you are gay or lesbian, they don't bother who you are. (...) So, in Benin the problem is the community. (...) If, like, two men kiss in the street, the community can get beating (...). And some time when they call the police to say the police must come, the police say they cannot waste their time to come. But sometime they can come and they come to lock you.

Experiences in Malawi have similarities with those in the countries already mentioned. Stephina (UK) described the situation in her country of origin stressing that the information available in the UK about Malawi does not correspond to social reality:

> In my country, they said, people are no longer put into prison and nobody is taken into custody. [But] my worry is if the community decides so (...) the government is not going to come to my rescue. (...) Recently there were so many reports of people being killed, like, there were videos everywhere of people being stoned by communities, because they are suspected that they are blood suckers. (...) Even the president says we are like dogs that eat our own vomit. So, the law would say one thing, but the reality is another.

Buba (Italy), from the Gambia, confirmed that, despite public announcements, nothing had changed in practice with the new President coming into post. Diamond

(UK) also referred to Tanzania as a society that is particularly homophobic and homophobia remains unpunished:

> It is very illegal. (...) They will just start beating you. They might even kill you. And they don't have anything for them to... go and complain or nothing. Because if you go and complain to police, they will torture you. (...) Even the family, family, people, anybody, nobody will give you support. (...) Because government itself, the president at the moment, he said that gay are like a cow, he has already mentioned us in the category of animals.

As Sandra (Germany), also fleeing Tanzania, confirmed:

> They will just start chasing you with stones and calling you a thief or someone will just say "a thief!", then everyone comes chasing you, they beat you, then they take tyres, put them around you, put some petrol over them and then light you openly on the street.

Similar patterns of social intolerance towards SOGI minorities were expressed in relation to Zimbabwe: '[t]hey are a strict Christian country, they don't accept that. And it is not only the government, it is the community' (Meggs, UK).

Pointing out the impact of well-reported homophobic events involving SOGI minorities, Ibrahim A. (UK) from Egypt explained that the absence of a law criminalising homosexuality does not ensure better treatment for SOGI minorities in Egypt:

> There is a continuous LGBT crackdown from the government since 2013, after the military coup. (...) There is no law that criminalises homosexuality but... we have the combatting prostituting and debauchery law, so the government applies the article of this law on homosexuals.

Moreover, new technologies are actively used to identify members of SOGI minorities:

> The internet revolution and the online platforms [were] somehow a way for LGBT community to communicate with each other. And it also start[ed] a new age of... criminalisation for LGBT. Because even the government was using the same platform to start to entrap gays and transgenders and take their activity online as an evidence even for their sexual orientation (Ibrahim A., UK).

Selim (UK) further explained this trend in Egypt (as well as in Dubai, where he lived for a few years):

> I have seen a lot of my friends getting killed and that is on daily basis (...). People disappear. (...) And, I don't even know how many times we used to switch off our phones right after, you know, someone has disappeared, one of the group disappears and that for us means is arrested, they are going to go through his phone and they are going to try and find us as well. So we just switch our phones off, we disappear for months. (...) Grindr on his phone, he is chatting to this guy for a while now and then finally they decided to go and meet, he goes to meet him and it was just the police.

Finally, Shany (Germany) stressed the total denial of their existence experienced by SOGI minorities in Morocco:

> The idea is lesbian or gay, it is a taboo (...) you go to the jail. (...) It's a big crime, it's a scandal. (...) You give no respect to the society because there is no lesbians and gays, they don't know this word. It's forbidden, it's not in the society.

5.2 Life in the Countries of Origin

Moving toward the Middle East, accounts of violence and abuses, including by family, were also given about Iraq and Syria. Fares (Germany) remembered that, in Iraq, one of his friends was beaten very badly by his parents when they found out about his sexual orientation and they stopped feeding him, as they considered his sexuality to be a shame for the family. Fares also emphasised the role played by religion in determining SOGI minorities' lives in Syria:

> In Syria, in the school we study the Koran. We should study that. They start to put in our mind LGBT or gays, LGBT community are something bad, they will go to hell and these things. And you shouldn't do that, and do this. (…) I thought that I'm totally alone in this world.

Diana (Germany), instead, pointed out the 'multifaceted' approach in Iran towards SOGI minorities:

> If someone is obviously gay or lesbian or something like that, it can turn into jail and then kill – so not be alive anymore. But that's also different levels. (…) And of course that's from the person who is [sexually] passive, that's killing. When [penetrative] active person is different. (…) Only transsexuality is acceptable – that is legal. (…) Many gay and lesbian people as trans also do these operations. Because they think if they change the sex, that would be better to live in Iran. (…) That is only legal. Socially, of course, that's taboo.

SOGI claimants from other regions, like Eastern Europe, Asia and the Caribbean, shared analogous difficulties and ill-treatment, whether or not criminalising laws are still in force in their country of origin. A few examples are illustrative. Referring to Russia, which is a member of the Council of Europe and ratified the ECHR, Veronica (Germany) explained: 'Other people are allowed to behave aggressively and say and beat, bad words, so openly, because they see what comes from the state. (…) That's hard to really live openly in Russia. And for men, I mean, worse'. Similarly, Prince Emrah (Germany) explained in relation to Turkmenistan:

> If I go to Turkmenistan, they will take me to jail again. (…) You cannot be openly manly, you cannot be openly feminine. You cannot go to the clubs as gay. When they see you, they catch you (…) they give you four years, five years to sit in the jail.

The persistence of 'cultural' beliefs about SOGI minorities was stressed by Sadia (UK) with reference to Malaysia: 'My uncle think it was the devil coming inside my body'. Such accounts confirm the strong influence that religion plays in that country in this respect. In fact:

> [They] do have laws that specifically legislate to curb LGBT people and its "lifestyle", especially Sharia law, because Malaysian society is predominantly Muslim and Malaysia made Islam as the official religion in its constitution. (…) Especially if you are trans, there is a specific Sharia law against cross-dressing in every 13 states, basically saying if you are caught dressing up as the opposite sex and doing immoral acts (loose term for prostitution), you can be prosecuted. And in three states it just simply stated that you can be prosecuted if you step out of the house while presenting as the opposite sex or crossdressing. And for gays or lesbians, who might be presenting too femme or butch respectively, they could be approached by self-righteous "religious police" offering unsolicited advice to return to the right path (Amber, UK).

Jamaica is another case in point. Angel (Germany) explained that:

The church uses the buggery law against every member of the LGBT community. (…) It's embedded in your mind from when you're a child that lesbians must die, gay men must die. And they don't say lesbians, they say "sodomite". They don't say gay men, they say "batty man". (…) I've had partners that I've had to tell people that she's my cousin. (…) You can't be a transgender in Jamaica, because a man can't put on a woman's clothes (…) you will die by the time you step through your door. Your neighbour will kill you. (…) When straight heterosexual people kill them, and no police is investigating, and on top of that the parents are not going to claim the body and bury it.

As Trudy Ann (Germany), also from Jamaica, summarised: 'As a man you can never be girly, you have to tug that out because you would be like dead meat'.

The pervasive legal and social homophobia and transphobia evident in these claimants' experiences throws doubt on the possibility of improving SOGI minorities' enjoyment of human rights through law alone, including by undertaking international commitments. A more encompassing cultural and social 'revolution' seems necessary. South African experience confirms this difficulty (Camminga 2018, 2019). As Junio (UK) explained:

There are different ways that they are treated. Firstly, they are met with the stigma of the community, even though there is a constitution that supports LGBT people. (…) LGBT people in South Africa have a difficulty to express themselves (…) they can't because of the community and the traditional leaders. (…) Then there is corrective rape that unleashes from the community to LGBT people and access to healthcare is very limited, jobs as well. (…) The police is not really doing much. (…) So, most cases go unreported for the sake of that fear.

The overall implications of past abuses and discrimination on the 'new' life in Europe are evident in a Syrian claimant's words:

[I]t was hard [to get used to life in Germany]. Because I saw the culture, it was a shock for me because in Syria we can't do anything, we cannot do anything to hang out, to kiss a guy or to hold his hand on the street. (…) Because if you do that you will go to the jail or the community will judge you. It's going to be really horrible (Fares, Germany).

Indeed, the habit of living one's SOGI in the 'closet' to avoid persecution makes living in a more open environment difficult at first. In sum, for many SOGI minorities, it was the social and cultural environment of their countries of origin, as much as the law, that made life intolerable. As Just Me (focus group no. 3, northern Italy) expressed very clearly, '[s]ome people live with that fear every day in Africa, day to day. It is always their secret, always afraid for people not to know about your sexual identity'. When the need to flee becomes overwhelming, new challenges lie ahead, as the next section explores.

5.3　'It Suddenly Happened'

The previous section has shown why, while some aspects of people's lives may be relatively satisfactory, the constant presence of homophobia and transphobia forces individuals to leave their country of origin. Yet, the decision to leave is rarely followed by an easy process of departure and travel towards a 'safe haven'. The main obstacle is the general lack of legal channels for escape, including to European countries, which forces claimants to find alternative solutions rather than use direct, safe and legally recognised pathways. As anticipated in Chap. 4, even legal channels such as family reunification are often not an option for SOGI claimants (Del Guercio 2018) owing to a still widespread heteronormative reading of the notion of family, which contrasts with our theoretical framework (Chap. 3).

The current extent of territorial and extraterritorial control of state borders, particularly those of the EU, means that it is increasingly difficult to reach a safer country in order to lodge an asylum application. This is not a new phenomenon, as historical analyses have confirmed (Scott FitzGerald 2019), in light of states' 'undeniable sovereign right to control aliens' entry into and residence in their territory'.[2] By applying an 'embodied border paradigm' in relation to EU migration and asylum law, Violeta Moreno-Lax demonstrates how external borders, set up at the European level inside and beyond the EU to exercise this sovereign right, now constrain all migrants (Moreno-Lax 2018). People seeking asylum, including SOGI minorities, are prevented from reaching Europe through the deployment of a variety of legal and institutional mechanisms and enforcement controls, not only at European borders but also in transit countries. In sum, these macro-level factors may suggest that European countries are primarily implementing their Refugee Convention-related obligations by pursuing their own internal interests, thus stretching the exclusionary rationale embodied in that Convention (Chap. 3) rather than adopting a human rights-based approach.

The international legal framework leaves states with significant room for discretion in this field. Doubts have been raised about whether IHRL includes an obligation to issue humanitarian visas, thus granting people who are in need of international protection a 'safe passage' to destination countries, even before the formal submission of an asylum application (Danisi 2019). Despite the fact that every individual, regardless of nationality, is entitled to enjoy certain human rights and freedoms, human rights treaties apply only 'within the jurisdiction' of contracting states. Unless the notion of 'jurisdiction' is framed along the lines of more progressive models based, for instance, on the impact of decisions refusing 'safe passage' in order to claim asylum,[3] human rights play a limited role, mainly through the principle of non-refoulement or procedural obligations once the asylum application is already submitted at the borders of the destination country or within its territory.[4] An obligation to issue humanitarian visas cannot be established under EU law either, as the CJEU found in *X and X*.[5]

---

[2] Taking into account the ECHR, for instance *Saadi v. UK*, Application no. 13229/03, Grand Chamber, 29 January 2008, para. 63.
[3] HRC, General Comment no. 36, 2018, paras. 5–7. For an analysis of this model, see Danisi (2019).
[4] For example, when a European country has control over a claimant's life, such as on high seas: *Hirsi and Others v. Italy*, Application no. 27765/09, 23 February 2012.
[5] Case C-638/16 PPU, *X and X*, 7 March 2017, ECLI:EU:C:2017:173, para. 51.

For people fleeing homophobia and transphobia, as for many others, such an obligation to issue humanitarian visas would help avoid the additional layers of violence and abuse that this section, through the personal accounts of SOGI claimants, explores. It should be noted, however, that it may be easier to cross European borders when exceptional situations arise, putting specific groups in a position of relative advantage for reasons unrelated to SOGI but that, nonetheless, may have a positive effect on people belonging to SOGI minorities. This was the case of Ibrahim (Germany): whereas humanitarian visas were issued for some people following the war in Syria, Ibrahim was not Syrian and was denied a visa in European embassies in Lebanon. Nonetheless, Ibrahim took the opportunity to escape homophobia and travelled to Germany via Turkey, Greece and Macedonia:

> Since I was 17, 18, I always had the dream to live in Europe, because I saw this parade on YouTube. (…) But I never believed that I would be here one day, until that day of what happened. In Syria, the war, the borders [were] opened. [H]ow should I come? I won't have a visa, I won't be able to come here. So, I guess sometimes war was positive for some people.

The same phenomenon occurred in Italy, where Anna, an LGBTIQ+ group volunteer, told us about the case of a bi-national couple where the Syrian partner in the relationship did not need to apply for asylum on SOGI grounds, as he had obtained international protection owing to war-related events in his country of origin. Similarly, the UK's Syrian Vulnerable Persons Resettlement Scheme (Chap. 4) takes people identified as vulnerable by the UNHCR, which may include individuals at risk owing to their SOGI.

Other useful mechanisms for protection are humanitarian corridors, which may have a general scope, as reported in Italy (for instance, Valentina, social worker) or may consist of more limited initiatives devised for SOGI claimants with NGOs support (Angel, Germany). These scenarios, however, constitute exceptions to the experiences of most SOGI claimants, especially if compared to other national experiences like Canada's dedicated resettlement programme (House of Commons Canada 2017). In the following sub-sections, we explore the experiences of forced departures and travel, including the treatment suffered in transit countries.

5.3.1 Forced Departures

Our data show that, most of the time, neither the decision to flee a country nor the final destination are planned by SOGI claimants. More often than not, these follow unforeseen events. As Shany (Germany) put it, after a family member discovered her sexual orientation, '[a]ll my life I was working, I didn't have any, any kind of any problem… [Other people] plan their coming (…) all their lives. This is the difference between me and them (…): I didn't plan it'. Not surprisingly, she continued as follows: 'it was something like, "I have to do it, I have no way". (…) The life in my place [was] not possible anymore'. Equally, Selim (UK) explained:

5.3 'It Suddenly Happened'

[Asylum] is a term that never crossed my mind before. Like it was nothing, it was never planned. I had a good life, I had a good career. Lots of people wanted to be in my position, but I was always unsafe because (...) you wake up every morning in the Middle East and you draw this line on your face that you are straight, but you are not.

A similar experience was shared by Diana (Germany): '[T]he goal was simply to leave Iraq. So that was not a decision where or where to go'. The most common experience is expressed well by Jayne (UK): 'It wasn't anything to do with choices at that point, I was kind of desperate'.

Nonetheless, our data include some SOGI claimants in all countries under comparison who had planned their destination and journey. For instance, Janelle said: 'I chose to come to the UK. I did my research in terms of gender identity, the laws of the country, and it was my place of choice'. The same experience was shared by Tiffany (focus group no. 2, Glasgow) who explained: 'I escape[d] from home, to go to UK because I know in UK... people with sexuality to live freely and openly'. Still, as Kamel explained, decisions may not be entirely freely made: 'Italy was not my choice, not at all. I have gathered information on all countries of the world in relation to my situation, but the only place I found doable was Italy'. Even when planned, there is no guarantee that the chosen destination will be reached. For instance, Alphaeus explained: 'When I reached [Germany] I struggled still, because I wanted to proceed my journey, to continue to go to Finland. (...) But the police told me "you're not going anywhere"'. In turn, Sadia remembered: 'No, I [didn't] have any idea about UK, but my sister just [told] the agency [to] give [me] any place for just a safe place'. What she meant by 'the agency' was not, however, clarified.

These accounts lead us to what some participants referred to as the common story of many claimants claiming asylum on grounds of sexual orientation (for instance, Diego and Riccardo, LGBTIQ+ group volunteers, Italy). As reported, such recurring scenarios generally involve two people, the claimant and their partner, who are found in intimate or sexual circumstances in someone's home (or less commonly, at school or at work). What follows may be expressed in the words of William (Germany): 'I was naked and my partner was also naked. (...) They forcefully entered. (...) They started beating me, shouting "you are promoting homosexuality in our village". (...) They dragged me outside [and continued] beating [me]'. Often, what happened to the partner is unknown and, even where the police intervenes, such accounts commonly include arbitrary mistreatment, interrogation to identify other LGBTIQ+ people, eventual release from imprisonment (sometimes after the payment of bribes), and an immediate attempt to escape the country, which, by that time, seems the only possible solution. As always William explained: 'I could not go back to the village because I was now a vagabond, I was now an outcast'.

In these particular circumstances, the option of resorting to humanitarian visas, even if available, was deemed problematic by some participants. Fred (Italy) explained: '[For visas] you need to wait and wait. But when a person experiences a problem like the one we [SOGI minorities] have and apply for a visa, when will it be provided?' The same difficulty is expressed by Fido (focus group no. 4, northern Italy):

> You know why people will not ask [a visa] from Nigeria, and come to Europe through flights or whatever (…)? Because when you are living your life, you don't have any problem, you would not think of going to Europe. (…) [T]he problem occurs immediately, no one out there would think "let me go to airport and go and prepare my visa and take flight", it is not possible when they are looking for you. The next opportunity is your road.

Our data also demonstrate the persistent and ongoing nature of persecution experiences in countries of origin before the final decision to flee. To use the words of Halim (Germany):

> I had certain incidents and threats from the government (…). I used to dismiss those fears and threats for a long time. However, by the end of 2014, I felt I [was] no longer safe in Egypt, [because it became] increasingly dangerous, friends of mine [were] arrested.

In other cases, relatives and friends play a key role. Sandra (Germany) explained that:

> I didn't know that I would be a refugee, but a friend of mine who is in France (…) he knew my problems, and he told me to leave the country (…) I had to quit my job, I had to quit everything and just not exist. (…) If it wasn't for him giving me a way out (…) I don't know, maybe I would still be living inside [my country].

When escaping persecution, protection is often sought and, sometimes, temporarily obtained through personal contacts or socio-economic connections in the country of origin, thus avoiding forced and immediate departure. A first example of this is provided by Sandra (Germany):

> I had to move [to the house of my best friend's sister] because I knew that nobody would ever suspect me being there. She took me in because she lived maybe 15 years in the states. (…) She's a lot open minded, so for her it was ok, and that's where I stayed all this time.

A second experience was shared by Marhoon (Germany), who came from a privileged and well connected family in his country of origin:

> When people see it [my name], immediately they change their attitude towards me. I'm respected automatically just because of my family name and title. I was caught once with a guy in a car kissing, having sex, not only kissing (…) by the police. I thought ok, I'm done, my family will disown me. (…) Then, once they saw my ID card, they said "ok, go home".

While these experiences are unusual, such 'private' and limited protection is immaterial for claiming and being granted international protection. In fact, the availability of a private, relatively safe environment, is no surrogate for state protection and does not reduce SOGI claimants' fear of persecution. In this respect, Sandra (Germany) herself pointed out that '[y]ou just wake up with a cancer. You don't plan to have it. So it's either you die or you survive from it'.

These experiences of forced departure are aggravated by the need to undertake dangerous routes, often with the involvement of smugglers and harsh treatment in transit countries – harsh treatment both for their 'refugeness' *and* as members of a SOGI minority, as our intersectional approach suggests (Chap. 3).

5.3.2 Journey Experiences

Travel experiences were described as extremely traumatic by professionals working directly with arrivals in Europe, in line with 'desperate journeys' of migrants already documented at Europe's borders (UNHCR 2019). For example, Susanna, a social worker in Italy, explained:

> We are talking about extremely vulnerable people, not only because they are claiming asylum on sexual orientation grounds, but also because they have gone through such a tough journey that they arrive here with an intermingling of psychological issues, including sometimes a certain amount of apathy, as well as restraint in showing their inner feelings.

According to Susanna, these psychological problems may also be related to sexual abuse suffered in transit countries that, in turn, may cause diseases or infections: 'Belonging to sexual minorities is an additional factor that generates a higher level of vulnerability. (…) These claimants appear to be more subject to sexual exploitation (…) especially those who are not able to hide their sexual orientation'. She provided the example of two men who, after arriving in Libya, were sold and raped before attempting to cross the Mediterranean Sea. As a consequence of sexual exploitation, the sole survivor who eventually arrived in Italy discovered that he was infected with HIV in Libya.

While only a few people felt sufficiently comfortable or secure to talk openly about their journey to Europe, and we avoided pushing them to do so because of the risk of re-traumatisation (Chap. 2), our data show that travel experiences varied according to the destination country. Lacking space to recount in full these experiences, we note that whereas the journeys of those arriving in Germany and Italy often involved smugglers, a significant number of journeys to the UK seemed connected to trafficking. For instance, Daphne (UK) said:

> I was brought here by somebody called (…) and he promised me to find me a job here. But, when we reach here (…), the job he offered me was prostitution. That is why I ran away from him and (…) I went to claim asylum.

Experiences of direct flights were reported most often by participants in the UK, and were rare for our participants in Italy. Sometimes, those were the result of a 'fortunate' chain of events. For instance, Halim (Germany) remembered:

> I didn't want to really leave but because of the threats I felt I had to, and around that time I got invited to a conference in Berlin and that was my visa out of Egypt and into Europe. (…) Somehow, it ended up being Berlin without me really planning to be in Berlin.

In her turn, Shany arrived in Germany because her job involved travel in Europe, while Mary and Zaro used their sporting achievements to secure invitation letters and apply for short-term visas to the UK. Others, like Veronica and Julia (Germany), fleeing Russia, used tourist visas, and yet others, like Fares (Germany), fleeing Syria, resorted to a student visa. In short, due to the lack of any systematic means of safe passage to Europe, SOGI claimants who flee are forced to use a range of ways to reach Europe and, only on arrival, submit applications for international protection.

SOGI claimants in Germany and Italy had generally taken different routes, in line with more general migratory flows.[6] In both cases, however, they were exposed en route, along with other people in need of international protection, to experiences of violence, extortion and abuse, as well as additional isolation. As Prince Emrah (Germany) recalled, '[t]alking is so difficult, not sleeping, not eating anything, sleeping with I don't know how many people, not counting. And I'm alone from Turkmenistan to Turkey. (…) I [could not] tell my feelings'.

Most of our asylum claimant participants in Germany followed the Balkan route, entering Europe by land via Eastern European countries. The length of some journeys was notable. While Tina took seven months to arrive to Germany via Greece, Bebars recalled his four-week travel from Syria to Germany: he went from Syria to Lebanon, Turkey, Greece, then he crossed Macedonia and Austria by train, bus, and on foot before he arrived in Germany. Sometimes the journey took even longer, as for those SOGI claimants fleeing sub-Saharan countries. For instance, a claimant who travelled to Germany from Uganda via Turkey, explained in detail:

> The best way was to go to Kakuma Camp (…) to seek for asylum in Kenya. (…) It's where I met fellow Ugandans who are also LGBT people. Some had been there for one week and they told me life was hard there, the camp was full. (…) I had to fly out of Kenya. I went to Turkey (…) I stayed on the streets for almost one week and a half. (…) Life was really hard. (…) There was a gay man that I came to know. He took me to his place. (…) He gave me another choice of life. [But] he started treating me badly, really, really badly. He could sometimes even send some guys to force me to have sex with them, (...) they raped me, forced me to have it. [After meeting two Syrian guys] we collected some small money. (…) So I ended up with these guys on the journey, on the same journey, on a small boat from Turkey to Greece, to a certain island in Greece. When we entered Greece (…) they welcomed us, they took some small care of us (…) we were given some bad food. (…) After we were released and we (...) proceeded to Macedonia, from Macedonia we just passed through, we entered Serbia. (…) We entered Hungary. (…) They detained me in Hungary, [but] they released us, they drove us to the next border. (…) When we reached Vienna, at the Bahnhof [train station] there were so many people and we heard that the German borders are closed. (…) Then after some time they boarded us in (…) a train. And they brought us to Germany.

William (Germany) confirmed that the journey appears to be a chain of causal events, where forced labour and sexual exploitation is often the price for a passage to Europe:

> I stayed with this man in this house surviving on the mercy of these people. (…) We went to a place called Izmir. (…) It's like, this was the place where people used to cross. (…) One day, we were crossing, we fell into the water and were rescued by the Turkish police, and they imprisoned us (…) they gave us some white papers, return. These papers were allowing us now to move. (…) When we crossed, we came to Greece. (…) It was a very big reception camp. (…) They took us to Athens. Now in Athens we slept on the street for two days in the city. Then we managed to board trains, which trains took us through Macedonia, they took us again to Serbia. In Serbia, we stayed there for two days again sleeping on the streets. Then (…) I reached Hungary. (…) I was not looking for good things to be in a good

---

[6] See Frontex: https://frontex.europa.eu/along-eu-borders/migratory-map/

5.3 'It Suddenly Happened'

life, but I was looking for a place where my life could be safe. And I said, since I'm here I'm going to stay here. Let me make this my home.

Yet, the discriminatory treatment suffered in Hungary motivated him to move to Germany.

In the hope of avoiding such violent and traumatic experiences, some SOGI claimants feel forced to resort to fake visas. As Diana (Germany) explained:

> I've heard a lot of disadvantages, that's a very difficult and dangerous way. That's why I said, okay, so I tried to find a direct route and I just want to go straight from Iran to that safe country. And that was – it costs more, but I found someone, there's just you pay and give you a fake visa. (…) I wanted to leave Iran because I could not live with the situation anymore. (…) My mother did not know that I go to Germany to claim asylum. She thought I have a tourist visa. I did not tell my family what would happen.

Most SOGI claimants interviewed in Italy, as nationals of sub-Saharan countries, arrived instead through the Mediterranean by sea. Ken explained his travel as follows: 'From Nigeria to Niger, from Niger to Algeria, from Algeria to Libya, then I got stopped in Libya for some time. Then from Libya to Italy [by boat]'. Dev and Fred, fleeing Cameroon, passed through Algeria, where they worked for five months, before reaching Libya. Mamaka had an even longer journey:

> I am from the Gambia. (…) When I have the problem in my country I moved to Senegal because it was the neighbourest country (…) I was there for a year but it could not be ok with me. So (…) I came to Mali. So it is from Mali I had the information that there is a road going to Italy (…) from Mali to a placed called Niamey [in Niger] (…). Then from Niamey to Agadez [in Niger], from Agadez to Sabha [in Libya] (…) I was almost two to three weeks, almost a month in Libya before I took the boat to Italy.

Similar journeys were described by other participants, including Buba, Bella, Diarra, Franco, Siri and Moses. As Moses recalled, '[m]y intention (…) was to just leave my country and go to a place where I could probably be safe from the horrors of my country'. Instead, he ended up spending eight months in Libya before being able to cross the sea.

During this kind of journey, episodes of violence, detention and extortion were frequently reported. According to Gbona (Italy), who reached Libya from Mali through the desert, 'along the way, there were some Arabs, they are in the desert. They went around, around and then stopped us, forced [us] to get off the car, and start beating… yes, beating'. As Nelo (Italy) also explained:

> Basically, I was just only run saving my life first, and when I got to Niger, to Libya, they were very angry because the money I was supposed to pay, I didn't pay… they have to keep me in different parts, called prison, they call it… kidnapping. (…) They will (…) beat you and tell you to call your people at home to send the money.

The lack of support from contacts in their country may lead to extended deprivation of one's liberty. So Odosa summarised his travel experience as follows: 'Oh, the travel. It is not good. (…) I spent close to six months (…) because of the delay and the kidnapping, the "trankey" [forced labour camp] in Libya. (…) From Nigeria to Italy, take like one month and some weeks, but because of the kind of problem I face along the road, that is why I use close to six months'.

Nice Guy (focus group no. 1, northern Italy) remembered the attempt to cross the sea as an experience of complete uncertainty: 'All I knew was that, OK, the boat is going to take me to Europe, I don't even know if it's Italy, France, Germany… No way, I don't know. In fact, it's just like being re-born, you know nothing'. For this final part of the trip, other SOGI claimants, like Nelo, Gbona and Moses, expressed mixed feelings following incidents on the high sea and subsequent rescues by NGOs ('the Swedish', 'the Norwegian' or 'the Dutch') or Italian coastguard vessels. For Gbona, 'Italy saved my life (…) we were on danger on the high sea with water rising and [the boat] going down', whereas for Moses:

> Seeing the sea alone is like death already, because (…) if anything should happen, there is no safety guarantee and so (…) I felt that, at least (…) I am going to be alive (…) when the rescue came. So I arrived in Italy [and said] "thank God, I still have a future ahead". (…) For a moment I was happy.

Nelo (Italy) explained that he discourages other people from coming to Europe to avoid such fear: 'The most scary part of it is when you're on top of the blue sea. (…) So that's what I'm always advising every day, "look, don't think of coming to Europe by land [and by sea], it's not good, it's dangerous"'. Nelo felt lucky to have arrived in Europe, but also said that 'due to the fact that I just came in, my head is still a mess'. This 'mess' can be insurmountable for people, such Alain A., who lost their partners in the high sea after the sinking of the dinghy used to cross the Mediterranean Sea. The short and long-term consequences of these traumatic experiences in terms of health appear self-evident (Chap. 9; Alessi et al. 2018).

From the above, it seems that belonging to a SOGI minority shaped our participants' journeys differently. On the one hand, it may influence the entire journey plan. For instance, Mary and Zaro (UK) explained that, in order to avoid raising suspicions, they travelled individually: 'First she… she went to Dubai, then I came, after three or four days I came, after her. Because we could not travel together'. On the other hand, SOGI aspects appear immaterial for some claimants, who see mere survival as their only need. According to Kennedy (Italy), who reached Libya from Nigeria, people simply hide their SOGI during the journey:

> I stayed in Libya four months. (…) What you are just thinking at that particular moment is let me get to (…) a place to just rest my head. (…) The second thing is (…) food. When you eat, you begin to think security. When you get security, then your mind calms down [and] you express (…) feelings, you know, with person that you love.

Similarly, Alain A. (Italy) pointed out:

> It is a very dangerous journey. For everyone, not only for LGBT, and it is not a journey where you get to know who is gay and who is not gay. Because it is just a journey, so we don't stay like to exhibit our characters, or our what we are. So, [in] my journey I didn't face a problem as an LGBT because I didn't identify myself as a LGBT.

For Ken (Italy), the reason to avoid mention of his SOGI was simply to avoid additional abuse: 'You don't talk about it, it is hell. No'. Yet, the negative effects of such repression and fear on the submission of the asylum claim at arrival are noticeable, as the next section will discuss.

5.3 'It Suddenly Happened'

Finally, it is worth noting that a significant exception to these general trends seems to relate to those transgender claimants who were mostly nationals of South American countries and claimed asylum after several years in Italy. As Valentina, a social worker in Italy, explained: 'They have no other way to be granted a permit to stay in Italy. (…) Many sex workers from South America would not claim asylum but would like to work in Italy, as it happens in other European countries'. Valentina also reported that, where other transgender claimants from the same countries have travelled to Italy through Eastern European countries after flying to Russia, border authorities often signpost people to NGOs, more as a result of practice than clear guidance but with positive implications in terms of addressing their reception needs. In her view, this is related to the 'visibility' of trans claimants, which distinguishes them from other SOGI minorities.

From the above analysis, one of the most difficult aspects of such journeys is certainly the treatment suffered in transit countries. This has an additional impact on the well-being and social experiences at and post-arrival of SOGI claimants. The countries of transit for claimants headed to Europe are often Turkey and Libya, which are also the primary recipients of the EU and its member states' assistance to neighbouring countries in the area of migration irrespective of their human rights record (Human Rights Watch 2019; United Nations Support Mission in Libya-Office of the High Commissioner for Human Rights 2018). In this respect, it is appropriate to explore, albeit briefly, how SOGI claimants experience and perceive these countries. Most importantly, the intersection of a variety of personal characteristics – being migrant and member of a SOGI minority – appears to render SOGI claimants more exposed to abuse in these transit countries than other migrants and refugees. This risk increases exponentially when they cannot leave these countries, or are even sent back to their countries of origin, especially as a consequence of EU-led externalisation migration policies (Liguori 2018).

Starting with Turkey, the prevalence of homophobia and transphobia that has been denounced at international level (Ramón Mendos 2019), combined with high levels of racism (UNHCR 2011), were confirmed by our participants. For instance, William (Germany), who arrived to Turkey from Uganda, explained:

> When I told [a Turkish man] that I'm gay he told me "that cannot happen. In Turkey I cannot even take you to the authorities because they cannot accept you". The next day he transferred me to another house. (…) He moved me out of his family, because he had two kids and a wife. (…) I stayed in fear, crying day and night, fearing the police because they could arrest me any time. (…) I could not work because I used to fear going to the streets. The Turkish people are not easy people. They are racists, they segregate Blacks, you're a Black man.

As for Libya, arbitrary detention is the rule for all people trying to migrate across the Mediterranean to reach Europe (MSF 2019; United Nations Support Mission in Libya-Office of the High Commissioner for Human Rights 2018). SOGI claimants communicated a striking level of fear at the prospect of being forced to stay in Libya. Despite the severity of the legal and social environment of his country of origin, Nelo (Italy) told us that: 'It's even better that you are recognised as a gay in

Nigeria than to be recognised as a gay in Libya, in Arab country'. In his view, violence in Libya reaches unimaginable levels.

In an attempt to explain the negative implications of such journeys and treatment in transit countries, Just Me (focus group no. 3, northern Italy) pointed out: 'Many people that died in my presence (…) even in Libya (…) they kill somebody from my back. (…) You see people die after passing through all this, you come here, Commission give[s] you negative. (…) If you are not strong, you will go mad'. Yet, these traumatic stories and consequences in terms of depression and anxiety are rarely considered and addressed at and after arrival in host countries (Piwowarczyk et al. 2017).

As we will explore especially in Chap. 7, the circumstances of the departure, aspects of the journey and the treatment in transit countries may however be, among others, at the centre of the credibility assessment at administrative or judicial level. For instance, during a hearing, an Italian judge focused a significant part of the questioning on the separation of the claimant from his partner in Libya and on the attempts made, at arrival and in Libya, to obtain any information about his partner's disappearance (Tribunal observation, northern Italy 2018). The claimant argued that, at arrival, he was too traumatised to seek information about his partner's fate from Italian authorities or from his smugglers. Any empathy, which common sense should require, aside from any theoretical approach or SOGI guidelines (Chaps. 3 and 4), was replaced by an evident 'disbelief'. Similar episodes show that decision-makers are not always aware of, or consciously ignore, the general condition of SOGI claimants on arrival in Europe and the reasons why they may not be able to express their SOGI immediately. The next section therefore aims to explore this particular aspect.

5.4 The Arrival in Europe

A complex mixture of feelings was shared by participants in relation to their arrival in Europe. Several asylum claimant participants described feelings of safety. This was true of Susan (focus group no. 3, Bavaria, Germany), who told us '[w]hen I came to Germany, I felt safe', as well as Silver (Italy), who said: 'When I arrived in Italy (…) I was very happy [and] I said "Why no one is looking at me? Why do not they beat me?"' Others remembered, instead, feeling fear and anxiety about the risk of being returned. As Miria (focus group no. 3, London, UK) explained: 'If it is going back to Uganda (…) I said I really tried to kill myself, I said, already in Uganda I was dead. Kill me here rather than spoiling your ticket'.

Related to their stressful experiences before and upon arrival, some SOGI claimants told stories of alcoholism and drug abuse. As Shany said: 'Mostly I wake up at six in the evening, but I was using a lot of marijuana, a lot of alcohol. (…) I [didn't] want to think nothing. (…) I [didn't] want to wake up because I just, like, think somebody in the door going to kill me. I was a paranoid'.

5.4 The Arrival in Europe

Above all, a feeling of bewilderment emerged. As Nelo (Italy) explained: 'We don't know many things about asylum or whatever. I've been to Niger, I've been to Libya, I never had to go to the courts, go to Commission, go to anything in order to stay'. This feeling may have been exacerbated in cases of collective arrivals. As Vincenzo, an LGBTIQ+ group volunteer in Italy, pointed out: 'At arrival the security approach is undeniable nowadays. (…) People probably get the perception of being only numbers and are put under control'. In such situations, the SOGI dimension does not receive the attention and care it warrants.

In the particular context of arrival, participants consistently raised at least three issues to assess how fair an asylum system is for SOGI minorities: (1) whether, and what, information is provided on SOGI asylum at the moment of first contact with national authorities; (2) the guarantee of individual assessments; and (3) whether the initial reception (or detention) takes SOGI into account. Before delving into these aspects, a brief clarification is needed. First, our survey confirmed that arrival is a key moment for SOGI claimants themselves, as 63% of respondents claimed international protection immediately after they reached their host country. Second, the conditions of arrival clearly vary between Germany, Italy and UK. As discussed in Chap. 4, the reason for this lies not only in the lack of harmonisation between EU countries in this specific area,[7] but also in geo-political factors that explain the different travel experiences of SOGI claimants arriving in these three countries (IOM 2019).

Regarding the general initial procedure, in Germany asylum applications can only be registered at the BAMF, but an asylum claimant can also report to a federal or local police, or at reception facilities (ECRE, AIDA & Asyl und Migration 2019, p. 18). While this reporting should happen 'immediately', there is no time limit for lodging an application. The situation of SOGI claimants interviewed in Germany confirmed that the bulk of applications were registered at the BAMF, after having been sorted and processed at the border.

Italy, in turn, has faced a high number of arrivals in recent years. As a result, most people claiming asylum, including SOGI claimants, followed a similar path for the submission and subsequent evaluation of their asylum request. On arrival at the border, by land or by sea, Italian authorities take charge and, afterwards, claimants' asylum requests are registered at the police local headquarters ('Questura'). As Jonathan, an LGBTIQ+ group volunteer, explained, SOGI claimants who are already in Italy or enter the country in a different way have less chance of being taken in charge by the authorities. It may therefore be more difficult for these claimants to receive initial support, at least in terms of accommodation.

The UK, in contrast, has not faced similar high numbers of arrivals. Excluding specific programmes such as the Syrian Vulnerable Persons Resettlement Scheme, asylum applications should be made on arrival or 'at the earliest possible opportunity' (UKVI 2016, p. 4). This means that if claimants do not apply on arrival or at the border, as was the case for some of our participants, they submit their

---

[7] In contrast to other aspects of the asylum process, as the CEAS shows (Chaps. 4, 6, 7 and 8).

application to offices 'in country', the most well-known being Lunar House in Croydon, South London. Once the application is submitted, a meeting with an immigration officer (known as a 'screening interview') takes place, followed by an asylum interview with a caseworker some time later (usually a few weeks, but sometimes months).

Taken this broad context into account, the situation that each SOGI claimant needs to face initially, including the nature of their first contact with authorities, varies in light of individual circumstances and according to the receiving country in question. Yet, from our data, some general trends emerge.

5.4.1 Information on SOGI Asylum

The importance of having knowledge on SOGI asylum to enable informed decisions is widely recognised. For instance, according to Jean, a member of the European Parliament, the access to 'quality information', which needs to be provided 'in a format they can understand', is essential in improving the system for (all) claimants. As Ibrahim (Germany) explained: 'I got informed a bit about asylum and I felt it more reasonable to stay and not be living in fear'.

Some SOGI claimants we met knew at the time of their arrival in Europe that they could make an application for protection on SOGI grounds. Such information is often shared through SOGI claimants and refugees already in Europe. For instance, Momo (Italy) explained that one of his friends in France instructed him: 'He explained me everything. You need to do this, follow this procedure, until you get international protection. In Africa you do not have such a thing [being protected on SOGI grounds]'. According to Jonathan, an LGBTIQ+ group volunteer in Italy, and Livio, a lawyer in Italy, the increasing exchange of information on SOGI asylum between potential claimants who are still in their countries of origin, asylum claimants (including SOGI), NGOs and other personal contacts in Europe, means there is a greater awareness of relevant procedures, which may on occasion also improve decision-making. A good example of this was provided by Kamel, who was granted refugee status in Italy after having prepared all the necessary material to support his claim before fleeing Libya. For these claimants, it may have been easier to tell their story at arrival. Wole (focus group no. 2, Glasgow, UK) explained: 'When I was back at home, I did a research and I found out that you can claim in the UK, so when I came in the UK, at the airport, I claimed directly for asylum protection'. Michael (UK) also recalled:

> When I came to… airport Heathrow, I ask officer (…) please can you help me with protection. And they asked me a lot of questions about why you ask about protection, why we should help you with asylum, and I answer them everything.

However, this openness does not necessarily secure advantages in relation to individual assessments and reception conditions. To use Michael's experience as an example once again: 'After that I had been in airport I didn't know anyone in Great

5.4 The Arrival in Europe

Britain (laughs) I didn't have any colleagues here, I didn't have any friends here'. He was eventually helped by an NGO.

Yet, most of our claimant participants identified the lack of information on SOGI asylum at arrival as one of the most problematic aspects of the system across Europe. According to our survey, 31% of respondents did not know they could claim asylum on SOGI grounds when they arrived. This lack of information not only prevents them requesting asylum on SOGI grounds as soon as possible, it also denies them reassurance that they are now safe if the reason for having fled their country is connected with their SOGI. As Ibrahim (Germany) confirmed, many SOGI refugees 'didn't know from the beginning that they can apply for asylum based on their sexual orientation'. This failure of communication may be expected given that the relevant legislation in Germany, Italy and the UK does not include a general duty to provide specific information on SOGI asylum at arrival, nor do relevant EU directives address this point. Yet, there is a general duty to inform claimants about the asylum procedure (for instance, Recitals 22 and 25 and Article 12 of the Procedures Directive), and its importance has been stressed also by the ECtHR in its jurisprudence.[8] In some cases, specific information is provided thanks to the involvement of NGOs. For example, in the UK, in 2014, the Scottish Refugee Council (with other agencies) published an information leaflet for SOGI asylum claimants arriving in the UK in 12 community languages (Scottish Refugee Council 2014). However, this example of good practice has not been taken forward elsewhere. The 2019 reform in Germany (Chap. 4), which restricts the role of NGO counselling as it happens already in AnkER Centres (ECRE, AIDA 2019, pp. 10–11), may therefore have a particularly negative impact on the right to receive adequate information on SOGI asylum.

More generally, according to Helena, an EASO officer, even when SOGI information is provided, there is lack of uniformity across Europe. Therefore, it is not surprising that a significant number of our participants were unaware of what 'asylum' is and what procedures apply, in general, and that SOGI asylum is possible. Shany (Germany) explained:

> Even the word asylum, I couldn't even find it in my mind in that time because I was like, you know, you using, this is like a big, big moment which like your brain is completely, it's not working, it's like plastic.

According to Gbona (Italy), at arrival, no one asked the reason why he fled his country of origin but only for basic personal details. Siri (Italy) became aware at arrival that he could apply for asylum in order not to be immediately returned to his country of origin, but no information on SOGI was provided to him. Giovanna, a lawyer who was involved as a volunteer in a few disembarkation operations, confirmed the way post-arrival situations are managed in Italy:

> Actually, after the disembarkation, only a few general pieces of information are requested, such as age or health records. Then, they are sorted into groups and asked whether they want to apply for asylum. If they don't, a return order is issued. There is no room for

---

[8] *M.A. and Others v. Lithuania*, Application no. 59793/17, 12 December 2018.

personal stories and, in that very particular moment, people just arrived have often no idea about refugee status, subsidiarity or humanitarian protection.

Participants in other countries, like the UK, shared similar experiences. Meggs, for example, explained:

> I didn't know it was called asylum, no, I didn't know. I just, when I got here I thought, since I am here, that is it, I will just have to find a place to live legally, and start my life all over again (…). That is what I thought, I didn't know there was this process, and how long it is, and how painful it is, I wasn't ready and prepared for that.

Success (Germany), in turn, explained: 'I was not bold enough to say that. Yeah. I was not bold enough, because I thought it was like Nigeria'. This fear may increase when different personal and cultural factors intersect, as our theoretical approach suggests (Chap. 3). For instance, in terms of relationship with fellow nationals, Lutfor (UK) recalled:

> No, I didn't hear anything about [being able to claim] the asylum and, being honest, when I was living with other guys [from Pakistan and India], I think they have no idea what is asylum (…) I didn't work, so I was living with them, I cooked for them, I ironed their clothes, cleaned the house (…) I was really scared to go out.

The difficulties faced by SOGI claimants are often aggravated by other elements. First, translation issues are a case in point. As Sadia (UK) stated:

> But that time also I am not doing any claim because I, I have a problem, language problem. I am not educated, so I have a problem. So I didn't understand, I didn't understand, I am just going there and sitting, I don't understand anything.

Second, other than facing unknown bureaucratic challenges, feelings of distress may hamper the identification of SOGI as a reason for claiming asylum. For instance, Miria (UK) explained:

> I had some problems. (…) Yes, I am a lesbian, but for that time I had no idea of that. And, you know, when you have a problem, you can't think about that thing at the same time, because I was struggling a lot. Yes, and my life was in danger, so when I came here I had to think about my life. Yes, I didn't think about of being a lesbian, I had to put that aside, because at that time that was not the issue. But, I was struggling.

The situation is even more complex when SOGI claimants are not identified by public authorities as soon as they arrive. For those who enter Europe in a group or are exploited after arrival obtaining accurate information about SOGI asylum can be particularly difficult. This trend is especially noticeable in the UK. Irma stated:

> No, I never knew that [SOGI asylum], I never knew that. Because, I mean, I never had the opportunity to talk to people. Where who brought me into the country, I was under like security, the woman was all the time, she was saying "I will report you back, I will send you back." (…) If I knew like that [SOGI asylum], I would have come out straight away with my sexuality.

Jayne, also an asylum claimant in the UK, explained:

> I had to stay with people I met from church, and surprisingly throughout the years no one said anything to me about asylum. Maybe those people were taking advantage to have me in the house, maybe babysitting, just so that I have somewhere to live.

5.4 The Arrival in Europe

A potential consequence of the lack of adequate information on SOGI asylum is the submission of a claim on grounds not related to SOGI (Chap. 7), but often connected to a particular situation of widespread violence in their country of origin. For instance, Fares (Germany), like other SOGI claimants, applied first on the basis of religious and political persecution due to the existence of political or religious conflicts. Likewise, Kennedy (Italy), fleeing Nigeria, explained:

> I did not see reason to tell them that it's [because I'm] gay, because I don't want any problem again to reoccur, whereby I will be running from Italy again to another place. So that is the reason why I told them, yes, it's Boko Haram.

Damiano, a lawyer in Italy, and Valentina, a social worker in Italy, highlighted a particular concern for SOGI claimants: the combination of the lack of information about SOGI asylum, the lack of knowledge about the treatment of SOGI minorities in the host country, internalised homophobia and/or the proximity of fellow nationals may nudge some SOGI claimants to rely on more familiar narratives of persecution as the basis of their claim. This makes it more important that authorities are sensitive to what may be the real reasons for claiming asylum in the initial screening, as well as during the main interview (Chaps. 6 and 7).

Titti, a decision-maker in Italy, also stressed this point:

> Let me give you an example. A claimant could say "I left my country because I was in conflict with my father" and, then, incidentally says that he left his [same-sex] "partner" in his country (…) This is a SOGI claim but he does not know that. (…) Probably, he does not have the tools to understand that the conflict with his father is based on his sexual orientation and that this is something wrong.

Without official information about SOGI asylum at the point of arrival, claimants had to rely on their own research or word-of-mouth information from other claimants. Alain A. (Italy) explained:

> When I came to Italy, first of all I had so much fear in me, like the fear I brought from my country was still in me. Yes, I knew like Italy protected gay people or the homosexual, but I didn't know, like, where to deal with my problem, with who to speak to. So, I was so afraid and I went to the internet (…) to do research on gay associations.

For some SOGI claimants, however, having the relevant information did not guarantee a smooth process. For instance, Nelo (Italy) was still traumatised by his past experiences when he found out about the possibility of claiming asylum on SOGI grounds. He found it difficult to trust anyone: 'And when they said, I actually have to think of it, like trying to understand if this is just a trick'.

For other claimants, instead, discovering that SOGI minorities enjoy higher levels of social and legal protection in European countries, at least to a certain degree and on paper, was a source of relief and empowerment. As Miria (UK) pointed out:

> When I saw people on the train free, for the first time to get that confidence, to know that lesbians are free here. (…) So, when I saw that I say what… oh this means LGBT here are free. Then my mind opened up, I started to know and I started to feel, what I am, to feel in my mind, I started to feel, feeling free.

In this respect, refugee community organisations and support groups, which are often the first and trusted point of contact for newly arrived asylum claimants, play a positive role, although their support can be limited in this initial phase for reasons such as lack of resources or trained staff (Chap. 6). For example, Diarra (Italy) recalled that he was not aware of the possibility of requesting asylum on SOGI grounds but, thanks to an information session on SOGI rights organised by a support group in his reception centre, he learned how SOGI minorities are treated in Italy. As he put it: 'Today I can say that I'm gay. After that meeting, I went to talk to the reception centre's staff'. This feeling of empowerment was also experienced by those claimants who were already aware that they could submit an asylum request on SOGI grounds and needed a safe environment to be able to gradually open up about themselves. As Ophelie (focus group no. 2, Glasgow, UK) confirmed:

> I did a research back home in Namibia so (…) I knew that you can claim asylum in Scotland. (…) The airport (…) was hectic, they didn't want to let us in and we (…) told them that "no, we can't go back because of my sexuality, I came with my partner". (…) [Scotland] is not an environment that we were used to, so we didn't, we were not open to show out our sexuality, because we were afraid of the same judgement we had home. (…) We had to hide (…) just stay indoors [and] not going out, until we met the LGBT Unity group. (…) It was fine, we were welcomed nicely.

To summarise, the lack of information on SOGI asylum and treatment of SOGI minorities before and at arrival may play a significant role in the submission of a claim in terms of content, timing and evidence. Surprisingly, as we will explore in Chap. 7, the lack of awareness of SOGI asylum is not duly considered by decision-makers, who sometimes also use it to cast doubt on SOGI claimants' credibility. The fallaciousness of such an approach was strongly criticised by Emily, a decision-maker in the UK:

> [Most people know they can claim on that basis] more now than before. We're seeing a lot more LGBT cases than ever before. [Decision-makers may ask] "if you've been here for 15 years, why have you never claimed asylum?" (…) I don't think I knew before this job that that is actually a specific reason for claiming asylum in this country, I've lived here for 28 years and I didn't know that!

As Giulia, an LGBTIQ+ group volunteer in Italy, stated: 'SOGI is not considered until there is a need to express it'. This need may arise during the initial individual assessment.

5.4.2 Initial Screenings

When a claimant receives appropriate information, the initial screening is more likely to run smoothly. For instance, Siri (Italy) remembered that, after he had disembarked, he was told simply that everyone in Italy is free to say whatever they want, as long as they are not breaking the law. As he explained: 'I was not told that I could be homosexual here. [But] when I was sent to Questura [police local headquarters] after 15 days and I was asked the reasons why I fled my country, I did not

5.4 The Arrival in Europe

hesitate'. When this sort of reassurance about speaking openly is not provided to claimants, it is more difficult for SOGI claimants to share their real stories at the first screening interview. The same is true when a strong securitisation approach is adopted at arrival, echoing the security paradigm that has characterised EU policies since Amsterdam (Kostakopoulou 2000). For instance, Mamaka (Italy) remembered that she was only fingerprinted, while no immediate access to an immigration office was granted. Again in Italy, another participant recalled that, despite her willing to share her story, only examinations of a medical nature were carried out at arrival:

> I told them that I was being raped and all, so they took me to one place, they snapped my picture and they took me to the hospital, check if I am pregnant, they found out that I was pregnant. (...) They put us on one big bus, so we spent almost a full day on the road. (...) The next day (...) they took me to Questura.

Although the duty of individual and objective assessment of all international protection claims is well established in ECHR[9] and EU law (EASO 2018), there were no accounts of any SOGI-friendly individual assessment at national level during the screening interview stage. The different logistics in each country also need to be considered. Whereas in all three countries under investigation the initial screening is carried out by national officers, in Germany and Italy it may take place in arrival/reception centres. No clear or direct questions on SOGI are asked at this stage, unless claimants self-identify as LGBTIQ+, as confirmed by our data. Taking the example of Italy, when a request is submitted to the police local headquarters ('Questura'), only general information is required: personal details, the presence of any family members in Europe, educational and family background, and travel details. While the form used for screening – the so-called 'C3' – expressly asks about the reasons for applying for international protection, these reasons are often not specified at this stage (Chap. 6).

The difficulty in talking about individual personal experiences in terms of SOGI was confirmed by other participants. For example, SOGI was not mentioned during these initial stages in the cases of Pato and Frank (focus group no. 3, northern Italy), Osa and Chima (focus group no. 4, northern Italy) or Bakary (focus group no. 2, northern Italy), who were hosted in temporary camps in southern Italy for a few days. However, it should be noted that for some people this was not an issue, because not addressing SOGI as soon as possible may be more consistent with a sensitive cultural-based approach. According to Jonathan, an LGBTIQ+ group volunteer:

> We have a very Western approach to this aspect (...). Many people can be MSM [men who have sex with men] or have adopted a similar behaviour (...) and, if you are asked "are you gay?", they might not answer "yes". I think it's a positive thing that it's not specified at this stage.

Whether or not such an approach should be followed as a rule is doubtful, individualised solutions being more appropriate to balance all general and personal factors at play. The perception of this initial stage of the asylum procedure shared by

---

[9] For example, *Sharifi and Others v. Italy and Greece*, Application no. 16643/09, 21 October 2014.

Nice Guy (focus group no. 1, northern Italy), who was asked to explain the reasons why he fled Nigeria after the arrival in a reception centre, offers a good overview:

> We come here the first time, as asylum seekers, we know nothing about the Italian system or anything. Then, like just I think within a week they gave us piece of paper to fill with our data and everything about our stories. A lot of us do not even know what we are writing. Some are still sick, very, very sick, they have other people write it for them. Some have other people advise them, ah don't write this, write this, and it is not right. They make blunders, big mistake. (…) Then they submit it, without nobody educating them about the concept of the form they are filling. (…) You cannot even get a copy of that form – you have just few days to submit it, and that's this. (…) They photostated [photocopied] the form (…) "go and write your story, go and write" (…) What can you write? (…) Then later, you start judging the same person by what the person wrote when his or her head was not in a stable state. It's not good. They should encourage them and inform them the minute they get here. Give them time to understand. Let them ask questions also.

This personal analysis of the shortcomings of this initial stage is enlightening. In addition to the lack of appropriate information on asylum (in general and specifically in relation to SOGI) and the delicate mental and physical condition of claimants, the importance of a number of other factors emerges strongly: the lack of support; the short time period between arrival and first screening; the level of education of claimants; the influence of other people claiming asylum on the grounds for persecution that are put forward; and the risk of authorities using the initial screening as the basis for denying international protection.

The lack of support received on arrival was indeed stressed by participants in all countries. Starting with Germany, Trudy Ann remembered when she arrived in Frankfurt with her girlfriend and they said at the airport that they were a same-sex couple:

> When we just arrived off the plane and go to the immigration part, we told the lady that we wanted to seek asylum. She was shocked at first (…) like she never know what we were speaking about. So I had to repeat it back three times.

The support in arrival or reception centres may also be problematic when SOGI is not taken into account. For instance, Jacqueline (Germany) explained: 'Generally in the camps they don't ask about your sexual preference or the reason why you came. That is saved for the big day [main interview]'. This lack of SOGI support played a bigger role in Italy where SOGI claimants' accounts are collected in reception centres, shortly after arrival. Silvana, a judge, and Valentina, a social worker, stressed that the staff of these centres are not adequately trained to explain to claimants that they can request asylum on SOGI grounds, or to identify such claims when individual stories are recorded (Chap. 6). Nelo, who shared his story only three months after arrival, pointed out that when he met trained and experienced staff in SOGI claims, it was not necessary for him to open up directly to be understood. As he told us:

> When they collected my story for the first time, I gave them part of it (…) when I was in the hotel [reception centre], I asked them not to go to Nigerians. (…) Specific[ally], I said, I don't want to go to Nigerians.

5.4 The Arrival in Europe

Because the staff at this point identified a potential SOGI claim on the basis of Nelo's plea, he eventually opened up about his reasons for fleeing Nigeria. Unfortunately, as we will explore in Chap. 6, staff in accommodation centres who are called upon to support asylum claimants in their claims procedure more often than not lack this ability to identify not-declared claims, being unprepared to deal with SOGI claims and, more generally, with people survivors of sexual and gender-based violence (UNHCR 2012b).

The level of education and how articulate claimants are, as well as the presence of other people from the same community, were also raised as important factors, which relevant authorities more often than not overlooked. As Ibrahim (Germany) put it: 'I am able, like I have a power of discussion and I have a power of communication with people. I can speak, or I know what I speak. But some other people don't know what to say'. When this 'power' is absent, other asylum claimants may play a significant part in SOGI claimants' narratives: Bakary (focus group no. 2, northern Italy) provided an example: 'When I arrived, I was given two papers. One for my personal details and the other for describing my personal history. (…) I asked a guy from Ghana how I should fill it'. In turn, Abdoul (focus group no. 2, northern Italy) found it difficult to give his account in the presence of other claimants with a similar cultural background:

> When we arrived (…) after three or four days, I was given a few forms for describing my story. (…) Frankly (…) there was a big community of people from the Ivory Coast. (…) When they know that you are gay… no, I couldn't.

In this initial phase, there were few mechanisms signposting SOGI claimants to relevant NGOs or support groups, or addressing the specific needs of transgender claimants. Whereas a few of our participants referred to the fact that some reception centre staff suggested SOGI claimants contact support groups, only Valentina, a social worker in Italy, pointed out that national authorities at the north-eastern border of Italy seem to routinely signal the arrival of transgender people to NGOs and specialised support groups. The potential empowerment of SOGI claimants through contacts with LGBTIQ+ actors is therefore far from being facilitated in all countries under comparison.

The lack of specific solutions and support for trans claimants, including in terms of health (Chap. 9), is combined with bad practices at the initial screening. As Kamel (Italy) recalled:

> I was asked if I was a boy or a girl. My documents, including my passport, signal that I am a woman, but I show myself as a man. I answered "I am trans", but [the officer] did not know what that means. (…) It was very bad. (…) I submitted my request, I was given a form (...) and then stop. I went out and I spent my days in the streets, without a doctor, hormones, nothing.

What is more, apart from a few exceptions, the initial screening appears to play no role in identifying appropriate accommodation in any country studied. There is no consideration of the need to provide queer spaces, where SOGI claimants can be free from repetitive heterosexual performances (Chap. 3). The suggestion given to Julian (focus group no. 5, Bavaria, Germany) by an officer is illustrative of the obligation imposed on asylum claimants to cope with non-queer spaces by erasing their SOGI:

> The first office I went to was the Bundesamt [federal office] in Bielefeld, that's where my asylum process started from. (…) And the first person who interviewed me, when (…) I explained to her the reason I don't want to go back home is because I'm a lesbian and I'm having so many issues at home. She did the paperwork for me to be transferred to Munich and she told me not to say it to anybody in those camps. Meaning, she was aware more than me that it could also be dangerous for me.

In light of this omission, we now consider how SOGI claimants are initially hosted in the countries under investigation.

5.4.3 Initial Reception and Detention

The EU Reception Directive omits any reference to SOGI (Ferreira 2018). Therefore, as further explored in Chap. 8, it is not surprising that no country involved in this research has any specific policy in place for the initial reception of those who identify as SOGI claimants. This lack of specific regulations or provision gives rise to a range of experiences that, more often than not, leave SOGI asylum claimants in 'vulnerable' situations at arrival. In light of the wide use of detention measures in the UK in comparison to Germany (at least until the 2019 reform, Chap. 4) and Italy, this lack of specificity does not relate only to reception centres but applies also to detention structures. While in Germany a threefold system of reception is in place (Chap. 8), Italy has shaped its system on the basis of an emergency rationale owing to collective migration flows and, more recently, to far-right political policies (ECRE, AIDA & ASGI 2019).

This state of affairs was confirmed by our participants. In most cases, SOGI played no role in the allocation of accommodation or reception conditions. For instance, Jacqueline (Germany), stressed that initial accommodation was chosen on the basis of her country of origin:

> They had something like a temporary camp, so I stayed there like, almost a week. And then we went to the police, they took… that's when they asked our names and then they took the fingerprints, and that's where they were selecting where you're supposed to go depending on your country. Like, where you're coming from. So, I was given a ticket to come to Munich with all the directions. That's how I ended up here. (…) They don't ask why you came or anything, it's about placing you somewhere and then other things will follow.

This signals a wider trend in Germany, which is based on a distribution system called 'EASY' (Chap. 8), given that Amis (focus group no. 2, Bavaria) also stated that most claimants from Uganda are transferred to Munich. The risk of placing claimants in the same persecutory environment from which they have fled is therefore very high. A less organised approach is identifiable in Italy, as Moses pointed out:

5.4 The Arrival in Europe

Moses: Initially, when we came it was a general camp. A big camp where there were up to like from 100, 150, a very big camp.

Interviewer: And did the authorities ask you "do you want to stay with people from your country or do you want to stay with other people"?

Moses: No, it was just normal distribution.

Yet, this 'normal distribution' – no matter on which basis it is carried out – does not reflect SOGI claimants' needs. In fact, by totally denying queer spaces, for SOGI claimants this initial accommodation was far from ideal. According to William (focus group no. 2, Bavaria, Germany): 'I was living with people that are not of my character, and anything maybe could happen to me. And I had stress, because of it not being open and always being in bed in that camp'. Equally, Jolly (focus group. no. 3, Bavaria, Germany) stressed:

> I felt some difficulties in me. As in, how to identify myself. Why? First of all I looked around, there were not only the White people around. My fellow Blacks were also there. So, I didn't know their background or where they came from, and I had a fear that maybe some of them came from my country, whereby they know maybe me. (…) So, that was really a very big fear in me and it really made me not open up as fast as possible. Until when I went for the interview.

These fears connected to entirely heteronormative spaces have to be added to the precarious conditions of these initial reception centres. As Sandra (Germany) pointed out:

> Then I got the shock of my life because that was a very huge place, where I was taken to. It was a big hall and there's were all kinds of people, all ages and all sexes. Kids, old, young, female, male, like, we're all there.

To make matters worse, what is intended as initial or provisional accommodation may end up as a long-term solution, coupled with restrictions on individual freedom of movement, something that, for instance, the 2019 reform in Germany further promoted by extending the length of stay in initial reception centres (Chap. 8). Ibrahim (Germany) explained:

> There was a lot of isolation in the beginning. Part of it is about moving to another place where I didn't know people and I had to start from the beginning. Part of it is frustration… the first three months, for example, I'm not allowed to leave Berlin. That was a rule, and it sounded very strange for me. It just sounded very absurd and medieval.

Although the limited contacts established in these initial camps may help in finding out about LGBTIQ+ associations and support groups (for instance, Bella, Italy), a feeling of isolation often prevailed. According to Sandra (Germany):

> We were just coexisting, nobody speaks to anyone, nobody tells anyone why they are fleeing, you just try to exist. (…) I felt empty, defeated, lost, tired, very, very tired. I lost all the motivation and all the thinkings that I had about life and what I wanted to achieve and everything. I was pretty much not thinking, my mind was just blank. I'm just sleeping and waking up not thinking about anything.

Edoardo (focus group no. 3, northern Italy) also recalled:

I am a little boy and to the place they took me to in the camp was bush, and... meeting new people and I don't know. I don't know how they behave, I don't know how they talk, I was like, early morning someone would come to, "come, you don't talk, you don't eat, you don't do this", I was like, many times because what I saw in the sea was in my head, I don't know how to talk it, because it is like my spirits have left, I am trying to recover myself. Like one month, so I was in the room all alone.

This feeling of isolation was aggravated by the often inadequate management of these centres, as we explore in greater detail in Chap. 8. Just Me (focus group no. 3, northern Italy) worried about this:

I was afraid. I was solely scared because I was like in a strange place. Nobody, no family, I never knew anybody. I was just all alone. I was transferred from Messina to Settimo Torinese after about two weeks, I was taken to Saluggia, so the condition in the camp was so grim, so horrible. They don't really care about us, anyway. (...) Due to my experience in the sea and the road to Libya, I was in kind of depression. So, the camp nurse take me to a psychiatric to have a look at me and see if they could help about my situation.

In turn, Halim (Germany) explained:

It was very hard for me to... I mean, in the beginning, arriving there, I didn't really know if I felt safe to disclose that I'm gay to people even who were there. Because there was no introduction, guidance, orientation or... it was just, you discover things yourself. And I had a flatmate and basically I didn't want to tell anybody, even the workers, because if it comes out I might be at risk, and I don't want people to be talking about me, people might harass me or whatever. (...) And then I had the problems inside also, not feeling safe, also tired and not having my own private space. That was the biggest problem.

A range of experiences were shared in the UK. As many of our UK claimant participants arrived through a variety of channels, often with the help of third parties, and did not immediately claim asylum, their initial reception often had a private dimension. In these cases, a set of different actors came into play. For instance, Luc explained that:

I start[ed] living with the man (...) with hope that he will help me, but I [didn't] know anything about asylum and they told me I should not tell anyone about my life. (...) One day when I know he is not around, I went to the one church in London. (...) I was living in that church (...) so I started working [there].

The religious nature of this support, however, inhibited him from being himself: 'Since then, I [didn't] want to tell anyone about who I am'. However, without such support, individuals may be left entirely alone. As Mary and Zaro said: 'We were homeless, we did not know if you come to airport you can call to the police (...) we are not that quick'.

While detention did not emerge as an issue in Germany or Italy, it was of great concern in the UK, where calls to address the needs of sexual minorities in detention have remained mostly unaddressed (Chaps. 4 and 8). What is more, when deciding to detain SOGI claimants, asylum authorities do not place enough weight on previous long stays and the degree of social integration those claimants may already have achieved. For instance, SGW (focus group no. 4, London), an asylum claimant who arrived in the UK as a student, explained:

5.4 The Arrival in Europe

> After spending (...) six years out [in terms of sexuality] (...) I decided I didn't want to go back to Jamaica because I had adapted so much to the (...) culture (...). I told the Home Office (...) I went down to Croydon, in person, to (...) state my situation, and then I was detained in Yarlswood for about six weeks. (...) It was a miracle that through Asylum Aid (...) I was able to get temporary release.

Lutfor (UK) elucidated:

> When I was in relationship, my boyfriend told me (...) that you can claim asylum based on your sexuality. (...) I didn't do any research or anything on any lawyer, I went, I make appointment to the Home Office, and I called them and I went for interview and they put me in detention for 22 days and I got a lawyer from legal aid, and interviewed and so that time I realised I should prepare for my case. I mean, I had the confidence that I am gay, I know this, so it would be easy to prove this. But I didn't know the system was too horrible.

Given the likelihood that SOGI minorities in detention may not feel able to disclose their SOGI as the basis for their asylum claim, it is particularly likely that their claims will also be jeopardised by relying on hearsay from other detainees, misinformation from detention centre staff with no training in RSD matters, and a lack of access to external sources of advice and information (as described in Chap. 4).

A final specific concern relates to people claiming asylum on gender identity grounds, where the lack of initial appropriate accommodation may be a serious obstacle to providing adequate support. Valentina, a social worker in Italy, recalled the case of a transgender claimant fleeing Cuba who arrived at the north-eastern Italian border: 'In that territory, all reception centres are reserved to men. They found for her an apartment managed by the Italian Red Cross. But it was absolutely personalised. There is no system in place, no reception protocols in this case'. Another transgender claimant, also remembered by Valentina, was less lucky on arrival in Tuscany, after having transited through Hungary and Austria: she was abandoned by the authorities, who failed to offer her any accommodation at all. The personal experience of Kamel, a transgender person claiming asylum in Italy, confirms the inadequacy of provision:

> They told me that it was difficult, they did not know where to put me, if in a male or female reception centre, because I've not undergone the operation yet. We went to Caritas, in many churches, but no one hosted me (...) until an association called me and said that a family could host me. (...) Now they are my family (...) I stayed at their place during the first two weeks.

The above experiences make it clear that domestic authorities still fall short in meeting the duty to consider the individual's condition in order to identify the most appropriate reception solution on arrival, as required by ECtHR jurisprudence.[10] Action, including specific amendments to the Reception Directive currently in force, seems more urgent than ever.

---

[10] *O.M. v. Hungary*, Application no. 9912/15, 5 July 2016, para. 53.

5.5 Concluding Remarks

This chapter has shown that the difficulties experienced by SOGI claimants start well before the evaluation of their asylum request, and have clear implications for the submission of an asylum application on SOGI grounds. Considering the limited literature dealing with these aspects, this analysis brought new insights and depth to our current understanding of SOGI claimants' legal and social experiences in their countries of origin, during their journeys, and at their arrival.

In many cases, the need to escape persecution forces SOGI claimants to leave their countries of origin and travel taking unknown routes, often at very short or no notice. This experience is often accompanied by the fear that one can never go back. Within a very short period of time, the new "unknown" takes the place of an entire life and all that one has experienced matters only insofar as it supports or undermines the claim. Yet, while persecution is an essential reason for flight, it is still only a fragment of a larger, fuller more complex life made up of many experiences. Persecution does not define the individual, although the assumption that it does is prevalent and unspoken during the assessment of the claim, as the subsequent chapters will show.

This is also why Marhoon, who submitted a *sur place* claim (Battjes 2013; UNHCR, 2012a, para. 57), said: 'I [was] very afraid of applying for asylum because (…) I'd seen a lot of terrible pictures and heard news about refugee camps and what's going on there'. He therefore tried other options, including scholarship applications, before reluctantly taking the asylum pathway. Making a related point, Anna, an LGBTIQ+ group volunteer in Italy, recalled the case of a bi-national couple where the Russian national did not want to apply for asylum because he knew that, if refugee status was granted, he would not be able to go back to his country and see his family again. As a consequence, he preferred to try other strategies to secure protection, such as entering into a civil union with a Syrian refugee in Italy. Fear of loss may therefore prevail over international protection needs.

Within European asylum systems as currently conceived, claimants' experiences are homogenised and individual needs and fears are not taken into account. The lack of alternatives to asylum is itself a major problem needing further investigation. As pointed out by Diego and Riccardo, LGBTIQ+ group volunteers in Italy:

> Why is it not possible to create humanitarian corridors? Why should they be forced to arrive in Italy to claim asylum? [We] have just received an e-mail from (...) a Sierra Leone's national, "how could I claim asylum in Italy?" (…) In this case, we can do almost nothing.

In this respect, the SOGI dimension of human corridors and the UNHCR's role in supporting these initiatives, as reported by Cristina (UNHCR officer, Italy), should be strengthened, and the possibility of issuing humanitarian visas considered. While a motion in this respect was adopted by the European Parliament, asking the Commission to prepare a draft for an EU regulation on humanitarian visas, thus bringing this matter under EU law with the consequent application of the EU

5.5 Concluding Remarks

Charter of Fundamental Rights,[11] developments remain dependent on the political agenda of EU's member states too often based on their border control interests (Balboni and Danisi 2019).

Overall, the detrimental effects of their journeys on SOGI claimants are striking. As Just Me (focus group no. 3, northern Italy) stated:

> If I have the freedom in my country, I don't think I will risk all the odd[s] to pass through the desert, to the sea, to Italy. So even to the European country that I can't speak their language. It is very difficult for me. Where I have nobody, it is like, if the life in my country was not so difficult about homosexual, I don't have to, I can't even imagine to take such risk.

Sometimes, such risk is undertaken for meeting basic survival needs, while totally ignoring the socio-cultural conditions of the chosen destination country. Nelo's experience (Italy) is a case in point:

> I feel lucky, very, very lucky because… I spent three days or four days in the desert. (…) Some of them died in the process. (…) When you are fighting with the Arabs (…) they see you like, like an animal. (…) I heard a lot of stories that in Libya there's a lot of opportunity to work. (…) The plan was not to come to Europe.

The difficulties we have discussed above relating to submission of SOGI claims at arrival, often owing to the lack of appropriate information and inadequate initial screening, were highlighted as a key concern. As Giovanna, a lawyer in Italy put it:

> The low percentage of SOGI claims and the fact that SOGI claimants are reluctant to manifest their personality, as well as the fact that they travelled to reach Europe, are all elements which should be clear enough to understand that, before submitting an asylum request, SOGI claimants really struggle with themselves.

The lack of a 'common language' preventing SOGI claimants from submitting their claims as soon as possible was expertly summarised by Valentina, a social worker in Italy:

> We should help these people to create a vocabulary, their vocabulary. They have never told themselves to anyone. I can see a comparison with the Italian trans community, with the European trans community and the north America's trans community, where no words existed to narrate oneself.

The 'trans' dimension, which still remains largely unexplored, thus brings specific difficulties, compounded by the absence of appropriate initial accommodation.

More generally, the current initial reception solutions are inadequate to address SOGI claimants' needs. As they stand now, initial reception centres often contribute to aggravating individual fears on arrival, hampering the likelihood that a full and frank claim for asylum will be made at the earliest possible opportunity. One solution may be to classify SOGI claimants as 'vulnerable', as Gisela, a lawyer in Germany, and several other participants suggested:

> [if] people [are] classified as a vulnerable group from the beginning, then they could be offered the corresponding information. Then maybe they would know before the interview

---

[11] European Parliament, Humanitarian Visas, 12 December 2018, 2018/2271(INL).

that they do not have to be afraid, that it is not punishable in Germany, that the interpreters actually should not talk about it.

Whether or not this classification would improve the life experience of SOGI claimants at arrival, as explored in Chaps. 3 and 4, is still debatable. It is instead certain that different factors influence their experience, thus confirming the need to elaborate specific solutions for SOGI asylum, both before and upon arrival, based on an intersectional and queer human rights approach (Chap. 11). The urgency of addressing SOGI-specific needs is indeed apparent also in the context of the procedures in place for the evaluation of SOGI asylum applications, which we explore in the next chapter.

References

Alessi, E. J., Kahn, S., Woolner, L., & Van Der Horn, R. (2018). Traumatic stress among sexual and gender minority refugees from the Middle East, North Africa, and Asia who fled to the European Union. *Journal of Traumatic Stress, 31*(6), 805–815.

Atak, I., Nakache, D., Guild, E., & Crépeau, F. (2018). *'Migrants in vulnerable situations' and the global compact for safe orderly and regular migration* (Queen Mary School of Law Legal Studies Research Paper No. 273/2018).

Balboni, M., & Danisi, C. (2019). Human Rights and EU External Policy: In Search of Unity. In Various (Eds.), *Liber Amicorum Angelo Davi. La vita giuridica internazionale nell'età della globalizzazione* (pp. 374–410). Napoli: Editoriale Scientifica.

Battjes, H. (2013). Accommodation: Sur place claims and the accommodation requirement. In T. Spijkerboer (Ed.), *Fleeing homophobia: Sexual orientation, gender identity and asylum*. London: Routledge.

Camminga, B. (2018). "Gender refugees" in South Africa: The "common-sense" paradox. *Africa Spectrum, 53*(1), 89–112.

Camminga, B. (2019). *Transgender refugees and the imagined South Africa: Bodies over borders and borders over bodies*. Cham: Palgrave Macmillan. https://doi.org/10.1007/978-3-319-92669-8

Danisi, C. (2018). What 'safe harbours' are there for sexual orientation and gender identity asylum claims? A human rights reading of international law of the sea and refugee law. *GenIUS – Rivista di studi giuridici sull'orientamento sessuale e l'identità di genere, 5*(2), 9–24.

Danisi, C. (2019). Crossing borders between international refugee law and international human rights law in the European context: Can human rights enhance protection against persecution based on sexual orientation (and beyond)? *Netherlands Quarterly of Human Rights, 37*(4), 359–378.

Del Guercio, A. (2018). Quali garanzie per il diritto all'unità familiare dei richiedenti e dei beneficiari di protezione internazionale con coniuge/partner dello stesso sesso? *GenIUS – Rivista di studi giuridici sull'orientamento sessuale e l'identità di genere, 5*(2), 59–73.

EASO – European Asylum Support Office. (2018). *EASO practical guide: Qualification for international protection*. Luxembourg: EASO.

ECRE – European Council on Refugees and Exiles, AIDA – Asylum Information Database. (2019). *The AnkER centres. Implications for asylum procedures, reception and return*. https://www.asylumineurope.org/sites/default/files/anker_centres_report.pdf

ECRE – European Council on Refugees and Exiles, AIDA – Asylum Information Database, & ASGI. (2019). *National country report: Italy, 2018 update*. ECRE – European Council on Refugees and Exiles. http://www.asylumineurope.org/sites/default/files/report-download/aida_it_2018update.pdf

References

ECRE – European Council on Refugees and Exiles, AIDA – Asylum Information Database, & Asyl und Migration. (2019). *National country report: Germany, 2018 update*. ECRE – European Council on Refugees and Exiles. https://www.asylumineurope.org/sites/default/files/report-download/aida_de_2018update.pdf

Ferreira, N. (2018). Reforming the common European asylum system: Enough rainbow for queer asylum seekers? *GenIUS – Rivista di studi giuridici sull'orientamento sessuale e l'identità di genere*, 5(2), 25–42.

Giametta, C. (2016). Narrativizing one's sexuality/gender: Neoliberal humanitarianism and the right of asylum. In F. Stella, Y. Taylor, T. Reynolds, & A. Rogers (Eds.), *Sexuality, citizenship and belonging: Trans-national and intersectional perspectives*. New York: Routledge.

House of Commons Canada. (2017). *LGBTQ+ at risk abroad: Canada's call to action: Report of the standing committee on citizenship and immigration*. Ottawa: House of Commons Canada.

HRW – Human Rights Watch. (2019). *No escape from hell*. https://www.hrw.org/sites/default/files/report_pdf/eu0119_web2.pdf

IOM – International Organization for Migration. (2019). *Flow monitoring – Europe*. https://migration.iom.int/europe?type=arrivals

Kostakopoulou, T. (2000). The 'protective union'; change and continuity in migration law and policy in Post-Amsterdam Europe. *JCMS: Journal of Common Market Studies*, 38(3), 497–518. https://doi.org/10.1111/1468-5965.00232

Liguori, A. (2018). *Migration law and the externalization of border controls: European state responsibility*. New York: Routledge.

Moreno-Lax, V. (2018). *Accessing asylum in Europe*. Oxford: Oxford University Press.

MSF – Médecins Sans Frontières. (2019). *Out of sight, out of mind: Refugees in Libya's detention centres*. https://www.msf.org/out-sight-out-mind-refugees-libyas-detention-centres-libya

Munir, L. P. (2019). Fleeing gender: Reasons for displacement in Pakistan's transgender community. In A. Güler, M. Shevtsova, & D. Venturi (Eds.), *LGBTI asylum seekers and refugees from a legal and political perspective* (pp. 49–70). Cham: Springer.

Odlum, A. (2019). To stay or to go? Decision-making of LGBTQI Syrians in mixed migration flows. In A. Güler, M. Shevtsova, & D. Venturi (Eds.), *LGBTI asylum seekers and refugees from a legal and political perspective* (pp. 71–94). Cham: Springer.

Piwowarczyk, L., Fernandez, P., & Sharma, A. (2017). Seeking asylum: Challenges faced by the LGB community. *Journal of Immigrant and Minority Health*, 19(3), 723–732. https://doi.org/10.1007/s10903-016-0363-9

Ramón Mendos, L. (2019). *State-sponsored homophobia 2019: Global legislation overview update*. ILGA. https://ilga.org/downloads/ILGA_World_State_Sponsored_Homophobia_report_global_legislation_overview_update_December_2019.pdf

Scott FitzGerald, D. (2019). *Refuge beyond reach: How rich democracies repel asylum seekers*. New York: Oxford University Press.

Scottish Refugee Council. (2014). *Asylum in the UK information for Lesbian, Gay, Bisexual, Transgender and Intersex (LGBTI) people*. Scottish Refugee Council.

Türk, V. (2018). Promise and potential of the global compact on Refugees. *International Journal of Refugee Law*, 30(4), 575–583.

UKVI – UK Visas and Immigration. (2016). *Information about your asylum application*. https://assets.publishing.service.gov.uk/government/uploads/system/uploads/attachment_data/file/513585/Point_of_Claim_English_20160401.pdf

UN. (2017). *International migration report*. https://www.un.org/en/development/desa/population/migration/publications/migrationreport/docs/MigrationReport2017_Highlights.pdf

UN Independent Expert on protection against violence and discrimination based on sexual orientation and gender identity. (2019). *UN rights experts urge more protection for LGBTI refugees*. https://www.ohchr.org/EN/NewsEvents/Pages/DisplayNews.aspx?NewsID=24764&LangID=E

UNHCR – UN High Commissioner for Refugees. (2011). *Unsafe haven: The security challenges facing lesbian, gay, bisexual and transgender asylum seekers and refugees in Turkey (Updated edition)*. Refworld. http://www.refworld.org/docid/524c114f4.html

UNHCR – UN High Commissioner for Refugees. (2012a). *Guidelines on International Protection No. 9: Claims to Refugee Status based on Sexual Orientation and/or Gender Identity within the context of Article 1A(2) of the 1951 Convention and/or its 1967 Protocol relating to the Status of Refugees (HCR/GIP/12/09)*. UNHCR – UN High Commissioner for Refugees. http://www.unhcr.org/509136ca9.pdf

UNHCR – UN High Commissioner for Refugees. (2012b). *Working with men and boy survivors of sexual and gender-based violence in forced displacement*. UNHCR – UN High Commissioner for Refugees. https://www.refworld.org/docid/5006aa262.html

UNHCR – UN High Commissioner for Refugees. (2019). *Desperate Journeys. Refugees and migrants arriving in Europe and at Europe's borders (January–December 2018)*. UNHCR. https://www.unhcr.org/desperatejourneys

United Nations Support Mission in Libya-Office of the High Commissioner for Human Rights. (2018). *Desperate and dangerous: Report on the human rights situation of migrants and refugees in Libya*. UN. https://www.ohchr.org/Documents/Countries/LY/LibyaMigrationReport.pdf

Winton, A. (2019). I've got to go somewhere': Queer displacement in Northern Central America and Southern Mexico. In A. Güler, M. Shevtsova, & D. Venturi (Eds.), *LGBTI asylum seekers and refugees from a legal and political perspective* (pp. 95–116). Cham: Springer.

Open Access This chapter is licensed under the terms of the Creative Commons Attribution 4.0 International License (http://creativecommons.org/licenses/by/4.0/), which permits use, sharing, adaptation, distribution and reproduction in any medium or format, as long as you give appropriate credit to the original author(s) and the source, provide a link to the Creative Commons license and indicate if changes were made.

The images or other third party material in this chapter are included in the chapter's Creative Commons license, unless indicated otherwise in a credit line to the material. If material is not included in the chapter's Creative Commons license and your intended use is not permitted by statutory regulation or exceeds the permitted use, you will need to obtain permission directly from the copyright holder.

Chapter 6
The Decision-Making Procedure

> *I am still waiting. And it's too much and it's too stressful for me. (…) They keep me as if we're in prison. I don't know what is going on.*
>
> (Mayi, focus group no. 4, Bavaria, Germany)
>
> *You cannot just sit in front of me and ask me question, and expect to know me (…) I might not trust you to tell you the truth.*
>
> (Nice Guy, focus group no. 1, northern Italy)
>
> *They are torturing us. Really torturing.*
>
> (Mary and Zaro, UK)

6.1 Introduction

Whereas in Chap. 5 we analysed pre-departure, journey and arrival experiences of SOGI claimants, we now turn our attention to the decision-making procedure. Whether they apply for asylum on arrival or later on, the initial screening is usually followed by a substantive interview. This is the essential moment when SOGI claimants have the opportunity to present their case. If the application is then refused, a judicial process is normally activated to appeal against the initial negative decision.

This chapter aims to analyse the most problematic aspects of these asylum procedures, as they emerged in our research as well as in the relatively limited available literature, and their impact on SOGI claims. These aspects include: the interview setting; the training and conduct of caseworkers, judges and other people working in this field, including interpreters; access to legal aid at all decision-making stages, including the appeal; and the quality of legal representation. The preparation of the asylum claim and – where applicable – of the appeal are also explored. In relation to all these aspects, the potential influence of bias of all actors involved in the asylum procedures is considered in detail.

This attempt to explore procedural issues, while leaving the substantial analysis of decisions on SOGI claims to the next chapter, takes into account the efforts already made at domestic level to integrate IRL and IHRL for setting up a fair asylum system and the positive influence of the EU's asylum framework, which takes the Refugee Convention as the cornerstone of its Procedures Directive (Chap. 4; ILGA 2014). In this respect, the UK is the only country under comparison that has made a clear commitment to 'continue (…) to ensure that the needs of all LGBT claimants are met in the asylum process, regardless of whether their claim was lodged on this basis' (Government Equalities Office 2018, p. 17). However, this commitment is absent in the Government's Progress Report published a year after it was made (Government Equalities Office 2019).

As a preliminary background for this analysis, we briefly outline the procedural aspects of the general asylum framework in force in each country analysed here. In Germany, the asylum decision-making procedure may be easily summarised through the following chart (Fig. 7):

As pointed out in Chap. 4, the administration of asylum is not homogeneous across Germany owing to its federal structure. The body responsible for the implementation of asylum procedures and refugee protection is the BAMF. As seen in Chap. 5, on arrival at Germany's borders, people claiming asylum are distributed throughout the federal states with no consideration of SOGI or other grounds for persecution. Despite often being 'severely exhausted [and] traumatised' (Noah, NGO social worker), asylum claimants are suddenly immersed in an unfamiliar process, that may last for many months, or even years, from their first interview through to – in the case of a refusal and appeal – their hearing before a judge. In practice, there is no time limit for the BAMF reaching a decision on asylum applications, although within 6 months of a claim being lodged it needs to state when the decision is likely to be taken (ECRE, AIDA & Asyl und Migration 2019, p. 24). However, under paragraph 75 of the Code of Administrative Court Procedure,[1] if the BAMF does not produce a decision within 3 months of receiving an asylum claim, claimants can make a claim against the authorities' failure to act.[2] In 2018, the average claim took approximately 8 months to process,[3] and this became almost 17 months for a final decision to be reached in cases where there was an appeal (ECRE, AIDA & Asyl und Migration 2019, pp. 20–21). The need to speed up the assessment of asylum claims is at the heart of the reform that, in 2017, introduced the so-called AnkER centres – a network of centres that gather all asylum-related stages within them (BAMF 2019). While in these centres applications may be

---

[1] Verwaltungsgerichtsordnung (VwGO).

[2] 'Untätigkeitsklage'. This was confirmed by the Federal Administrative Court (BVerwG), 1 C 18.17, judgment of 11 July 2018.

[3] However, the length of the procedure varies according to country of origin. Data from the BAMF from the third quarter of 2018 shows that claimants from Syria (5 months), Iraq (6.1 months) and Iran (6.8 months) were under the 8 months threshold on average, while claims from Pakistan (11.7 months), Afghanistan (11.3 months) and Russia (13.5 months) took much longer (ECRE, AIDA & Asyl und Migration 2019, p. 21).

6.1 Introduction

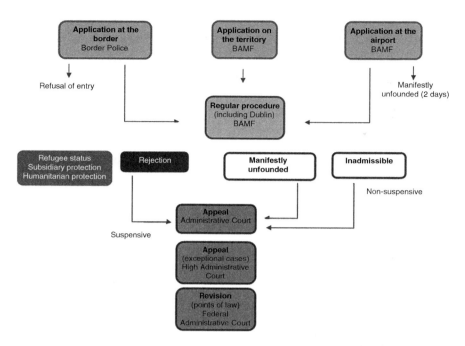

Fig. 7 Asylum decision-making procedure in Germany. (Source: ECRE, AIDA & Asyl und Migration 2019, p. 13)

decided within a few days (Chaps. 4 and 8), this system has a particularly negative impact on the fairness and the quality of the asylum procedure in relation to all aspects explored in this chapter (ECRE, AIDA 2019).

In Italy, the procedure starts when the asylum application is registered at the police local headquarters ('Questura') using the 'C3' form (Chap. 5). As Roberto and Titti, decision-makers, emphasised, the way in which this form is completed may heavily influence the procedural arrangements adopted to assess a SOGI claim. Owing perhaps to the lack of a common language between those who fill the form (the Questura's officers) and SOGI claimants, only relatively 'visible' causes of 'vulnerability' tend to be reported at this stage, such as pregnancy or underage status, but not SOGI. The submission of the C3 form is followed by an interview with the territorial commission after an indeterminate number of months, depending on the general flow of arrivals and number of pending applications to be processed. In recent years, territorial commissions have been under great pressure, to the point of being expected to carry out 12–15 main interviews each day (Filippo, senior judge). Although this means that each individual member of a territorial commission listens to four-five claimants in 1 day (Titti, decision-maker), raising doubts about the commission's ability to fully engage with claimants' testimonies, a claimant may still wait for more than a year before being interviewed. In the case of a refusal at this administrative stage, the right to appeal exists for all claimants, despite the fact that this right has been seriously undermined by the 2017 and 2018 reforms of the asylum legislation (Chap. 4 and Sect. 4.4, below; Palermo 2018). In order to speed up the assessment of asylum claims, these reforms introduced new procedures, including the concept of 'safe country of origin' and a new border procedure,[4] which provides for a nine-day examination of applications submitted at designated border areas or transit zones, or made by people coming from a 'safe country of origin'. A good summary of the different procedures in place after these legislative amendments is provided by the following chart (Fig. 8):

Finally, in the UK, applications are processed through a number of routes. These include the regular route, in which claimants are dispersed across the country pending a decision by a regional office or the Home Office, and other specific procedures, such as in the case of people arriving from 'safe countries' or whose applications are clearly unfounded and for which there is no in-country appeal (so-called 'accelerated procedures'; ECRE, AIDA & Refugee Council 2019). Perhaps

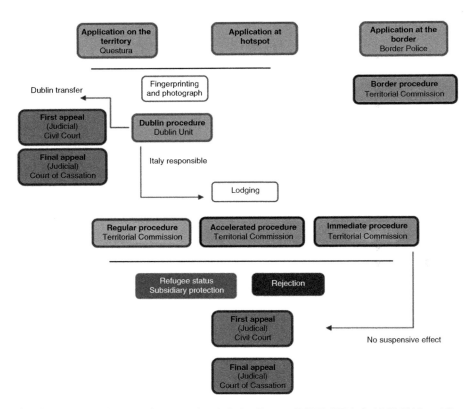

Fig. 8 Asylum decision-making procedure in Italy. (Source: ECRE, AIDA & ASGI 2019, p. 17)

---

[4] Article 28-bis (1-ter) of the Procedure Decree, inserted by Decree Law no. 113/2018 (converted into Law no. 132/2018).

6.1 Introduction

to an even larger extent than in Germany and Italy, the time taken to process an asylum application varies greatly, although all asylum cases 'have a deadline of 182 days between the moment that someone claims asylum until the moment they should receive a decision' (Qasim, decision-maker).[5] Similarly, when the initial decision by the Home Office is a refusal, most claimants can appeal to the First Tier Tribunal. A judicial review – but only of the process, not the substance of the case – is sometimes a final resort before a case becomes Appeal Rights Exhausted (ARE). At this point a claimant may be able to submit a fresh claim if the Home Office accepts the existence of new evidence. This might apply in SOGI cases where, for example, a country of origin introduces new legislation criminalising homosexuality, as happened in Nigeria in 2014.[6] Again, a good summary of the asylum procedures in the UK is provided by ECRE (Fig. 9):

In all these countries, as well as across Europe, time and waiting are key issues for SOGI claimants. To give an example from our survey, 51% of respondents who lodged an appeal against a negative decision reported that they had waited more than 6 months for their hearing. As Joachim, an NGO worker in Germany, put it, timing 'is very much a double-edged sword for LGBTI people'. While quicker procedures may have positive effects in terms of the well-being and mental health of SOGI claimants, a short process does not always correspond to a fair process in SOGI cases, considering the time needed to adequately prepare for the asylum interview (Sect. 6.2.1). Nevertheless, as Thomas, an NGO volunteer in Germany, explained in relation to the first period of the NGO's activity between 2015 and 2016:

> Waiting times were so insanely long between the first interview and the second. During this period, the refugees were doomed to inaction. And that is of course a real psychological problem. We have partly tried with work permits, but it was difficult.

For some SOGI claimants, the wait for a decision can feel unbearable. For example, Halim felt lucky to have been granted refugee status in Germany within less than a year. Nevertheless, he also felt that the whole period was 'like a very long time (…) a waste of time and energy. (…) I lived that year with a feeling of uncertainty, not knowing what to expect, what's going to happen next'. Susanna, a social worker in Italy, also reported the pain of a claimant who, after another postponement of a hearing, simply stated: 'I cannot wait anymore, I do not know anymore what I shall do with my life'. The wait was particularly traumatic for those separated from their children and who needed a grant of asylum before their children reached adulthood in order to bring them to Europe through family reunification (Stephina, UK). Yet, for people like Bella, claiming asylum in Italy, 10 months waiting were tolerable because her accommodation centre had arranged training activities for all residents and she was able to learn Italian.

---

[5] However, in May 2019, the Guardian reported that the government had abandoned its six-month target (https://www.theguardian.com/uk-news/2019/may/07/home-office-abandons-six-month-target-for-asylum-claim-decisions)

[6] The Same-Sex Marriage Prohibition Act was passed into law by the Nigerian president in January 2014.

Fig. 9 Asylum decision-making procedure in the UK. (Source: ECRE, AIDA & Refugee Council 2019, p. 13)

As many of our participants pointed out, SOGI claimants may need time to come out and reveal the real reasons for requesting asylum in Europe. For instance, Bakary (focus group no. 2, northern Italy) was asked to complete the C3 form only 4 days after arrival, when he was not ready to discuss the real reasons for having escaped his country of origin. Moreover, as Thomas (NGO volunteer, Germany) pointed out, shorter assessment periods may prevent a comprehensive preparation of the claimant 'to just have a fair chance in the process'. In this respect, it is noticeable that the expected CEAS reform at EU level will not bring benefits for asylum claimants. In fact, as Jules, staff member at ILGA-Europe, highlighted, 'the reform is now focused on accelerating procedures and making it quicker (…). But, in the cases of (…) LGBTI asylum seekers, this becomes extremely problematic especially considering that (...) a vast majority of asylum seekers who arrive are traumatised in some form or another'.

With this background and difficulties in mind, this chapter is structured as follows. Section 6.2 investigates how SOGI claimants are prepared for the main administrative interview and for judicial hearings, including access to legal aid. The quality of legal aid provision during this preparatory phase is also considered. Section 6.3 examines the procedures around the main interview, paying attention to the individual experiences of SOGI claimants, while attempting to identify any specific procedural arrangements that are in place to assess SOGI applications in these countries. Other than the interview setting and the conduct of the interview, this section also explores the selection and training of administrative decision-makers and, where possible, the existence and influence of any bias on their part. The same aspects are analysed in Sect. 6.4 in relation to the judicial adjudication of SOGI claims. Section 6.5 investigates the collection and use of Country of Origin Information (COI) in light of its fundamental role in the assessment of SOGI claims. Section 6.6 examines interpretation issues, transversal to both the administrative and judicial procedures. Finally, Sect. 6.7 explores other procedures in place in the countries under comparison, namely accelerated procedures and Dublin transfers, in light of their particular impact on SOGI claims. While all sections highlight elements that may shape a fair asylum procedure for SOGI claimants, the chapter ends with some final remarks that take into account participants' calls for an overall improvement of the procedural aspects in SOGI asylum.

6.2 The Preparation of Asylum Claims and Legal Aid

The preparation of SOGI claimants for the main interview and judicial hearing(s) was widely identified by our participants as a key aspect of a fair asylum procedure. According to Roberto, a decision-maker in Italy, whether SOGI claimants are briefed in reception centres about what an interview entails, and have discussed their stories with staff and written them down, can be the most influential factor in ensuring a positive RSD experience and outcome. In turn, Qasim, a decision-maker in the UK, explained that when claimants arrive 'with lots of information, really professionally sort of organised information, their interviews [are] really, really easy as well and straightforward'. Yet, this kind of preparation is not standard practice for SOGI claimants, especially those who, for various reasons, are not accommodated by the state during the application or, even if the state takes charge of them, are held in reception centres that do not offer the necessary social or legal services.

6.2.1 The Preparation for the Main Interview and Judicial Hearing(s)

Despite the evident role it can play in a successful claim, preparation can be an issue in all countries under investigation. In Germany, while in some areas NGOs and support groups provide advice to SOGI claimants assessed through the regular procedure, their support is increasingly hampered by the creation of the AnkER centres (mainly in Bavaria). Claimants who are hosted in these centres receive all information on the asylum process by the BAMF. Independent advice is rarely available, not least because of the short time between arrival at the centre and the main interview. As our participants confirmed, the gathering of evidence is severely jeopardised by this system (Nina, legal advisor; Frank S., legal advisor). In such circumstances, claimants are often still in 'flight mode', unable to relax, concentrate or present their claim to the best of their ability, while no connections to local LGBTIQ+ community for advice and evidence can be established. Following the adoption of the 2019 reform (Chap. 4), no improvements are expected as this approach seems to apply more generally. In fact, the law now requires that the Federal Office provide voluntary and independent legal advice on the asylum procedure through group and individual counselling sessions, with the potential involvement of welfare organisations. This move has been already criticised, as it risks undermining the role of NGO counselling, which, if adequately provided, is often an essential part of a fair and efficient asylum procedure (ECRE, AIDA 2019).

In Italy, at least in principle, a combination of services in accommodation centres, which are publicly funded but provided by private entities, along with support by associations and LGBTIQ+ groups, is available to prepare SOGI claimants for their interview(s) and hearing(s). If we look at the situation on the ground, however, most participants, with few exceptions, reported that the quality of services provided in accommodation centres was unsatisfactory for different reasons. Some participants did have a positive experience, such as Alain A., who remembered 'I had a meeting with my legal operator [advisor], we did the story, she wrote everything in Italian, we tried to read [the story]'. Yet, many other participants complained about the lack of an adequate number of legal advisors in these centres, or the inexperience of the staff running these centres in dealing with SOGI claims. According to Susanna, a social worker:

> The management of reception centres was also given to private individuals or companies that were not previously involved in community work (…) and they want to make profit. So, they save money by not providing a psychologist, a cultural mediator [mediatore culturale], a lawyer [in] many facilities that are totally isolated from society.

Diego and Riccardo, LGBTIQ+ group volunteers, reported that the accommodation centres are often packed and in-house legal advisors, even if very competent, are not able to provide appropriate support to all claimants. As one of the participants in focus group no. 4 in northern Italy, Bubacan, explained: 'the [reception] centre's lawyer cannot but work superficially, cannot pay regular and specific attention to everyone, owing to the amount of people under their mandate'. Many SOGI

6.2 The Preparation of Asylum Claims and Legal Aid

claimants did not meet an advisor at all. In this respect, Cedric (focus group no. 5, southern Italy) remembered that 'they [the managers of the reception centre] can tell you that lawyers are available but you never see them', whereas Fred (focus group no. 5, southern Italy) simply affirmed '[m]y camp did not even have a lawyer to tell my story'. This is also why associations and support groups in Italy play a central role at this stage. It is no coincidence that the number of SOGI asylum support groups has rapidly increased between 2016 and 2019 (Il Grande Colibri 2019). Thus, Antonella, who leads a support group that offers psychological support, legal advice and cultural mediation, recalled that some claimants expressly asked her to carry out simulations of the main interview, in order to test answers to the most recurrent questions. This is also why a significant part of her support aims to train claimants to understand 'decision-makers' own mental schemes' (Antonella, LGBTIQ+ group volunteer). As an example, she explained that a lot of effort is placed on remembering dates and places and on reporting all facts without contradictions and through a 'European lens'. This voluntary support is even more fundamental when SOGI claimants are not hosted in reception centres. As Jonathan, an LGBTIQ+ group volunteer, pointed out, in these situations associations support SOGI claimants during the entire procedure, from the submission of the application and the request of a permit to stay, to the preparation of the narrative to be articulated during the interview and the collection of evidence.

Equally, in the UK, voluntary and non-governmental organisations (NGOs) play a fundamental role. Many individuals seek information, advice and support from voluntary organisations, ranging from larger or national ones, such as Refugee Action, to local ones supporting particular refugee communities or working in particular areas, such as the Somali Women's Support Group or Southwark Refugee Communities Forum. SOGI organisations also play an important role and, again, these range from national – for instance, Stonewall, UKLGIG and Stonewall Cymru – to local and grassroots organisations like Brighton & Hove LGBT Switchboard and the Lesbian Immigration Support Group in Manchester. These have been complemented by a number of asylum support groups set up by SOGI claimants, such as African Rainbow Family in Manchester, Out and Proud in London, the LASS group in Sheffield or Reach Out in Leeds (as reported by Janelle). Research dating as far back as 2009 pointed out that SOGI claimants rely mostly upon personal relationships or social networks in the absence of more traditional support from family and ethnic networks (Bell and Hansen 2009, p. 43), therefore it is unsurprising that, for many participants, these organisations and support groups provide more than procedural and legal advice.

The complexity of this preparatory work across all countries under comparison, extending well beyond simply giving information about the asylum process, was well expressed by Noah (NGO social worker, Germany). After reporting that a significant number of people arrive totally unprepared at the main interview, he highlighted the need to establish a relationship of trust as a precondition for a successful preparation:

I have to take away the fear from the people, reduce the boundaries of shame, establish a bond of trust that enables them to express themselves on things that may have traumatised them in their lives, which still move them today.

Nonetheless, much of the time this dedication is absent in the asylum system. As Bakary (focus group no. 2, northern Italy) recalled:

When I arrived, my friend helped me to write down my story in order to fill the C3 form, he told me how to proceed. (…) it's the cooperative [reception centre] that should (…) support you in improving the narrative of your personal account, because we come, we arrive here, after facing several difficulties; it is clear that you are not able to express yourself, the cooperative must look for someone who can help improving how to present your story (…) rather than simply submitting your story as you can write.

In the face of this lack of support in preparing claimants for the interview, individuals are likely to look to other claimants for advice as the only available option. However, being advised by other claimants may backfire in being perceived negatively by decision-makers. As Halim, claiming asylum in Germany, where he works for an NGO, pointed out:

[T]he interviewer (…) asked him [Halim's client] who gave advice about asylum and he mentioned that he got counselling from people including myself about how the process goes. I think people have the right to get counselling and the information about the asylum process. Then he considered this a manipulation of asylum, "Asylbetrug" he said, and it was rejected.

In some circumstances, the lack of support services and failure to provide accurate information about asylum procedures may result in some claimants feeling insecure to the point of fabricating or embellishing elements of their narrative. The peculiar submission of Abdoul's (focus group no. 2, northern Italy) claim is illustrative. As he put it:

a person told me to use a story of gays. Ah! Since I was ashamed to declare who I really was, he did not know [that I was actually gay]. Hence, I was obliged to write down that story (…) without being forced to disclose my real identity.

In light of the central role they play in all three countries for the preparation of SOGI claimants, NGOs and support groups are often, at least indirectly and informally, involved in the decision-making process in a number of ways.

A primary way is certainly the provision of supportive statements. While the value attributed by decision-makers to evidence provided by third parties is examined in Chap. 7, it is nonetheless important to highlight here how participants justified this proactive intervention of associations and support groups during the preparation of administrative interviews and judicial hearings. Diego and Riccardo, LGBTIQ+ group volunteers in Italy, explained that their involvement in the asylum procedure became necessary due to the assumption that claimants needed to prove their SOGI. In this respect, their project – called 'Immigrazioni e Omosessualità' (IO – Immigration and Homosexuality) – made a clear choice: alongside providing a safe space where claimants could learn Italian and gain self-confidence before sharing their stories, IO supports them by issuing a statement on their involvement in the project's activities. As Diego emphasised, decision-makers will never find in

6.2 The Preparation of Asylum Claims and Legal Aid

these statements 'what [claimants] like [in terms of partners], [but] these simply describe the life of a person', in light of the experiences which claimants shared with the project's volunteers. Significantly, according to Diego, once these statements are produced, decision-makers' questioning during the asylum interview is often more pertinent and less intrusive of claimants' privacy. Other support groups adopt a different approach. For example, Zouhair, claiming asylum in Germany and who now works for an NGO, affirmed that his group usually sends letters where it is written that 'he or she… is gay or lesbian'.

Another fundamental aspect of the role of support groups was shared by Valentina, a social worker in a trans association in Italy. Besides discussing the testimony with a claimant before the main interview, her association – MIT – collects information on the socio-cultural environment of the relevant country of origin, as well as on the rights granted to transgender people in Italy. This information is then made available to the decision-makers. Perfectly in line with a human rights approach to asylum (Chap. 3), she stressed that decision-makers may ignore these rights, for example, the law allowing gender reassignment, but should be aware of the availability of appropriate health services and legal guarantees in force in Italy to adopt informed decisions. Considering that all asylum applications followed by MIT, including the case of a claimant from Nigeria who recently started the male-to-female (MtF) transition process in Italy, have been successful, this approach certainly helps to fill the existing gap in the training of decision-makers on SOGI-related rights (Sect. 6.2.3).

The lack of training, coupled with the (still) widespread stereotypes of SOGI minorities in the decision-making process (Sect. 7.5 of Chap. 7), may prompt other associations involved in the preparation of SOGI claimants to encourage claimants to 'fit' specific categories in order to maximise their chances of receiving a positive decision. Jonathan, an LGBTIQ+ group volunteer in Italy, provided a powerful example connected to the 'invisibility' of bisexuality in asylum decisions (Rehaag 2009): 'More than once I suggested to avoid bisexuality and to say they're gay'. Although conforming to certain Western-informed categories may indeed increase the chances of a successful application, it also undermines the agency of SOGI claimants. Despite the good intentions behind this type of instructions, claimants may disapprove of such strategies. William, who claimed asylum in Germany, reacted to a suggestion aimed at boosting his gay appearance for the interview as follows: 'you cannot make someone who has been one year in Germany like someone who has grown [up] seeing gay, or someone who has grown [up] with gays in a gay lifestyle. You cannot change in one year, no no no no'. In so doing, NGOs and support groups risk reproducing decision-makers' disputable stereotypical assumptions on SOGI minorities (McGuirk 2018), rather than trying to eradicate them.

During this preparatory period, members of support groups, as well as reception centre staff if they are appropriately trained, may shape the procedural aspects of SOGI claims' assessment. This outcome can be achieved indirectly, by providing information to SOGI claimants about their rights, but also directly, by communicating with relevant decision-makers in order to request SOGI-friendly arrangements. Giulia, an LGBTIQ+ group volunteer in Italy, explained that she would inform claimants that they are entitled by law to change interpreters if they perceive biased or stereotyping behaviour, and that they should sign the record of the interview only after having had it carefully translated. Nonetheless, as she explained and other participants confirmed, many claimants get in touch with support groups only after a first refusal by the administrative bodies, once these basic rights have already been ignored. Moreover, in focus group no. 5 in southern Italy, it emerged that even those who are aware of these rights may not 'dare' to invoke them owing to the power imbalance in the interview setting. In Cedric's own terms, 'I considered that, maybe, if I contested, I could be seen as a rebel, thus I agreed with everything they did'. In contrast, Dev recalled: 'We redid my transcript, she [the interviewer] said to be in a rush but I said "no, we are going to spend all the time required to redo it" and so we did'. That is why, Alain A., a refugee in Italy, stressed the importance of also being 'psychologically prepared' to face, among other things, the presence of an interpreter with a similar cultural background (Sect. 6.6).

In order to address some of these issues, Zouhair explained that, before the interview takes place, his group informs relevant asylum authorities in Germany about the need to secure a 'sensitive interpreter'. The same approach is adopted in some areas of Italy, where staff in reception centres and support groups developed the habit of informally giving the territorial commissions advance warning of the upcoming interview of a person claiming asylum on SOGI grounds (Chiara, NGO worker; Cristina, UNHCR officer). In some circumstances, this preliminary communication is also necessary to speed up the process. As Diego (LGBTIQ+ group volunteer) explained, a request to bring forward the interview date was submitted to the relevant territorial commission on behalf of a lesbian claimant from Cameroon who, due to her appearance, was continuously discriminated against by other female guests in their accommodation centre. Bringing forward the interview was an effective way to limit the time she spent in that reception centre before a final decision on her application was taken.

Finally, despite preparatory efforts, some volunteers or staff of reception centres reported the importance of accompanying SOGI claimants on the day of their interview to support them psychologically. Yet, this is not always permitted except in exceptional individual circumstances (for instance, when the claimant is an unaccompanied child, their guardian may assist). Mara, a lawyer in Italy, explained that, owing to the particular situation of 'vulnerability' of a gay claimant from Pakistan, she asked and obtained authorisation for a member of the support group to attend his main interview before the territorial commission. Considering the power dynamics during the interview process, this simple but fundamental entitlement emerged as one of the possible recommendations for rendering the asylum system for SOGI claimants fairer (for instance, Thomas, NGO volunteer, Germany; Daniele, decision-maker, Italy; Giuseppe, lawyer, Italy). The empowering effect of such a measure is already visible at the appeal stage, where volunteers and support groups assist SOGI claimants on the day of tribunal hearings (for instance, Court observation, Hesse, 2018; Tribunal observation, northern Italy, 2018).

According to Damiano, a lawyer in Italy, the impact of all this 'laborious' voluntary work is shown by the high percentage of recognition of SOGI claims at

6.2 The Preparation of Asylum Claims and Legal Aid

administrative level during recent years. Based on the experiences of SOGI claimants, it is clear that NGOs and support groups also play a significant role in the preparation of judicial hearings, especially in relation to those who have their first contact with LGBTIQ+ associations only after the administrative refusal of their asylum application (for instance, Odosa, Italy). According to Antonella, an LGBTIQ+ support group volunteer in Italy, when SOGI claimants get in contact with associations only after filing a judicial appeal, their preparatory work consists of understanding the reasons for the refusal and drafting appropriate answers to the most problematic points. Equally, Noah, NGO social worker (Germany), explained that, during the 6–12 months before the hearing:

> [They] collect (…) write down, capture in detail (…) which things were asked in the interview, which were not. (…) That means [that] you have a lot of preparation, [especially because] it depends more on the credibility. People who have fled or migrated here do not have the evidence, unless they have physical scars and a credible narration.

In the UK, the support at his stage seems to be more encompassing. Organisations such as Asylum Aid, Refugee Action and the Refugee Council provide a range of resources to help individuals navigate the asylum system (Asylum Aid 2018). In this context, Denise and Umar, legal advisors, explained that, besides providing letters of support, their preparatory work is focused on the need to demonstrate that SOGI claimants have a general support network, attend meetings and take part in demonstrations in the UK, such as Pride. This also includes the identification of appropriate witnesses, although in their view some judges look at witnesses positively, while others do not: 'we know with a couple of judges that [a witness] has had an effect' (Denise and Umar, legal advisors). The preparatory work also aims to address issues that, without the adoption of an intersectional approach (Chap. 3), may not seem reconcilable in terms of the relationship between religion and sexual orientation. As Debbie, an NGO worker, explained 'we try now to help people to verbalise, to give people sort of arguments to verbalise why it can be reconciled. But it did seem to be something that was used [by Home Office interviewers] to just… to shake them [claimants] up'. However, for a range of reasons, this initial preparation of the case is not always carried out as it should. For example, Irma, who claimed asylum in the UK, experienced a number of problems at all stages of her application and the appeal process: some of her paperwork went missing, her solicitor went on holiday immediately before the hearing date, and an expert report was submitted late. Irma also reported that on the day of the hearing the barrister found the material prepared by an NGO 'no[t] good'. As she recalled, she was 'really angry with them', taking into account that her case was a 'good one' and should not have been rejected again.

Irrespective of the preparatory activities of NGOs and support groups, it seems that during the appeal procedure claimants become more confident. As Giovanna, a lawyer in Italy, put it, during the appeal 'claimants tend to have a chance to talk, to explain their stories after having had the time to elaborate them [and] to become familiar with the [surrounding] society'. In fact, SOGI claims fail at first because people are still often in hiding and/or do not have evidence. By the time they get to the appeal, they may be more confident and provided with better evidence.

Consequently, preparation at this stage is often accompanied by a greater willingness and ability on the part of SOGI claimants to fight for their rights. Perhaps it is also this increased awareness that explains why relationships with lawyers, who sometimes tend to make decisions about aspects of the claim without consulting their clients (pointed out, among others, by Susanna, social worker, Italy), may be particularly problematic during the appeal, as the next section explores.

6.2.2 Access to, and Quality of, Legal Representation

Our fieldwork confirmed that asylum claimants experience serious difficulties in accessing legal representation across Europe. Only 54% of claimants responding to our survey had a legal advisor or representation during the asylum procedure. This data is consistent with the different provisions and practices that emerged in our three country case studies.

In Germany no legal aid is available for initial claims, only for the appeal stage. According to Evelyne and Anne, lawyers in Germany, legal advice is nonetheless provided by advice centres, volunteers and non-governmental institutions like Caritas. As Ibrahim, a claimant now working for an NGO, confirmed, in some federal states the financial support for legal advisors has been reduced, leading them to work fewer hours than in the past. This general framework causes financial hardship to claimants, who cannot consequently ensure access to adequate representation in the early stages of their asylum claim.

By contrast, in Italy, while as a general rule legal aid is not granted during the administrative procedure, asylum claimants who are hosted in accommodation centres are entitled to receive legal assistance from the staff. However, often these staff do not have any legal training and, according to some claimants, the limited legal assistance provided in these centres is sometimes offered against payment. Bakary (focus group no. 2, northern Italy), for instance, told us that 'yes, you need to pay 150 Euros, so every month when they give you the pocket money, you give back 15 Euros'. In contrast, during the appeal stage, all claimants with insufficient financial resources may apply for, and usually receive, state legal support (so-called 'gratuito patrocinio').

Free legal assistance is available in the UK to people claiming asylum who cannot meet the costs of representation. Yet, in practice, access to good legal advice is difficult for many of them. Problems arise because of the low level of funding available to solicitors working under a legal aid contract and because there are not enough high quality solicitors with legal aid contracts to meet demand. It seems that few claimants receive legal advice prior to their screening interview.[7] Since 2014,

---

[7] Legal aid expenditure was significantly reduced through the 2012 Legal Aid, Sentencing and Punishment of Offenders Act (LASPO). The loss of this funding 'threatens the existence of legal firms who represent asylum seekers, and the loss of representation to those in desperate need'

the Home Office has funded Migrant Help to provide asylum support, but this no longer includes advocacy either in relation to decision-making or appeal stages (ECRE & Refugee Council 2016, p. 54).

Irrespective of access to legal aid, a general problem arises from the fact that asylum systems do not always allow lawyers to be present during the main interview (also called administrative or substantive interview in some countries), unless authorised on a case-by-case basis, as was reported in Italy. Lawyers are instead entitled to attend the substantive interview in Germany and the UK, where such attendance is however not usually covered by legal aid, thus in practice lawyers only tend to attend if privately funded. Even when they do attend, the lawyer's role in the interview may be limited. Yet, as Giuseppe, a lawyer in Italy, explained, the best thing for all asylum claimants would be to have the lawyer with them during their main interview. In fact, lawyers are in the best position to intervene when answers are reported or transcribed inaccurately, strengthen claimants' confidence, and even stop the interviewer in case of inappropriate questions (something reiterated by Damiano, lawyer, Italy; Diana, Germany; Thomas, NGO volunteer, Germany; and Sofia and Emma, NGO workers, Germany). The case of Alphaeus, who claimed asylum in Germany, is illustrative:

> In my big interview [I was] mentioning the date of when my mum died. The interviewer (…) instead of 1996, he wrote 2006. (…) I just thank God that my lawyer was there. (…) He told them "No, this is not real. See what you've done here". So he managed to correct them.

The positive effect of having legal assistance is even more evident when we look at the active role played by certain lawyers at judicial hearings. For instance, during a tribunal observation in northern Italy in 2018, the lawyer intervened to challenge those questions that were perceived (also by the claimant) as irrelevant in the context of his overall story, while trying to direct the judge's attention towards his LGBTIQ+ activism. The need for a change was therefore widely shared in this matter. Consequently, Allan, a lawyer in the UK, affirmed in light of his multi-year experience that 'having good legal representation from the outset does make a huge difference (…) no question'.

It should also be recognised that, in addition to the appeal, sometimes lawyers' support is essential in other areas of SOGI asylum, like accommodation. For example, only the intervention of a lawyer allowed Ken, who claimed asylum in Italy, to move out of the reception centre where he was continuously discriminated against by other asylum claimants (Chap. 8). In the UK, the Asylum Support Appeals Project fulfils this role, by helping people claiming asylum to obtain housing and welfare support, including by providing free representation at the First Tier Tribunal.[8]

Overall, this shortage of free legal provision is unsurprising given that, under EU law, the obligation to grant legal aid relates only to the appeal stage (Article 20 of

---

(Asylum Aid 2013). Two of the main not-for-profit advice organisations – Refugee and Migrant Justice and the Immigration Advisory Service – closed in 2010 and 2011.

[8] http://www.asaproject.org/about/representation

the Procedures Directive). Yet, even when legal aid is available and legal representation granted, our data shows that, despite some important exceptions consisting of highly qualified lawyers and legal advisors, the quality of representation does not always reach adequate standards across the three countries under comparison.

First, besides a lack of contact between lawyers and claimants in preparation of the initial claim, there is a clear problem in relation to the preparation of the appeal hearing. Very limited contact between claimants and lawyers was reported before the hearings. Betty (focus group no. 3, Bavaria, Germany), for example, told us that 'it is one year and one month, but I've never got anything like a paper from my lawyer'. In other cases, claimants were neglected, as, for instance, Zaro (UK): 'weekly we try to call [the solicitor], trying to meet with her, she ignoring us'. During a tribunal observation in northern Italy in 2018, the lawyer asked the SOGICA researcher to contact the claimant, because the lawyer had never called them before, all contacts having previously been managed by the reception centre's staff. A similar disinterest emerged during other judicial hearings we observed (for instance, Court observation, Hesse, Germany, 2018), including the failure to ensure preliminary contact with tribunals as requested by claimants themselves (for instance, Court observation, Hesse, Germany, 2018, when the lawyer did not ask for a joint hearing of a couple, despite her clients' express request). Other observations also showed a lack of preparation by lawyers and, often, a total reliance on support groups' preparation of the claim (for instance, Court observation, Hesse, Germany, 2018; Tribunal observation, northern Italy, 2018).

Where, instead, there is good engagement between claimants and their lawyers, a process of empowerment may take place. For instance, Buba, an unaccompanied child in Italy, recalled that he only obtained free legal assistance after the refusal of his asylum application by the administrative body, which did not determine that he was underage until a volunteer discovered it. Together with his legal representative, Buba analysed the negative decision and collected appropriate evidence, including medical reports and pictures of his scars, and was eventually able to cogently present his claim before the judge. In fact, as Sean, a lawyer in the UK, pointed out, for legal representation to be of good quality it is essential to spend a considerable amount of time together with the claimant:

> [For] LGBT cases (…) it might take you five hours just to build the relationship with the client. Ten hours after that to take a detailed statement, four hours after that to go through the statement and look at difficulties and contradictions and gaps, and to bring some experience to that (…) You can't ask [some kind of] question[s] on hour one or even on day six, but weeks later (…). So it is about exploring and spending the time that you need to get as much as you think you need.

Nazarena, a lawyer in Italy, also confirmed that, by following this approach, SOGI claimants may articulate experiences that they were not able to share before, including the real reason for fleeing their country of origin when not disclosed any earlier. Sean asserted as well that to 'strike a relationship' one needs to also be gender-aware, something that tallies with our intersectional and feminist approach

6.2 The Preparation of Asylum Claims and Legal Aid

(Chap. 3). That is why Sean always asks female clients whether they are comfortable with talking to a man, giving them the option of having a female advisor instead.

Nonetheless, it is true that, in some cases, despite the willingness and the availability of lawyers, SOGI claimants find it difficult to 'open up'. In this respect, the cooperation with NGOs or staff in reception centres remains fundamental. The case of a lesbian claimant retold by Celeste, a social worker in Italy, is illustrative. The claimant was convinced that she had to talk only about the sexual aspects of her relationships in line with her understanding of being lesbian: 'She always referred to herself by using the expression "I do lesbian", not "I am" lesbian'. Despite the availability and the efforts of the lawyer, only the intervention of Celeste changed the situation. So, during a long talk between them before the hearing, Celeste explained again why the claimant's initial claim was refused and what questions were to be expected by the judge. It was only thanks to the clarifications provided about the meaning of 'being in a relationship' that the claimant was eventually able to argue effectively before the judge. In other words, a cultural mediation process was necessary to build a case that would otherwise have been unsuccessful. Yet, it is noticeable that this approach may nonetheless reinforce the recognition of refugee status largely on a Western identity basis, as further explored in Chap. 7, in contrast with the queer perspective we advocate (Chap. 3).

Second, the lack of effective communication between legal representatives and claimants was a widespread point of concern. For example, Stephina, a claimant in the UK, told us that when she went to court for her hearing, she could not speak: 'I didn't, I wasn't given a chance to speak and explain some things for myself (…) I followed what my lawyer said… "you say this, you don't say that", so I went with the mentality of "yes sir", he said this and he said not this'. Maria (focus group no. 5, Nottingham, UK) was asked by her lawyer not to mention sexuality as the real ground for requesting asylum, despite the negative implications she feared for the assessment of her claim. Something worse happened to a claimant in the UK, who was involved in focus group no. 3 in London, who discovered after a period of 2 years that her fresh claim, which was supposed to have been submitted, had never been filed: 'Over two years I have been in lie (…). When we phoned him, I went to his office, he said "oh, I don't think I believe you, you were a lesbian"'. For people who have used their own initiative to bring about changes in their lives, the requirement to hand over control to advocates can be difficult. In this respect, Meggs (UK) pointed out: 'Maybe it is one of the mistakes that I did, I didn't kind of do my own research and find out what is really needed, what are they going to ask or what kind of evidence they really required'. In some cases, however, what might be perceived as a lack of energy in pursuing a claim may be motivated by other legitimate reasons. In this respect, the experience of Deirdre, a lawyer in the UK, is enlightening:

Sometimes I would say to a client, "I am not necessarily sure you are ready for this interview and this interview is the most important thing. I think you should go to your GP, I think you should get referred to mental health services, I think we should say to the Home Office, you need a bit more time".

Third, the substantial amount of money that good legal representation costs, mainly in Germany and the UK, is problematic, especially in light of the lack of work opportunities for asylum claimants (Chap. 9). Fees may even be charged for initial consultations (Marlen, legal advisor, Germany), although some lawyers stressed that charging for initial advice can help claimants save 'a lot of money in the long run by being properly advised on the merits', rather than being more concerned 'by the offer of "free" consultations where applicants are then advised to go ahead with expensive poor claims' (Barry, lawyer). Some participants also believed they needed to pay a private lawyer to improve their chances of securing international protection during the administrative process. For instance, Diana (Germany) had paid 700 Euros for a lawyer in the belief that 'it would be easier if you have someone like that (…). That was not a social lawyer or refugee advocate'. For some claimants, a private lawyer remained essential even when reception facilities offered legal support. According to Nice Guy (focus group no. 1, northern Italy):

There's a difference (…). If you are using a camp lawyer, it's free. If you are using your personal lawyer, you have to pay (…) by yourself. But most of the time, the personal lawyer works better than the camp's lawyer.

This perception puts many SOGI claimants under serious financial pressure. In Germany, a questionable system is in place: claimants can apply for legal aid to pay for a lawyer, but legal aid is granted by the same judge who has to decide on the appeal itself, depending on how that judge rates the chances of success of the appeal (ECRE, AIDA & Asyl und Migration 2019, p. 29). Not surprisingly, Barbara, a lawyer, affirmed: 'There was a time, I used to feel that legal aid, if I get that, I've already won'. Far from being compliant with the right to access to a fair asylum procedure (for example, Article 13 ECHR), Thomas, an NGO volunteer, explained that, in practice, claimants need to pre-finance their legal representatives and are only reimbursed in case of success. As further confirmed by Halim, who claimed asylum and worked for an NGO in Germany, the money to anticipate the payment of legal support must come from claimants' monthly welfare income, which is intended to cover basic expenses, including food. This disproportional burden is clear in Tina's account: 'Every month I give 50 Euros from the money government pays me. They pay me 100 Euros every month'. The involvement of LGBTIQ+ support groups sometimes addresses this problem by co-financing initial fees (Sofia and Emma, NGO workers, mentioned the Rainbow Foundation in this respect), which may amount to up to 500 Euros (Noah, NGO social worker).

In Italy, where almost all participants had obtained legal aid to cover their representation by a lawyer, cases of misconduct emerged. Although they had already been paid by the state, we were told of some lawyers asking for additional money, which claimants are unlikely to have. Disturbingly, despite these fees, which may amount to 600 Euros for a first appointment according to Jonathan, an LGBTIQ+

6.2 The Preparation of Asylum Claims and Legal Aid

group volunteer, most lawyers do not have specific competences in SOGI claims, as reported to us by Cristina (UNHCR officer), among others. The case of Franco, who was in touch with a lawyer for 2 years and was never clearly told why his application was rejected, is illustrative:

> I don't know the woman [lawyer]. Someone pushed me. I said no, I don't have choice, before I lose they said 30 days [to appeal]. I pay a lot. She said 550 euro. (…) Yes, I make "campagna" [working in farms]. She never tell me to go to court. (…) She always tell me "Non preoccupare" [do not worry], "Io devo parlare con il giudice" [I have to talk with the judge]. [On the day of the hearing] The police [stopped me], but lawyer don't want to come down (…). After that (…) negative [RSD outcome]. (…) She asked for the rest of the money. I said "no".

The cost of legal advice and representation was also a concern in the UK. Retaining a good private lawyer was expensive, especially when SOGI claimants were not supported by specific entities – for instance, Ibrahim A. was supported by Amnesty International and by Freedom House, through a programme called Dignity for All. As Ali explained: 'even after I got the refugee status I kept paying her by month, [but] it was worth it at the end because she did a hard job (…). I think at some stage we were meeting every week'. For Amber, who was pushed to choose a specific firm for its expertise with Malaysian claimants, legal fees amounted to GBP 3,000. They could not afford to pay the entire amount, until that firm decided to take their case *pro bono*. The preparation of their appeal was indeed meticulous:

> I had to come to the office about once a month or every two weeks or so to sit down and talk to my lawyer about my background. After we're done with the statement, I focused on documenting all the articles and pictures of what was asked by my lawyer after the statement completion as supplementary evidence. (…) It was very detailed and long, and it took me months to complete.

In comparison to others participants, Amber's and Ali's experiences of legal representation are, however, uncommon. According to Wendy and Justina, NGO workers in the UK, many solicitors are not prepared in this area and provide poor advice for high fees. In this respect, Seth, another NGO worker in the UK, summarised what happens to most claimants: 'Quite often, they have spent all their money on a claim that is going to go nowhere, and then when they do finally get the right advice, they have got no money left'. Overall, the experience in the UK seems to suggest that the quality of representation is not determined by whether the client is legally aided or paying privately. As Barry, a lawyer, put it: 'Some legal aid lawyers provide excellent advice, some provide poor representation. It is the same for those who are paid privately'. The consequences of this state-of-affairs are well described by Jayne, who was not lucky enough to meet an experienced lawyer:

> I remember first thing when I walked into the interview room, I was asked if I had brought a witness statement, and I was like "what is that?" (laughs). I had no clue. (…) The solicitor (…) just helped me to give me the numbers to call the Home Office and then he just left. [I] wanted just to have an idea of what I should expect, just to prepare myself psychologically, but… he just said "oh, they will just interview you, about your life generally".

From the perspective of those working on legal aid contracts, it is noticeable that funding is increasingly inadequate as a result of successive cuts to legal aid that have indirectly affected asylum work. As Sean, a lawyer, told us:

> We set up [the law firm] in 2003, predominantly doing legal aid work. Then when the cuts came in, we had to take on private work, to support ourselves and also the legal aid rates were cut... So, in reality, doing legal aid work is not really viable financially.

Financial issues may also prevent the collection of appropriate evidence on claimants' countries of origin. As Sean also explained:

> If you apply to the Legal Aid Agency, say, for GBP1,100 to buy an expert report on the... treatment of LGBT victims of hate crime in [the] Gambia over the last 12 months, the Legal Aid Agency will say "No", because we don't even know that it is an issue in your case yet. (...) So, it is very difficult to get funding for specific expert evidence in advance. (...) A lot of the country-based reporting that we do get evidence of is after the refusal, because the Legal Aid Agency will fund it.

A similar situation applies to psychiatric and medical reports providing evidence of torture, as Deirdre, a lawyer, explained:

> So the way that legal aid works is that until something is in dispute, you can't put forward expert evidence. So I couldn't get an expert psychiatric report on a client until after the Home Office decision letter, because the legal aid agency would say to me "but you don't know that the Home Office don't believe her".

All the above contributes to the likelihood that claimants in the UK will be refused at the initial decision-making phase on evidentiary grounds but may then be successful on appeal when they have been able to commission corroborating reports. Strikingly, some decision-makers are not aware of these dynamics. For instance, Adrian, a judge in the UK, told us that 'I am a strong believer in legal aid... I haven't noticed a falloff in quality as a result [of cuts to legal aid] by and large'.

Fourth, nationality can be relevant to the selection or provision of solicitors. When the lawyers available are from the same ethnic or religious community, there may be negative implications for claimants who are not (yet) open about their SOGI. As previous research has reported, sometimes lawyers are 'arranged through members of the applicant's extended family, so gay applicants that are supported by their community are unlikely to be able to come out to their lawyer' (Miles 2010, p. 30). This general difficulty was confirmed, among others, by Ashley, a psychotherapist in the UK:

> After their initial experiences, maybe at the Home Office interview (...) of interpreters (...), their fears about information getting back to people in their community or back home [prevent] at their initial meetings with their lawyers [the] disclosure around sexuality. [Therefore] that part of the story is delayed and not in their initial claims and that adds to the issue of credibility.

From the discussion above, overall access by SOGI claimants to legal representation of high quality seems therefore difficult across Germany, Italy and the UK, especially when legal aid is not effectively granted to cover the time needed to prepare such complex cases. When high quality representation is accessible instead, even good lawyers may find it difficult to rectify initial wrong advice at a later stage

6.2 The Preparation of Asylum Claims and Legal Aid

of the procedure. Bearing in mind this general state of affairs, a wide range of unethical conduct and working methods were described by our participants. Giulia, an LGBTIQ+ volunteer in Italy, shared the case of a lawyer who forgot to submit the appeal on time with very negative consequences for the claimant, who had to leave the accommodation centre and, only after a while, was able to start a fresh claim. The case of Amadin, who claimed asylum in the UK, is even more concerning:

> So my lawyer make a mistake (…) because there is a confusion between Benin City who is a city in Nigeria and the Benin country. (…) The lawyer got some evidence online, where he put, I don't know what he put because he no tell me what he was putting, so I did not know what he knew. (…) So my lawyer was not ready to defend the country issue. (…) So now, the lawyer dropped me and I get a new lawyer now, who are preparing the case and they are doing a country report.

In other cases, lawyers failed to inform claimants about the day of the hearing (as reported by Juliet, Germany) or did not follow up the claim, despite having been already paid by a support group (Louis, NGO volunteer, Germany). Giulio, an LGBTIQ+ group volunteer in Italy, gave us another worrying example of the poor quality of some legal representation:

> [Asylum appeals] are considered easy ones (…) they just copy and paste, submit the same documents. [In SOGI claims] they find also difficult to understand the difference between being persecuted for being gay or for being perceived as gay… (…) So, in the appeal form, they simply write "gay claimant" although he might not be gay (…). The judge will then see a contradiction with negative consequences for the claimant.

Lawyers themselves are critical of their colleagues' work. According to Mara, a lawyer in Italy, lawyers who submit an LGBTIQ+ association membership card as part of their documentation to the judge damage the claimant's case because they are indirectly suggesting that homosexuality needs to be proved (Chap. 7). Similarly questionable advice was reported in the UK. Sean, a lawyer, recalled the case of a lesbian claimant:

> The number of errors that she suffered at the hands of her previous solicitors were significant such as: not being advised why witnesses might be necessary at a hearing; not having the witness statements prepared for her witnesses in advance of the hearing; getting to court and then her star witness can't make it, and the advisor from the same [law firm] says "we don't want an adjournment, we are just going to press on". Wow – that is basic, basic stuff! And now she finds herself a year, six months on, living off nothing, separated from her son, and her story is compelling.

The worst experiences were perhaps those where claimants were unable to find a lawyer to represent them and invest time in their case (Joyce, focus group no. 5, Nottingham, UK, among others). As Leon, LGBTIQ+ community project staff member in Germany, told us, '[w]e have many cases where several of the lawyers (…) tell us that, from their point of view, this is hopeless'. As Meggs (UK) put it:

> I was told we are supposed to appeal again that [but] he said, "oh no, we don't have a case. (…) Just go and find new evidence, if you find it, come back to me", and I didn't know what new evidence would that be. Don't know what is fresh claim or what I have to look for, yes. So if we didn't have like the kind of organisation First Wednesday, Lesbian Immigration

Support Group, where you meet and they tell you like this is how it is done, I wouldn't even know until today. Because I didn't know what I was looking for.

In these cases, the claimant's only option was to lodge an appeal without legal representation to the best standard possible for a non-legal professional. Irma (UK) represented herself and became homeless after seeing her appeal rejected. The case of Daphne (UK) is also illustrative. When her solicitor abandoned her before the hearing, she led her own appeal. After explaining what had happened to the judge, he adjourned her case for 2 weeks, however she was still unable to find a legal representative, so her appeal was refused. Incredibly, when she finally found a solicitor to take her case to judicial review, she was eventually given refugee status after a total of three refusals and more than 6 years in the asylum system.

Denise and Umar, legal advisors in the UK, explained one reason why law firms are reluctant to take cases based on sexual orientation-related persecution, particularly fresh claims:

> If [a sexuality case] has been refused, then it really needs some real… detailed and really kind of concentrated work in order to try and make it a success. (…) If you are in a private practice and (…) you are looking at your profit, then some of these cases are not the kind of cases that you would want to take on because they require a lot of work that you are not necessarily going to be paid for by through legal aid.

According to Sean, a lawyer in the UK as well, it is not only about profit:

> Those fresh claim cases add a layer of complexity and difficulty to an original asylum claim. Because if you have got a new client who hasn't claimed asylum yet, you can sit down and say "Right, this is the process, this is what is going to happen. Let's take your story". (…) With a fresh claim you have got to do all of that, you have got to identify what went wrong in a previous claim, turn that around, explain this is the actual story and the corroborating evidence, and why it wasn't done before or what was missed and that there might have been delay for personal reasons, reluctance to talk about things. It may be a solicitor's incompetence, [or] they haven't done it because they feel restrained by the fixed fee (…). And then you put it altogether and you present the fresh claim in person but in Liverpool.

Negative attitudes also emerged during hearing observations in tribunals. For example, during a tribunal observation in northern Italy in 2018, we observed the completely passive behaviour of a substitute lawyer before the judge, and failure to intervene on the claimant's behalf. The situation appears even more problematic if coupled with the influence of strong bias against SOGI claims. As one of the lawyers contacted for carrying out that observation expressly affirmed, 'SOGI claimants always tell the same stories', thus assuming that – at least as a starting point – all his clients lie to obtain international protection.

The difference between legal representation of good or poor quality is captured in the account given by Jayne (UK):

> I have never been to court, I don't know what to expect, what do they expect me to do, what shall I bring with me. Just general information. So, I remember all [the solicitor] said was just prove you are a lesbian. (…) the day before my hearing I went to the office tearful to the receptionist to say, I have court tomorrow (…) and I don't know what to do. (…) One of the solicitors came and said "oh, you shouldn't worry, your solicitor will be at the court

6.2 The Preparation of Asylum Claims and Legal Aid 201

tomorrow". I went home, the following day I went to court (…) one lady came and said (…) "I am going to represent you" (…) She doesn't know anything about my case, there are some things that I requested that they don't get like discussed, in front of people, and… boom [they were discussed publicly], because she didn't know anything. (…) At some point the judge asked her a question and she said, "I am sorry but I have only been given the file this morning, so I really haven't had time to go through this file." (…) Now I started the journey of a fresh claim. And it was a totally different experience altogether, because I could sit two or three hours with [the lawyer] asking me personal… questions, getting deep into my case, asking me about my relationships, I didn't know all that would be relevant to my case.

Perhaps not surprisingly, decision-makers are conscious of the differences in the quality of legal representation. Harry, a senior judge in the UK, told us that while some lawyers do their job very well, at 'the other end of the spectrum are unscrupulous people who prey upon the most vulnerable in our society, take their money and do a dreadful job for them'. Equally, according to Silvana, a judge in Italy, SOGI claimants too often lack adequate legal representation, which is clearly reflected not only in the lack of contact with their clients, but also by their usual 'copied and pasted' appeals. Training and preparation of lawyers, as well as of any other staff working with SOGI claimants, thus remains a highly problematic aspect which needs specific investigation.

6.2.3 *Training of Volunteers, Lawyers and Staff Working with SOGI Claimants*

Concerns about the lack of training of SOGI asylum of volunteers, lawyers and staff working in the field were widely reported, particularly in Germany and Italy (Helena, EASO staff member; Angel, Germany; Kadir, NGO worker, Germany; Emilia, judge, Germany; Nazarena and Giuseppe, lawyers, Italy). The rules currently in force, including at EU level, do not establish any obligation to train staff working with SOGI claimants on the specificities of these claims. The same is true for lawyers, whose basic legal training does not cover SOGI claims specifically, and for volunteers, who often are not trained at all. Only a few of our participants received training on SOGI asylum (for instance, Knud, NGO worker, Germany; Juliane, public official, Germany). Even when training on asylum is offered, for instance concerning the CEAS, this does not cover the grounds considered here.

From a positive perspective, various kinds of SOGI asylum training are provided by support groups across the three countries under comparison, sometimes in cooperation with local/national/European/international institutions, for anyone who is willing to be involved on a voluntary basis. For example, Giulia, an LGBTIQ+ group volunteer in Italy, recalled a training course organised in 2017 by local associations in central Italy, in cooperation with the UNHCR, as a fundamental moment in her involvement with SOGI claimants. On that occasion, she learned it was possible to alert territorial commissions in advance of the interview date to ensure

SOGI-friendly procedural arrangements on the day (Sect. 6.3). Still in Italy, before launching their new support groups, some leaders organised training courses on the basics of SOGI asylum by inviting experts in the field or attending training with 'experts' (for instance, Anna and Vincenzo, LGBTIQ+ group volunteers; La Migration 2018). As Vincenzo put it: 'I needed to be trained to avoid damaging or not supporting entirely people who arrive with problems that I was unable to understand'. Perhaps even more interesting, owing to the lack of training available to staff working in reception centres, a few support groups took the initiative of offering training to local reception centres, not only on SOGI asylum but also on SOGI equality – an offer that some centres accepted (for instance, Giulia, LGBTIQ+ group volunteer). Yet, as Vincenzo (LGBTIQ+ group volunteer) pointed out, most staff working with SOGI claimants are not 'craving for training, but need mechanical tools to make their work easier'. Consequently, in his view, only those people who already have an interest in this topic choose to be involved in voluntary training courses; thus the challenge is engaging the remaining staff working with SOGI claimants but without an interest in improving their knowledge and expertise in this field.

In the Italian asylum system, we also heard of the specific problem of accommodation centre staff not possessing a legal education or previous experience with refugees or migrants (for instance, Vincenzo, LGBTIQ+ group volunteer). This hampered their ability to elicit claimants' stories in an appropriate way, with negative consequences for the asylum procedure, especially in terms of subsequent assessment of credibility (Chap. 7). The different degrees of SOGI asylum expertise of staff may be attributed to the particular individual or entity managing a given accommodation facility. Many participants shared the view that, as such facilities are run by private companies, their managers did not find it profitable or, more simply, were not aware of the need to train their staff in general and, more specifically, on SOGI asylum (Nazarena, lawyer; Roberto, decision-maker; Silvana, judge; Susanna, social worker). For these participants, finding competent staff in reception facilities was indeed a kind of lottery. Positive experiences were nonetheless found among this specific group of professionals. For example, Nazarena, a lawyer, explained that the staff with whom she cooperated at accommodation centres had begun to compile information about claimants' countries of origin in order to better understand their experiences.

Lack of training facilitates the prevalence of practices based on bias, prejudices and stereotypes. For instance, the lack of basic understanding of transgender issues was at the core of experiences of discrimination against transgender claimants. Kamel, who submitted an asylum request in Italy by using identity documents where his sex at birth was signalled, reported the ignorance of the staff met at the police headquarters: 'I said "I'm trans" and she did not know what trans means [while] keep saying "are you a man or a woman?"'. He felt very hurt. More strikingly, as Kamel also explained, this same problematic attitude towards transgender claimants was observed in relation to staff who already dealt with gay claimants. Another relevant case was mentioned by Giulia, an LGBTIQ+ volunteer in Italy. Despite the obligation to respect the right to privacy of claimants, a reception centre staff member had shared details about a gay claimant with other users of the centre, and as a result he experienced discrimination. As confirmed by Cristina (UNHCR officer, Italy), this was not an isolated episode. Lawyers also fall prey to bias and prejudice, leading some to treat SOGI claimants arriving from particular countries with suspicion (for instance, Tribunal observation, northern Italy, 2018).

For these and other reasons, while pointing out a general need for both basic (on asylum) and specialised (on SOGI issues) training of all categories working with SOGI claimants, our participants also drew our attention to particular areas of need. For instance, Cristina (UNHCR officer, Italy) emphasised the importance of multidisciplinary training also covering basic concepts, such as SOGI and equality, in order to promote and consolidate an anti-stereotyping approach within the asylum system, consistant with our theoretical underpinnings (Chap. 3). This view was shared by Louis (NGO volunteer, Germany), who pointed out the need to sensitise people working with asylum claimants in a way that can help them understand claimants fleeing homophobia or transphobia *without* forcing them to come out. According to Nazarena (lawyer, Italy), training should include background information on COI (Sect. 6.5) and on claimants' cultural background, not simply on legal matters. Finally, Evelyne and Anne (lawyers, Germany) pointed out the need to involve claimants in training all people working with SOGI, as well as therapists or psychologists to support these people in how to manage the emotional consequences of their job. In this respect, it is noteworthy that positive experiences on training carried out at EU level included topics like how to create a safe space and how to help SOGI claimants to be open about their stories. Of course, while being relevant for all those considered in this section – volunteers, lawyers and staff – these general recommendations need to be tailored, taking into account the specific role played by these actors in the SOGI asylum procedure (Chap. 11).

In brief, while we heard of the provision of one-off training, we found little evidence in the three countries under examination of mandatory, systematic and continual SOGI-specific training for those working with SOGI claimants, except where volunteers, lawyers and staff autonomously choose to attend available training on SOGI asylum. Some participants also expressed doubts on the real effect generated by widespread specific training, other than producing greater awareness on SOGI asylum. In fact, the working conditions in the asylum sector remain 'hard' in the context of large migration flows and involve actors that may not support SOGI equality. In relation to the latter aspect, Celeste (social worker, Italy) told us of a lesbian claimant who was accommodated in a facility run by the Catholic Church. Irrespective of the background training of the staff, she decided to avoid any reference to her grounds of persecution for 'safety' reasons.

Beside this, even for the most sensitive and experienced SOGI asylum advisors and representatives, the impact of work of this nature can have an effect on the individual that in turn affects their ability to do their job. For example, Deirdre, a lawyer in the UK, explained that:

> [T]hat's the risk that you become so exposed to it (…) that you do to protect yourself and how you are feeling, you almost try and close the door and it is just words (…). And we

have to be so careful of our staff with that, because as soon as that starts to happen, quality just goes.

As Helena (EASO staff member) explained, almost everyone who has been in the asylum system for more than 2 years has had vicarious trauma or a 'burn out', so the easiest response is to stop believing in claimants' stories. Yet, apart from some institutions' measures mitigating against the risk of burn-out of their staff (for instance, the psychological support offered by the UNHCR, as reported by Cristina, UNHCR officer, Italy), there is no obligation whatsoever in the legislation of the three countries under comparison, nor under EU law, to provide appropriate support or risk-management measures. Similar concerns emerged in relation to decision-makers involved in the main asylum interview, to which we now turn.

6.3 The Main Interview: Actors and Procedures in SOGI Asylum

The key moment for all asylum claimants is indubitably their main interview. As Evelyne and Anne, lawyers in Germany, pointed out:

> [we] often have clients from all sorts of countries saying, "Yes, I was in the hearing with the judge". Those are not judges. But they have the feeling that this is an incredibly important person. (…) They have a huge respect. They do not sleep for days before this interview (…) they have dark circles under their eyes because they did not sleep all night. Eat nothing, drink nothing (…). And [often] there is no one who somehow creates a pleasant atmosphere.

In spite of the differences between Germany, Italy and the UK, a common pattern emerges. Asylum systems should provide an environment in which claimants feel comfortable about self-identifying as members of a SOGI minority and revealing the real grounds for their asylum request, in line with the UNHCR SOGI Guidelines. Instead, no asylum system under investigation here has in place formal procedures addressing the specific needs of SOGI claimants at the main interview. Even the simplest possible measure, consisting of a formal preliminary communication mechanism to inform the relevant administrative body that an interview with a SOGI claimant will take place in order to identify the most appropriate interviewer/decision-maker (as pointed out, for instance, by Cristina, UNHCR officer, Italy), is absent in all countries.

In addition to the lack of specific measures, the entire interview process seems designed to unveil false claims. As Sean (lawyer, UK) put it, often the starting point is '"[y]ou are a liar, convince me otherwise" (…) rather than having an open mind, asking, "tell me your story, let me understand it, and let's explore it"'. Moreover, as David (official, UK) confirmed, SOGI claimants are not always recognised as complex cases: 'I think there are seven types which are automatically perceived to be complex, pregnant women being one, for example. I don't think LGBT is one'. That is why this section places particular attention on the actors involved in the interview process. After analysing the interview setting and the – general or informal – procedures in place for reaching a decision on asylum applications, we move on to the selection and the training of interviewers and decision-makers, how these actors carry out an interview with a SOGI claimant and, finally, the influence – if any – of bias during the interview, in light of the experiences of our participants.

6.3.1 The Interview Setting

As anticipated in Chaps. 1 and 4, despite some similarities, each country under investigation has shaped its asylum system differently, especially at administrative level. Here we aim to identify any specific, even informal, procedural arrangements in place for managing these particular claims.

In Germany, the BAMF is responsible for the asylum interview ('Anhoerung'), which in most cases is carried out by a single officer. When there is an indication that the claimant belongs to a 'vulnerable' group, a specialised decision-maker may be called to process the claim. In line with Article 12 of the Procedures Directive (Chap. 4), vulnerable groups include unaccompanied children, victims of torture, traumatised asylum claimants and victims of gender-specific persecution, which may also cover SOGI claimants on a case-by-case basis.[9] The involvement of a specialised officer ('Sonderbeauftragter') can be also requested before the interview. Some criticism has emerged in relation to the effective availability of these officials in every BAMF office, as well as the quality of interviews (ECRE, AIDA & Asyl und Migration 2018, p. 45). Moreover, according to a local survey involving several NGOs in North Rhine-Westphalia (Held et al. 2018), most SOGI claimants are not aware that they can ask for a specialised officer and, when requested, their involvement was not always guaranteed.

Our participants in Germany shared contrasting views on this subject. Although the existence of specialised officers was widely reported, some doubts were expressed in relation to their number (for instance, Evelyne and Anne, lawyers; Noah, NGO social worker), availability across Germany (for instance, Frank S., legal advisor) and the regularity of their involvement in processing SOGI claims (among others, Marlen, legal advisor). Where and when this procedural arrangement is adopted, it seems to be based on informal grounds. In this respect, Sabrina, an NGO worker, explained that, during a meeting with BAMF, 'it was virtually decided that we could inform the BAMF if we knew of any such case, and then a specialised officer would be appointed for the interview, or at least included in the decision-making process'. Sandra, who claimed asylum in Germany, confirmed that her lawyer requested a specialised officer and one was appointed. The officer was a man, and, in line with EU law norms on this matter (Article 15(3)(b) of the

---

[9] Statistics in this respect, however, are not available: see responses 8, 11 and 12 in the answer to the FOI request submitted in Germany (BMI 2019).

Procedures Directive), Sandra was given the possibility to choose the gender of her interviewer. To this, she answered:

> If it's gay or lesbian, I feel like I'm home. Someone I can be open about anything, because he or she would understand. So, for me, if it's a man or a woman... as long as he's from my group.

In her view, sexual orientation played a more important role than gender in terms of the choice of the interviewer, which highlights the importance of the intersectional approach to our analysis adopted in Chap. 3. For other participants, or in specific contexts in Germany, this choice still remained problematic. A striking example was provided by Tina. She was not aware of this possibility and, despite being interviewed four times, only the last interview was carried out by a woman and then she finally felt 'free' to talk. Equally, Mayi (focus group no. 4, Bavaria), who was interviewed by a male officer, explained:

> I did not give them everything. Because myself, I was feeling ashamed. Maybe I thought they would judge me (...). I didn't have a choice. And when you are talking to them, the way they look at you, it's like "what are you talking?" Really, you feel fear.

In turn, Shany recalled that, being in detention at the time of the interview, she had 'no choice' and experienced a particularly distressing situation:

> I'm sitting and then I need to say my story in Moroccan [Arab] and they are two men [the interviewer and the interpreter], I mean, like not women, I mean, how can you bring men? It was like horrible. (...) It's just like you can't, because there is two men and I got small, my confidence is low, it's going down. (...) I see father, I see jail, I see knives, I see that I'm there, I see everything then (...) I would never do it if I have this kind of interview (...). I would stay in the desert, maybe living alone with animals. (...) I never have any conversation with Moroccan men.

A distinct situation is in place in Italy, where the UNHCR is directly involved in the administrative decision-making process, as discussed in Chap. 4. The presence of the UNHCR staff in the territorial commissions brings the attention of these bodies to the specific needs of SOGI claimants. An informal procedural arrangement was consistently reported across Italy. When the presence of a SOGI claimant is known via the C3 form, there is a high chance that the interview will be carried out by the UNHCR representative or otherwise by another territorial commission member specialised in SOGI issues (among others, Giuseppe, lawyer; Maria Grazia and Roberto, decision-makers; Celeste, social worker). The same arrangement takes place if a SOGI case is communicated in advance, mainly by the accommodation centre's staff, NGOs or support groups, or when SOGI is visible (for instance, when transgender claimants are already transitioning, as reported by Valentina, social worker). When the SOGI nature of the case is not known or communicated in advance, the interviewer may decide to stop and postpone the interview to ensure that the most competent member of the territorial commission is involved. As Daniele (decision-maker) pointed out, this system clearly favours SOGI claimants who are already open about their story or are sufficiently prepared for the interview. A similar informal arrangement is also used for other specific categories identified as 'vulnerable', like victims of trafficking. The ongoing discussion about the

6.3 The Main Interview: Actors and Procedures in SOGI Asylum

replacement of the UNHCR representatives with human rights experts may not, therefore, lead to an improvement of the overall process insofar as SOGI asylum is concerned (Roberto, decision-maker), unless the new professionals are required to have an equal level of expertise and are employed with the same UNHCR mandate, which is clearly based on a human rights reading of the Refugee Convention, in line with our theoretical underpinnings (Chap. 3). Finally, our participants confirmed that a general measure adopted in the daily activities of territorial commissions for all claimants, as required by law, irrespective of their persecution grounds, is to ensure that participants are offered interviewers of the same gender (for instance, Daniele, decision-maker). Yet, this is not always possible, especially when the commission member most competent on SOGI asylum is not of the same gender of the participant. Moses, claiming asylum in Italy, explained that he was not comfortable at all with 'a woman asking such questions... it wasn't really easy for me'. Considering that he waited 10 months for the interview, however, he decided not to risk further delays by asking for a male interviewer.

Moving to the UK, no separate process for SOGI claims is in place, but the activity of the Home Office is informed by specific SOGI guidance, namely the 2011 guidance on gender identity and the 2016 guidance on sexual orientation (Chap. 4). Both documents show a high degree of sensitivity to the particular issues likely to affect SOGI claimants. For instance, claimants should be 'given respect and referred to by their chosen name and gender identity' (Home Office 2011, p. 12). The 2016 sexual orientation guidance emphasises, in turn, that caseworkers should avoid stereotyping such as requiring familiarity with the 'gay scene' and should allow the claimant to provide a narrative without expecting 'milestones such as first romantic encounters' (Home Office 2016, p. 27). Equally, they should recognise that claimants may find it difficult to talk about their sexual orientation (Home Office 2016, p. 13). In our fieldwork specific contrasting views emerged in relation to how the processing of SOGI claims is supervised. Olivia (government official) explained that in Scotland and Northern Ireland all SOGI claims are subject to the Second Pair of Eyes procedure, consisting mainly of an evaluation of the quality of the decision-making process by a more senior colleague. As Olivia pointed out, according to available records, final decisions did not change most of the time, 'but it may well be that that [more senior colleague] goes back to the decision-maker to say, "here is another aspect that you have not actually considered"'. While the value of this procedure is apparent for SOGI claims, it does not seem to be mandatory across the UK (David, official). As for the right to choose the gender of the interviewer, it is granted so far as Home Office's resources allow it. For instance, when Amber was asked during the screening interview if they had any preference in this respect, they were told that the Home Office would try to accommodate the request 'depending on available staff'. Finally, it is worth noting that, once an interview is scheduled, claimants are not always given appropriate resources to reach the venue. The case of Selim is striking. After waiting for 7 months, he could not afford the price of the train ticket. To avoid seeing the interview postponed for months or years, he sold his engagement ring.

An important question to consider in all countries under comparison is whether the interview is carried out by the same person who eventually takes a final decision on the case. In Germany, cases are often decided by designated decision-makers rather than the person who interviews the claimant (Gisela, lawyer), even when a specialised officer is involved. In Italy, instead, given the particular composition of territorial commissions, the interviewer corresponds, at least informally, to the officer deciding on the case. In fact, whereas the law establishes that, within territorial commissions, decisions are taken collectively, in practice it is the officer who individually interviews a claimant who, afterwards, reports directly to the entire commission and drafts a decision to be jointly discussed. As Titti, a decision-maker, explained, after interviewing a claimant, she usually drafts a decision consisting of three main parts: applicable law, facts of the case and credibility of the claimant. When the entire commission reunites after each member's interviews, reasons for the drafted decision are explained in order to reach a unanimous decision. During this discussion, it may happen that, when a SOGI case is reported, the most competent member of the commission in this area asks for a second interview to be scheduled with the claimant *if* it is perceived that the interview was not carried out appropriately (for instance, Maria Grazia, decision-maker; Cristina, UNHCR officer). Equally, a second interview may be scheduled when, from the account of the interviewer, doubts arise about the existence of a potential non-declared SOGI claim or when the interviewer is not able to report accurately the case while proposing a rejection (for instance, Daniele, decision-maker). In all other circumstances, if a consensus is reached, the drafted decision is adopted by the territorial commission. In very exceptional situations, where the members of the commission do not agree, it is possible to issue a dissenting separate opinion. According to some participants, the collective approach to decision-making is not only an essential guarantee of a fair decision-making process for SOGI claimants, but also stimulates all members to operate appropriately to avoid seeing the decisions they draft refused (Roberto, decision-maker). Finally, in the UK, most cases are decided by an officer who is different from the interviewer (Olivia, government official). Alternative experimental models have been tested, such as the pilot scheme called the Early Legal Advice Project, in which individual case owners were more likely to cover all aspects of a case. Yet, these experimental models were not adopted permanently, for reasons such as cost and the longer time that decisions took to be made (Home Office 2013).

On the need to have – or not – a single caseworker for the entire administrative procedure in order to improve the fairness of the SOGI asylum system, some contrasting views were held by our participants. According to Roberto (decision-maker, Italy), there are no advantages at all to having a single caseworker. As he explained, every system should be based on collective decision bodies or on discussions between peers before reaching a final decision or, at least, on referrals to senior caseworkers. In fact, there is a widespread belief that involving different caseworkers contributes to the objectivity of decisions (for instance, Evelyne and Anne, lawyers, Germany). Yet, for some participants, a collective decision-making system is problematic. According to David (official, UK), the involvement of different

6.3 The Main Interview: Actors and Procedures in SOGI Asylum 209

caseworkers leads to a decision process that appears as a 'transaction [in which] the [final] caseworker is reviewing the material (...) and saying "does this [claimant] meet [certain] tests"'. In turn, for Daniele, decision-maker in Italy, when the interviewer is not the decision-maker, the latter can never properly evaluate the claimant's credibility. In his view, the decision-maker needs to focus also on elements like demeanour or non-verbal communication, which are essential factors in complex applications, such as those based on SOGI grounds. In any case, as Daniele further pointed out, in this area the fairness of the evaluation process always depends on the ability of the single caseworker to avoid being influenced by bias, prejudices and stereotypes, that is, an approach based on some of our theoretical underpinning (Chap. 3). That is why their selection and training, to which we now turn our attention, remain fundamental.

6.3.2 *The Selection and the Training of Caseworkers*

In light of the differences that have emerged so far in our analysis, it is not surprising that each country under investigation has its own rules and practices on the selection and training of interviewers and decision-makers.

Starting with Germany, there is no indication that the BAMF, when hiring its officers, requires that they undergo a particular training covering SOGI asylum or possess particular high level qualifications. Data shows that most caseworkers did not complete any or the full training programme, 'with new staff members only being trained in "crash courses" and getting basic training only after they have started their job' (ECRE, AIDA & Asyl und Migration 2019, p. 20). Having regard to the caseworkers who process SOGI claims, the so-called 'special officers', the German government explained that BAMF officers should complete specific training on 'vulnerable' groups, which also contains modules on gender, gender identity and sexual orientation, and receive appropriate references to documents and publications such as those issued by the EASO (BMI 2019, pp. 2–3, 18). Yet, most of our participants claiming asylum in Germany were not heard by special officers, being interviewed by officers who had therefore not received specific training. From their perception, the training of the BAMF officers in SOGI asylum is indeed very poor. An example of this was provided by Ibrahim, who still remembered that:

> When I first applied (...) she asked me "why are you here? Why are you applying for asylum?" In English. I said "because of my sexual orientation". She said to me "what?". I had to let her see a picture of two gay men kissing so she understood.

Although signs of improvement had been noticed (Knud, NGO worker), the pressure caused by a high number of asylum applications in 2015 and 2016 was reported as one of the main reasons for shorter intensive training programmes for newly-arrived caseworkers (for instance, Elias, lawyer). Serious consequences from the lack of specific training have followed. Speaking about one of his clients who was hiding his sexual orientation from his family, Frank S. (legal advisor) recalled that when the claimant's mother arrived in Germany a few months later and was interviewed in the context of her asylum application, the interviewer revealed to her the son's sexual orientation, thus violating the son's right to privacy. Specific concerns were also reported in relation to the correct use of information about claimants' countries of origin (Sect. 6.5). In this respect, Noah (NGO social worker) noticed that most decisions related to Jamaica are copied and pasted: 'Besides the individual rejection reasons, which are derived from the interview, [BAMF decision-makers state that] "in Jamaica, the situation is not as bad as shown, because (…) the Ministry of Justice set up a programme that should sensitise the local police [and] protect them"'. This mechanistic use of COI reflects poorly on the training of the decision-makers.

In Italy, the particular composition of the territorial commissions shapes both the selection mechanism and the training available to each member. Following the 2017 reform (Chap. 4), if we exclude officers serving as presidents and the UNHCR representatives, whose selection and training follow different paths, 250 new officers were selected through a national public competition in 2018. The evaluation was mainly based on legal knowledge of the asylum legal system, thus excluding people with other university studies (Vincenzo, LGBTIQ+ group volunteer). In the context of the training programme organised by the National Commission of Asylum in cooperation with the UNHCR, successful candidates specifically addressed SOGI asylum through a format consisting of general information and case-study analyses with the involvement of SOGI experts. As Cristina (UNHCR officer) explained, a transgender activist was invited as well, not only for the information they could offer, but also to address, directly and indirectly, potential stereotypes and prejudices in newly-appointed officers. This initial training has been followed by periodic refresher trainings. This development was seen as positive by our participants, because it came after a period where the high number of applications, and the consequent setting up of new territorial commissions on an emergency basis, hampered the implementation of specific training on SOGI asylum. In fact, one of the decision-makers who was employed in that precise period explained that, in light of her legal background and her activism on SOGI equality, she was appointed by the local municipality but, except for a few days of individual coaching by the UNHCR representative in her Commission, she had received no comprehensive training before starting her new role. As she summarised, 'I really felt like I was thrown into the deep end' (Maria Grazia, decision-maker).

At least in principle, the employment and the coordinated and intensive training of the new caseworkers in Italy may improve the poor level of preparation of decision-makers reported by some participants (among others, Anna and Giulio, LGBTIQ+ group volunteers). The involvement of professional staff with an expertise in asylum would potentially lead to fairer evaluations and better-motivated outcomes (Silvana and Maurizio, judges). These opinions were also based on the premise that the new staff replaced police officers and local authorities' representatives who, irrespective of their background, were mainly perceived as pursuing security or locally-based interests and being influenced by bias and prejudices (for instance, Maria Grazia, decision-maker). A number of examples connected with the

6.3 The Main Interview: Actors and Procedures in SOGI Asylum

former composition of territorial commissions were attributed to the lack of, or poor, training. For instance, Mara (lawyer) recalled that the decisions of some territorial commissions show a clear lack of knowledge about the situation of SOGI people in their countries, leading to the use of 'copied and pasted' information on the claimant's country of origin, without paying attention to the specific region and situation at stake, thus similar to Germany. It is worth noting however that, due to the role internationally fulfilled by the UNHCR, even when specific training is not available, the UNHCR representatives within most territorial commissions provide a sort of ongoing training to all other members and staff. In fact, in case of doubts on how a case should be managed or which form of protection should be granted, the UNHCR representatives are regularly consulted (Titti, decision-maker). For this reason, their own training becomes fundamental. As several participants explained, the UNHCR representatives are continuously trained on different aspects of the asylum process, including SOGI asylum. Moreover, thanks to their periodic rotation across different territorial commissions, the risk of burn-out is also somewhat reduced.

In the UK, repeated calls for better training on SOGI claims for Home Office decision-makers led to some improvements (Gray and McDowall 2013, p. 23). Thanks to its activities, the UKLGIG 'had extensive input into compulsory training for all UKBA decision-makers and into an Asylum Policy Instruction on sexual identity asylum claims' (House of Commons Home Affairs Committee 2013, pp. 86–87). Despite this, in 2016 it transpired that university education did not seem to be a requirement for being selected as a caseworker, it being only incidental that most caseworkers have university degrees (Khan 2016, pp. 277–282). In the same year, a parliamentary report recommended that the Home Office improve staff training and potentially appoint specialised caseworkers in SOGI cases (APPG on Global LGBT Rights 2016, p. 6). While the reduction in the seniority and expertise required of asylum decision-makers as a cost-saving measure contrasts with Home Office reassurances about the delivery of appropriate training on SOGI asylum (Home Office Minister 2018), our participants shed light on the kind of programmes in place to train interviewers and decision-makers. According to Olivia (government official), a foundation training programme is given over a period of 5 weeks. While the first 3 weeks are dedicated to decision-making, the principles of the Refugee Convention and immigration rules, the subsequent 2 weeks cover specific types of asylum applications, including those based on SOGI grounds. Qasim, a decision-maker who was trained in 2017, confirmed this in detail:

> We looked at some of the feedback that previous LGBT applicants have given regarding their experience of the asylum process, including their criticisms of the Home Office. We then had further group discussions around what an LGBT asylum applicant would find difficult in an interview environment, why an LGBT person may not want to disclose their sexuality, and how we as interviewers can help applicants to explain any shame or stigma they may have felt as a result of their sexuality. We also looked at the difference between someone's identity as a gay person and their conduct, why someone might be at risk as a result of either of these factors and the reasons why someone who is gay might not want to get involved in a gay relationship. We also explored how we would conduct an LGBT interview (…) and we completed case studies to prepare us for dealing with LGBT applicants.

We also of course looked at what factors we would need to consider in order to decide whether an LGBT person should be granted asylum in the UK. This includes looking at the degree of risk for LGBT people in their country and whether internal relocation within their own country or sufficiency of protection is available.

This foundation programme is followed by periodic refresher training, but enrolment is voluntary. A sort of mentorship scheme, consisting of an experienced officer following the newly arrived caseworker for a certain period, is also organised. As Emily (decision-maker) explained, 'at the beginning you get every decision checked by a technical expert, until you're ready to be signed off'. Overall, by taking the training and this mentorship into account, as Olivia (government official) pointed out, 'it probably takes about six months for a decision-maker to become (…) more competent, confident'. Although this training appears satisfactory, as David (official) reported, caseworkers who are relatively new do not always 'feel that their training was adequate' and lack adequate mentoring. The consequences for him are evident:

> If you have got volumes of demand coming in, time limits on decisions, lots of very new people with little experience and the people who have been bumped up to be their immediate managers, you know, are equally not especially experienced, (...) you are giving people a challenge which they can't meet.

As a result, David favoured a focus on 'quality assurance' and more effective mentoring of more junior caseworkers.

In light of data collected across the three countries here analysed, a few more aspects concerning the selection and training of decision-makers should be highlighted. First, while suggested by some claimants (for instance, Ibrahim A., UK; SGW, focus group no. 4, London, UK), the specific recruitment of people belonging to SOGI minorities as caseworkers in SOGI cases was deemed unfeasible by other participants, partly because of employees' right not to reveal their SOGI (in contrast to perceptions of the rights of the claimants whose claims they assess). In fact, Olivia (government official, UK) argued that 'my team is a diverse team, and they do their job regardless of who they are speaking to'. Second, it was widely stressed that, once decision-makers are appointed, they should be able to rely on adequate support and periodic breaks to reduce the risk of burn-out. For example, Roberto (decision-maker, Italy) told us that 'I cannot imagine someone who interviews claimants for 40 years (…) you certainly die before'. Third, as for the kind of training organised for new caseworkers, participants highlighted the need for knowledge and tools that go beyond legal notions, and which considered the concrete experiences of SOGI people (among others, Chiara, NGO worker, Italy). As Maria Grazia (decision-maker, Italy) pointed out, many decision-makers still do not have direct experience of SOGI minorities and should be taught about the meaning of SOGI to break down the 'stereotyped, generical, unreal idea' they may have. In order to be effective, such training should directly involve SOGI refugees. Fourth, the importance of training was often related to the development of caseworkers' ability to recognise SOGI claims even when they are not raised by the claimants. This seems to be the real challenge, but which may help to effectively implement an approach

6.3 The Main Interview: Actors and Procedures in SOGI Asylum   213

compatible with our theoretical underpinning (Chap. 3). The example reported by Titti (decision-maker, Italy) is illustrative:

> Once, I was interviewing a male claimant who was talking about many different things and at some point, despite the presence of the interpreter, I noticed that he mentioned a male partner, not a female one, but he promptly corrected himself. The interview went on for a while and he never mentioned his partner again. I didn't treat this episode as a slip, but as a sign that he was ashamed to talk about certain life experiences. (…) After the end of the interview, I contacted the accommodation centre to ask if they had checked or prepared the claimant somehow. [They did not] In that moment, all [his fear of persecution] was clear to me. (…) It was unnecessary to ask "Are you homosexual?".

All these dynamics require a multi-dimensional and multi-disciplinary training, which in turn can ensure an effective and fair interview.

6.3.3   *The Conduct of Interviews*

Other than the relevant provisions of the Procedures Directive (2005 original version for the UK and 2013 recast version for Germany and Italy, Chap. 4) and the jurisprudence of the CJEU, there are no common standards between the three countries explored here for the conduct of an interview with a SOGI claimant. Bearing in mind that the Refugee Convention leaves this matter to the discretion of contracting states, the general standards recommended by the UNHCR SOGI Guidelines have not provided enough common ground for harmonisation of interview procedures. Crucially, according to our data, differences exist even within each country. A variety of aspects need to be analysed.

To start with Germany, no list of specific questions is provided to interviewers, with all questioning individually tailored (BMI 2019, pp. 13, 16). SOGI claimants shared a general feeling of disempowerment in this stage of the procedure. One example was provided by Alphaeus, who was informed of his second interview only the day before it was scheduled:

> [The BAMF stated] "Before we ask you further questions you have to sign this document". I was like "what is the document all about?" They told me "this document, it's about asking permission from your embassy, from the Ugandan Embassy, to give us authority to take you back to your country. (…) If you don't sign it, we don't proceed. (…) Failure to do so, that means you're not co-operating." (…) I had no option other than to sign.

According to Evelyne and Anne (lawyers), sometimes the interviewer's cultural and social background hampers SOGI claimants from opening up. Recounting the case of a gay claimant coming from an Islamic culture, who was severely traumatised by his life in a small village, they explained how a cultural awareness and sensitivity could diminish this risk:

> He saw the worst things. And there was the interviewer with a headscarf. Not the interpreter, but the interviewer was wearing a headscarf. And he (…) was practically unable to speak. (…) That's such a sensitive area. (…) [Then the interviewer should ask]: "Is it alright

for you? Have you experienced things that you do not want to tell me now because of my religious attitude? That's no problem, we can swap the interviewer".

As for the length of interviews, they range from a few hours (for instance, Trudy Ann was interviewed for 'only' 3 h) to almost a day (for example, Alphaeus was interviewed for 9 h). Evelyne and Anne also gave the case of a claimant who had been repeatedly raped over the years and was interviewed for more than 9 h with no break, ignoring the risk of re-traumatisation (UNHCR 2012b).

The wish to create a safe environment for SOGI claimants sporadically emerged in our fieldwork in Germany. For instance, Sandy (focus group no. 1, Hesse) reported that the interviewer approached her at the end to say 'Miss X, you don't have to worry no more, you're safe'. By contrast, in other cases, no efforts were made. Veronica waited with her partner and her two children for 5 h for the interview to take place:

> And it's already five-thirty in the evening. (…) Of course, they [children] are all a bit nervous because five hours and no food and decision-maker (…) did not ask me so much. (…) I also felt that she is not so open to conversation. (…) It is already almost night, eight o'clock in winter [when the interview finished], totally dark. We have nothing to eat, we should go to the train station and we do not even know where to go, which direction, it is raining.

Diana reported that the lack of support after the screening interview made it impossible for her to open up again:

> At that time, I told them I'm a lesbian, like that. (…) So me, I was waiting to hear from them, that (…) maybe they could give me organisations that, maybe you can go to these people, they can take care of you (…). But they didn't tell me anything, so when I went back, I started growing fear in me, not to come out, to talk. (…) So when I was called to the second interview, so I said "maybe if I talk it again, no-one can help me, so it is maybe better for me to keep quiet, not to tell them". (…) I didn't open up. (…) No-one is there to help you.

Cases of multiple interviews were also reported (for example, Tina was interviewed four times before a final decision was reached), in spite of the acknowledged risk of re-traumatisation (Alessi et al. 2016, 2018; Bögner et al. 2007). We were also told of the (unusual) involvement of claimants' children during interviews (Harriet, focus group no. 2, Bavaria), potentially violating claimants' and their children's right to privacy. Finally, interviewees' right to read and sign the minutes of the interview was sometimes rendered meaningless because of language issues, as highlighted by one of our participants: 'even if you could read German, you will not be able to understand what you read. And it doesn't make any sense' (Emroy, focus group no. 1, Hesse). For these reasons, the previously mentioned option of being accompanied, by support group volunteers and/or to be assisted by a lawyer during the main interview is particularly important for these participants (Sect. 6.2).

In Italy, the presence of the UNHCR representatives may be the basis for a more sensitive approach towards SOGI claimants, beyond the already mentioned frequent allocation of these claims to the most competent member of territorial commissions. First, there is no indication that the interview is carried out on the basis of a

6.3 The Main Interview: Actors and Procedures in SOGI Asylum

pre-established list of questions, commissions generally preferring an open approach based on the specific circumstances of the case. As Titti (decision-maker) confirmed, questioning cannot but be case-specific. Second, particular attention is given to creating a supportive environment. While Cristina (UNHCR officer) explained that 'sometimes there is no need to ask many questions', Titti also shared with us the general approach she adopts during interviews:

> At the very beginning, I introduce myself as a member of the UNHCR in order to make it clear that I do not have any prejudices based on gender, culture or religion. I show them pictures about the UNHCR (…). At that point, I can see that the claimant is more confident (…). I also ask if it is ok that I'm a woman and specify that they can choose [another interviewer] with no consequences for the final decision (…) I also ask them if they have questions for me, as I have for them [and] some claimants asked me questions to know who they were talking to. (…) I think all this is very important (…) in order to establish trust.

In turn, Maria Grazia (decision-maker) recalled that she usually started interviews by trying to provide as many guarantees as possible in relation to the claimant's privacy and the confidential nature of the interview. Once she also revealed her own (non-heterosexual) sexual orientation when she noticed that a gay claimant was embarrassed and afraid to speak about themselves. Although she expressed doubts about the appropriateness of such an initiative, that claimant eventually opened up. The value of this kind of attention to detail was confirmed by some claimants. For example, Dev explained that:

> When he heard that I was a bit depressed, he asked me if I were ready, and that I needed to be reassured before starting [the interview]. He offered me a glass of water. (…) After the interview ended he asked me if I really felt well, and added that, if it were just for him (…), he would have granted me international protection.

Third, a certain awareness of the existence of cultural differences emerged. According to Titti (decision-maker), when people coming from some specific countries are interviewed, she does not even use the word 'gay' because 'it is equal to mention "the devil"'. Similarly, due to the cultural background of certain male claimants, she knows they may not feel able to look her in the eyes as that may be perceived as a form of disrespect, and not 'a sign of a bogus SOGI claim'. Crucially, thanks to the collective discussion between all members of the territorial commissions before adopting a final decision (Sect. 6.3.1), these cultural aspects are often cross-checked by the most competent caseworker in SOGI claims (confirmed by Roberto, decision-maker, among others). Finally, as for the length of the interview, there were a variety of experiences. Very short interviews were reported (Wilson, focus group no. 3, northern Italy, was interviewed for only 1 h, and Gbona, for one hour and a half), alongside questionings lasting many hours (for instance, Dev was questioned for 6 h). Perhaps coincidentally, the longest and most detailed interviews saw the involvement of the most competent member of the commission in SOGI cases. Significantly, due to the complexity and the length of these interviews, Roberto (decision-maker) explained that, if he has advance notice, he prefers to start his working day with a SOGI claimant or to postpone these interviews when there is not enough time to carry them out properly.

Despite attempts to create a friendly environment for SOGI claims, some criticisms remain in Italy. As Giovanna (lawyer) confirmed, asylum claimants, including those fleeing homophobia and transphobia, face a sort of inquisitorial approach. In the legitimate attempt to investigate the position of the claimant, by asking for instance locations and dates, interviewers are sometimes eager to identify inconsistencies. The feeling of being under investigation was widely shared. For instance, Edoardo (focus group no. 3, northern Italy) noticed that 'when I was telling her, she was like going to the Google to confirm so many dates (…) trying to get if this is true'. Other claimants stressed the irrelevant nature of some questions asked (Nice Guy, focus group no. 1, northern Italy) or the lack of mutual understanding, sometimes based on the differences in interviewer-claimant social and educational backgrounds (Chap. 7). Odosa, for example, could not work out what information the interviewer wanted from him, after he reported that he was caught by the police 'for being gay', thus forced to run away. His feeling of distress, mixed with incomprehension, was evident: 'I don't know, I don't, he [the interviewer] might have explained his self but because of things that was in my head, I can't just remember everything'. Equally, Nazarena (lawyer) reported that questions are too often aimed at ascertaining credibility and are not pertinent or related to the available COI. It is no coincidence that, in her view, many negative decisions are justified by saying that the claimant gave a 'generic and contradictory account', without explaining why that particular account is not consistent with available COI, as research has also shown (Busetto et al. 2017). For Giulio (LGBTIQ+ group volunteer), one problem is that territorial commissions rarely stop and postpone the interview in case of doubts, instead preferring to reject the claim.

Finally, although claimants have the opportunity to revise the minutes at the end of the interview, too often claimants simply feel obliged to sign, irrespective of their accuracy (Giovanna, lawyer). In fact, Water (focus group no. 4, northern Italy) alleged that the minutes were not read point-by-point, but only summarised.

It should be noted that most of these good practices and criticisms reflect local experiences and, consequently, the activity of specific territorial commissions. Yet, macro-level factors may hamper the general implementation of the positive procedural arrangements already in place. First, the necessity to assess a high number of asylum claims every day may lead to the lower quality of the process. As Titti (decision-maker) reckoned, with this imposed rhythm, 'how could you summarise the life of a person in half an hour?' Second, the 2017 reform introduced the obligation to video-record the interview so that it can subsequently be used for the appeal process, if necessary. Some of our participants expressed a positive opinion about this development, not least because it may avoid the risk of re-traumatisation (Silvana, judge). Instead, for other participants, this new procedure risks having a specifically negative impact for SOGI claimants and their willingness to open up on camera for reasons that include concerns about confidentiality of the recording within the asylum system (for instance, Mara, lawyer).

Moving on to the UK, past research has showed that interviewers often apply the inquisitorial approach of a criminal court when carrying out asylum interviews (Cohen 2002; Gill and Good 2019). Earlier research has also indicated a tendency

6.3 The Main Interview: Actors and Procedures in SOGI Asylum

on the part of caseworkers to refuse SOGI claims in the belief that any erroneous decisions will be corrected at appeal stage by tribunal judges (Miles 2010, p. 22). Yet worryingly, at the same time, a 'deference of appellate courts to first decision and fact-finding' has also been identified (Millbank 2009, p. 33). Consequently, whereas civil servants rely on the judiciary to be the ultimate arbiter, the judiciary in turn relies on civil servants to have made a sound initial decision.

In relation to this initial interview process, contrasting views emerged in our fieldwork. Starting with the existence or not of a friendly environment during the interview, Amber remembered that:

> [The interviewer] came herself to get us (…) from the waiting area, she called me by my name properly and asked if it was the right way [to pronounce it] and I assured her that she is correct, and we walked to the interview room together. [She] was very friendly, welcoming and cheerful, and that made the whole interview process easier.

Even more importantly, Amber being a transgender claimant, the interviewer always referred to her as a female: 'She didn't make any errors because it just flow naturally and she just, labelled, put my gender as female, instead of asking what is your gender, so she knows already'. In turn, Janelle explained: 'The person who interviewed me was very nice. So I felt very calm, because I was very frightened, I was shaking, and she said she will try to make it as comfortable as possible, which she did'. By contrast, Selim's experience was less positive:

> She didn't look at me the whole time, she was just taking [notes], writing down what I was saying and she asked me to slow down, you know, when you are telling a story, you get excited and you know, and then she was like "no, slow down because I need to write it down". And then you break down the story and then you lose the point and you are, like, what was I saying, it was just a mess.

The perspective of an interviewer is particularly valuable in this context. Emily, a decision-maker who told us she found SOGI claims 'harder' to handle, also said:

> I get the file and go through it. (…) Everyone's preparation is slightly different but generally you need to be sure that you've… every aspect of their claim, so that you can make a good decision at the end. (…) Every case is different. You have to make it personal, as personal as you can with them because they're talking to a stranger about quite private parts of their life… and also they're probably sitting there thinking this is the person making a decision on my life, I can't really inform how they're feeling (…). If you get someone who's giving one-word answers, it's very hard to try and decide on that basis, so you're just trying to get people to talk, really. It's quite difficult. (…) You're asking people to relate very difficult periods of their life (…) They're coming from countries where they don't talk about it… so it's very difficult to try to navigate.

In light of this challenge, Emily usually adopts an open approach:

> I say "I'm happy to listen, if there's anything you want to tell me, that's fine", I prefer people to just, free recourse of memory and then if they stop or if they're struggling I say "is it just easier if I ask a direct question" and most of the time they say "yes, please", and then I say specifically "I'm not looking for details of what they've done to you specifically", you try and guide them, you say "I'm going to ask who they are, what they're like, the location, days, things like that", and then they usually calm down a bit.

Yet, other experiences show that direct questions on specific aspects of claimants' lives, including in relation to religion, first sexual experiences or the involvement in the gay scene in the UK, are usually asked (Chap. 7). As Ibrahim A. explained, 'she [the interviewer] wasn't rude. (…) She didn't like humiliate me with any word or anything, but she provoked me (…). She kept asking me about very detailed information which I don't have'. Whereas for claimants these questions appear irrelevant or even offensive, Olivia (government official) defended such an approach at least indirectly:

> If you were living in a country where it is illegal, you would expect somebody to be able to say how they felt about it [SOGI]. (…) And then maybe their first encounter, how did it happen, how did you tell your parents, people find out, were you scared, you know, it is illegal there, how did you go about it, things like that. But, you know, nothing sexual. (…) If somebody just says, "oh, yes, I was about 15, and yes I felt fine about it", you would expect more detail. Like, I say to some people "do you remember your first kiss?" (…) they are going to remember details about it.

This problematic expectation may be greater in certain cases. Although it echoes an intersectional approach (Chap. 3), Emily (decision-maker) explained that there are

> lots of variations in how people express their sexuality (…) so you have to take… the individual circumstance of the claimant into account. You know, their education background, their history, the country, the sort of the society that they grew up in. I mean, if for example you get someone from like a really middle-class background in Pakistan, then you would expect them to be able to talk a bit more freely about how they were living, because amongst middle class families in Pakistan it is a little bit more accepting.

This approach is sometimes coupled with other general disputable attitudes, when SOGI claimants in the UK are not offered a 'safe' environment. As Edith explained:

> The Home Office where you go to sign [in], it is not a very homely place, you just feel like it is stressing, the whole situation is stressing, so sometimes I even get sick when I am going there. So… they did an interview, but I said I can't finish the interview because already I was sick [and] he wants for me to sign, I said I can't sign it. (…) And they didn't even offer me even a glass of water or anything.

Finally, in relation to the length of interviews, it is variable as observed in Germany and Italy, but so is the number of interviews carried out per day/week. Emily (decision-maker) reported the existence of a guideline suggesting a time of '2.5 to 3 hours', which allows decision-makers to interview at least six people a week. Yet, as she pointed out, while trying to respect these indications, she does not 'know how you're supposed to assess someone in 2 h. Everyone's different, so you have to try to do your best to get as much information [as you can]'.

In short, with a few exceptions mainly connected to the Italian (formal and informal) procedural practices, none of the systems under investigation may be described, at least in relation to the interview process, as entirely SOGI claimant-friendly. In particular, the risk of re-traumatisation is rarely considered, while an environment that is conducive to self-identification is absent. As Mariya, an NGO worker in Germany, pointed out, the 'interview-hearing situation [is] simply an imposition

6.3 The Main Interview: Actors and Procedures in SOGI Asylum

(...) and a totally exhausting and re-traumatising situation for people who like to leave their story behind them, to experience (...) a new non-discriminatory life'. It is no surprise that, according to her experience as well as our data, claimants often perceive the interview as 'a humiliation', with negative implications also for their self-confidence, well-being and integration. Winifred (focus group no. 3, Bavaria, Germany) affirmed that she has 'never felt safe' during the asylum process. Sandra, also claiming asylum in Germany, chose 'to forget, just to make [herself] feel better'. Rather than being an occasion for claimants to share the reasons why they believe that they risk persecution if returned to their countries of origin, interviews often focus largely on ascertaining claimants' SOGI.

What is more, these dynamics may be further aggravated by the vivid influence of bias and prejudices of caseworkers in carrying out their responsibilities (Chap. 7, especially in relation to how these intertwine with stereotypes in SOGI claims). In all the countries under comparison, our data has pointed to the significant influence of bias in the way interviewers and decision-makers conduct interviews, probably owing to the unconfirmed assumptions on the 'abuse' of the asylum system (McFadyen 2016; Veglio 2017). In particular, the belief that many SOGI claims are fabricated is still strong, thus influencing the line of questioning (Rousseau and Foxen 2006). An example in this respect relates to the intervention of the Home Office's presenting officer during a hearing (Upper Tier Tribunal observation, London, 2018): 'Isn't it correct that your claim for asylum came at a moment when you had exhausted all other possibilities of getting leave to remain in the UK?'. In the same case, the Home Office complained that the claimant was not active in the 'LGBT community'. While this bias ostensibly derives from the inquisitorial approach emerged above, for some participants, its roots lie in the increased number of SOGI claims. For instance, Celeste, a social worker in Italy, explained that, in the past few years, SOGI claims were considered extremely vulnerable cases with few doubts about their authenticity but, more recently, territorial commissions are increasingly cautious to avoid granting refugee status to 'bogus claimants'. This approach is particularly evident in the UK. According to Sean, a lawyer:

> Our collective understanding and feeling is that the Home Office is a beast, it is a terrible, terrible beast and they will do everything they can to refuse cases, even the strongest cases where we will say to a client "we will win this", and the Home Office refuse and you appeal and then you win.

For Joseph, an NGO volunteer in the UK, this attitude is the result of the previous Home Secretary Theresa May's policy aimed to 'create a hostile culture [that] when it comes to LGBT stuff it just becomes homophobic'. In this kind of situation, according to Siri, who claimed asylum in Italy, there is no room for taking into account the particular feelings experienced by many SOGI claimants during the interview:

> At first you feel a pressure deep inside. (...) You have a hard time expressing yourself, sometimes there are words that you would like to let out [but] – because of that pressure – you simply can't let out. Maybe also other people shake when they are speaking in front of the commission, and those who are listening have the feeling that you may not be telling the truth.

As explored elsewhere in relation to asylum claims submitted by women on the basis of sexual violence (Baillot et al. 2012, p. 19), one reason for this attitude is that caseworkers may be vulnerable to 'case hardening'. Consequently, the intersection between a hostile climate and the pressure to deliver more with less resources may make it harder for interviewers and decision-makers to connect emotionally with asylum claimants, including those with SOGI claims, thus preventing them from carrying out an individual assessment as required by our theoretical underpinnings (Chap. 3).

Other specific kinds of bias towards SOGI claimants also emerged. These include at least two different, but interconnected, beliefs in terms of 'similar' stories (Chap. 7) and of 'countries of origin'. First, a bias seems to exist in relation to claimants who arrive from a particular country. In Germany, Barbara (lawyer) mentioned Cameroon or Pakistan in this respect, while Julian suggested that this bias may also be frequent in relation to Uganda: 'My interviewer was really biased. I entered and he said "oh, you're from Uganda, I guess you're now going to tell me that lesbian story". Before I could even start'. For many participants in Italy, SOGI claimants from Nigeria and the Gambia are usually viewed with greater suspicion (Giulia, Diego, Riccardo and Giulio, LGBTIQ+ group volunteers; Chiara, NGO worker; Celeste, social worker; Damiano, lawyer). Roberto (decision-maker), for example, did not hide the fact that, when a Nigerian male claimant alleges persecution on grounds of his sexual orientation, he needs to ask more questions 'because many SOGI claims are fake'. As he said:

> Since I'm here, I have only heard a Turkish national claiming asylum for being transgender (…) a Somali national for being homosexual, no one from Eritrea. It's clear that the great weight of some nationalities [in SOGI asylum] makes you be more doubtful.

Following the same problematic line of reasoning, Daniele (decision-maker) added that it is 'informally known' that, for people coming from specific countries, it is particularly difficult to expose themselves as belonging to or being associated with SOGI minorities. In his view, this is the case for claimants coming from Mali, who may perceive this kind of request as a shame, but not for Nigerian nationals, who appear to submit such a claim 'more easily'. According to Nazarena (lawyer), this attitude does not have negative implications only for the number of refusals, but also for the rate of recognition of refugee status in opposition to other forms of international protection (equally, Mara, lawyer; Maria Grazia, decision-maker). People from some countries appear to deserve refugee status more than claimants from other countries, irrespective of a thorough and individual analysis of the risk of persecution and the relevant COI (Sect. 6.5).

While preconceptions based on nationality or ethnicity are apparent, a lack of knowledge of SOGI, in general and SOGI from different cultural perspectives, has an equal negative influence in the conduct of interviews. Kennedy, who claimed asylum in Italy, pointed out that the interviewer 'did not even know anything about LGBT', while Damiano (lawyer, Italy) shared his impression that many caseworkers are ignorant of the number of LGBTIQ+ people there are in society. He remembered the case of a member of a territorial commission who believed that SOGI claims were 'too many' because they hear an average of five SOGI claimants per week, out of a total of 60 claimants. For Anna, an LGBTIQ+ group volunteer in Italy, the interviewers' 'lack of belonging' to a minority group themselves may prevent them developing 'empathy' with SOGI claimants. A good example in this respect was provided by Julian, who claimed asylum in Germany:

> He said "what makes you think Bayern [Bavaria] or Munich is interested in lesbians?" (…) "What makes you think you will even be safe here?" (…) Now, imagine you're really stressed. Someone is already biased, you are feeling it and you have to go ahead and tell your story. You're already frustrated.

The situation with transgender claimants is often more problematic. The NGO Transgender Europe (TGEU) has reported that trans asylum claims are often mistakenly treated as sexual orientation-based claims because of lack of knowledge on the part of the interviewer (TGEU 2016, p. 6) or incredulity if the claimant has not had hormonal treatment or surgery, with clear implications for the outcome of the interview. In this respect, Prince Emrah's interview in Germany is illustrative, not least in terms of the distress caused to asylum claimants by the lack of a queer approach:

> They asked me about my gender so much. They said to me, "do you want to change from your body? What do you want to change? Or do you want to cut? Do you want to, I don't know, operations? In the future what will you do here?" With my gender…it's like…why don't they stop, I don't think it's important to ask. What I'll be, I'll be. It's important I'm queer and I'm here. So I will, I will not cut, I will put my boobs, or not, it should not interest them. It's my own life.

For the sake of completeness, it is worth noting that particular forms of bias have also emerged amongst other participants (Sect. 6.2) as well as asylum claimants themselves, thus leading to complaints about some procedural aspects of the interview. This is especially the case regarding the relationship between SOGI and religion, in cases where the interviewer has an obvious religious background. The case of Selim (UK) is illustrative of this:

> I still remember my feeling in the interview, my interviewer is a covered woman, so she is Muslim, she is covered, and the questions the interviewer asked are very personal, and please don't take it as an offence, one of the questions like what did you used to do when you get aroused or you get, how can I say like she is asking me if I used to masturbate how can I tell a covered woman that I masturbate. It was just, it felt uncomfortable (…). But then the question is (…) how far does she know about the gay culture.

In short, despite the improvements noticed in terms of training and, sometimes, of procedures, patterns of bias still permeate the asylum system of Germany, Italy and UK in different ways. Those caseworkers who were aware of their impact on the interview process and the decision, also recognised the difficulty in remaining totally uninfluenced by 'external factors' (for instance, Daniele, decision-maker, Italy; Vincenzo, LGBTIQ+ group volunteer, Italy; Bilal, presenting officer, UK). As Deirdre, UK, told her client in trying to explain the lottery effect prevalent in the asylum system: 'Sometimes you will be lucky (…) and get somebody who is just nice at the Home Office'. We explore this lottery effect in terms of the assessment of SOGI claims in Chap. 7, while in the next section we investigate the appeal process for those who are not so 'lucky' and whose applications are rejected.

6.4 The Judicial Procedure

In all the countries we consider, asylum claimants may appeal against a rejection of their claim in accordance with international, European and domestic guarantees. In particular, it is worth remembering that the ECHR protects the right to an effective remedy (Article 13), which, when applied to asylum claimants, is often read in combination with the right to life (Article 2) and the prohibition of torture and degrading or inhuman treatment (Article 3). Contracting states, like Germany, Italy and the UK, thus need to ensure that all claimants have, at least, access to an independent authority that can review the risk of being returned to a country where they might be exposed to the risk of death or torture, degrading or inhuman treatment. In turn, if we look specifically at the Procedures Directive, member states 'shall ensure that an effective remedy provides for a full and *ex nunc* examination of both facts and points of law' (Article 46(3)), at least in appeal procedures before a court or tribunal of first instance. The importance of effective access to an appeal procedure is evident in light of some trends on the significant number of positive decisions against administrative refusals. For instance, according to Sabrina, an NGO worker in Germany: 'You can see that in the judgments, which are loads in the administrative court, and where a large number of, I believe, 30% are then granted a positive decision'. This high success rate in appeals suggests that decision-making standards at the BAMF are poor and that the BAMF generally decides too many claims negatively (NDR 2019). Similarly, in the UK the fact that over two thirds of refusals are over-turned on appeal (ECRE, AIDA & Refugee Council 2019, p. 10) chimes with concerns from NGOs 'about an apparent over-reliance by the Home Office on asylum appeals to correct straightforward failures by caseworkers' (Freedom from Torture 2016, p. 49). Yet, this right is ensured and enjoyed in different ways in Germany, Italy and UK, some of which may have a particular impact on SOGI claimants, as we explore in the following sub-sections.

6.4.1 The Appeal Setting

Starting with Germany, when an asylum request is rejected, a claimant can appeal against that decision before the relevant administrative court among the 51 administrative courts ('Verwaltungsgerichte') that deal with asylum matters. These appeals usually have suspensive effect, unless they are rejected as 'manifestly unfounded' or 'inadmissible' (on Dublin cases, Sect. 6.7). If the administrative court also rejects the claim, further appeals are possible but, in practice, only in exceptional circumstances (Evelyne and Anne, lawyers; ECRE, AIDA & Asyl und Migration 2018,

p. 16). In fact, it seems that a second instance appeal is only allowed in case of procedural errors or 'fundamental questions' raised by the appeal rejection. According to Emma, NGO worker, and confirmed by Oscar, a judge, since most cases are rejected on credibility grounds, it is hard to argue for the necessity of a second instance examination. If the appeal before the administrative court is successful, the judge also decides on the kind of international protection to be granted (Chap. 4). Other than the length of the appeal procedure, which takes more than a year in some cases (for instance, Veronica and Julia), the essential obstacle to appeal is the short deadline for submitting the application before the administrative court. Indeed, if viewed in the broader context of asylum claimants' conditions and bureaucratic delays, a deadline of 2 weeks is generally difficult to meet. For example, Ayeta (focus group no. 4, Bavaria) received her rejection letter when the 2 weeks were already over: 'So I had to go to the Caritas where I stayed and they had to get me a lawyer, so the lawyer wrote to the Bundesamt [federal office]. There, they accepted the late appeal'. Noah (NGO social worker) explained that many claimants cannot read properly in German or experience feelings of shame, which may mean they are less likely to take action within the given time limits. Moreover, while it seems that BAMF notifies decisions through post without using recorded delivery, thus generating confusion in relation to the date of notification, in collective reception centres it is not unusual for letters to be lost or held up (ECRE, AIDA 2019, p. 9). In cases of unfounded or inadmissible claims, the deadline is even shorter, which amplifies these problems. As Kadir, an NGO worker, pointed out, in this process the psychological implications are often neglected: 'It's a week and you have to react. And first of all handle the shock that you have been rejected and then react quickly, find a lawyer and file an appeal'.

In terms of internal organisation, it is worth noting that some administrative judges in Germany consistently deal with cases relating to the same country of origin (for instance, Evelyne and Anne, lawyers; Court observations, Hesse, 2018). By encouraging expertise, this system has a great advantage according to Noah (NGO social worker): 'You can figure out with time what arguments you can get through in court or what boxes you need to tick, what do they ask, what do they want'. Yet, being overexposed to SOGI claims coming from the same country may lead to 'case hardening', that is, as already explored above, a general unwillingness to believe claimants when stories have a range of similar elements or entail high degrees of violence and distress (Baillot et al. 2013). Moreover, this procedural arrangement does not seem to produce any degree of consistency across Germany. As Oscar, a judge, affirmed, 'we may have judgments from different administrative courts on a nearly identical situation with different results. But it is quite normal in asylum'.

While in Italy an appeal against a refusal of an asylum request is allowed within 30 days of the notification of the negative decision, the 2017 reform radically changed the applicable judicial procedures. The elimination of the second instance appeal on merits effectively means that asylum claimants can only submit an appeal against judicial first-instance negative decisions to the Supreme Court, which carries out an evaluation of procedural legitimacy, but not on the substance of the claim. This aspect of the reform was widely criticised (De Santis 2018) and worried a number of our participants, because it may be unconstitutional. In fact, although the Italian Constitution does not impose a two-instance process to have an appeal examined on the merits, this reform is clearly discriminatory in comparison to other judicial processes, which are all based on the possibility of a two-instance appeal plus a legitimacy review by the Supreme Court. Consequently, as our participants also pointed out (for instance, Nazarena, lawyer), people claiming asylum are treated differently to other parties in court cases, in potential violation of Article 3 of the Italian Constitution. Some judges, however, defend this aspect of the reform by arguing that the more appeals are granted and the claimant tells their story, the greater the risk that the claimant's testimony will contain inconsistencies (Silvana).

In parallel, the 2017 reform introduced two additional novelties. From an institutional point of view, it set up specific sections in the main tribunals to cover only matters of asylum and migration. Although in practice a single judge follows the entire appeal procedure within these specialised sections, all asylum decisions are adopted collectively by three judges, in contrast to the previous system with only one judge deciding on each case. From a procedural perspective, there is the concrete danger that claimants are no longer heard live by the first instance judge, because the same 2017 reform introduced the mandatory recording of the main administrative interview. This recording should be used subsequently by the first instance judges to decide on the appeal. This aspect of the reform was criticised both as a violation of the fundamental right to defence and the right to asylum (Nazarena, lawyer), as well as removing the scope for judges' empathy for, and understanding of, SOGI claimants (Vincenzo, an LGBTIQ+ group volunteer; Palermo 2018). Moreover, as Damiano explained, this procedure is an evident additional obstacle to a safe environment:

> Besides someone [the interviewer] they never met before, they see a camera, a tape recorder, and are told "This recording will be seen by the judge, by the lawyers" (…) They will be afraid that someone will see this video-recording.

In addition, there is no certainty that judges will watch the video-recording of the interview, especially in light of the limited amount of time available (for instance, Nazarena, lawyer). Some Italian courts resisted this reform and have continued offering a hearing to claimants, whether or not the video-recording of administrative interviews was available (for example, Filippo, senior judge). According to Silvana, a judge, for those claims where credibility is an issue, such as SOGI ones, hearings with claimants may be nonetheless necessary in order to allow judges to form an opinion on whether or not the claimant is credible. Yet, Silvana also explained that, in line with the jurisprudence of the CJEU, there is no need to hear the claimant, including in SOGI cases, if judges have all the necessary evidence to hand, such as a detailed transcript of an interview carried out well by the territorial commission. This judicial discretion to hold a hearing or not introduces an element of 'lottery' in the appeal system (Cristina, UNHCR officer), especially when claimants were not adequately interviewed in relation to SOGI elements or were not able to reveal the real reason for fearing persecution (Livio, lawyer). As Filippo, a senior judge, affirmed: 'Sometimes holding a new hearing is not necessarily a guarantee of

6.4 The Judicial Procedure

recognition of international protection or of a better understanding of the story. Yet, it is certainly a clear assumption of responsibility [by the judge]'. In any case, as Silvana effectively summarised, even with the new system, the competence of the judge in asylum matters is always the key to a fair appeal procedure. Due to the 2017 reform, the new specialised and collective decision-making mechanism may foster this expertise.

Finally, as anticipated in Sect. 6.1, the UK system allows an appeal against negative decisions to the First Tier Tribunal but there are restrictions on further appeal stages. Claimants whose case becomes ARE may be able to submit a fresh claim but, given the elements that emerged above, our participants are cautious about the real prospects of success in such cases. According to Sean, a lawyer, the way 'fresh claims' are usually treated is clearly intended 'to stop people having a further appeal', as both the Home Office and judges rarely agree that a claimant has a fresh claim. The long time that the appeal process takes was widely criticised by our participants (for instance, Ernest, judge), with the entire asylum procedure in the cases of Daphne and Junio taking, respectively, more than six and eight years. An important factor characterising the UK appeal system is the presence of the Home Office Presenting Officer or legal representative at most appeal hearings, which often contributes to the hostile atmosphere encountered in UK hearings (Braganza 2019). As a participant in our surveys pointed out:

> The UK Home Office representatives are often hostile, implicitly or explicitly homophobic, and aggressive. Even if sexuality has been accepted prior to appeal, there can be questioning about credibility, about relationships, etc. For example last week I was at an appeal where (…) the [Home Office presenting officer] also repeatedly told the appellant to "speak up" and "stop mumbling". The appellant was a 21 year old lesbian (for whom English was not first language) who had escaped forced marriage (imposed to try and "cure" her of being a lesbian) and sexual violence (S110, NGO volunteer, UK).

The awareness of some UK judges of the need to create a 'safe environment' at the appeal stage is valuable in this context. Adrian, a judge, clearly supported the need 'to create an atmosphere where [SOGI claimants] will feel able to talk about it and in some cases that may mean that we will ask for a closed court and so forth'. Reassuringly, the reason given for this was not SOGI prejudice but claimants' needs. As Adrian further explained:

> There should not normally be closed courts because being gay is not anything to be ashamed of in any way but some people feel incredibly sensitive and… also if they are not used to the British system they may feel less confidence in how things work, so judges have to be quite sort of open and creative in these sorts of cases.

With this overview in mind, we now look at how members of the judiciary are prepared for deciding asylum cases. With the exception of the UK, judges are not specifically selected for asylum or immigration purposes. In Germany and in Italy they simply follow the ordinary selection process for joining the judiciary, while in the UK they are appointed through the Judicial Appointments Commission and must meet the statutory qualification necessary for sitting in the Immigration and

Asylum Chambers. One important question thus arises: are there any specific procedural arrangements or training for judges deciding on SOGI cases?

In Germany, there is no evidence of specific procedures for selection or training of judges dealing with SOGI claims, as asylum is only one of the areas under judges' mandates. This was confirmed by a judge, Emilia, who explained that the judicial body tasked with the training of judges offers educational sessions on a variety of subjects, but no training on SOGI asylum had been organised until then. Enrolment on training courses is, in any case, voluntary. The lack of specific training was commented on by lawyers (for instance, Elias and Barbara), but judges themselves may not see the need for training. Oscar, a judge, stated: 'The interest in the judiciary would be rather low. After all, there are very few homosexuals who make asylum applications'. Besides such a biased assumption, this appears more worrying when we consider that university law studies generally do not cover immigration and asylum as a compulsory subject.

In Italy, by creating specialised asylum sections in some tribunals, the 2017 reform aimed to ensure that judges who join these units have specific competences in migration and asylum, as well as in foreign languages to communicate with asylum claimants in case of hearings. Yet, many participants asserted that, in practice, there are no guarantees that only experienced and trained judges will be selected (for instance, Mara and Nazarena, lawyers), especially when there are no judges interested in this field of law. In fact, Filippo, a senior judge, reported that in his tribunal it was impossible to find a sufficient number of judges to set up the new specialised section. Consequently, as Filippo explained, the youngest judges were appointed simply by virtue of 'their knowledge of foreign languages'. In other tribunals, judges working on family issues are usually called on to cover asylum and migration issues as well (for instance, Silvana and Maurizio, judges). In relation to both newly appointed judges and judges working on family issues, there is no evidence of any intensive training on asylum, including SOGI asylum. Yet, at a more general level, it seems that in recent years specific training on different aspects of asylum, including SOGI claims, has been organised by the national judicial training body in cooperation with the UNHCR (Silvana, judge). However, judges enrolled on it on a voluntary basis, so there is no guarantee that all judges working with SOGI claimants will have attended this training. Perhaps surprisingly, if compared with the German case, specific training is felt as a priority by some judges, like Filippo (senior judge), who see their role as 'not appropriate to deal with such a complex area', one that in his view requires other, non-legal, expertise to deal with claimants' suffering and trauma.

While there is general selection for judges who work with asylum claimants in place in the UK, there is no specific selection for dealing with SOGI claimants. The Tribunals Committee, which is the body with overall responsibility for the training of tribunal judges, may organise specific training sessions in cooperation with relevant NGOs. For example, participants mentioned asylum training with EASO (Alex, judge) and a one day-training session on SOGI issues, including asylum, with Stonewall (Ernest, judge). Adrian, a judge, reported that cycles of one-day training are organised on different subjects and are compulsory for all judges,

6.4 The Judicial Procedure   227

including a training on transgender issues held in 2017, whereas others are attended on a voluntary basis. Yet, according to other participants (for instance, Bilal, presenting officer; Allan, lawyer), judges do not appear adequately trained in SOGI asylum, nor in SOGI issues more generally. This was confirmed by the fact that some of them ignore the existence of rules in the Equal Treatment Bench Book or the Home Office's SOGI guidance. Some examples of the impact of the lack of comprehensive training of judges on the judicial decisions reached in SOGI cases, mixed with personal bias and prejudices, will be explored in Chap. 7. That impact is also evident in the way hearings are conducted.

6.4.2 The Conduct of Hearings and the Adoption of Decisions

Looking now at the ways in which hearings of SOGI claimants are carried out as well as the decision-making process in tribunals, our data provides a mixed picture with negative experiences coupled with positive attitudes that are more in line with a human rights reading of the Refugee Convention. Owing to the different characteristics of each judicial system in question, a country-by-country investigation is particularly appropriate here.

To begin with Germany, our data shows the existence of encouraging decision-making processes along problematic lines of questioning. Examples of promising approaches include the attitude adopted by a judge during a hearing (Court observation, North Rhine-Westphalia, 2019), where she carefully introduced herself and explained the entire procedure and its consequences to the claimant. As Noah (NGO social worker) explained, when a case is well prepared, 'these are the moments of joy, that the judge opens the file, checks the personal data, closes the file, says: "That's clear" and he grants it. Then (…) no further check is made'. More importantly, both judges interviewed in Germany (Oscar and Emilia) adopt an approach that seems, in principle, to conform to the notion of refugee enshrined in the Refugee Convention. According to Oscar, 'two things always run in parallel', namely the research and the evaluation of relevant COI (Sect. 6.5) and the examination of the specific circumstances of the claimant. These are investigated by reading the transcript of the interview(s) prepared by the BAMF, which also serves as a basis for the choice of questions to be asked during the hearing. As Oscar pointed out, these questions aim to ascertain the credibility of the claimant or aspects that were not clarified at the BAMF interview. These include basic information, such as the reasons for fleeing one's country and the individual process leading to the decision to escape. Oscar emphasised that, although administrative decisions are often based on the lack of credibility, they do not provide appropriate evidence that all efforts were made to clarify the claimant's account, which is 'bad work from the Federal Office'. This might also be why, during most hearings observed in Germany, claimants were asked several questions to clarify apparent inconsistencies in the decision taken by the BAMF. Sometimes questions did not appear focused on claimants' SOGI, but were mostly aimed at checking the plausibility of the story (for instance, Court observation, Hesse, 2018). Other times, questions moved on to relationships, first sexual encounters, visits to gay bars, as well as intimate aspects, in the attempt to assess the credibility of claimants' testimonies (for instance, Court observation, Hesse, 2018). Therefore, overall judges do not seem to favour an open narrative (with some exceptions, for instance, Court observation, Hesse, 2018), even though this approach is more consistent with a SOGI-friendly asylum system (UNHCR 2012a, para. 60). Yet, significantly, by confirming the reliance on the individual circumstances of the claimant, another judge – Emilia – emphasised the role of COI. In this respect, she investigates whether or not in the claimant's country of origin 'possible and reasonable' forms of protection exist, or whether the required level of persecution – curiously identified as a 'gradual concept' (not an isolated understanding however, see Danisi 2019) – is reached, taking into account the personal circumstances of the claimant. From a negative perspective, some disrespectful attitudes to claimants were witnessed. For instance, in a Court observation in Hesse, in 2018, the judge failed to address the claimant directly and only addressed the lawyer and the interpreter (also Court observation, Hesse, 2019). Moreover, when additional evidence was produced at the appeal stage, the new material was analysed with suspicion. This was the case in another hearing (Court observation, Hesse, 2018), where the judge scrutinised a letter provided by a support group and asked detailed questions in a way that seemed to question the letter's authenticity. Finally, it is noticeable that, although the BAMF is expected to attend hearings, it is rarely present (except for one Court observation – Hesse, 2019 – out of ten observations carried out in Germany), while on some occasions there were no witnesses heard (for instance, another Court observation, Hesse, 2019). The duration of hearings appears overall very variable.

Experiences in Italy were also mixed. Here, judges are under considerable pressure to decide on a substantial number of appeals against territorial commissions' refusals in a (much criticised) new time frame of 4 months (Various 2018). During observations carried out in tribunals in 2018, it was noticed that several hearings a day were usually scheduled with the same judge, one every 15 or 30 min. In this respect, Maurizio, a judge in one of the newly-established specialised sections on immigration and asylum, referred to an average of 60 new appeals every week and an average of 20 or 25 cases decided each week. No specific procedural arrangements emerged for SOGI claimants, and in general the approach adopted in these appeals depends on the individual judge appointed. According to Filippo, a senior judge, his usual approach with asylum claimants is to start by attempting to reassure them and to make sure that they understand that it is essential 'to be precise and say the truth'. Then, claimants are asked if they confirm the account shared at the main interview or whether they want to clarify or specify some points. As Filippo explained, he tends to let the claimant talk, rather than ask direct questions about partners or feelings during relationships. It happened that, in some cases, claimants directly signalled problems with interpretation or the transcript of the main interview, thus clarifying inconsistencies emphasised by the administrative body. In other experiences, less open lines of questioning emerged. For instance, Maurizio (judge) told us that he usually asks questions to verify unclear or doubtful aspects of the main interview, often with the aim of assessing the credibility of the claimant. As he explained, in this process there is room to provide new evidence and, as has happened on occasion, a claimant may put forward SOGI grounds for persecution for the first time at this stage.

It is worth noting that, in Italy, the judge in charge of an asylum appeal may delegate the conduct of the hearing to an honorary judge ('giudici onorari', GOT), who then provides a transcript that the judge in charge of the case uses to discuss the final decision, sitting in a composition of three judges. The choice as to whether to delegate the hearing is based on a number of factors. Our participants mentioned that, given the high number of appeals, this choice is sometimes inevitable. In some tribunals, instead, this is a matter of practice, irrespective of the kind of claim at stake. Yet, as Maurizio explained, in light of credibility issues, he tries to hear SOGI claimants himself as much as possible. In fact, as he put it, 'the perceptions gained during the hearing are invaluable and cannot be transcribed'. Importantly this support staff may not have received appropriate training. In this respect, Filippo (senior judge) mentioned that some training is provided to GOT by simply having them assist a number of hearings of asylum claimants by a judge.

Disparities between hearings held by support staff and judges were evident at our observations in tribunals in Italy. Two hearings, observed in the same tribunal in northern Italy in 2018, are illustrative in this respect. A first hearing, which was indirectly observed thanks to the support of the interpreter (Chap. 2), was held in a private room with the sole presence of the (male) claimant, the interpreter, the lawyer and the (female) GOT. Worryingly, in terms of the rigour and therefore the fairness of proceedings, it lasted less than 15 min. The GOT mainly asked the (non-professional) interpreter to swear and, in a perfunctory manner, as to whether the SOGI claimant wished only to confirm the declarations made at the main interview or wished to add something about his fear of persecution. No evidence was requested, except for a single question on the claimant's integration in Italy. A second hearing with a (female) GOT, which was directly observed by us in a private room with the presence of the (male) claimant, the (non-professional) interpreter and the lawyer, showed a slightly more positive, though still problematic, approach. With no introductions of any kind, the GOT asked questions on specific circumstances reported by the claimant at the main interview. These questions were related to the family's lack of acceptance of his homosexuality, the claimant's relationship with a partner in his country of origin (including dates), the circumstances of his escape from Nigeria, the separation from the partner after the journey by boat in the Mediterranean, and the level of integration in Italy, which was deemed 'essential' for a positive outcome of the case. Some of these questions were irrelevant to an assessment of the fear of persecution, being based on minor aspects of the travel towards Italy, or inappropriate from a SOGI perspective. For example, by relying on a stereotyped notion of SOGI identity in contrast to a more nuanced analysis (Chap. 3), the claimant was asked 'are you truly homosexual?' and whether or not he had had any homosexual 'affective' relationships after his arrival in Italy. An equally problematic approach was discernable in relation to evidence (Chap. 7). In particular, the GOT in this hearing wished to be reassured that the support group that wrote a declaration for him was one dedicated to supporting mostly, if not only, SOGI claimants. Allowing the intervention of one of the group's representatives, she asked how they can 'certify' that only 'gay claimants' are supported. The influence of bias in the GOT's questioning here is evident.

A more sensitive approach was perceived in a third hearing, observed in a different tribunal in northern Italy in 2018, where the (male) claimant was not heard by a single judge but by a panel composed of three immigration and asylum judges (two women and one man). Importantly, no sexual-related questions were asked in this hearing. After starting the hearing by verifying that the claimant did not need clarification on any points, the judges asked for further information relating to aspects of the claimant's personal circumstances (as reported at the main interview) that appeared contradictory. Overall, the hearing appeared to focus on identifying minor inconsistencies in the claimant's story, rather than establishing the credibility of the claimant. Examples of questions included 'How could you forget to leave the door open while spending time with your partner?' or 'In what moment of the day your neighbours discovered you?', both aimed at finding reasons for inconsistencies emphasised by the administrative body. At the end, the transcript of the hearing was read point by point aloud by one of the judge and, although it was checked in Italian, some errors were corrected.[10]

Following the Italian 2017 reform, once judges have all the necessary material at their disposal and, if deemed necessary, the hearing has taken place, a decision is made. Analysis of the available case law (Danisi 2020) and participants' views indicate that too often judicial decisions are formulaic, in particular, COI is 'copied and pasted' from one decision to the next. According to Filippo (senior judge), the new collective decision-making procedure is to be welcomed in this respect. Judges are required to report every case to their colleagues for a joint discussion with references to case law and relevant COI. As a result, the overall quality of decisions improves and the influence of individual bias is better controlled, as we saw above in relation to administrative caseworkers, leading to a fairer Italian judicial asylum system also for SOGI cases.

Data on the UK is also rich. No specific procedures are in place for SOGI claimants making an appeal in the UK. While our approach would suggest the adoption of specific individualised measures (Chap. 3), according to Harry (senior judge), such arrangements would be unnecessary because 'LGBT isn't thought of as anything unusual or special really'. On judges' approach to SOGI asylum cases, some of our participants gave positive accounts. According to Bilal (presenting officer), almost all judges now introduce themselves and explain carefully every aspect of the appeal, while trying to reassure claimants throughout the hearing. In this respect, the case of Irma is illustrative. At her hearing, she did not have a lawyer and the questioning by the Home Office representative upset her to the point of crying.

---

[10] It is only fair to point out that, according to lawyers who had been involved in other hearings with the same judges, this kind of long and detailed hearing is uncommon. The presence of a SOGICA researcher, duly authorised, might have influenced the conduct of the hearing and the subsequent positive outcome, as the claimant's lawyer argued.

6.4 The Judicial Procedure

Showing a sensitive approach, the judge told her 'I will be your barrister and your solicitor because, why, you don't have a solicitor to help you… and I will'. In turn, Lutfor, who faced hard questioning from the Home Office representative and expressed fear, explained that the judge reassured him by reprimanding the presenting officer for their inappropriate manner. Less positive experiences were shared by other participants, including Gary and Debbie (NGO workers), who found that the appeal system is not 'genuinely impartial'. Christina, for instance, explained that they never had the opportunity to talk during the hearing, even to correct errors made by the judge about her story. Judges also seem to have limited time to prepare before the hearing, owing to the lack of cooperation with the Home Office. In this respect, as Harry (senior judge) confirmed, judges usually receive the claimant's bundle only the day before the hearing:[11]

> It can be very frustrating… (…) And it is disgraceful, it shouldn't happen, they have got loads of time and some people just fail to do so. Fail to file and serve their documents. (…) But the barrister wants the case to go ahead anyway… and of course you know if you have, if you have dealt with one Cameroonian asylum which is based on LGBT, you know what the issues are anyway, so it is hardly likely that anything startlingly new is going to come out of the documentation. Because they normally just turn on credibility.

Overall, as Ernest (judge) said: 'I'm personally quite unhappy about how inconsistent the judiciary is'. This inconsistency in the decision-making process is likely to lead to inconsistent outcomes, as Chap. 7 will explore in detail.

Inconsistencies and unfair treatment may also be attributable to the Home Office representative at the hearings. It is worth noting that in 2019, the ICIBI launched an inquiry and call for evidence addressing 'what is working well and what is working not so well' in the work of Home office presenting officers (ICIBI 2019). It is true that, sometimes, the Home Office is unrepresented (for instance, Tribunal observation, Manchester, 2018) or unprepared (for example, Tribunal observation, London, 2018, where the Home Office presenting officer asked the judge for time to read the relevant papers). And this is generally due to capacity and resourcing issues. Yet, when the Home Office presenting officer or barrister is present, their manner towards the claimant could often be described as sceptical or incredulous, unsurprising given the inquisitorial nature of the judicial system, as emerged during the hearings observed in 2018. Judges and Home Office presenting officers recurrently question the nature of support organisations, aiming to verify whether they 'accept' only LGBTIQ+ people and 'certify' asylum claimants' SOGI (for instance, Upper Tier Tribunal observation, London, 2018; Tribunal observation, Manchester, 2018). What is striking in all these direct experiences is that, in most cases, the judge did not intervene to prevent inappropriate questions to the claimants. Indeed, on

---

[11] According to Bilal, a presenting officer, 'the appellant's bundle (…) have a huge amount of background material, that is called the objectable background evidence and then the main bulk of it should be the subjective material. That will have the appellant's witness statement (…) and any evidence that they have managed to get hold of… either about their claim or about matters contiguous to that perhaps, mental health issues or health issues or anything like that. So they differ in quality and quantity, but that is the usual structure'.

occasion, judges gave the impression of taking the Home Office's side. For instance, in a First Tier Tribunal observation in London (2018), the judge requested clarifications on the streets where gay clubs were located, and asked what was the difference between 'gay venue and gay bar'. In this kind of dialogue, the imbalances of power felt by claimants become evident. For example, during that same observation, when one of the witnesses mentioned that they had met the claimant to look for a Christmas tree, the judge asked 'I just have one question out of straightforward interest, from your statement, what is camp about Christmas?' The sense of relief when the Home Office does not adopt this kind of approach was well expressed by Janelle:

> After court I felt a relief. I was just actually happy I don't have to say anything, because I was worried on my way to [tribunal location], my belly was hurting. (…) I am like "oh my God, they are probably going to ask me a lot of questions", I was preparing myself mentally, physically to answer questions, and when I got there and I spoke to the barrister, the barrister says Home Office has nothing to ask you. I took a deep breath and I said, "Amen".

Coming to the adoption of decisions in the UK, the approach of a judge, Adrian, is instructive. To decide on an appeal, he explained that he first looks at the declarations of the claimant at the main interview, taking into account the quality of the interview. Then, he examines witnesses' statements and verifies inconsistencies and the plausibility of the claimant's story. He also looks at the claimant's social life and what 'benefit from living in a free society' they have had. As he explained, a balanced approach is required. For instance, 'in South Asian community, probably more Bangladesh perhaps than India… there is social disapproval, so there may only be a relatively small group of people who they can socialise with. I mean, you just have to be aware of things like that'. Although in apparent tension with the cultural anti-essentialist approach we adopt in our analysis (Chap. 3), Adrian's statements reflect an effort to embed his decision-making practices in a degree of cultural awareness. Adrian said he would not give weight to evidence such as participating in gay Pride events or submitting explicit videos: 'if you were making that kind of material in a country where you could face the death penalty (…) it is completely insane'. Furthermore, he pointed out that 'no one has any ability to know a person's sexual orientation, the only relevance in our field is if that is the claimed cause of persecution'. However, despite the generally recognised reliance on objective evidence, other factors may influence some judges. For instance, although a claimant had permission to appeal, the judge in question affirmed that, irrespective of the number of witnesses and the evidence provided, he could not ignore the fact that two judges had previously found the claimant not credible (Tribunal observation, Manchester, 2018). The overall fairness of the process is therefore seriously undermined.

Before moving on to other procedural aspects, a final point should be stressed. Like caseworkers, judges bring their own attitudes, experiences and values to bear in decision-making. Previous research has found that, in light of their very limited or absent training on asylum SOGI issues, bias and prejudices may have a stronger influence on the judiciary than at administrative level (Jansen 2014, p. 45). As Chap. 7 will further explore, too often disbelief is the starting point in asylum claims and

6.4 The Judicial Procedure

this is reflected in the way hearings of SOGI claimants are carried out (Nana, focus group no. 3, Bavaria, Germany; Evelyne and Anne, lawyers, Germany; Thomas, NGO volunteer, Germany). For example, during a Court observation (Hesse, 2018) which involved a claimant applying for protection for the second time, the judge made it clear that he did not believe him and potentially intimidated the witness by telling him that he could receive a 12-month prison sentence if false information were provided. The existence of this kind of biased preconception is confirmed by the words of Oscar, a judge in Germany: 'And the more you have listened to asylum seekers from a country, the sooner you will notice whether this really happens [claimants using fake stories] or if that is more likely. These are stories that are passed on from asylum seeker to asylum seeker and which they always try to use here [in court] So, typical stories'. Similar examples were also found in Italy (Maurizio, judge) and in the UK, where Bilal (Home Office presenting officer) said: sometimes 'evidence doesn't seem to persuade some judges at all'. Such bias in hearings may have racist undertones. In this respect, Joseph, an NGO volunteer in the UK, noticed that: 'if you take lots of witnesses to court, if they are White and middle-class, they are believed.' He described a case in January 2019 where a Pakistani couple gave evidence to support two Pakistani claimants: 'The judge said they weren't worth much [as witnesses]'.

Bias on the part of asylum judges may lead to insensitive and unfair reactions. For example, Filippo, a senior judge in Italy, made it clear that some colleagues are not willing to hear asylum claimants because they sell each other 'absurd stories', especially when they arrive from particular countries, like Nigeria. Another example is that of a judge responding to a claimant facing trauma generated by his journey to Europe (Chap. 5):

> My client (…) said, "There was water everywhere". And then the judge said: "Yes, I'm sure you were on the sea". And he said: "Yes, in the boat the water came in". And then it went on, [saying] that he sleeps badly because of that and always dreams and his friend or brother, I do not know, has died. And then the judge says: "Yes, I sleep badly too" (Evelyne and Anne, lawyers, Germany).

SOGI-specific bias has also emerged. This tends to be connected with the lack of knowledge of SOGI experiences and concepts, something that is illustrated by cases where the judge does not understand the concept of bisexuality (Elias, lawyer, Germany) or the difference between sexual orientation and gender identity, for example, by asking a claimant 'Are you gay or a trans woman now? What is it now? You have to commit yourself!' (Noah, NGO social worker, Germany). During one hearing in Germany (Court observation, Hesse, 2018), a judge stated openly: 'this story is so deceitful, it's unbelievable! [The claimant] has five children and tells me that he is gay all the way! That is unbelievable!' Claimants' desires and interests are totally neglected or misunderstood in such cases. In fact, as Emroy (focus group no. 1, Hesse, Germany) said, 'my son is because I want a child, and which gay person or which human doesn't want a child?'

Insensitivity in hearings sometimes becomes open homophobia or transphobia. During the hearing in Italy of a lesbian claimant from Nigeria, Mara (lawyer) was explaining to a senior judge that the claimant had been discovered with her girlfriend and seriously beaten. Mara made it clear that the claimant was traumatised and had been through a difficult recovery and an equally difficult pathway to self-acceptance. At that point, the judge intervened saying 'well, that's not really a trauma…' and pointed out that she (the judge) would have reacted in the same way as the alleged persecutor of the claimant if she had found her young daughter in bed with a girlfriend. While this example confirms the still widespread lack of empathy amongst decision-makers, the sexuality or gender identity of the judge is no guarantee of an impartial hearing. According to Allan (lawyer, UK), gay judges 'are very much imposing their own gaydar or lesbian-dar or whatever you call it-dar on somebody. They are sitting there and they might be gay or lesbian themselves, but they are very much judging the person'.

In sum, subjective factors may still influence decision-makers, both at administrative and judicial level, thus shaping the way interviews and hearings are carried out. For this reason, the availability and the correct use of objective information on countries of origin becomes even more essential in SOGI claims. In the next section, we thus turn our analysis to COI.

6.5 Country of Origin Information

As many of our participants emphasised, COI is an essential element for the evaluation of every asylum application, irrespective of the grounds of persecution. According to the definition of a refugee, individuals who fear persecution need to demonstrate that the protection available if returned to their country of origin, if any, is insufficient. Therefore, other than assessing the individual circumstances of a claimant (Chap. 7), decision-makers need to verify whether those circumstances are consistent with the information available on the country of origin in question. Inevitably, the sources and the quality of this information become crucial to the grant or refusal of refugee status or any other form of international protection. In this respect, SOGI claims pose particular challenges to decision-makers, primarily because most COI sources do not have specific information on the treatment of SOGI minorities (Jong 2008) or, if they do, relevant data 'privileges certain voices over others' (McDonald-Norman 2017). In other words, against the principles underlying our theoretical approach to SOGI asylum (Chap. 3), the risk of homogenisation of SOGI minorities is very high. Indeed, no obligation to collect SOGI-specific COI exists at EU or national level, although the increasing role of EASO in the collection of information on refugees' countries of origin has progressively led to the gathering of evidence on SOGI minorities in a more consistent way (EASO 2015). Yet, as Helena (EASO staff member) confirmed, this material has not reached a satisfactory level of detail and completeness. It is therefore no surprise that significant disparities emerge not only between the countries under investigation, but also within each country, considering the lack of guidance for, or the inconsistent material available to, decision-makers. In this area the UK appears to play a significant

6.5 Country of Origin Information

role with the potential to influence decision-makers in Germany and Italy, as well as in other European countries.

In Germany, the BAMF includes specific departments working on COI and producing background papers, sometimes for internal use only, and has set up a specific database to support decision-makers' assessments.[12] This database, however, does not hold extensive information on SOGI. Moreover, when publicly available, relevant sections often focus on sexual orientation issues, in this way marginalising transgender minorities (Huebner 2016, p. 247). Although, during the appeal, courts may request specialist reports from experts, there is no guarantee that SOGI-specific reports are commissioned. Given that relevant material in foreign languages is not generally consulted (Kalkmann 2010) and Google is used to find the 'best article' that confirms the decision-maker' view on a specific case (Gartner 2015, p. 14), there are also serious doubts about the fairness of the assessment of SOGI claims in Germany. Yet, according to the response provided by the German government to a parliamentary request, a less instrumental and more objective use of COI is emerging as decision-makers are said to draw on reports by the BAMF, the EASO, the UNHCR and, more generally, the UN, as well as on cases decided by administrative courts (BMI 2019, p. 14). This broad and contrasting picture on COI was confirmed by our participants. While Evelyne and Anne (lawyers) defined the BAMF's reports as accurate but 'cautious', Elias (lawyer) and Thomas (NGO volunteer) emphasised that their confidential nature prevents open consultation. In light of these pitfalls, it is promising that judges, like Oscar, usually consult a variety of sources on the relevant country of origin, other than BAMF's relevant reports, for reaching an informed decision:

> I inform myself about the respective country (...) in a very detailed way and the more detailed the better. That means that I also watch a lot on the Internet and I also read many reports, newspaper articles, the Foreign Office, Amnesty International (...) they write country information and individual information. (...) Most of the time, the truth is, I estimate a lot, so somewhere in the middle. Amnesty always writes "all very bad", Foreign Ministry writes "everything is fine". And probably it will then hit somewhere in the middle.

As Oscar also pointed out, finding information on some countries may require greater research, as is the case with Jamaica, the country of origin of only a small number of asylum claimants in Germany. Gisela (lawyer) confirmed this disparity of information with the example of Uganda, for which information is usually available, in contrast to Somalia, for which there is little accessible material. While she relies on the UK Home Office's COI for her clients' appeals, which is deemed 'much more accurate and up to date' than the BAMF's reports, in her experience, many decision-makers usually only use sources available in German.

As anticipated, a further problem is that decision-makers in Germany often read COI in a way that supports their own position in an inappropriate way. Kadir (NGO worker) provided two different, but equally illustrative, examples in this respect. In one case, a worrying parallel between members of a sexual minority and murderers

---

[12] https://milo.bamf.de

was made. So, in light of the difference between rural and metropolitan areas in Pakistan, a gay claimant from that country was told 'you could have fled to Karachi. Karachi has about 20 million inhabitants, even murderers can hide there'. In another case, following the rejection of his asylum request, a claimant was given a country report on the economic development of his country and the increasing availability of employment options, although he had not applied to stay in Germany on economic grounds but because of SOGI persecution.

The situation in Italy is similar. The Italian asylum system does not have a department that gathers evidence on countries of origin, if we exclude the unsuccessful attempts of the National Commission of Asylum to draft national COI (among others, Roberto, decision-maker). It is thus no surprise, in line with past research (Busetto et al. 2017), that most participants stressed a lack of detailed information on the treatment of SOGI minorities in their countries of origin (for instance, Maria Grazia, decision-maker). Consequently, the use of a variety of sources was reported, suggesting that, apart from perhaps the UNHCR representatives, decision-makers had their own approaches to finding and consulting relevant COI. For instance, Roberto (decision-maker) usually looks for information using Refworld and Google. Daniele (decision-maker) consults EASO material, NGO reports, and the jurisprudence of the ECtHR and CJEU. In Daniele's experience, if no information is available, the decision may be suspended for the time needed to collect appropriate material. In his view, in light of the expected reform of the CEAS (Ferreira 2018; ILGA Europe 2016), EASO reports will probably become the primary source of COI in Italy in due course. In addition, Titti (decision-maker) referred to the UK Home Office's COI, as well as non-institutional online databases such as Asilo in Europa and Melting Pot Europa. She also emphasised the importance of consulting media from the claimants' countries of origin, because these may provide an understanding of the social environment and the discrimination prevailing in their communities. Here Titti gave the example of Ukraine, where the President often states that SOGI minorities are protected by law and a Pride march had been organised but where negative attitudes towards SOGI minorities remain prevalent. By consulting a survey carried out in Ukraine, Titti established that more than 50% of Ukrainian citizens (still) believe that homosexuality is 'an incurable disease', thus raising doubts about the existence of a 'safe' social environment for SOGI minorities. As for the COI used specifically by judges, the collection of case law on asylum applications from specific countries carried out at national level by the self-governing judicial body ('Consiglio della Magistratura') was widely reported (Titti, decision-maker; Maurizio, judge). According to Nazarena (lawyer), while only some judges use diverse COI sources similarly to administrative decision-makers, most of the time in both administrative and judicial decisions, as well as in appeals prepared by lawyers, COI sources are not specified. When they are specified, sources are inappropriate (for instance, travel guides like 'Viaggiare sicuri') or insufficiently specific (for example, Amnesty International).

If we look at the responses provided by judges in Italy, approaches to COI depend on individual background and training. Silvana referred to Refworld and COI-net as main sources, arguing that EASO material is often too broadly framed to provide

6.5 Country of Origin Information

SOGI-related information. Filippo mentioned an online migration network of lawyers, academics, judges and public administration officers providing, among other material, information on countries of origin called 'Malta'. Filippo also mentioned travel guides, but emphasising that 'working with COI can be an endless job, [because] one can never be sure about their trustworthiness'. He observed that some judges in Italy tend to repeat information on countries of origin that had already been used by other colleagues in earlier decisions. Consequently, as other participants confirmed (Giovanna and Mara, lawyers), COI mentioned in much case law is out of date. It is no coincidence that, in 2019, the Italian Supreme Court found that judges should avoid 'generic' and 'stereotyped' references to the claimants' country of origin, and should identify specific and up-to-date COI for each case.[13] This obligation derives from the general 'duty-power of cooperation' of judges (Flamini 2018), which the Supreme Court has repeatedly emphasised in its case law (Chap. 7). As Filippo stressed, echoing Nazarena (lawyer), the problem is that very often territorial commissions are not clear about what COI is used to deny an asylum request. In Filippo's view, this lack of information does not reflect inexperience or incompetence but might simply be a consequence of the 'hellish rhythms' imposed on the commission. For all these reasons, COI provided by lawyers or support groups is particularly welcomed by members of the commissions and judges because it facilitates their work (Sect. 6.2). For example, in the case of a transgender claimant from Cuba, Valentina (social worker) provided original material collected by local contacts in that country that showed abuses by the police against SOGI minorities, despite the absence of any discriminatory legislation. In this light, it was suggested that one way to greatly enhance the quality of COI in use would be to fund social and ethnographic research in claimants' home countries, thus shedding light on social perceptions of these minorities (Vincenzo, LGBTIQ+ group volunteer).

Compared with Germany and Italy, at first sight the UK asylum system appears very advanced in relation to COI and SOGI. There is a growing number of SOGI-specific Country Policy Information Notes (CPIN) that, being publicly available, are also in use in other European countries, as discussed above.[14] In the past, there have been concerns regarding the regularity with which this material is updated (UKLGIG 2013, p. 31). At the same time, some Country Information and Guidances have been found to be problematic. An example is the guidance on Jamaica, which was for a long period on the list of 'safe countries' (Sect. 6.7).[15] The guidance clearly mentions that, according to the Jamaican Offences Against the Person Act of 1864, '[w]hosoever shall be convicted of the abominable crime of buggery [anal intercourse] committed either with mankind or with any animal, shall be liable to be imprisoned and kept to hard labour for a term not exceeding ten years' (Home

---

[13] Supreme Court, decision no. 11312, 26 April 2019, pp. 3–4.

[14] Publicly available at https://www.gov.uk/government/collections/country-policy-and-information-notes

[15] Although the Supreme Court found that it could not be considered 'safe' already in 2013: *R (on the application of Brown) Jamaica* [2015] UKSC.

Office 2017, p. 10). Equally, the guidance recognises that lesbians risk violence 'up to and including "corrective" rape and murder' with insufficient state protection. Yet, the same guidance also quotes a Tribunal ruling saying that:

> Not all lesbians are at risk. Those who are naturally discreet, have children and/or are willing to present a heterosexual narrative for family or societal reasons may live as discreet lesbians without persecutory risk, provided that they are not doing so out of fear.[16]

The obvious question is whether anyone at risk of corrective rape or murder would *not* hide their sexuality through fear of persecution (Weßels 2012, p. 821). These logical inconsistencies, however, are far from being duly considered. In fact, 'discretion reasoning' according to the *HJ (Iran)* ruling is generally emphasised in all the CPIN and Home Office guidance also identifies countries where relocation is an option for SOGI minorities (UKLGIG 2013, p. 22). The guidance on Iran is a case in point. Despite the severity of punishments in case of same-sex sexual relations, the Home Office guidance on Iran excludes internal relocation to escape persecution but, simultaneously, also says that 'some evidence suggests that homosexual and bisexual persons who do not openly reveal their sexual orientation and keep a low profile are able to move freely within society' (Home Office 2019b, p. 9).

For reasons connected to 'discretion', relevant guidance often recognises criminalisation and discrimination but not to the level of persecution. For example, although the Home Office guidance on Bangladesh includes serious concerns about human rights and violence against SOGI minorities, it then distinguishes between different groups to identify persecution (Home Office 2020, p. 11). On the one hand, the Home Office's guidance states that 'an LGBTI person who is open' may be at risk of persecution. On the other hand, it requires that where a person does not openly express their SOGI, 'consideration must be given to the reasons why they do not' and, consequently, shall bear the burden of demonstrating that they would be at real risk of persecution on return (Chap. 7). What is more, past research emphasised that these country guidance documents do not always include information on specific groups within SOGI minorities (ICIBI 2014, p. 31), for instance in relation to transgender or lesbian people, leading to the risk of the absence of evidence being interpreted as absence of persecution (Bach 2013). In this respect, however, it is worth noting that the last available guidance tends to avoid homogenisation of SOGI minorities and provides specific details on particular groups in countries of origin (Home Office 2020, para. 7). Moreover, both the Home Office's 2016 Sexual Orientation guidance and the 2011 Gender Identity guidance point out that there may be a lack of country of origin supporting evidence, with the Gender Identity guidance stating that 'absence of specific legislation on transgender men and women in particular may be an extension of their general marginalisation' (Home Office 2011, p. 15).

Based on our data, these CPIN and guidance documents are widely used in UK decision-making (for instance, in four different judicial hearings that we observed – Tribunal observations, London 2018; First Tier Tribunal observation, Birmingham,

---

[16] *SW (lesbians – HJ and HT applied) Jamaica CG* [2011] UKUT 251 (IAC).

6.5 Country of Origin Information

2018 – related to Kenya, Albania and Malawi). Our data also shows the existence of some gaps and mixed views on the real value of these CPIN and guidance documents. According to one decision-maker, consulting Home Office material in advance of an interview is fundamental to identify appropriate questions for the claimant (Emily, decision-maker). For instance, when the relevant guidance suggests that SOGI claimants cannot relocate to other parts of their countries of origin, in her view there is no need to further investigate that option. More generally, the availability of up-to-date COI usually depends on the specific country under examination. In fact, as Emily explained, COI on countries from which SOGI claimants commonly arrive may contain detailed information on the treatment of SOGI minorities, while there might be a lack of SOGI-related information in relation to less common countries of origin. In these cases, reports by the US government may be consulted, although Emily explained that these are often too general and 'basic'. Worryingly, another decision-maker explained that, when information is lacking, his research includes academic sources as well as news about 'Pride events' or the existence and activities of 'any LGBT societies' in the claimant's country of origin (Qasim, decision-maker). COI was equally challenging for judges. For instance, Amadin, who claimed asylum in the UK from Benin, explained that the judge in his case had confessed to being 'confused' by the contradictory evidence she had found by searching online for information about gay acceptability in Benin. Amadin's case was also set back by his lawyer's confusion of information about Benin (Amadin's country of origin) with information relating to Benin City (a city in Nigeria) (Sect. 6.2). During the appeal stage, lawyers may contribute to filling evidentiary gaps, given that – in contrast to Italy for example – in the UK the judge does not play an active role in gathering information and relies primarily on lawyers' 'bundles'. For instance, during a judicial hearing observed in 2018, the lawyer provided evidence on the treatment of gay men in Tanzania from NGO sources, such as Human Rights Watch and the Human Dignity Trust. In other cases, even the use of tourist guides by the Home Office's presenting officer was reported (Allan, lawyer). Finally, regarding the updating of available COI, concerns were expressed as to the capacity of the Home Office to ensure that this is done consistently:

> I find it quite difficult to get my head around how it is that, a team of 14 or 15 is responsible for producing all of this material which is essentially life changing material for thousands of people (…). You need to get really good up-to-date stuff, but if you have got an expert, and we try to find the people who are most expert to inform the reviews, you need to listen to them and there is a risk that if the expert is saying something that the Home Office doesn't like the sound of, they are not necessarily going to be quite so receptive (David, official).

In addition, material that is not available in English is not necessarily taken into account, thus limiting the sources of information and adding further concerns about the value of the COI used (David, official). That is perhaps why, although Emily and Qasim (decision-makers) stated that they usually consider the information provided in such guidance, their assessment is always based on the individual circumstances of SOGI claimants. As Qasim (decision-maker) put it:

Someone from (…) say… Jamaica, is not going to be able to display all of the thoughts and processes and emotions that the guidance tells us they should be doing. Again it depends on the kind of society they grew up in… it depends on, yes, their own experiences in their childhood… you have just got to look at the individual aspects of the case on a case-by-case basis and judge according to that.

According to the Refugee Convention and UNHCR guidelines, a case-by-case analysis is indeed the method that should always be adopted, irrespective of more or less detailed COI. Consequently, criticising the general UK approach in this field, Roberto, a decision-maker in Italy, pointed out that 'the main problem with COI is that too often information on a country is used to support a specific position, not as a helpful tool for reflecting on a case'. In fact, as Chap. 7 will investigate, once a claimant is deemed credible, there is the risk that COI is used to deny the fear of persecution on the basis of 'objective' evidence in an exercise of detachment from 'personal' circumstances. It is perhaps no surprise that, according to Nath, a lawyer in the UK, 'where there is a little information, [decision-makers] tend to give the benefit of the doubt (…) so paradoxically sometimes you are quite happy when there is no guidance'. Conversely, when 'objective' evidence related to the country of origin is available, this evidence may be given more weight than evidence submitted by claimants. For instance, in a case involving a Nigerian claimant, the Tribunal of Bari (Italy) reversed the territorial commission's decision in the belief that the lack of proof should have been afforded less weight than the objective situation of discrimination faced by sexual minorities in that country.[17]

In sum, while COI is undoubtedly important, its gathering, production and use raise doubts across all countries under investigation, particularly when the individual circumstances of a SOGI claimant are outweighed by general, but not necessarily relevant, information about the country of origin in question. Our survey confirms this conclusion, by signalling an even more worrying trend. For 50% of respondents who work with or support LGBTIQ+ people claiming asylum, COI is the second main problem at the appeal stage in SOGI claims – second only to credibility (75%). Similar concerns emerged in relation to interpretation, to which we now turn our attention.

6.6 Interpretation

An important component of a fair asylum system is access to an interpreter for all claimants to ensure that they can both understand the proceedings and be understood. This guarantee is protected and further specified at European level. Whereas the ECtHR has emphasised in its jurisprudence 'the importance of interpretation in order to ensure access to the asylum procedure',[18] the Procedures Directive provides

---

[17] Tribunal of Bari, decision of 23 September 2014.
[18] For instance, ECtHR, *M.A. and Others v. Lithuania*, Application no. 59793/17, 11 December 2018, para. 108 ff.

6.6 Interpretation

for specific obligations on member states in this respect. According to Article 12(1)(b), claimants 'shall receive the services of an interpreter for submitting their case to the competent authorities whenever necessary', to be paid for by public funds. Equally, according to Article 15, member states shall select an interpreter for the interview who can ensure appropriate communication in the language preferred by the claimant and, wherever possible, of the same sex, if the claimant requests it.

Yet, when we look at our data, the failure to implement these guarantees across Europe was evident. According to our survey, only 43% of those respondents who had an interpreter for their interviews or court hearings (73% of the total) declared being happy with the interpreting service. The situation is not any more positive in our country case studies, both from a general asylum perspective and a more specific SOGI dimension. While Germany and Italy appeared less compliant than the UK in this area, probably for linguistic reasons, two distinctive features emerged. On the one hand, where possible, claimants preferred to avoid interpreters to enable more direct communication (for instance, Diarra, Italy; Harriet, focus group no. 2, Bavaria, Germany). As Tina, who claimed asylum in Germany, explained:

> You can't translate something you really would like to express… the way you feel, it can't be translated. That's what I felt, like I wish I could… I know the language to express deeply how really I… that I really have here [within myself]. But I have not got that chance.

The inability to talk directly to the interviewer or the judge, also given the fact that judicial proceedings are carried out in German or in Italian, appeared to create feelings of disempowerment in SOGI claimants, which were sometimes aggravated by interpreters' attitudes. Owing to power differentials within the system, often coupled with time constraints, many claimants explained that they did not 'dare' asking to change interpreters, despite this being a legal entitlement (for instance, Odosa, Siri, Mamaka, Franco, all claiming asylum in Italy). On the other hand, a low level of linguistic competence by national authorities working with asylum claimants was reported (for instance, Gisela, lawyer, Germany), which clearly hampers direct conversations. These linguistic barriers, coupled with the use of a third language, such as English, which is then translated by interpreters into the claimants' native language, risk seriously undermining effective communication (Giuseppe, lawyer, Italy).

Rigorous selection and training of interpreters is an essential component of a fair asylum system. In Germany, although the presence of a 'language mediator' ('Sprachmittler*innen') is provided for by law, for BAMF interviews freelance interpreters are usually employed but no specific professional qualifications or state examinations are required (ECRE, AIDA & Asyl und Migration 2019, p. 25). Nonetheless, as the 2019 ECRE/AIDA report states, in recent years the BAMF announced new measures to improve the quality of interpretation services. In particular, language mediators are now obliged to acquire, at least, a C1 certificate in German and to complete an online training programme. This training includes general themes relating to the asylum process and the treatment of claimants with symptoms of trauma, in order to develop psycho-social competences and to acquire knowledge of professional ethics (BMI 2019, p. 14). In addition to a formal complaint system, the BAMF also introduced a 'code of conduct' containing a number of principles, such as integrity, professional and financial independence and neutrality, to which language mediators should commit.[19] These improvements seem much needed in light of our participants' strong concerns about the qualifications of interpreters used by the BAMF. According to Barbara, Evelyne and Anne, all lawyers, many people are not qualified as interpreters but are simply 'language mediators', and so more likely to accept lower fees than trained professionals. Other claimants reported the lack of interpreters/language mediators for some languages. Sylvia told us that, although she asked to be interviewed in Luganda, no Lugandan interpreter was provided for her. She was asked to use English during the interview. As she put it, 'I felt like I had no choice, but forced myself to express my story in English. But I don't think I even said the right things I had to say. That was not fair'. This corresponds to experiences in some of the hearings observed during our fieldwork, where the quality of English interpretation was poor (Court observation, Hesse, 2018), including the use of offensive terms to identify SOGI minorities (Court observation, Hesse, 2019). Judges were only rarely proactive in ensuring that claimants understood every question before recording their answers (for instance, another Court observation, Hesse, 2019). In this context, not surprisingly, no SOGI-specific training for interpreters was reported (for instance, Kadir, NGO worker).

In Italy, the selection of interpreters varies for different stages of the asylum procedure. According to our data, a combination of formal procedures and informal practices are in place. At the administrative interview, interpreters are provided by territorial commissions through private companies. During the appeal, instead, claimants often need to find an interpreter in case a hearing is scheduled. Sometimes reception centres and support groups help asylum claimants in this respect, while on other occasions claimants rely on personal contacts or pay a professional. Although public funds are theoretically available to cover these expenses, bureaucratic delays may prevent their use in practice (for instance, Giuseppe, lawyer). In addition to general concerns over the lack of interpreters from specific countries or with knowledge of specific dialects (Nazarena, lawyer; Daniele, decision-maker), this twofold 'selection' process generates concerns. While some SOGI claimants welcomed the possibility to choose their own interpreter for the tribunal as it meant they could appoint someone they trusted and avoid using people from their communities serving as interpreters (for instance, Nicola and Giulio, LGBTIQ+ group volunteers), this mechanism may undermine the quality of interpretation. Much of the time interpretation is indeed provided on a voluntary basis by Italian contacts. However, when no one is available, claimants have to rely nonetheless on people from their same community, even if with no qualifications at all. According to Filippo (senior judge), this practice violates the most basic principles of justice: 'neutrality, impartiality and independence'. Moreover, an interpreter chosen by the claimant may be perceived as less neutral and trustworthy by judges, as we saw in a Tribunal

---

[19] Following the introduction of these measures, more than 2100 interpreters were declared unfit for further employment by the BAMF, most of them apparently due to insufficient language skills (ECRE, AIDA & Asyl und Migration 2019, p. 25).

6.6 Interpretation

observation in northern Italy in 2018. At the same time, when appointing the interpreter is left to reception centres, there is no guarantee that SOGI dimensions are considered (Silvana, judge). In fact, this consideration depends on the professionalism of the specific centre in question (Sect. 8.2 and Chap. 8).

In relation to the administrative interview, the provision of an interpreter by the state is positively evaluated given most claimants' lack of resources. However, since there are no provisions for verifying interpreters' qualifications or experience, professional and ethical standards cannot be guaranteed (Livio, lawyer). As a remedy, Roberto (decision-maker) explained that informal procedural arrangements are sometimes adopted in territorial commissions. For example, when he knows in advance that an interview with a SOGI claimant is scheduled, he submits very specific requirements in order to have the most qualified interpreter among those usually employed, namely the one 'with the right attitude' towards these claims. Yet, these informal procedural arrangements are left to the initiative and discretion of caseworkers, which in turn depends on their training on, and understanding of, SOGI asylum. After the interview, interviewers may report inaccurate or inappropriate interpretation services to the president of the territorial commission, to prevent the interpreter in question being employed again (for instance, Maria Grazia, decision-maker). In relation to the selection process, participants commented on the increasing employment of former asylum claimants as interpreters. On a positive note, as Roberto (decision-maker) explained, their employment may be a useful way to remedy the imbalance of power experienced by many asylum claimants. It is nonetheless true that the risk of re-traumatisation (Titti, decision-maker) as well as lack of legal, psychological and social competences (Vincenzo, LGBTIQ+ group volunteer) can be high. Despite any inadequacies, in Roberto's view some SOGI claimants trust the interpreter 'no matter what', just 'because they do not trust the interviewer'. As he put it, unless evident signs of homophobia or transphobia emerge, 'the interpreter is always a person of the community, someone who speaks their language, while the interviewer is always a White person who is examining them'. The experience of Mamaka, who claimed asylum in Italy, is noteworthy in this respect:

> I was not thinking that I would meet someone who speaks my language (…) I was expecting to speak English. So when I met him (…) he also gives me the courage. We will understand each other because he also went to my country.

Overall, this data shows that, in both Germany and Italy, basic standards are not consistently met. For instance, although asylum claimants are entitled to ask for an interpreter of a specific sex, we heard from participants that these requests are not always properly addressed (for instance, Maurizio, judge, Italy; Evelyne and Anne, lawyers, Germany). Often claimants themselves are not in a position to postpone their interviews to wait for an appropriate interpreter to become available (for instance, Ibrahim, Germany). The case of Trudy Ann, who claimed asylum in Germany, is illustrative. No one asked if she preferred a female interpreter/language mediator before the interview and no female was available that day. As she explained, 'with the interpreter I never feel really comfortable because he's a man, so I can't really express myself in the way I want to express myself'. Yet, Water (focus group no. 4, northern Italy) asked for and obtained a male interpreter, explaining that he did not feel confident speaking with a woman. Despite the above-mentioned CEAS obligation, it is therefore evident that no automatic mechanisms are in place to ensure an interpreter of the same sex of the claimant. This right is only granted where interpreters of both sexes are available to interpret in a particular language (Titti and Daniele, decision-makers, Italy).

In Germany and Italy, concerns were also reported in relation to the quality of interpretation from both a general and a specific SOGI point of view. In Germany, among many cases of interviews that had been poorly interpreted (including by William and by Nina, a legal advisor), Angel described how the interpreter himself stopped the interview because he did not feel able to translate adequately: 'He said he hasn't spoken English in a couple of years, so he understands English but not as much. So he said he didn't think it was fair to me, for him to continue the interview'. Always in Germany, we also heard of interpreters behaving in an unprofessional manner, asking questions in the place of the interviewer (Amis, focus group no. 2, Bavaria). As previous research has pointed out, interpretation can be a difficult task when terms used are intimate, colloquial or relate to a subcultural scene, which the interpreter feels embarrassed or ashamed to use (Hübner 2016, p. 250). Lack of understanding and erroneous translation of SOGI terms were also reported (for instance, Frank S., legal advisor; Halim). Marhoon remembered that his interpreter was not aware of the word 'gay', so the interview was postponed:

> When I told this woman that I'm gay in English, she didn't understand. And when I used the Arabic term for homosexuality in Arabic which is "mithli", she didn't understand. (…) I have to wait for another 3–4 weeks. But I'm glad I did it, because if I had carried on with that, they might have misunderstood my whole story.

Diana mentioned that, during the interview, the interpreter 'did not want to understand what is called the transition of man to woman, woman to man. And that is totally like a violence for a refugee, if that happens'. Finally, Trudy Ann recalled:

> I said to him "she's a butch", he said "I don't know what a butch is" [and] when I told him that I would take pills to kill myself (…) because of my lifestyle. He did not interpret that part.

Similarly, in Italy, decision-makers reported on the difficulty of working with non-professional interpreters who frustrated their efforts to ask questions in a sensitive way, with some interpreters going so far as to answer questions themselves or summarise complex answers by the claimant in just a few words (Daniele and Maria Grazia, decision-makers). One decision-maker offered an enlightening example in this respect: some interpreters may translate a claimant's statement 'I have had sex with men' with 'I'm gay' (Titti, decision-maker), with potentially negative implications in terms of credibility (Chap. 7). Giulio (LGBTIQ+ group volunteer) referred to interpreters who had no understanding of bisexuality or transsexuality. The situation may be worse in tribunals, especially when voluntary interpreters are brought along by claimants (for instance, Silvana, judge). Where they were not professionals in the field, basic mistakes would often be made. For example, during a Tribunal

6.6 Interpretation

observation in northern Italy in 2018, a friend of the claimant who was serving as an interpreter did not translate parts of his personal account and, when she did, the meaning had been changed (for instance, 'friend' in English was translated with the Italian word for 'partner'). In this situation, it was only the readiness and ability of one of the panel of three judges to detect linguistic discrepancies and to ask further specific questions to clarify the claimant's story that prevented this mistake damaging the claimant's credibility.

Other concerns in both Germany and Italy were reported in relation to the background of the interpreters and the problematic relationship with SOGI claimants. Ibrahim (Germany), as several others, shared the fear that when interpreters have the same socio-cultural background of the persecutors of a SOGI claimant, they may replicate homophobic or transphobic attitudes. In Germany, Joachim (NGO worker) recalled the use of offensive terminology, 'either out of own prejudice or out of ignorance', while Knud (NGO worker) reported the case of an interpreter in court who 'as soon as he heard what it was about, had no more interest'. More worryingly, the BAMF legitimises this kind of approach by not adopting adequate countermeasures in such cases (Knud, NGO worker). In Italy, Giulio (LGBTIQ+ group volunteer) explained that, in some cases, during the preparatory meeting before the interview or the hearing, interpreters refused to fulfil their role because 'they do not talk about homosexuality, or use this word'. Giovanna (lawyer), confirmed this by telling us about a former claimant who now serves as an interpreter: although he 'does not even want to hear about SOGI claimants', he had worked on several SOGI claims. It is therefore promising that, when such attitudes emerged during an interview, most decision-makers would suspend the interview (Jonathan, LGBTIQ+ group volunteer).

Finally, in some circumstances, an interpreter having the same background as a SOGI claimant was identified as an obstacle to the claimant being open about their real fear of persecution (for instance, Ibrahim, Shany, Prince Emrah, all claimants in Germany). Fares (Germany) expressed this feeling in the following terms:

> I was thinking to come out and say that I'm gay. I was like, for one week, I was thinking, should I say something? I want to say something, I want to be myself, but at the same time no. Psychologically I was really ready to say that, but when I saw this translator, every door was blocked, I cannot say anything anymore.

Despite the criticism this may raise from a theoretical perspective (Puar 2007, 2013), our data suggests that such experiences were more common when interpreters showed a religious background. For example, Gisela (lawyer) reported the case of a young claimant from Iraq, who, in Germany, was given an interpreter wearing a headscarf: 'that looked so strictly Islamic (…) he simply did not dare to say [his SOGI]'. Similar cases were reported in Italy. Valentina (social worker, Italy) recalled the experience of a Russian gay claimant with an orthodox interpreter from Ukraine, who could barely translate apparently because she was too embarrassed by the SOGI nature of the claim. Sometimes, being aware of their rights, claimants felt able to overcome such situations. As Moses (Italy) summarised: 'For the fact that I was here, I knew I was safe, that he [interpreter] couldn't really do anything'. Other positive experiences were reported, for instance, by Mamaka (Italy), who recalled that her interpreter was male with a similar socio-cultural background and, after the end of the interview, approached her to say: 'I am very sorry about what happened, what makes you to leave your country'. In turn, Cristina (UNHCR officer) remembered an interpreter from Iran who, despite admittedly struggling to accept same-sex relationships, tried to increase his understanding of SOGI matters by connecting with people belonging to SOGI minorities.

Similar problems concerning interpretation also emerged in others settings, including arrival and reception centres. On a general negative note, Livio (lawyer, Italy) recalled the case of a cultural mediator who was tasked with collating asylum requests in an arrival centre in Italy, and who suggested to newly arrived migrants that they claim asylum based on a fabricated story. One claimant was only able to correct his false account and avoid the likelihood of being identified as 'not credible' after meeting with a lawyer before his main interview. On a more positive note, in Italy, Chiara (NGO worker) and Celeste (social worker) explained that they specifically identify the most appropriate interpreter for SOGI claims by choosing, among those available, the interpreter closes to the claimant in terms of ethnic background, as long as they have not adopted discriminatory attitudes in the past. An interpreter who was called on to translate in therapy sessions with a lesbian claimant, but displayed a homophobic attitude, was promptly removed from that position. A similarly positive approach to the selection of interpreters was also reported by some lawyers (for instance, Damiano).

Apart from some negative experiences reported by claimants (Sadia, Mary and Zaro, all claiming asylum in the UK), there were more accounts of satisfaction with interpretation services in the UK. As Olivia (government official) explained, the Home Office has a database of interpreters who are checked before being employed and whose proficiency is constantly monitored. If any issues arise, the matter is reported to the Home Office's interpreters unit. Similar checks to ensure that a person meets the required standards are carried out in relation to external interpreters as well, needed for less common languages. A code of conduct is available for interpreters, but it seems that asylum claimants are often unaware of it and of what to expect from interpreters (ECRE, AIDA & Refugee Council 2019, p. 22). Asylum claimants are usually asked at the screening interview whether they wish to be interpreted by a man or a woman, but some concerns have been raised in this respect in light of the low number of such requests (ICIBI 2017). One senior judge, Harry, described interpreters used in tribunals as adequate for their role, while another judge made it clear that if an interpreter shows embarrassment or disapproval, the hearing is usually suspended (Adrian). As many claimants in the UK are able to communicate in English, Nath (lawyer) explained:

> Even if it is not great, I encourage them to go without an interpreter. (…) Also because it is very much about your feelings and emotions and so on, it will necessarily get distorted in one way or another, when it gets interpreted it is not, it is just not going to be the same… there is a lot of body language.

Yet, while recognising that some claimants are comfortable talking with interpreters of their own country of origin, Nath suggested that, in relation to interpretation as well as other aspects of the claim, preparation always remains the key factor:

> I spend so much time with my clients before getting to the interview, that I am, I have got quite a good feeling of whether or not they can do it without an interpreter... and obviously if they can't, then you just go with one.

Even where preparation and high quality interpretation services are provided, asylum claimants, including SOGI ones, risk being deprived of their rights when their requests are assessed through special procedures, to which we now turn.

6.7 Other Procedures

Before concluding, we consider some special asylum procedures that may apply to SOGI claimants in particular contexts. These include, amongst others, accelerated procedures, which often involve asylum requests from nationals of countries identified as 'safe', and Dublin transfers, which are based on the implementation of the Dublin Regulation (III) as a key instrument of the CEAS framework currently into force (Chap. 4). Albeit briefly, it is necessary to assess whether or not these procedures are appropriate for SOGI claimants given their specific needs.

As for accelerated procedures, their negative effects are primarily connected to the obstacles they pose to the identification of SOGI claimants' specific needs. For example, in Germany, if specific conditions are met, claimants may be assessed by special officers within a few days (ECRE, AIDA & Asyl und Migration 2019, p. 50), especially in the context of the new 'AnkER centres'. Given the speed of these assessments, claimants may not be in contact with social services, which are usually called upon to identify vulnerabilities and reception needs, or with NGOs to be supported or prepared before the interview. Considering the importance of preparation as well as the time often needed by SOGI claimants to reveal their real grounds of persecution, many participants in Germany expressed serious concerns about the effects of this new system on SOGI claimants (Nina, legal advisor; Frank S., legal advisor; Mariya, NGO worker; Sofia and Emma, NGO workers). While Halim, claiming asylum in Germany, where he works for an NGO, provided examples of the inconsistencies between decisions adopted through accelerated procedures, by referring to different results in two very similar cases of gay activists from Egypt, Thomas (NGO volunteer) emphasised their social cost. As he put it, '[t]hat's the next level of exclusion'.

The general inequity of accelerated procedures was confirmed in the UK in relation to the so-called Detained Fast Track ('DFT') when it was suspended in 2015, precisely because the England and Wales Court of Appeal found it to be 'structurally unfair'.[20] On the same basis, despite the attempts of the government to draw up a new Fast Track system for 'detained foreign criminals and failed asylum seekers' (UK Ministry of Justice 2017), the High Court ruled out any revival of the DFT in 2019.[21] Also in 2019, there was confirmation of the inappropriateness of these procedures for SOGI claimants when the case of a woman who applied for asylum on sexual orientation grounds while she was in detention was heard by the England and Wales High Court (Administrative Court).[22] As a result of the rejection of her asylum request through DFT and, in appeal, by the First-Tier Tribunal, the claimant had been returned to Uganda. After 6 years, the High Court held that the woman must be brought back to the UK to have her asylum claim fairly heard. It recognised that she required a longer timeframe to obtain relevant evidence. More broadly, as Amanda (NGO worker, Brussels) emphasised, it is not only a matter of proof but also of the environment generated by these procedures, which inhibits self-identification in SOGI claimants.

Accelerated procedures usually apply to claimants coming from so-called 'safe countries', whose claims have a reduced likelihood of being accepted (Joachim, NGO worker, Germany; Thomas, NGO volunteer, Germany; Gisela, lawyer, Germany). Whereas the concept of 'safe country of origin' is problematic overall (Costello 2016), when examined from a SOGI perspective, it is even more troubling when countries classified as 'safe' criminalise same-sex acts. For instance, participants in Germany pointed to the example of Senegal, among others, which criminalises same-sex acts and yet is treated as a 'safe country of origin'. This effectively places an extra evidentiary burden on SOGI claimants coming from those countries, who are expected to challenge the assumption that their countries of origin are safe. Considering that the timeframe to appeal in these cases is generally shorter than in ordinary procedures (Frank S., legal advisor), additional barriers to a fair procedure are clearly in place for SOGI asylum claimants coming from those countries.

The situation in the UK is somewhat different. Section 94(4) of the Nationality, Immigration and Asylum Act 2002, contains a list of designated states. A state is included on the list (that is, it is 'designated') if the UK government believes that 'there is in general in that state or part of it no serious risk of persecution of persons entitled to reside in that state or part of it' (Home Office 2019a, p. 7). Claims from

---

[20] '[T]he time limits are so tight as to make it impossible for there to be a fair hearing of appeals in a significant number of cases (…) The system is therefore structurally unfair and unjust': *The Lord Chancellor (appellant) v Detention Action (respondent) and the Secretary of State for the Home Department (interested party)* [2015] ECWA Civ 840, 45.

[21] Consultation on Tribunal Procedure (First-Tier Tribunal) (Immigration and Asylum Chamber) Rules 2014 and Tribunal Procedure (Upper Tribunal) Rules 2008 in relation to detained appellants, Tribunal Procedure Committee, 12 June 2019, available at https://www.gov.uk/government/consultations/consultation-on-tribunal-procedure-first-tier-tribunal-immigration-and-asylum-chamber-rules-2014-and-tribunal-procedure-upper-tribunal-rules-200

[22] *PN v Secretary of State for the Home Department* [2019] EWHC 1616 (Admin). The consequences of her removal, once arrived in Uganda, were reported by Bulman (2019).

individuals from these states will be designated 'clearly unfounded' – meaning there is no right of appeal from within the UK – unless the caseworker finds reasons to designate the application otherwise (ECRE, AIDA & Refugee Council 2019, p. 54). Countries like India or South Africa, where 'corrective rapes' affecting lesbian women are still reported, are included in this list (Strudwick 2014). Significantly, as far as SOGI claimants are concerned, in 2013 the Parliamentary Home Affairs Committee raised concerns about the impact of the credibility assessment for LGBTI claimants from countries designated as safe (House of Commons Home Affairs Committee 2013). The government responded: 'we agree. With specific reference to LGBTI related claims, there are further instructions relating to claims from some of the States designated under section 94(4) of the Nationality Immigration and Asylum Act 2002. Where there is strong objective evidence that members of the LGBTI community would be at risk of persecution in these countries, a grant of asylum would be appropriate' (UK Government 2013, p. 13). Also in 2013, the Court of Appeal in England and Wales found the designation of Jamaica as a 'safe country' unlawful because of the violence experienced by SOGI minorities and the lack of state protection against it in that country.[23] Therefore, as Olivia (government official) confirmed, even when the safe country concept applies, every claim needs to be evaluated on a case-by-case basis: 'we have a SPoE [Second Pair of Eyes] process for NSA [Non-Suspensive Appeals] or safe countries…'[24] That is probably why our research found that, in practice, the application of the 'safe country' concept and a list of 'designated' states is not currently a determining factor in SOGI asylum claims in the UK. Indeed, only an individual examination would be in line with the ECHR and EU law (Article 36 of the Procedures Directive).

Considering these pitfalls and the need to review the specific circumstances of each claimant, it is regrettable that the reform adopted in Italy in 2018 introduced, for the very first time in the Italian legal order, a list of safe countries allowing accelerated procedures, including at the border.[25] As a result, in October 2019, a first list of 13 'safe countries of origin' was drafted and includes Algeria, Morocco, Tunisia, Ghana and Senegal, countries with poor human rights records insofar as SOGI minorities are concerned (Ramón Mendos 2019). Considering that territorial commissions need to decide on these applications within 5 days as a rule, the quality of examination of claims relating to countries designated as 'safe' will in all likelihood decrease and there will be a heavier burden of proof for the claimant (Chap. 7).

If accelerated procedures and the 'safe country' concept are inherently unfair for SOGI claimants, there are also strong concerns about the application of the Dublin Regulation to these claimants. This is confirmed by our survey, given that (at least) 17% of respondents were transferred between EU member states under this Regulation. The Dublin Regulation establishes the criteria and mechanisms for

---

[23] *R (JB (Jamaica) v SSHD* [2013] EWCA Civ 666.

[24] 'A certification decision must be authorised by an accredited caseworker. This is referred to as a second pair of eyes (SPoE)' (Home Office 2019a, p. 22).

[25] See Decree Law no. 113/2018 (converted into Law no. 132, 1 December 2018), so-called 'Decreto Salvini'.

determining the EU member state responsible for examining an application for international protection lodged in one of the EU member states. Similarly to other claimants, when SOGI minorities request asylum in an EU country, it may happen that, following the rules of the Dublin Regulation, another member state is instead responsible for the evaluation of their claim. For example, in light of the importance attributed to family reunification in the Regulation, irrespective of the country where these requests are submitted, SOGI claims may potentially be examined by the member state where the claimant's family members have been already granted or have applied for international protection. Nonetheless, considering the likely heteronormative reading of the notion of family when the Dublin Regulation is applied to SOGI claimants, doubts have been raised about the fair application of this element of the Dublin Regulation from a SOGI perspective (Del Guercio 2018). Consequently, when a SOGI claim is submitted, there is a higher risk that, according to the Dublin Regulation, the first member state of access to Europe will be the country responsible for evaluating the claim (Danisi 2018).

It is not surprising, therefore, that during our fieldwork concerns were expressed in particular in relation to the transfer of SOGI claimants to Italy, Greece or Eastern EU member states, these countries often being the first member states through which claimants enter the EU (for instance, Evelyne and Anne, lawyers, Germany; Knud, NGO worker, Germany; Chiara, NGO worker, Italy). The problem here is not (only) whether the country identified as responsible for evaluating a SOGI asylum claim protects or not SOGI minorities, considering that all EU member states should – at least as a matter of law – offer a minimum level of protection to these minorities. The primary issue in SOGI claims is rather whether or not the designated country makes a fair evaluation of the asylum request and has in place adequate services, including accommodation, to address SOGI specific needs (Oscar, judge, Germany). Barbara (lawyer, Germany) expressed concerns about the alarming level of homophobia in countries like Hungary, raising doubts about the fairness of Dublin transfers of SOGI claimants to that country. Moreover, as Sabrina (NGO worker, Germany) pointed out, many claimants are so traumatised that a transfer can have a serious impact on their mental health (Chap. 9). In this situation, as she further explained, only the use of 'psychiatric statements' prevented Dublin transfers to Italy or Hungary from taking place.

It is nonetheless particularly difficult to appeal against such transfers. An example of this is the case of a male gay claimant whose hearing was observed in Hesse, Germany, in 2018. He had applied for asylum in Greece, where he experienced violence – including rape – before and after obtaining refugee status. He had not received any support from the Greek authorities. On the basis that Greece is a 'safe country' for asylum claimants, including SOGI, the judge did not ask the claimant any questions, not even related to the SOGI nature of his claim, and stated: 'I assume that this [abuse] does not happen everywhere in Greece. Greece is a member of the European Union and I assume that there is protection available'. The appeal was rejected, although the claimant was able to remain in Germany on separate grounds. In other cases, despite mental health concerns, Dublin transfers have been allowed. For example, Chiara (NGO worker) and Susanna (social worker), both in Italy,

6.7 Other Procedures

reported the transfer from Austria to Italy of a gay claimant from Morocco who had made several suicides attempts. On his arrival in Austria across the Italian border, he had found a SOGI asylum association, dedicated accommodation and mental health support. Despite his specific circumstances, the Austrian authorities decided that Italy was the EU member state responsible for evaluating his asylum request. With no specific and individual guarantees or assurances from the Italian authorities, he was sent to Venice and, from there, to Sicily. Thanks to the efforts of the Austrian SOGI asylum association, the claimant was referred to a support group in Italy, which then followed his asylum procedure while making sure his health issues were properly addressed. Yet, as Chiara pointed out: 'he is very traumatised, especially because he lives in a reception centre [for male claimants], where he constantly fears abuses by other guests (…) also due to the violence he already suffered in Lybia, where he was raped'. Franco (Italy) was another claimant sent back to Italy twice from Austria. As he explained, the reception conditions in Austria were very poor: 'they treat us as a prisoner, but they don't beat'. Remarkably, neither authority took his grounds for persecution into account when they considered his case under the Dublin Regulation.

Our participants also reported a lack of sensitive Dublin transfers, especially in relation to SOGI claimants sent back to Italy. For instance, Kamel (Italy) recalled a gay claimant from Germany who was transferred by flight to Rome with a voucher for one meal and without contacts of any kind. The claimant only avoided becoming homeless thanks to local associations in Rome, which found him temporary accommodation. In turn, Valentina (social worker, Italy) recounted the cases of several transgender claimants who, after obtaining visas to remain in Italy, tried to travel to the Netherlands to claim asylum there because of the availability of good quality trans-dedicated social services in that country. Yet, apart from a specific few whose medical issues presented obstacles to their transfer, they were all returned to Italy under the Dublin Regulation (Article 12). Only the intervention of an association defending transgender people's rights ensured that the Italian authorities and reception centres where they were eventually hosted addressed their specific needs, at least in part. In one case, Valentina reported that, owing to the violence they had already experienced in a reception centre in Italy, the transfer of a transgender claimant from the Netherlands was halted. A final concern is that, when claimants who belong to couples have to be transferred under the Dublin Regulation because they may not be legally recognised as partners, they risk being separated and sent to different countries if they entered the EU via two different member states. Gisela (lawyer, Germany) explained that, in at least one case, German authorities eventually decided to keep two claimants together after positively evaluating the 'informal' evidence of their relationship (mainly pictures taken in their home country).

Perhaps not surprisingly in light of the patterns of arrivals in the UK explored in Chap. 5, Dublin transfers do not seem to be a particular issue there as far as SOGI claimants are concerned. Only Denise and Umar (legal advisors) reported the case of a gay couple from Syria who risked being sent back to Croatia, as their first country of entrance into the EU. In their view, one of the reasons for the limited relevance of Dublin transfers in the UK may be that many SOGI claimants submit *sur place* applications in the UK, meaning that no other EU member state had previously been identified as responsible for their asylum applications. Indeed, as Oliver, an NGO worker, put it, 'Dublin is very, very rare'.

Overall, these experiences should prompt EU member states to invoke more often the 'sovereignty clause', and claim jurisdiction of a claim where there is a risk of exposing SOGI claimants to degrading treatment, at least in terms of lack of appropriate services in the country of destination. This would be in line with the case law of the CJEU[26] and the ECtHR.[27] The much awaited reform of the Dublin Regulation needs to review the current criteria by avoiding a heteronormative perspective, while addressing the specific needs of asylum claimants, including SOGI claimants, and ending the practice of inhumane transfers of people between EU countries.

6.8 Concluding Remarks

This chapter has examined procedural aspects of SOGI asylum as applied in Germany, Italy and the UK, having regard to the Refugee Convention and the European asylum and human rights frameworks. It has also examined the role played by different actors in applying or setting up informal procedural arrangements, aimed at improving the fair assessment of SOGI claims, while addressing people's specific needs. Our empirical data confirmed the perception of these claims as particularly complex ones and findings on aspects already explored in past research (Buscher 2011; Jansen and Spijkerboer 2011). Overall, by comparing these countries' practices, our analysis has demonstrated that procedures play a fundamental role for better decision-making but, as currently regulated at EU and domestic level, they still fail to fully comply with the UNHCR guidance (UNHCR 2012a).

Some of the problematic areas that emerged across all countries under investigation include: a lack of specific procedures, the long duration of the process, imbalances of power, the impact of bias, a lack of cultural awareness, and poor quality services, especially in terms of legal advice and interpretation. Training is needed to address gaps in knowledge and understanding of SOGI as concepts and as life experiences, although it cannot be the only answer to all these shortcomings in domestic asylum systems (LaViolette 2013). In addition, we found a generally low standard of COI in Germany and Italy, but better provision and practice in COI in the UK. However, commenting on this UK practice, Roberto (decision-maker, Italy) emphasised the risk that COI is used to turn individual assessment into an 'automatic box-ticking exercise', thus providing clear solutions ('modelli matematici') to life changing decisions. Overall, many doubts were raised about whether

---

[26] Joined cases C-411-10 and C-493-10, *N.S. v United Kingdom and M.E. v Ireland*, 21 December 2011, para. 94 ff, ECLI:EU:C:2011:865.

[27] For instance, *Tarakhel v. Switzerland*, Application no. 29217/12, Grand Chamber, 4 November 2014, para. 109.

European asylum authorities are correctly implementing the Refugee Convention, read in line with the UNHCR SOGI Guidelines and in light of our theoretical and analytical frameworks (Chap. 3), when SOGI claimants are involved. We also came across some positive practices, especially in Italy, for instance in terms of the designation of the interviewer in SOGI claims and of administrative and judicial collective decision-making in many asylum claims. Yet, these were not common to all countries analysed, nor were they applied consistently within each country.

Factors such as Brexit, the rise of anti-immigration political parties, the media portrayal of immigration flows, and the lack of investment and resources, cast doubts on the likelihood of positive developments in this area, despite the range of actions that might easily be taken (Chap. 11). Moreover, the future reform of the CEAS, which might lead to improvements to many of the procedures analysed above (at least in Germany and Italy) if these are implemented in a human rights compliant manner (Chap. 3; Ferreira 2018; Velluti 2014), is today uncertain. Despite these macro-level changes and the persistent impact of biased attitudes, on the ground some decision-makers are clearly worried by the role to which they have been assigned. As Filippo, a senior judge in Italy, explained: 'it's [asylum] a situation of extreme difficulty. I feel a profound discomfort (…) for this task [and] I wonder if the judiciary is the authority best placed to deal with it'.

In turn, SOGI claimants do not feel their suffering is properly addressed by the existing systems. As Nice Guy (focus group no. 1, northern Italy), put it:

> People come here, they keep preparing for Commission, Commission, Commission, many of them, a week to the Commission, they have sleepless nights, they are so scared. They get there and… the Commission is not friendly, that is just issue, it is not friendly. They just put you in front of somebody as if you are doing a job interview and start bombarding you with questions.

Their frustrations sometimes lead them to blame themselves for 'being' what they are. As Lutfor, who claimed asylum in the UK, explained:

> Do you know how hurtful I was, how ashamed I was, of me how much I have to struggle, how much feel guilty about myself, then slowly, slowly I accept myself but it is still every time I have sex, I feel guilty. (…) I don't hurt anyone, [but] sometimes I blame the system, sometimes I blame myself.

Whether or not these life experiences are duly considered in the assessment of their claims in Germany, Italy and UK will be addressed in the next chapter.

References

Alessi, E. J., Kahn, S., & Chatterji, S. (2016). 'The darkest times of my life': Recollections of child abuse among forced migrants persecuted because of their sexual orientation and gender identity. *Child Abuse & Neglect*, 51, 93–105. https://doi.org/10.1016/j.chiabu.2015.10.030

Alessi, E. J., Kahn, S., Woolner, L., & Van Der Horn, R. (2018). Traumatic stress among sexual and gender minority refugees from the Middle East, North Africa, and Asia who fled to the European Union. *The Journal of Traumatic Stress*, 31(6), 805–815.

APPG on Global LGBT Rights. (2016). *The UK's stance on international breaches of LGBT rights*. APPG. https://www.appglgbt.org/lgbt-report-2016

Asylum Aid. (2013). *Policy briefing: Legal aid*. http://d2t68d2r9artlv.cloudfront.net/wp-content/uploads/2013/08/LegalAidBriefing.pdf

Asylum Aid. (2018). *Your asylum appeal hearing. Information to help*. https://www.asylumaid.org.uk/goingtoappeal/

Bach, J. (2013). Assessing transgender asylum claims. *Forced Migration Review, 42*, 34–36.

Baillot, H., Cowan, S., & Munro, V. E. (2012). 'Hearing the right gaps': Enabling and responding to disclosures of sexual violence within the UK asylum process. *Social & Legal Studies, 21*(3), 269–296. https://doi.org/10.1177/0964663912444945

Baillot, H., Cowan, S., & Munro, V. E. (2013). Second-hand emotion? Exploring the contagion and impact of trauma and distress in the asylum law context. *Journal of Law and Society, 40*(4), 509–540. https://doi.org/10.1111/j.1467-6478.2013.00639.x

BAMF – Bundesamt für Migration und Flüchtlinge. (2019). *Branch offices in AnkER facilities*. BAMF - Bundesamt Für Migration und Flüchtlinge. http://www.bamf.de/EN/DasBAMF/Aufbau/Standorte/ASinAnKEREinrichtung/aussenstelle-in-anker-einrichtung-node.html

Bell, M., & Hansen, C. (2009). *Over not out. The housing and homelessness issues specific to lesbian, gay, bisexual and transgender asylum seekers*. London: Metropolitan Support Trust.

BMI – Bundesministerium des Innern, für Bau und Heimat. (2019). *Kleine Anfrage der Abgeordneten Ulla Jelpke u.a. Und der Fraktion DIE LINKE: Situation von LSBTI-Geflüchteten* (BT-Drucksache19/10308). https://www.ulla-jelpke.de/wp-content/uploads/2019/06/19_10308-LSBTI-Gefl%C3%BCchtete.pdf

Bögner, D., Herlihy, J., & Brewin, C. R. (2007). Impact of sexual violence on disclosure during Home Office interviews. *The British Journal of Psychiatry: the Journal of Mental Science, 191*, 75–81. https://doi.org/10.1192/bjp.bp.106.030262

Braganza, N. (2019). Human dignity – A lesser right for refugees? *European Human Rights Law Review, 19*(2), 144–154.

Bulman, M. (2019). Gay woman unlawfully deported from UK was 'gang-raped and fearing for her life' after removal to Uganda. *Independent*. www.independent.co.uk/news/uk/home-news/home-office-uganda-woman-deported-home-office-gang-rape-a9019356.html

Buscher, D. (2011). Unequal in exile: Gender equality, sexual identity and refugee status. *Amsterdam Law Forum, 3*(2), 92–102.

Busetto, E., Fiorini, A., Pieroni, E., & Zarrella, S. (2017). Le informazioni sui Paesi di origine nella procedura di asilo: Sempre più rilevanti, ancora poco considerate. *Diritto, Immigrazione, Cittadinanza, 19*(1). https://www.dirittoimmigrazionecittadinanza.it/archivio-saggi-commenti/saggi/fascicolo-2017-n-1/61-le-informazioni-sui-paesi-di-origine-nella-procedura-di-asilo-sempre-piu-rilevanti-ancora-poco-considerate

Cohen, J. (2002). Questions of credibility: Omissions, discrepancies and errors of recall in the testimony of asylum seekers. *International Journal of Refugee Law, 13*(3), 293–309.

Costello, C. (2016). Safe country? Says who? *International Journal of Refugee Law, 28*(4), 601–622. https://doi.org/10.1093/ijrl/eew042

Danisi, C. (2018). What 'Safe Harbours' are there for sexual orientation and gender identity asylum claims? A human rights reading of international law of the sea and refugee law. *GenIUS – Rivista di studi giuridici sull'orientamento sessuale e l'identità di genere, 5*(2), 9–24.

Danisi, C. (2019). Crossing borders between international refugee law and international human rights law in the European context: Can human rights enhance protection against persecution based on sexual orientation (and beyond)? *Netherlands Quarterly of Human Rights, 37*(4), 359–378.

Danisi, C. (2020). *SOGICA – Table of Italian SOGI asylum case law*. http://www.sogica.org/database/danisi-italian-sogica-case-law-table-2019/

De Santis, A. D. (2018). L'eliminazione dell'udienza (e dell'audizione) nel procedimento per il riconoscimento della protezione internazionale: Un esempio di sacrificio delle garanzie.

References

Questione Giustizia. https://www.questionegiustizia.it/rivista/articolo/l-eliminazione-dell-udienza-edell-audizione-nelpro_547.php

Del Guercio, A. (2018). Quali garanzie per il diritto all'unità familiare dei richiedenti e dei beneficiari di protezione internazionale con coniuge/partner dello stesso sesso? *GenIUS – Rivista di studi giuridici sull'orientamento sessuale e l'identità di genere,* 5(2), 59–73.

EASO – European Asylum Support Office. (2015). *Researching the situation of lesbian, gay, and bisexual persons (LGB) in countries of origin.* EASO – European Asylum Support Office. https://www.easo.europa.eu/sites/default/files/public/Researching-the-situation-of-LGB-in-countries-of-origin-FINAL-080515.pdf

ECRE – European Council on Refugees and Exiles, & Refugee Council. (2016). *Country report: United Kingdom. 2016 Update.* http://www.asylumineurope.org/sites/default/files/report-download/aida_uk_2016update.pdf

ECRE – European Council on Refugees and Exiles, AIDA – Asylum Information Database. (2019). *The AnkER centres. Implications for asylum procedures, reception and return.* https://www.asylumineurope.org/sites/default/files/anker_centres_report.pdf

ECRE – European Council on Refugees and Exiles, AIDA – Asylum Information Database, & ASGI. (2019). *National country report: Italy, 2018 update.* ECRE – European Council on Refugees and Exiles. http://www.asylumineurope.org/sites/default/files/report-download/aida_it_2018update.pdf

ECRE – European Council on Refugees and Exiles, AIDA – Asylum Information Database, & Asyl und Migration. (2018). *National country report: Germany, 2017 update.* ECRE – European Council on Refugees and Exiles. http://www.asylumineurope.org/sites/default/files/report-download/aida_de_2017update.pdf

ECRE – European Council on Refugees and Exiles, AIDA – Asylum Information Database, & Asyl und Migration. (2019). *National country report: Germany, 2018 update.* ECRE – European Council on Refugees and Exiles. https://www.asylumineurope.org/sites/default/files/report-download/aida_de_2018update.pdf

ECRE – European Council on Refugees and Exiles, AIDA – Asylum Information Database, & Refugee Council. (2019). *National country report: United Kingdom, 2018 update.* ECRE – European Council on Refugees and Exiles. https://www.asylumineurope.org/reports/country/united-kingdom

Ferreira, N. (2018). Reforming the Common European Asylum System: Enough rainbow for queer asylum seekers? *GenIUS – Rivista di studi giuridici sull'orientamento sessuale e l'identità di genere,* 5(2), 25–42.

Flamini, M. (2018). Il ruolo del giudice di fronte alle peculiarità del giudizio di protezione internazionale. *Questione Giustizia.* http://questionegiustizia.it/rivista/2018/2/il-ruolo-del-giudice-di-fronte-alle-peculiarita-del-giudizio-di-protezione-internazionale_544.php

Freedom from Torture. (2016). *Proving Torture: Demanding the impossible – Home Office mistreatment of expert medical evidence.* http://www.refworld.org/docid/58495c5f4.html

Gartner, J.L. (2015). (In)credibly Queer: Sexuality-based Asylum in the European Union'. In A. Chase (Ed.) *Transatlantic Perspectives on Diplomacy and Diversity* (pp. 39–66). New York: Humanity in Action Press.

Gill, N., & Good, A. (Eds.). (2019). *Asylum determination in Europe: Ethnographic perspectives.* Palgrave Macmillan. https://doi.org/10.1007/978-3-319-94749-5

Government Equalities Office. (2018). *LGBT action plan.* Her Majesty's Stationery Office. https://assets.publishing.service.gov.uk/government/uploads/system/uploads/attachment_data/file/721367/GEO-LGBT-Action-Plan.pdf

Government Equalities Office. (2019). *LGBT action plan: Annual progress report 2018 to 2019.* Her Majesty's Stationery Office. https://assets.publishing.service.gov.uk/government/uploads/system/uploads/attachment_data/file/814579/20190702__LGBT_Action_Plan__Annual_Report__WESC.pdf

Gray, A., & McDowall, A. (2013). LGBT refugee protection in the UK: From discretion to belief? *Forced Migration Review,* 42, 22–25.

Held, N., Rainbow Refugees Cologne-Support Group e.V., Aidshilfe Düsseldorf e.V., You're Welcome – Mashallah Düsseldorf, Kölner Flüchtlingsrat, Projekt Geflüchtete Queere Jugendliche, & Fachstelle Queere Jugend NRW / Schwules Netzwerk NRW e.V. (2018). *Projektbericht: Erfahrungen mit der Anhörung von LSBTIQ* Geflüchteten*. https://schwules-netzwerk.de/wp-content/uploads/2018/10/Projektbericht-zur-Anh%C3%B6rung-von-LSBTIQ-Gefl%C3%BCchteten.pdf

Home Office. (2011). *Gender identity issues in the asylum claim: Transgender*. GOV.UK. https://www.gov.uk/government/publications/dealing-with-gender-identity-issues-in-the-asylum-claim-process

Home Office. (2013). *Evaluation of the early legal advice project*. GOV.UK. https://www.gov.uk/government/publications/evaluation-of-the-early-legal-advice-project

Home Office. (2016). *Asylum policy instruction. Sexual orientation in asylum claims. Version 6.0*. GOV.UK. https://assets.publishing.service.gov.uk/government/uploads/system/uploads/attachment_data/file/543882/Sexual-orientation-in-asylum-claims-v6.pdf

Home Office. (2017). *Country policy and information note Jamaica: Sexual orientation and gender identity (Version 2.0)*. GOV.UK. https://assets.publishing.service.gov.uk/government/uploads/system/uploads/attachment_data/file/594901/Jamaica_-_SOGI_-_CPIN_-_v2_0.pdf

Home Office. (2019a). *Certification of protection and human rights claims under section 94 of the Nationality, Immigration and Asylum Act 2002 (clearly unfounded claims)*. GOV.UK. https://assets.publishing.service.gov.uk/government/uploads/system/uploads/attachment_data/file/778221/certification-s94-guidance-0219.pdf

Home Office. (2019b). *Country information and guidance Iran: Sexual orientation and gender identity*. GOV.UK. https://assets.publishing.service.gov.uk/government/uploads/system/uploads/attachment_data/file/810845/CPIN_-_Iran_-_SOGI_-_v3.0__June_2019__EXT.PDF

Home Office. (2020). *Country policy and information note Bangladesh: Sexual orientation and gender identity*. GOV.UK. https://assets.publishing.service.gov.uk/government/uploads/system/uploads/attachment_data/file/660538/Bangladesh_-_SOGI_-_CPIN_-_v3.0__Nov_2017_.pdf

Home Office Minister. (2018). *Immigration: Asylum claims*. House of Lords.

House of Commons Home Affairs Committee. (2013). *Asylum. Seventh report of session 2013–14*, Volume I. House of Commons.

Hübner, K. (2016). Fluchtgrund sexuelle Orientierung und Geschlechtsidentität: Auswirkungen von heteronormativem Wissen auf die Asylverfahren LGBTI-Geflüchteter. *Feministische Studien*, 34(2). https://doi.org/10.1515/fs-2016-0005

ICIBI – Independent Chief Inspector of Borders and Immigration. (2014). *An investigation into the Home Office's handling of asylum claims made on the grounds of sexual orientation March–June 2014*. ICIBI – Independent Chief Inspector of Borders and Immigration.

ICIBI – Independent Chief Inspector of Borders and Immigration. (2017). *An inspection of asylum intake and casework. April – August 2017*. ICIBI – Independent Chief Inspector of Borders and Immigration.

ICIBI – Independent Chief Inspector of Borders and Immigration. (2019). *Call for evidence: The work of presenting officers*. GOV.UK. https://www.gov.uk/government/news/call-for-evidence-the-work-of-presenting-officers

Il Grande Colibri. (2019). *SOGI asylum support groups in Italy*. https://www.ilgrandecolibri.com/en/migrants

ILGA – International Lesbian, Gay, Bisexual, Trans and Intersex Association. (2014). *Laying the ground for LGBTI sensitive asylum decision-making in Europe: Transportation of the recast asylum procedures directive and the recast reception conditions directive*. http://www.refworld.org/docid/5433a7634.html

ILGA Europe. (2016). *Protecting the rights of LGBTI asylum seekers and refugees in the reform of the Common European Asylum System*. ILGA Europe. https://www.ilga-europe.org/resources/policy-papers/protecting-rights-lgbti-asylum-seekers-and-refugees-reform-common-european

Jansen, S. (2014). *Good practices related to LGBTI asylum applicants in Europe*. ILGA Europe. http://www.ilga-europe.org/resources/ilga-europe-reports-and-other-materials/good-practices-related-lgbti-asylum-applicants

References

Jansen, S., & Spijkerboer, T. (2011). *Fleeing homophobia: Asylum claims related to sexual orientation and gender identity in Europe*. Vrije Universiteit Amsterdam. https://www.refworld.org/docid/4ebba7852.html

Jong, A. de. (2008). *An analysis of the coverage of LGBT issues in country of origin information reports produced by the COI service, UK Border Agency. Report for the Advisory Panel on Country Information*. UK Border Agency.

Kalkmann, M. (2010). Questionnaire European Research Project. In S. Jansen, T. Spijkerboer (Eds.) *Fleeing Homophobia, Seeking Safety in Europe, Best practices on the (legal) position of LGBT Asylum Seekers in the EU Members States*. Vrije Universiteit Amsterdam. https://www.sogica.org/wp-content/uploads/2017/04/Kalkmann_Questionnaire-Fleeing-Homophobia_-2010.pdf

Khan, T. (2016). *Investigating the British asylum system for lesbian, gay and bisexual asylum-seekers: Theoretical and empirical perspectives on fairness*. PhD thesis. University of Liverpool.

La Migration. (2018). *Manuale per operatori*. La Migration. https://arcigaypalermo.wordpress.com/2018/10/15/la-migration-il-manuale-per-operatori/

LaViolette, N. (2013). Overcoming problems with sexual minority refugee claims: Is LGBT cultural competency training the solution? In T. Spijkerboer (Ed.) *Fleeing homophobia. Sexual orientation, gender identity and asylum*. London: Routledge.

McDonald-Norman, D. (2017). No one to bear witness: Country information and LGBTQ asylum seekers. *Refuge*, 33(2), 88–100.

McFadyen, G. (2016). The language of labelling and the politics of hospitality in the British asylum system. *The British Journal of Politics and International Relations*, 18(3), 599–617. https://doi-org.ezproxy.sussex.ac.uk/10.1177/1369148116631281

McGuirk, S. (2018). (In)credible subjects: NGOs, attorneys, and permissible LGBT asylum seeker identities. *Political and Legal Anthropology Review*, 41, 4–18.

Miles, N. (2010). *No going back. Lesbian and gay people and the asylum system*. Stonewall. https://www.stonewall.org.uk/sites/default/files/No_Going_Back__2010_.pdf

Millbank, J. (2009). The ring of truth: A case study of credibility assessment in particular social group refugee determinations. *International Journal of Refugee Law*, 21(1), 1–33.

NDR. (2019). *BAMF-"Skandal" wird immer kleiner*. https://daserste.ndr.de/panorama/archiv/2019/BAMF-Skandal-wird-immer-kleiner,bamf204.html

Palermo, P. (2018). Orientamento sessuale e identità di genere nel sistema dell'asilo in Italia anche alla luce della riforma Minniti. *GenIUS – Rivista di studi giuridici sull'orientamento sessuale e l'identità di genere*, 5(2), 43–58.

Puar, J. K. (2007). *Terrorist assemblages: Homonationalism in queer times*. Durham: Duke University Press. https://doi.org/10.1215/9780822390442

Puar, J. (2013). Rethinking Homonationalism. *International Journal of Middle East Studies*, 45(2), 336–339. https://doi.org/10.1017/S002074381300007X

Ramón Mendos, L. (2019). *State-sponsored homophobia 2019: Global legislation overview update*. ILGA. https://ilga.org/downloads/ILGA_World_State_Sponsored_Homophobia_report_global_legislation_overview_update_December_2019.pdf

Rehaag, S. (2009). Bisexuals need not apply: A comparative appraisal of refugee law and policy in Canada, the United States, and Australia. *The International Journal of Human Rights*, 13(2–3), 415–436.

Rousseau, C., & Foxen, P. (2006). Le mythe du réfugié menteur: Un mensonge indispensable? *L'évolution psychiatrique*, 71, 505–520.

Strudwick, P. (2014, January 4). Crisis in South Africa: The shocking practice of 'corrective rape' – Aimed at 'curing' lesbians. *Independent*. http://www.independent.co.uk/news/world/africa/crisis-in-south-africa-the-shocking-practice-of-corrective-rape-aimed-at-curing-lesbians-9033224.html

TGEU – Transgender Europe. (2016). *TGEU trans asylum brochure*. http://tgeu.org/wp-content/uploads/2016/10/TGEU_TransAsylumBrochure_WEB.pdf

UK Government. (2013). *The Government response to the Seventh report from the Home Affairs Committee session 2013–14 HC 71: Asylum*. UK Government.

UK Ministry of Justice. (2017). *New fast-track immigration appeal rules proposed*. GOV. UK. https://www.gov.uk/government/news/new-fast-track-immigration-appeal-rules-proposed

UKLGIG – UK Lesbian and Gay Immigration Group. (2013). *Missing the mark. Decision making on lesbian, gay (bisexual, trans and intersex) asylum claims*. UKLGIG.

UNHCR – UN High Commissioner for Refugees. (2012a). *Guidelines on International Protection No. 9: Claims to refugee status based on sexual orientation and/or gender identity within the context of Article 1A(2) of the 1951 Convention and/or its 1967 protocol relating to the status of refugees (HCR/GIP/12/09)*. UNHCR – UN High Commissioner for Refugees. http://www.unhcr.org/509136ca9.pdf

UNHCR – UN High Commissioner for Refugees. (2012b). *Working with men and boy survivors of sexual and gender-based violence in forced displacement*. UNHCR – UN High Commissioner for Refugees. https://www.refworld.org/docid/5006aa262.html

Various. (2018). Special Issue 'L'ospite straniero: La protezione internazionale nel sistema multilivello di tutela dei diritti fondamentali. *Questione Giustizia*. http://www.questionegiustizia.it/rivista/2018-2.php

Veglio, M. (2017). Uomini tradotti. Prove di dialogo con richiedenti asilo. *Diritto, Immigrazione, Cittadinanza*, 18(2). https://www.dirittoimmigrazionecittadinanza.it/archivio-saggi-commenti/saggi/fascicolo-2017-n-2/72-uomini-tradotti-prove-di-dialogo-con-richiedenti-asilo

Velluti, S. (2014). *Reforming the Common European Asylum System – Legislative developments and judicial activism of the European Courts*. Berlin: Springer.

Weßels, J. (2012). HJ (Iran) and HT (Cameroon) – Reflections on a new test for sexuality-based asylum claims in Britain. *International Journal of Refugee Law*, 24(4), 815.

Open Access   This chapter is licensed under the terms of the Creative Commons Attribution 4.0 International License (http://creativecommons.org/licenses/by/4.0/), which permits use, sharing, adaptation, distribution and reproduction in any medium or format, as long as you give appropriate credit to the original author(s) and the source, provide a link to the Creative Commons license and indicate if changes were made.

The images or other third party material in this chapter are included in the chapter's Creative Commons license, unless indicated otherwise in a credit line to the material. If material is not included in the chapter's Creative Commons license and your intended use is not permitted by statutory regulation or exceeds the permitted use, you will need to obtain permission directly from the copyright holder.